Computers in Education 5–13

Exploring the Curriculum

This book is one of a series designed to assist teachers to review practice in schools and classrooms. The series has been prepared by members of the Open University team for the course: *Applied Studies in Curriculum and Teaching*. Each volume follows a common sequence of issues relating to the nature of an area of specialization, its place in contemporary society, its treatment in schools, particular features of its teaching and learning, and consequences for organization and evaluation.

The titles in the series are:

J. Brown, A. Cooper, T. Horton, F. Toates and D. Zeldin (Eds.):
Science in Schools
A. Cross and R. McCormick (Eds.): *Technology in Schools*
V. J. Lee (Ed.): *English Literature in Schools*

Computers in Education
5–13

edited by
Ann Jones and Peter Scrimshaw
at the Open University

Open University Press
Milton Keynes · Philadelphia

Open University Press
Open University Educational Enterprises Limited
12 Cofferidge Close
Stony Stratford
Milton Keynes MK11 1BY, England

and

242 Cherry Street
Philadelphia, PA 19106, USA

First published 1988

British Library Cataloguing in Publication Data

Computers in education 5–13.
  1. Education——Data processing
  I. Jones, Ann, *1954–*   II. Scrimshaw, Peter
  370'.28'5   LB1028.43
    ISBN 0–335–15549–9
    ISBN 0–335–15543–X Pbk

Library of Congress Cataloging in Publication Data

Computers in education, 5–13.

  1. Computer-assisted instruction.
I. Jones, Ann, 1954– . II. Scrimshaw, Peter.
LB1028.5.C5725 1987   372.13'9445   87–22109
ISBN 0–335–15549–9
ISBN 0–335–15543–X (pbk.)

Printed in Great Britain at The Alden Press, Oxford

Contents

Acknowledgements

The editors and publisher gratefully acknowledge the following for permission to reproduce the articles in this collection:

1.1 Bruner, J. (1986) *Towards a Theory of Instruction*, Harvard University Press, Cambridge, Mass, pp. 45–53, 156–163.

1.2 Woods, R. G. and Barrow, R. St. C. (1975) *An Introduction to Philosophy of Education*, Methuen & Co, London, pp. 143–155.

1.3 Ross, A. (1984) 'How does information retrieval help children's learning?', in *Making Connections*, Council for Education Technology, London, pp. 18–22.

2.1 Peterson, L. (1984) 'Creating a convivial communications society', in *Telecommunications Policy* vol. 8 No. 3, pp. 170–172.

2.2 Marx, G. T. (1985) 'The new surveillance'. Reprinted with permission from *Technology Review*, copyright, 1985.

2.3 Commissioned for this collection.

2.4 Weizenbaum, J. (1976) 'Against the imperialism of instrumental reason', in *Computer Power and Human Reason*, copyright © 1976, W. H. Freeman & Company, USA. Reprinted with permission.

2.5 Mitchie, D. and Johnston, R. (1984) 'A metaphor upside down', in *The Creative Computer*, Penguin Books, Harmondsworth, pp. 137–165.

3.1 Feickert, D. (1985) 'Britain's miners and the new technology' in Radical Science Collective (eds) *Issues in Radical Science 17*, Free Association Books, London.

3.2 Howard, R. (1985) 'UTOPIA: where workers craft new technology'. Reprinted with permission of *Technology Review*, copyright 1985.

3.3 Cockburn, C. (1984) 'Women and technology: opportunity is not enough'. Macmillan, London, Basingstoke and USA.

4.1 Papert, S. (1980) 'Computers and Computer Culture', in *Mindstorms*, Harvester Press, Brighton, pp. 30–37.

4.2 Ball, D. (1986) 'The use of microcomputers to support mathematical investigations', in *Exploring Mathematics with Microcomputers*, Council for Educational Technology, London, pp. 84–94.

4.3 Commissioned for this collection.

4.4 Sharples, M. (1983) 'The use of computers to aid the teaching of creative writing' in *AEDS Journal*, vol. 16, No. 2.

5.1 Cummings, R. (1985) 'Small-group discussions and microcomputer', in *Journal of Computer Assisted Learning*, Vol. 1, pp. 149–158.

5.2 Leonard Huber 'Computer learning through Piaget's eyes'. Reprinted by special permission of *Classroom Computer Learning*, 1985, by Peter Li, Inc., 2169 Francisco Blvd. East, Suite A–4, San Rafael CA94901.

5.3 Johnson, R. T. et al. (1985) 'Effects of co-operative, competitive, and individualistic goal structures on computer-assisted instruction', in *Journal of Educational Psychology*, Vol. 77, No. 6, pp. 668–677. Copyright 1985 by the American Psychological Association. Adapted by permission of the publisher and the author.

5.4 Turkle, S. (1984) 'Child programmers: the first generation', in *The Second Self: Computers and the Human Spirit*, Simon & Schuster, New York, pp. 91–134.

6.1 Fraser, R. et al. (n.d.) 'Learning activities and classroom roles with and without the microcomputer', an ITMA paper.

6.2 Lesgold, A. M. (1985) Excerpt from 'Computer resources for learning', in *Peabody Journal of Education*, Vol. 62, No. 2, pp. 60–74.

6.3 Self, J. (1985) 'A perspective on intelligent computer-assisted learning', in *Journal of Computer Assisted Learning*, Vol. 1, pp. 159–166.

7.1 Phillips, R. J. (1985) 'ITMA's approach to classroom observation', in Alexander, K. and Blanchard, D. (eds) *Educational Software – A Creator's Handbook*, Tecmedia Ltd, Loughborough, pp. 109–115.

7.2 Kerry, T. (1984) 'Self-report case-studies: an experiment in own classroom data collection by teachers', in *Westminster Studies in Education*, Vol. 7, pp. 103–111.

7.3 Atkins, M. J. (1984) 'Practitioner as researcher: some techniques for analysing semi-structured data in small-scale research', in *British Journal of Educational Studies*, Vol. 32:3, pp. 251–261.

7.4 Blease, D. (1986) 'Choosing educational software', in *Evaluating Educational Software*, Croom Helm, Beckenham, pp. 54–95.

8.1 Seely Brown, J. (1983) 'Process versus product: a perspective on tools for communal and informal electronic learning', in *Report from the Learning Lab: Education in the Electronic Age*, Educational Broadcasting Corporation. Reprinted in *Journal of Educational Computing Research*, Vol. 1, No. 2, 1985.

8.2 Feurzeig, W. (1986) 'Algebra slaves and agents in a logo-based mathematics curriculum', in *Instructional Science*, Vol. 14, pp. 229–254. Reprinted by permission of Martinus Nijhoff Publishers, Dordrecht.

8.3 Commissioned for this collection.

8.4 Commissioned for this collection.

Preface

This reader has been assembled to help teachers wishing to use computers in a learner centred way with children aged five to thirteen. We take a learner centred approach to education to involve an interest in the development of:

— problem-solving skills
— creativity
— effective cooperation
— decision-making skills
— independent learning strategies
— a capacity for systematic enquiry
— information handling ability.

Many of the articles are about the ways in which these target aims can be conceived, built into CAL packages and pursued in the classroom. However, we have also included a number of articles on the social context of computer use, in work and beyond. Although our main concern is with the skills that individuals need to develop their full potential, this can only be properly understood within the context of the groups and society to which the individual belongs. In particular we need to ask whether computers are equally enabling (in terms of individual development) to all groups within society, whether they merely accentuate patterns of disadvantage that already exist, or create different patterns. Consequently the teacher needs not only to consider the classroom situation, vital though that is, but should also see how the development of such skills and capacities is distributed within society, and how these capacities might be used or misused in adult life. To some degree both of these are the result of work in today's classrooms. To that extent they are the responsibility of the teacher.

Ann Jones and *Peter Scrimshaw, March 1987*

1 WHAT CAN BE LEARNED FROM COMPUTERS?

This section looks at learner centred aims. We have selected papers which attempt to disentangle what such aims actually mean and in later sections will consider the role of computers in achieving them.

Bruner recognizes that gaining information is fundamental but emphasizes that children may fail to grasp its provisional nature—and so gain a purely static conception of knowledge and theory. Problem-solving assumes access to relevant information, as does sensible decision-making. Systematic enquiry is in part the categorization of available information and the search for what is missing. In that sense, concern with facts is not an alternative to more exploratory approaches, but a prerequisite of them.

Independent learning assumes that the child has a capacity for both systematic enquiry and problem-solving. But there is also an assumption of self-confidence and an ability to find useful information independently. Woods and Barrow argue that creativity requires a sound grasp of the activity concerned. It also assumes that children can learn for themselves. For them the link between knowledge and creativity is that the first is a prerequisite of the second.

These views naturally have implications for the organization of learning, as Bruner's paper indicates. Many of the issues he raises are taken up in later sections. However, the paper by Ross not only discusses the concepts of problem-solving and information retrieval further, but also illustrates how children can use databases co-operatively as an aid to problem-solving and hypothesizing more successfully.

1.1 Instruction and learning
• Jerome S. Bruner

SEQUENCE AND ITS USES

Instruction consists of leading the learner through a sequence of statements and restatements of a problem or body of knowledge that increase the learner's ability to grasp, transform, and transfer what he is learning. In short, the sequence in which a learner encounters materials within a domain of knowledge affects the difficulty he will have in achieving mastery.

There are usually various sequences that are equivalent in their ease and difficulty for learners. There is no unique sequence for all learners, and the optimum in any particular case will depend upon a variety of factors, including past learning, stage of development, nature of the material, and individual differences.

If it is true that the usual course of intellectual development moves from enactive through iconic to symbolic representation of the world[1] it is likely that an optimum sequence will progress in the same direction. Obviously, this is a conservative doctrine. For when the learner has a well-developed symbolic system, it may be possible to by-pass the first two stages. But one does so with the risk that the learner may not possess the imagery to fall back on when his symbolic transformations fail to achieve a goal in problem solving.

Exploration of alternatives will necessarily be affected by the sequence in which material to be learned becomes available to the learner. When the learner should be encouraged to explore alternatives widely and when he should be encouraged to concentrate on the implications of a single alternative hypothesis is an empirical question, to which we shall return. [. . .]

It is necessary to specify in any sequences the level of uncertainty and tension that must be present to initiate problem-solving behavior, and what conditions are required to keep active problem-solving going. This again is an empirical question.

Optimal sequences, as already stated, cannot be specified independently of the criterion in terms of which final learning is to be judged. A classification of such criteria will include at least the following: speed of learning; resistance to forgetting; transferability of what has been learned to new instances; form of representation in terms of which what has been learned is to be expressed; economy of what has been learned in terms of cognitive strain imposed; effective power of what has been learned in terms of its generativeness of new hypotheses and combinations. Achieving one of these goals does not necessarily bring one closer to others; speed of learning, for example, is sometimes antithetical to transfer or to economy.

THE FORM AND PACING OF REINFORCEMENT

Learning depends upon knowledge of results at a time when and at a place where the knowledge can be used for correction. Instruction increases the appropriate timing and placing of corrective knowledge.

'Knowledge of results' is useful or not depending upon when and where the learner receives the corrective information, under what conditions such corrective information can be used, even assuming appropriateness of time and place of receipt, and the form in which the corrective information is received.

Learning and problem solving are divisible into phases. These have been described in various ways by different writers. But all the descriptions agree on one essential feature: that there is a cycle involving the formulation of a testing procedure or trial, the operation of this testing procedure, and the comparison of the results of the test with some criterion. It has variously been called trial-and-error, means-end testing, trial-and-check, discrepancy reduction, test-operate-test-exit (TOTE), hypothesis testing, and so on. These 'units,' moreover, can readily be characterized as hierarchically organized: we seek to cancel the unknowns in an equation in order to simplify the expression, in order to solve the equation, in order to get through the course, in order to get our degree, in order to get a decent job, in order to lead the good life. Knowledge of results should come at that point in a problem-solving episode when the person is comparing the results of his try-out with some criterion of what he seeks to achieve. Knowledge of results given before this point either cannot be understood or must be carried as extra freight in immediate memory. Knowledge given after this point may be too late to guide the choice of a next hypothesis or trial. But knowledge of results must, to be useful, provide information not only on whether or not one's particular act produced success but also on whether the act is in fact leading one through the hierarchy of goals one is seeking to achieve. This is not to say that when we cancel the term in that equation we need to know whether it will all lead eventually to the good life. Yet there should at least be some 'lead notice' available as to whether or not cancelation is on the right general track. It is here that the tutor has a special role. For most learning starts off rather piecemeal without the integration of component acts or elements. Usually the learner can tell whether a particular cycle of activity has worked—feedback from specific events is fairly simple—but often he cannot tell whether this completed cycle is leading to the eventual goal. It is interesting that one of the nonrigorous short cuts to problem solution, basic rules of 'heuristic,' stated in Polya's noted book[2] has to do with defining the overall problem. To sum up, then, instruction uniquely provides information to the learner about the higher-order relevance of his efforts. In time, to be sure, the learner must develop techniques for obtaining such higher-order corrective information on his own, for instruction and its aids must eventually come to an end. And, finally, if the problem solver is to take over this function, it is necessary for him to learn to recognize when he does not comprehend and, as Roger Brown[3] has suggested, to signal incomprehension to the tutor so that he can be helped. In time, the signaling of incomprehension becomes a self-signaling and equivalent to a temporary stop order.

The ability of problem solvers to use information correctively is known to vary as a function of their internal state. One state in which information is least useful is that of strong drive and anxiety. There is a sufficient body of research to establish this point beyond reasonable doubt.[4] Another such state has been referred to as 'functional fixedness'—a problem solver is, in effect, using corrective information exclusively for the evaluation of one single hypothesis that happens to be wrong. The usual example is treating an object in terms of its conventional significance when it must be treated in a new context—we fail to use a hammer as a bob for a pendulum because it is 'fixed' in our thinking as a hammer. Numerous studies point to the fact that during such a period there is a remarkable intractability or even incorrigibility to problem solving. There is some evidence to indicate that high drive and anxiety lead one to be more prone to functional fixedness. It is obvious that corrective information of the usual type, straight feedback, is least useful during such states, and that an adequate instructional strategy aims at terminating the interfering state by special means before continuing with the usual provision of correction. In such cases, instruction verges on a kind of therapy, and it is perhaps because of this therapeutic need that one often finds therapy-like advice in lists of aids for problem solvers, like the suggestion of George Humphrey[5] that one turn away from the problem when it is proving too difficult.

If information is to be used effectively, it must be translated into the learner's way of attempting to solve a problem. If such translatability is not present, then the information is simply useless. Telling a neophyte skier to 'shift to his uphill edges' when he cannot distinguish which edges he is travelling on provides no help, whereas simply telling him to lean into the hill may succeed. Or, in the cognitive sphere, there is by now an impressive body of evidence that indicates that 'negative information'—information about what something is *not*—is peculiarly unhelpful to a person seeking to master a concept. Though it is logically usable, it is psychologically useless. Translatability of corrective information can in principle also be applied to the form of representation and its economy. If learning or problem solving is proceeding in one mode—enactive, iconic or symbolic—corrective information must be provided either in the same mode or in one that translates into it. Corrective information that exceeds the information-processing capacities of a learner is obviously wasteful.

Finally, it is necessary to reiterate one general point already made in passing. Instruction is a provisional state that has as its object to make the learner or problem solver self-sufficient. Any regimen of correction carries the danger that the learner may become permanently dependent upon the tutor's correction. The tutor must correct the learner in a fashion that eventually makes it possible for the learner to take over the corrective function himself. Otherwise the result of instruction is to create a form of mastery that is contingent upon the perpetual presence of a teacher. [. . .]

Thought in the classroom

Consider now (another) problem: how to stimulate thought in the setting of a school. We know from experimental studies like those of Bloom and Broder[6] and of Goodnow and Pettigrew[7] that there is a striking difference in the acts of a person who thinks that the task before him represents a problem to be solved and not that it is controlled by random forces. School is a peculiar subculture where such matters are concerned. By school age, children have come to expect quite arbitrary and, from their point of view, meaningless demands to be made upon them by adults—the result, most likely, of the fact that adults often fail to recognize the task of conversion necessary to make their questions have some intrinsic significance for the child. Children, of course, will try to solve problems if they recognize them as such. But they are not often either predisposed to or skillful in problem *finding*, in recognizing the hidden conjectural feature in tasks set them. But we know now that children in school can quite quickly be led to such problem finding by encouragement and instruction.

The need for this instruction and encouragement and its relatively swift success relates, I suspect, to what psychoanalysts refer to as the guilt-ridden oversuppression of primary process and its public replacement by secondary process. Children, like adults, need reassurance that it is all right to entertain and express highly subjective ideas, to treat a task as a problem where you *invent* an answer rather than *finding* one out there in the book or on the blackboard. With children in elementary school, there is often a need to devise emotionally vivid special games, story-making episodes, or construction projects to re-establish in the child's mind his right not only to have his own private ideas but to express them in the public setting of a classroom.

But there is another, perhaps more serious difficulty: the interference of extrinsic with intrinsic problem solving. Young children in school expend extraordinary time and effort figuring out what it is that the teacher wants— and usually coming to the conclusion that she or he wants tidiness or remembering or doing things at a certain time in a certain way. This I have referred to in earlier chapters as extrinsic problem solving. There is a great deal of it in school.

There are several quite straightforward ways of stimulating problem solving. One is to train teachers to want it, and that will come in time. But teachers can be encouraged to like it, interestingly enough, by providing them and their children with materials and lessons that *permit* legitimate problem solving and permit the teacher to recognize it. For exercises with such materials create an atmosphere by treating things as instances of what *might* have occurred rather than simply as what did occur. Let me illustrate by a concrete instance. A fifth grade class was working on the organization of a baboon troop—on this particular day, specifically on how they might protect against predators. They saw a brief sequence of film in which six or seven adult males go forward to intimidate and hold off three cheetahs. The teacher asked what the baboons had done to keep the cheetahs off, and there ensued a lively discussion of how the dominant adult males, by showing their formidable mouthful of teeth and making threatening gestures, had turned the trick. A boy raised a tentative hand and asked whether cheetahs always attacked together. Yes, though a single cheetah sometimes followed behind a moving troop and picked off an older, weakened straggler or an unwary, straying juvenile. 'Well, what if there were four cheetahs and two of them attacked from behind and two from in front. What would the baboons do then?' The question could have been answered empirically and the inquiry ended. Cheetahs *don't* attack that way, and so we don't know what baboons *might* do. Fortunately, it was not. For the question opens up the deep issues of what might be and why it isn't. Is there a necessary relation between predators and prey that share a common ecological niche? Must their encounters have a 'sporting chance' outcome? It is such conjecture, in this case quite unanswerable, that produces rational, self-consciously problem-finding behavior so crucial to the growth of intellectual power. Given the materials, given some background and encouragement, teachers like it as much as the students.

To isolate the major difficulty, then, I would say that while a body of knowledge is given life and direction by the conjectures and dilemmas that brought it into being and sustained its growth, pupils who are being taught often do not have a corresponding sense of conjecture and dilemma. The task of the curriculum maker and teacher is to provide exercises and occasions for its nurturing. If one only thinks of materials and content, one can all too easily overlook the problem. I believe that it is precisely because instruction takes the form of telling-out-of-the-context-of-action that the difficulty emerges. It is a pitfall of instruction by the 'third way.' The answer is the design of exercises in conjecture, in ways of inquiry, in problem finding. It is something that the good teacher does naturally at least some of the time. With help from the curriculum maker's exercises and conjectures, it is something that ordinary teachers will do much more of the time.

The personalization of knowledge.   Let me turn now to a third problem, one that is particularly important in social studies: the personalization of knowledge, getting to the child's feeling, fantasies, and values with one's lessons. A generation ago, the progressive movement urged that knowledge be related to child's own experience and brought out of the realm of empty abstractions. A good idea was translated into banalities about the home, then the friendly postman and trashman, then the community, and so on. It is a poor way to compete with the child's own dramas and mysteries. A decade ago, my colleague Clyde Kluckhohn wrote a prize-winning popular book on anthropology with the entrancing title *Mirror for Man*. In some deep way, there is extraordinary power in 'that mirror which other civilizations still hold up to us to recognize and study . . . [the] image of ourselves.'[8] The psychological bases of the power are not obvious. Is it as in discrimination learning, where increasing the degree of contrast helps in the learning of a discrimination, or as in studies of concept attainment, where a negative instance demonstrably defines the domain of a conceptual rule? Or is it some primitive identification? All these miss one thing that seems to come up frequently in our interviews with the children. It is the experience of discovering kinship and likeness in what at first seemed bizarre, exotic, and even a little repellent.

Consider two examples, both involving film of the Netsilik. In the films, a single nuclear family, Zachary, Marta, and their four-year-old Alexei, is followed through the year—spring sealing, summer fishing at the stone weir, fall caribou hunting, early winter fishing through the ice, winter at the big ceremonial igloo. Children report that at first the three members of the family look weird and uncouth. In time, they look normal, and eventually, as when Marta finds sticks around which to wrap her braids, the girls speak of how pretty she is. That much is superficial—or so it seems. But consider a second episode.

It has to do with Alexei, who, with his father's help, devises a snare and catches a gull. There is a scene in which he stones the gull to death. Our children watched, horror-struck. One girl, Kathy, blurted out, 'He's not even human, doing that to the seagull.' The class was silent. Then another girl, Jennine, said quietly: 'He's got to grow up to be a hunter. His mother was smiling when he was doing that.' And then an extended discussion about how people have to do things to learn and even do things to learn how to feel appropriately. 'What would you do if you had to live there? Would you be as smart about getting along as they are with what they've got?' said one boy going back to the accusation that Alexei was inhuman to stone the bird.

I am sorry it is so difficult to say it clearly. What I am trying to say is that to personalize knowledge one does not simply link it to the familiar. Rather one makes the familiar an instance of a more general case and thereby produces awareness of it. What the children were learning about was not seagulls and Eskimos, but about their own feelings and preconceptions that, up to then, were too implicit to be recognizable to them.

There is, perhaps, another route to personalizing knowledge, and it is one that will repel some scholars. Let me propose a view. Our population becomes increasingly urban, and it is characteristic of urban life that it is marked by a certain protective anonymity. Our great metropolitan areas have not only a problem of urban rot and urban renewal at their centers, but a problem of increasing blandness and remoteness from life at their bedroom-suburban peripheries. The close-knit, nearby, extended family of grand-parents and maiden aunts of the small towns and farms is almost extinct. For the middle class—which is, thanks to our genius in the distribution of wealth, increasingly large and dominant—there is a remoteness from the immediate tragic forces in life, a remoteness that is reinforced by the great cosmetic urge of our mass media of communication, our advertisers, our very affluence. We may be suffering a loss of moral richness at the periphery of our cities. At the center, in our slums, the problem is quite different and in the short run far more serious: it is a problem of loss of hope. Why should the negro child in central Harlem take the school as a vehicle to salvation? To him, school is an abstract and an alien proposition. What has it to do with him, his life, his aspirations?

Yet, for all our deep worry over hopelessness in the city and suburban provincialism outside, neither seems to blunt one particular human capacity that overrides both: the sense of drama, the mysterious device by which we represent most vividly the range of the human condition. I took a group of fourteen-year-olds to see Peter Ustinov's *Billy Budd* on film. The intensity of the discussion of moral philosophy on the way home convinced me that we have overlooked one of our most powerful allies in keeping alive our engage-ment in history, in the range of human life, in philosophy. Drama, the novel, history rendered with epic aids of its patron goddess Clio, are all built on the paradox of human choice, on the resolution of alternatives. They are in the best sense studies in the causes and consequences of choice. It is in their gripping quality, their nearness of life, that we can, I would urge, best make personal the dilemmas of the culture, its aspirations, its conflicts, its terrors. I should like to propose that we examine afresh the acting of drama, the use of theatre, the examination of the mythic and the tragic and the comic in their most powerful expressions. In some considerable measure we have intellec-tualized and made bland and good-natured the teaching of the particulars of history, of society, of myth. I would urge that in fashioning the instruction designed to give children a view of the different faces and conditions of man, we consider more seriously the use of this most powerful impulse to represent the human condition in drama and, thereby, the drama of the human condition.

Just as concepts and theory serve to connect the facts of observation and experiment in the conventional disciplines of knowledge, so the great dramatic themes and metaphors provide a basis for organizing one's sense of man, for seeing what is persistent in his history and his condition, for introducing some unity into the scatter of our knowledge as it relates to ourselves.

NOTES AND REFERENCES

1. Bruner, J. S. (January 1964) 'The course of cognitive growth', *American Psychologist* 19, 1–15.
2. Polya, G. (1957)(2nd ed.) *How To Solve It*, New York, Doubleday.
3. Brown, R. (1965) 'From codability to coding ability', Ch. 7 in *Social Psychology*, New York, Free Press of Glencoe.
4. For full documentation, see:
   Bruner, J. S. (1964) 'Some theorems on instruction illustrated with reference to mathematics', *Sixty-third Year-book of the National Society for the Study of Education* [Part 1], Chicago, University of Chicago Press, pp. 306–35.
5. Humphrey, G. (1948) *Directed Thinking*, New York, Dodd, Mead.
6. Bloom, B. S. and Broder, L. J. (1950) *Problem-Solving Processes of College Students*, Chicago, University of Chicago Press.
7. Goodnow, J. and Pettigrew, T. F. (1955) 'Effect of prior patterns of experience on strategies and learning sets', *Journal of Experimental Psychology* 49, 381–9.
8. Levi-Strauss, C. (September 1965) Smithsonian Centennial Lecture, Washington, D.C.

1.2 *Creativity*

- ## R. G. Woods and
  ## R. St. C. Barrow

[. . .] We thus arrive at the view that a creative person in any sphere is one who tends to produce original work that represents his own way of looking at things in that sphere. The obvious and crucial question now arises as to whether that is all that there is to being creative, or whether we have to add some reference to the quality of the work produced. If we do not add reference to quality as another condition of creativity certain consequences have to be accepted. First, virtually anybody who had a spark of independence in him (so that his way of looking at things could indeed be said to be his own) could be said to be creative. The very fact that I know very little about painting, with the result that any daub I produce on a canvas is very much my own, would paradoxically make me a creative painter. The mere fact of my sitting down to write a novel would turn me into a creative novelist. For what I wrote would be a product that was my own and was original in some degree; it would be consciously produced and there need be no problem about tendency, since presumably I could then write another novel. This consequence, I suggest, is quite unacceptable. I do not know how to paint, my novels have no merit whatsoever: I am neither a creative painter nor a creative novelist.

  Secondly, though obviously related to the first point, if any distinctive product consciously produced is evidence of creativity then the assumption from which we started—that it is desirable that people should be creative—is thrown right open to question. It is one thing to say that it is desirable to produce creative writers and scientists if we have in mind examples such as Shakespeare and Einstein (examples which carry the implication of quality), quite another if we have in mind virtually anybody who puts pen to paper or has an idea. The only way in which one could defend the thesis, that creativity without reference to standards or quality was a normative concept or a desirable quality, would be to argue that the mere fact that somebody produces something original is a praiseworthy feature of that individual. The reader must decide whether a scientist who produces a theory that is absurd but original (because nobody else would countenance such absurdity) is to be praised on that account, whether an artist who produces a smashed pane of glass, smashed in a subtly distinctive way, is therefore to be admired, or whether a photographer who takes a series of photographs without removing the cover from the camera lens is on that account alone to be revered. For myself, I claim emphatically that none of these three people are *necessarily* to be admired, and that therefore either we cannot necessarily attribute creativity to them, or else 'creative' must be understood as a purely descriptive value-free term, and it is a separate question as to whether we wish to promote such creativity.

Thirdly, if we do not write into the concept of creativity some reference to quality, then the word is in fact redundant. All novelists would be creative, since no two novelists have ever written the same book and no novelists (or at any rate very few) have ever written books that are not their own work. All people who thought at all would have a claim to be creative thinkers, since despite the fact that we may group ourselves in broad categories (e.g. some of us socialists, some conservatives) no two people think exactly alike; every individual, by the mere fact of being a unique personality, is in some respect a distinctive or original thinker. If the word 'creative' were redundant, it would make no sense to talk of promoting creativity. The demand for creative persons would simply be a demand for novelists, scientists, mathematicians and so on.

We therefore have to add as another necessary condition of being creative that the individual should produce good work. And this is where the problem really starts, because in some spheres at least it raises the fundamental question of what the criteria are for good work. In the sphere of science and mathematics the problem is less great: a creative scientist is one who makes advances in scientific knowledge which are genuine advances in knowledge. One can judge that the Russian scientists who produced the sputnik were creative because the sputnik, to put it crudely, worked. But in the sphere of art assessing creativity will involve reference to aesthetic criteria which are notoriously difficult to assess. This is why in the example of the photographer who does not remove his lens cover I had to write that he was not 'necessarily' creative. My point there was that the fact that he was being original would not alone make him creative. But some people might accept that, and go on to argue that he was none the less creative because his blank photographs were works of art. If that seems preposterous to some readers one has only to think of John Cage's piano concerto, heralded by many as an artistic work of quality, which consists of the pianist sitting at the piano with the lid down over the keys and playing not a note. We cannot, unfortunately, go into the question of aesthetic standards here. The point to be stressed is that given that there are some standards, that there is a distinction between good art and bad art, then the mere fact that I produce a colour pattern that nobody else has done does not make me creative: the pattern must have some quality; it must come up to certain standards.

If the analysis of creativity given above is acceptable, then certain things follow from it. The first point is that one part of what it means to be a creative artist, scientist or whatever, is that one is a good artist, a good scientist, or whatever. The converse of course is not true: I may be a good mathematician without being a creative one, because I may not produce any original work in mathematics. But if I am a creative mathematician then I shall both produce original work and work that is good work according to the standards of mathematics. It follows from this that in order to assess whether a man is a creative scientist we shall need to refer to different criteria than those that we shall need to refer to to assess whether he is a creative photographer. Maths, science, novel writing, photography and so on are distinct activities and to be good at any one of them requires distinct talents and reference to distinct standards and ways of proceeding. And it follows from this that there is no necessary reason why an individual who is creative in one respect or sphere should be creative in any other. It therefore does not make much sense to refer to one individual simply as creative or more creative than another. When we do pick out an individual such as Leonardo da Vinci as creative, without specific reference as to what spheres he is creative in, we mean not that he had some quality (creativity) that, say, Beethoven lacked, but that he showed himself to be creative in many spheres. Da Vinci was not more creative than Beethoven, as one might say he was more good-tempered. He was creative in more spheres.

How do these points affect the stress on creativity in education? Before going any further we may as well face the fact that despite the impression one may get from some educational writings, virtually nothing is known about what as a matter of empirical fact produces creative people in various spheres. That is to say virtually nothing is known about how one may best hope to produce a Shakespeare or an Orton, a Mozart or a Cage, a Darwin or an Einstein. It well may be that such people are born and not made at all. There is, of course, a certain amount of evidence (though not a great deal even here) to suggest that where children are given a certain amount of scope for free expression in the art room they grow up less restricted in their artistic expression than those who are not given such freedom. Or that children who are encouraged to partake in problem-solving situations are less ill at ease than adults in problematic situations. Such considerations may be very important from an educational point of view, but it should now be clear that to make either of these assertions is not really to say anything about creativity. One is hardly surprised at the suggestion that those who are brought up to express themselves freely in paint or to take a delight in problem solving should tend, as adults, to feel free to express themselves in paint and enjoy problem solving. But the questions still remain as to how important these things are, as to whether there are not other things equally important even in the sphere of painting for example, and as to whether such children can be called creative. To express oneself is not to be creative, despite the fact that to be creative involves among other things expressing oneself. To solve problems seems an admirable thing to do, but practice in solving problems in school does not automatically mean that one will be able to solve any problem as an adult.

If our intention is to promote creativity then clearly we have to meet the following requirements:

1 We have to avoid instilling in children the idea that everything is known and determined, and that they must subserve the acknowledged experts in any field and cannot follow their own distinctive way of looking at things.
2 We have to promote ingenuity and imagination so that individuals are capable of making the imaginative leaps necessary for breaking new ground in any sphere.
3 We have to produce skill and understanding in any given sphere, for without these how, except by chance, is the individual going to be a good scientist, artist or whatever; how is he going to have the excellence that is a part of creativity?

Once these considerations are spelt out one immediately has grave doubts about a lot of so-called creative activity in schools, for it neither is creative nor is there any reason to suppose that in isolation it will promote creativity. What, for instance, could be meant by a 'creativity hour' or a lesson simply entitled 'creative activity'? As we have seen, it does not make sense to talk of creativity in a vacuum: individuals can only display creativity in various spheres of activity. The idea of children being creative, as opposed to having a creative maths lesson or a creative writing lesson and so on, is a simple nonsense. This is a small point, of course, since presumably what is meant by a creativity hour, in most cases, is that it is an hour in which children may practise being creative in various spheres, or, perhaps specifically the impli-cation is that they are doing art and craft as opposed to maths and science. But small though the point may be it is symptomatic of the confusion that seems to surround the notion of creativity in schools. In order to avoid that confusion let us proceed by considering creativity in respect of various spheres one by one.

What are we to say in respect of artistic creativity when, for example, Anderson remarks that 'the creative environment must provide freedom for each person to respond truthfully with his whole person as he sees and understands the truth'?[1] Clearly the reply must be that this is indeed one thing that the creative environment must provide, but it is not all that it must provide. If children are simply given access to the materials for painting and left to respond truthfully with their whole person (the very idea of which, incidentally, I find perplexing in reference to *young* children: does not a truthful response involve the idea of considerable self-awareness?) they are not necessarily being creative. What is happening in such a situation is that the first of the three requirements outlined in the last paragraph but one is being met: the children are being encouraged to paint as they feel inclined and not in response to the instructions of others. It is possible that they are being imaginative and that therefore the second requirement is being met, although in terms of promoting creativity it is not at all clear how one does best promote ingenuity and imagination; obviously not by restricting the free expression of the child completely, and that is why one accepts a degree of freedom as a necessary part of the creative environment. But placing all the stress on a complete freedom of expression would seem to be self-defeating. For in these circumstances how is one to judge between the imaginative and the unimaginative piece of work? Either one argues that any sincere expression of oneself is imaginative, or one has criteria for distinguishing between imaginative self-expression and unimaginative self-expression. And if there are criteria for imaginative work, there seems no reason to suppose that children will necessarily become imaginative simply because they are free to express themselves. But it is the third requirement that is all important and *that* requirement is not being met at all. How are children expected to become creative artists if they are brought up under the impression that anything they do with their heart in it is creative? How does one expect to produce a creative composer or painter if one does not teach the child how to compose and how to paint and if one does not familiarize him with what has already been done in those fields and with what at the present time counts as music or painting?

Much the same may be said of 'creative writing'. Insofar as an emphasis on creative writing means that there is a case for suggesting that repeated corrections of stories, on the grounds that they are mispunctuated or misspelt, may stunt the child's enthusiasm and spontaneity, it obviously cannot be dismissed as an absurd idea. But it is not true that any spontaneous writing is creative writing, and it therefore does not follow that a systematic acceptance of anything the child writes promotes creativity. It is no doubt true that spelling and the accepted rules of grammar have got very little to do with being creative. It is probably also true that some creative artists have not been particularly gifted as spellers and grammarians. It is certainly true that some creative writers, such as Joyce, have deliberately abandoned conventional rules of grammar and spelling to a large extent. But it is equally true that many creative artists have emerged from a schooling that taught them to spell and punctuate, that much creative work has been written according to such rules, and that there is a limit beyond which not even a Joyce can go if his work is to be read by others. Certainly if one wants to produce creative writers one does not want to curb their spontaneity. All that is being said here is that it is not in fact clear that some concern with such things as spelling and grammar need curb spontaneity, that, more importantly, spontaneity alone does not produce creative writing, and that treating children's spontaneous writing uncritically and indiscriminately as creative cannot help to

promote creativity in that sphere in that child. To become a creative writer
he needs to acquire skills, understanding of other creative works and
familiarity with what has been written. He needs knowledge and critical
standards, neither of which are promoted by creative writing lessons understood as spontaneous writing lessons. The only way out of this impasse is to
argue, as Britton has done, that the definition of literature is a piece of writing
that is written for its own sake and involves the writer in reflecting on his
own past experience.[2] If that is what literature is, then children may be said to
be writing literature. The reply to this is that this is not in fact what most of us
mean by literature, but that if we accept the definition it becomes, as White
has pointed out, an open question as to whether there is necessarily any
value in people writing literature.[3]

Even more obviously if we wish to produce creative mathematicians or
scientists, it is insufficient simply to leave children to proceed as they see fit.
What usually seems to be meant by creative maths lessons is lessons in which
the child is encouraged to discover for himself from certain data certain
solutions rather than being simply given the answer (with or without the
explanation). Now there may be very good grounds for advocating this
discovery method, but the fact remains that such a procedure does not mean
that the child is being a creative mathematician, that such a procedure alone
cannot produce creative mathematicians and that, for what it is worth,
creative mathematicians can, as they have done throughout history, arise
without having had the benefit of such teaching methods. The situation is
quite simple: to be a creative mathematician is to be a good mathematician
and to have the ability and the originality to go beyond the current bounds of
mathematical knowledge. If all we wanted from maths lessons was a host of
creative mathematicians it would still be an open empirical question as to
how much in practice one needed to instil mathematical knowledge in order
to cover the ground and to what extent one could do this without stunting the
originality and questing frame of mind that are also necessary for creativity.

It seems fairly clear that the term 'creativity' is currently being used in a
variety of senses and that it covers a number of different ideas that are not all
equally valuable. [. . .]

We must distinguish clearly between spontaneous self-expression,
ingenuity, problem-solving and creativity. When Wyn Williams argues that
an emphasis on discovery methods is 'vital because it emphasises the need for
children to be creative',[4] he is confusing the issue. It does not necessarily do
any such thing, nor is there any obvious reason to accept the assumption that
we need creative people. Creative scientists have an obvious utilitarian
value, but why in point of fact do we need to be so concerned about producing creative artists?

The situation, then, is this. To be creative in any specific sphere demands
knowledge and understanding of that sphere. Any education that ignores
this point is not making a realistic effort to promote creativity in various

spheres. Originality is also a necessity, and it well may be that the American educational situation prior to the launching of the Russian sputnik was such as to curb originality and the tendency to attempt to break new ground in the scientific sphere. It may also be that discovery techniques and problem-solving activity will sharpen the tendency towards originality, or at least avoid the stultifying effect that traditional inculcation of information may have. All that can be said here is that these are empirical points and there is not as yet any convincing evidence that such teaching techniques make a material difference in terms of producing creative scientists. Such techniques may of course be advocated for reasons that have nothing to do with creativity (for example that the child understands better what he sees for himself, that his interest is sustained, that he thinks for himself) but that is a separate question.

NOTES AND REFERENCES

1. Anderson, H. H. (1959) 'Creativity in perspective' in Anderson, H. H. (Ed.) *Creativity and its Cultivation*, New York, Harper & Row, p. 253.
2. Britton, J. (1963) 'Literature', in *The Arts and Current Tendencies in Education*, London, University of London Institute of Education, p. 42.
3. White, J. P. (1972) 'Creativity and education', in Hirst, P. and Peters, R. (Eds) *Education and the Development of Reason*, London, Routledge & Kegan Paul.
4. Williams, W. (1970) 'The proper concerns of education', in Rubenstein, D. and Stoneman, C. (Eds) *Education for Democracy*, Harmondsworth, Penguin, p. 163.

1.3 *How does information retrieval help children's learning?*

- A. Ross

USING THE REAL WORLD

Much of children's learning is based on direct experience. They discuss their families, the weather, the local street and its shops, litter and traffic, and so on. British primary schools have a particularly good reputation for harnessing these experiences. They often encourage children to observe and describe their social and physical environment carefully, to collect both objects and information, and to use many of the so-called 'basic skills' in their responses and explorations. The emphasis is two-fold: firstly, to build on the direct and concrete experiences of children, and to use their findings as a starting point for further discovery; and secondly, to stress learning through performing a process rather than through acquiring facts about a process. Thus in primary school children learn a good deal about the world by observing, describing and analysing that which is near to them, and, in the process of doing this, acquire skills that will help them better observe, describe and analyse other aspects of the world which they may meet up with later.

ANALYSING AND CATEGORIZING

Children learn not just by looking and describing what is seen. They learn by thinking about their observations—by arranging them into mental categories of alike and unlike, by constructing abstract generalizations about events that will in future help them to learn quickly, classify and predict. We expect even very young children to learn in this way: think of the enormous range of physical appearance in various breeds of dog, and of how soon young children can categorize all of them as 'dog'. Or how children learn to predict that hot stoves, and then hot things in general, are potentially hurt-ful. Primary-school children learn to classify and sort an extraordinary variety of items, events and people. This process continues through life in the way that we all consider the social and scientific world about us.

MAKING HYPOTHESES

The way in which we sort out what we observe is by the process of making and testing hypotheses. Hypotheses are generally based on casually acquired personal experiences.

[If, for example] in a young child's experience of his own family and relatives, the father and other male adults go out to work, while mothers and other married females work at home, the child may make the very reason-able hypotheses that in all families adult females do housework, and adult males are in paid employment. The specific information has been generalized with a universal rule. Only later may fresh information challenge this rule. [. . .]

TESTING HYPOTHESES

[. . .] Hypotheses are constantly being tested and found wanting. Fresh hypotheses are then framed to meet the new evidence. Some hypotheses are very persistent, and it may take more than mere casual observation to find them wanting. Galileo and the testing of the acceleration of falling bodies of different weights from the tower of Pisa is an example of the disproving of a long and widely held hypothesis.

The philosopher Karl Popper has advanced the notion that all human understanding of the physical and social world is based upon the building and testing of hypotheses, and that hypotheses can only be proved false. No hypotheses, he argues, can be proved true. Hypothesis succeeds hypothesis, each new stage being more precise and refined than the previous stage. Even should the 'final' hypotheses be in fact true, we would have no way of knowing that we had reached this stage.

PROBLEMS: A RANGE OF RESULTS

Making hypotheses can be difficult. One reason is that there is often a range of observations, scattered about. For example, the various properties of a dog are not found in all dogs: we recognize an animal as a dog if it has a sufficient number of doggy features. We all recognize a family, but it can be very hard to define exactly what is meant by a family if we are to cover the full range of families. Most children, for example, generalize from their own experiences and those of their peers, and imagine that all families have children as members. If children measure the length and areas of horse-chestnut leaves, they find that the majority of leaves fall within a narrow band of lengths and areas. But there is a considerable minority that are larger, smaller, longer or shorter. The range of results makes it difficult to come to a generalized conclusion about dogs, families or horse-chestnut leaves.

PROBLEMS: MAKING GENERALIZATIONS

To generalize, it is useful to have more than simply one's own experiences and observations. We need an exchange of information, so that one person's false inference can be countered by the experiences of others. One problem in learning, therefore, is to listen to and evaluate the observations of other people, and to be prepared to modify or even abandon hypotheses as new information becomes available. This open-mindedness must be matched by an ability to investigate and share in a social manner, in discussion and argument with one's peers.

PROBLEMS: LARGE NUMBERS

The more experiences one tries to bring together, and the greater the scatter or range of observations, the more difficult it is for primary-school children to generalize. Sharing information and making hypotheses from the evidence of three or four people is fairly easy: when it comes to a classful of experiences, problems of handling numbers arise. When the teacher tries to bring in even more observations—which is necessary in order to continue hypothesising and testing—it can become very difficult. Sometimes statistics help—fractions, percentages, pie-charts and histograms; at other times probability language is used—most, many, a lot of, sometimes, usually, etc.

INFORMATION RETRIEVAL—BANKING INFORMATION

Information retrieval with a microcomputer can begin to meet some of these problems. Collecting together a body of information, for example, means that larger numbers of observations can be collated, which can be quickly and accurately searched through. Large numbers will not be such a problem if the information is held electronically, in a form that can rapidly be made accessible—unlike the casual sampling of the memories of a class (sometimes unreliable, often volatile, and on occasions distorted by absences), or lists on paper (dog-eared, mislaid and misread), the datafile on tape or disc can be read easily, quickly and reliably.

Much discussion and sharing of ideas is essential to agree on the nature of what data is to be collected, and the standard of observation that is required; and this social interaction of a class or group engaged in building or interrogating a database should not be overlooked. It is in the discussion about how to proceed and the debate about the significance of what has been found that learning occurs.

INFORMATION RETRIEVAL—TESTING HYPOTHESES

Children using an information-retrieval system should always be talking and discussing together what they are doing. Sometimes discussions will be about advancing and testing hypotheses: could it be that there is some association between one finding and another? Sometimes the discussion will be to do with logic: how can we ask to find the information we need? Some discussions will be between the two: what exactly do we mean when we categorize groups in this way? At a later stage, talk will be focused more upon significance: what have we found? How does this match our expectations, what we thought we would find? An example can be seen in the work of a group of nine-year-olds trying to discover which conkers were stronger. A group advanced the theory that the older the conker, the stronger it would be. The range of results from testing was not easy to handle in its raw form—some old conkers were strong, some weak, and vice versa. What, they argued, do we mean by a 'strong' conker, or an 'old' one? Definitions were arrived at in order to test the hypotheses. When the analysis tended to contradict the original theory, much debate followed on what new generalization should be used to supplant it.

INFORMATION RETRIEVAL—AN INTERACTIVE PROCESS

Information retrieval can thus greatly enhance the learning process. In particular, it should be seen as an interactive inquiry, encouraging a dialogue not just between child and machine, but also between child and child, child and teacher. By liberating the class from the drudgery of number-crunching, and enabling children to have a sufficiently large body of data from which to generalize with confidence, it can enormously enlarge the range and depth of learning activities in the primary curriculum.

2 COMPUTERS AND HUMAN VALUES

The papers in this section demonstrate the great diversity of ways in which computers will affect adult life outside work. They also indicate something of the complexity of the relationship between values and computer use. Many different ways of using computers are discussed and evaluated, including the following:

- development of software that individuals can customize to meet their own needs.
- production by individuals or small communities of local magazines, new kinds of games or community databases.
- more comprehensive and effective methods of checking on the activities of people without them being aware of it.
- devices to enable people to type out sentences in English that are then transformed into Braille script.
- coupling an animal's visual system and brain to a computer.
- 'therapeutic' programs that respond in some approximately appropriate way to people's worries or fears.
- systems that can recognize spoken words.
- programs that allow a painter to use the computer to paint in light rather than using conventional methods.
- designing programs that create works of art without further human intervention, in accordance with rules provided by the artist who developed the program.

Clearly many of these projects require people with the skills indicated in the Preface. But is the unreflective learning of these skills automatically desirable? Weizenbaum argues that just to encourage problem-solving or information-handling skills is not sufficient. University teachers and their students are also faced by the moral and social question of what problems the skills are used to solve, and with what results. You might wish to consider how teachers at school level could try to develop the sort of attitudes to computer use that this section implies are needed.

2.1 **Creating a convivial communications society**

• Lorne Peterson

Almost every commentator has assured the public that the computer is bringing on a revolution. By the 1970s it should have been clear that revolution was the wrong word. And it should not have been surprising to anyone that in many cases the technology has served as a prop to the status quo.

The Soul Of A New Machine, *Tracy Kidder*

Kidder's astute observation raises a vital question: how can we shape and use computer and communications technologies so that they serve as helpful tools for developing a convivial and democratic society?

Most of us, especially government policy makers, have not been asking this question. Not much thinking is being done about how to develop and shape communications technology in the context of the culture that we wish to create and nurture. Governments tend to focus on such questions as: how can computer-related technology be used to maximize industrial productivity and establish an economically sovereign and internationally competitive nation-state?

Industrial productivity and economic independence are important matters, but we let them overshadow and exclude equally vital concerns about the personal and cultural aspects of the new computer technologies. Consequently, we are navigating without charts of the social dangers and the life-enhancing opportunities of computer and communications technology.

If we want the new computer technologies to serve us within the context of the culture we wish to develop, we need to find a way of placing economic matters and strategies in their proper proportions. Gail Stewart, an Ottawa-based economist and public policy consultant, has suggested that this can be done by building policies for computer communications technologies upon a social strategy, in which industrial and economic strategies would become subsumed.

In other words, priority would be given to forming a social strategy, and economics would move from being a primary objective to being a necessary condition in the development and use of the new technologies. This approach, says Stewart, raises a new set of questions, which are society-oriented rather than merely market-oriented.

First, what kind of society do we want?
Second, what kinds of communications policies are needed to enable us to work towards that society?
Third, what kinds of communications tools and systems do we need to aid us in attaining our social and cultural aims?

Gail Stewart and other observers of communications technology have pointed to Telidon. Canada's version of videotex, as an example of how the social and cultural potential of a new technology is neglected when it is developed within a narrow industrial strategy.

Telidon technology could be used to develop a decentralized communications medium, like the telephone, that would allow people to create information and to communicate directly with each other. Instead, Telidon is being introduced as a centralized information medium, like TV, where a few large-scale electronic publishers sell information services to many users.

'When we get a new invention like Telidon', says Stewart, 'we put it in a narrow single strategy (increase our manufacturing capacity and export sales). Our primary concern must be the development of a structure of communications capabilities for Canadians, not the development of a specific manufacturing capability.' A broad social strategy is needed to guide the development of communications tools and networks, in ways that would foster the development of the Canadian community.

Stewart sees citizens playing a principal role in the designing of a social strategy for new communications technology; because citizens are responsible for their communities and for their governments. At the same time, governments have a responsibility to consult with citizens about what they want.[1]

In the designing of a social strategy, what may be needed 'is a process of *country talk*, rather than opinion polls or referenda', says Stewart. Citizens could meet in their communities and have conversations about how they want to use computer communications technologies.

'One way of doing this', she says, 'is to put questions on the public agenda'. For example, if citizens are concerned about how they could have more access to communications systems, they could hold a public seminar on that question. Government officials, telephone company managers and computer communications designers could be invited to the seminar. 'Then I bet you would very quickly have that question out as a real, live issue'.

But would government or industry people really listen to what citizens say?

'Governments are not accustomed to citizens planning themselves how they want the country to develop', says Stewart. 'So, their first reaction might be to dismiss it as some kind of community activity. Governments must become more respectful of the citizenry, and help citizens to develop their competence as managers of society.'

Policy makers are out of step with the new culture that is now unfolding— a culture which involves extending and broadening the rights and responsibilities of citizenship. We are entering a post-industrial society where a primary concern is how people can be active participants in developing and applying new technology, rather than being passive recipients of technology and its effects.

This view is expressed in a Vanier Institute of the Family (VIF) report. *A Familial Perspective on Micro-Computer Communications*. (VIF is an Ottawa-based national association that was established to promote the well-being of families). The report states that there is a need to approach computer-related technology in new ways and ask such questions as: 'what impacts will persons, families, community-groups, educators and learners have on the development of micro electronics?'.

Alan Mirabelli, VIF co-ordinator of communication and primary author of the report, says the tremendous power and low cost of micro computers, which makes them accessible to most people, is creating a new cultural opportunity—'what do I or what does my group create using this powerful instrument?'. From a cultural viewpoint, 'the real driving force of this technology is the development of software and new applications'.

These are activities that can be decentralized. 'It can be a "mom and pop" operation or a single individual working at home', says Mirabelli. 'The basic idea is that production is no longer separated from consumption. If I produce a piece of software for my terminal, it is because I have a use for it'.

Even when you produce a piece of software to sell to others, says Mirabelli, each buyer can customize it to suit his needs. 'This creates a different mentality in how one perceives products and services. You are no longer dependent on a large corporation, such as IBM'. (This assumes you learn how to program your computer, rather than just buying off-the-shelf software).

Once you and your family learn how to program, you can ask: how can we use our computer so that it serves our needs? 'This is a major leap forward for a society that is accustomed to consuming products. We should recognize that this is one of the more appropriate scenarios.'

Another appropriate scenario is the creation of cottage-type industries in communities, either in homes or community-based work places. People could, for example, use micro computers to produce magazines, community databases, games and art. Mirabelli thinks decentralized work activities are more likely to begin happening in community centres, which would be equipped with computers and communications technology, because the social isolation of working at home would be too great.

From a public policy perspective, says Mirabelli, we need 'policies of cultivation' which enable and encourage experiments in homes and communities aimed at developing new and socially beneficial uses for computer-related technology. He stresses, however, that you cannot regulate or set policies for innovation. 'All you can do is set policy which is broad enough to enable people, rather than restrict people.'

The problem, he says, is that governments have no experience in making policies that are enabling. He believes that social strategies for the development of computer communications technology will be more appropriate if each family and community creates its own policy.

Gail Stewart's view is similar. She says a social strategy has to come from members of the community. Then, we as citizens must tell government and industry how we want the new technologies to serve us.

Once we have found answers to such questions as 'what purpose do we want this technology to serve', says Stewart, 'we can give our specs to government and industry. It's like giving an architect the specs for a house you want. Before you can give him the specs, you have to know what kind of design you need.'

The exact opposite of this democratic process is now happening. Governments and industry are designing communications tools and networks without seriously consulting the public. They seem to be forgetting that citizens are the primary social navigators and that they are supposed to be serving our needs.

This situation will only change when we as citizens start acting as navigators, rather than as victims. As Marshall McLuhan once said: 'We're in a kind of big spaceship with everybody a crew member and no passengers'.

NOTES AND REFERENCES

1. The Regional Municipality of Ottawa-Carleton is exploring the use of a community consultation process as an alternative to conventional public participation practices.

2.2   *The new surveillance*

• Gary T. Marx

Most of us see computerized dossiers, x-rayed luggage at airports, credit
checks, video cameras in banks and stores, and electronic markers on consumer goods as the normal order of things. We think of these technologies as
essential to life as we know it, not as threats that enhance surveillance and
social control. However, many of these familiar systems have the potential
to do just that. Indeed, most of them are so subtle, diffuse, and voluntary
that we are unaware of the extent to which surveillance has become
embedded into everyday life.

Clearly these new forms of surveillance can be immensely beneficial. For
example, the life of an elderly heart-attack victim who lived alone was saved
when her failure to open her refrigerator sent an alarm through her telephone
to a central monitor. A corrupt judge was caught when he took a bribe from
an undercover police agent who tape-recorded the encounter. Serious crimes
have been solved because of tips received on citizen hotlines. Advanced
emergency systems that give a caller's location and phone number the instant
an operator answers have saved lives. Satellite photography has monitored
industry's compliance with emission standards. Credit cards have revolutionized travel and retail merchandising. Computer-matching programs
may save tax dollars, and citizens may feel safer because of video surveillance in banks and stores.

Yet as large databanks and their management have become central to the
workings of the modern industrial state, people have surrendered traditional
notions of privacy for the sake of efficiency, and the information-gathering
powers of the state and private organizations have extended deep into the
social fabric. In focusing on the power of these surveillance techniques, I do
not suggest that we are hapless victims of technological determinism who
can do little more than bemoan our loss of liberty. The fact that technology
can be misused does not necessarily mean that it will be. Government legislation, good program design, and intelligent management have reduced the
potential for errors and abuse. The United States has more restrictions on the

use of surveillance technologies than most countries. Furthermore, some potential for surveillance has been neutralized by countersurveillance devices—such as the detectors that warn drivers of police radar units. However, there is often a significant time lag between the appearance of a new technology and its regulation, and regulation when it does come is often weaker than desirable. For example, many states still do not regulate the use of lie-detector tests.

I do not argue that more harm than good now comes from these new technologies. My point is simply that in our eagerness to innovate and our infatuation with the efficiency and gimmickry of technical progress in day-to-day transactions, the potentials for negative results from these new developments simply have not received enough attention. More should be done to safeguard privacy now, and still more as new technologies are perfected and more widely applied.

A NEW ERA OF TRANSACTIONAL ANALYSIS

While adding immensely to the services rendered to consumers and companies, computer databanks have greatly increased the amount of personal information that is recorded and analyzed. The computers of the five largest credit-screening companies contain records on more than 150 million individuals, and most credit-card purchases are now approved electronically. The health records of nine out of ten working Americans are computerized through their insurance policies. Even pharmacies have begun to keep computerized records of patients' use of prescription drugs. As electronic funds transfer has become central to banking, individual financial transactions have become part of long-lived computer records. And the size and reach of police databases, such as the FBI's National Criminal Justice Information Center, continue to grow.

Many similar records, including bank statements, health-care histories, and credit ratings, existed before the advent of computers. But electronic data processing allows these vast databases to be cross-checked. Bits of scattered information that in the past represented no threat to an individual's privacy and anonymity now can be correlated, such as the timing of phone calls, travel, and bank deposits. A thriving new computer-based data-scavenging industry now sells—chiefly for marketing but for other uses as well—information gleaned from sources such as drivers' licences, vehicle-registration and voter lists, birth, marriage, and death certificates, land deeds, telephone and organizational directories, and census records.

State and federal governments have established more than 500 programs to compare information from two or more sources, and private interests match records even more extensively. Consider the following examples:

A resident of a Massachussets nursing home lost her eligibility for government medical assistance because a computer determined that she had more than the minimum amount permitted in her savings account. What the computer did not know was that the money was held in trust to be used for her burial expenses. Such burial contracts are exempt from asset calculations. Another woman was automatically eliminated from welfare roles because a loan for her son's college education had been temporarily deposited in her bank account.

A welfare recipient in Washington, D.C., obtained employment and repeatedly notified the welfare department of her new status. However, she continued to receive welfare checks in the mail, and she eventually cashed them to pay off doctor bills incurred from a serious illness. Finally, a computer match linking employment and welfare records resulted in her indictment on a felony charge. Her case was dismissed, but before her trial, a newspaper published her name (along with those of 15 others) in an article describing the 'successful' results of computer matching.

Residents of New York City cannot purchase a marriage license or register a deed for a new home if they have outstanding parking tickets. Such computer matching of disparate data is a pointed example of its inherent threats to civil liberties.

Profiling, in which disparate clues are used to assess whether a person or event fits a model of known or suspected violators, is also increasingly common. For example, the Educational Testing Service used computer profiling in an effort to discover cheating on Scholastic Aptitude Tests in 1982. The ETS sent some 2,000 form letters alleging 'copying' to students who had taken the tests, noting that a statistical review had 'found close agreement of your answers with those on another answer sheet from the same test center. Such agreement is unusual and suggests that copying occurred.' Students were told that in two weeks their scores would be canceled and colleges notified unless they provided 'additional information' to prove they had not cheated.

TRACKING PEOPLE'S WHEREABOUTS

Modern surveillance technologies now allow organizations to monitor people's movements to a degree previously imagined only in fiction. Aircraft that can spot a car or person 30,000 feet below have been used to monitor drug traffickers. Satellites may soon be used for this purpose as well. The CIA has apparently used satellite photographs to monitor antiwar demonstrations and civil disorders. Computer-enhanced satellite photography can identify vehicles moving in the dark and penetrate most camouflage materials.

One-way video and film surveillance has expanded rapidly, as anyone who ventures into a shopping mall or uses an electronic bank teller should realize. Many stores use closed-circuit television to monitor the activities of both customers and employees. The cameras often have 360-degree movement and may be concealed inside ceiling globes with amber or mirrored surfaces.

Other devices now in use include sensitive miniature but powerful radio transmitters; tape recorders the size of a match box; video cameras the size of a deck of cards; instruments for detecting motion, air currents, vibrations, odors, and pressure changes; and voice-stress analyzers. A light amplifier developed for use in the Vietnam War requires only starlight, moonlight, or a street lamp several hundred yards away to provide enough illumination for a variety of film and video cameras and binoculars. Attached to a telescopic device, the amplifier increases the latter's range to over a mile.

The National Security Agency can simultaneously monitor 54,000 telephone transmissions to and from the United States. The agency operates beyond the usual judicial and legislative controls, and can apparently disseminate its information to other government agencies at will.

The Crime Control Act of 1968 makes it a felony for a third party—except for government agents under strictly defined conditions and with a warrant—to place electronic listening devices on telephones or in rooms. Yet this law does not apply to information transmitted in digital form. Thanks to technological changes since this law was enacted, an increasing proportion of telephone calls, including more than half of all long-distance hookups, is now transmitted in digital form. These messages, as well as all cellular mobile communications, conversations on cordless telephones, and communications among computers appear to be exempt from the wiretap law. In addition, automatic telephone switching technology now records when, where, and to whom calls are made.

Devices that can transmit information on the location and physiological condition of the wearer—such as pulse-rate monitors developed to improve health care—are now being used to permit continuous remote surveillance of criminals. In at least four jurisdictions in Florida and New Mexico, some offenders must wear an anklet containing an electronic transmitter. If the wearer goes outside a specified territory, the signal is interrupted, alerting the computer. This 'electronic leash' is being used in other contexts as well, such as to allow police supervisors to determine the exact location of patrol cars at all times.

Indeed, the Hong Kong government is testing an electronic system for monitoring where, when, and how fast a car is driven. The information will be used to levy a road-use tax to help reduce Hong Kong's high concentration of cars. Low-frequency signals from wire loops set into streets trigger a car's small radio receiver, which then transmits an identification number to a central facility. A similar system could also be used to enforce speed limits and monitor individuals' movements.

Much has been written of the electronic office, where data-processing machines do routine tasks and electonic mail substitutes for letters and telephones. We forget, however, that these systems that make possible so much efficiency also allow monitoring of employees' productivity and behavior, including workers' time away from their stations and access to restricted areas. Surveillance of factory workers has likewise expanded with computerized electronic devices that measure work pace, detect mistakes, and deter thefts by detecting the location of tagged material.

The last decade has seen the increased use of supposedly scientific 'inference' or 'personal truth' technology. These systems, based on body clues, include polygraphs and analyzers of voice stress, blood, and urine. Some proponents even claim that brain waves can provide clues to certain internal states, such as a person's degree of concentration or surprise.

Rising public concern about drunk driving has led to broad police use of roadblocks to screen large segments of the population. And determining the amount of alcohol in a person's system has now become easy: an officer need only hold a microphone-like device in front of a suspect.

New technology is also providing decentralized and inexpensive ways for each of us to help keep our neighbours safe and honest. For example, states have established many hotlines for anonymous reporting. These include a turn-in-a-poacher program in Connecticut and a program in Washington State that encourages motorists to report—sometimes on their mobile telephones—other motorists who improperly drive in expressway lanes reserved for car pools. Many federal agencies also maintain hotlines on which citizens can report abuses. For example, all 19 inspector general offices have set up telephone lines for receiving people's allegations of fraud, waste, mismanagement, and other abuses.

Many companies urge employees to report dishonesty among colleagues, and some support WeTiP, a nonprofit organization that operates a nationwide 24-hour toll-free hotline for reporting any kind of suspicious activity. TIP (Turn In a Pusher) uses anonymous reporting to help combat illicit drug use in hundreds of communities. A television program called 'Crime Stoppers USA,' seen in over 450 cities, is the video equivalent of the old-style reward posters. The program re-enacts 'the crime of the week' to encourage witnesses of unsolved cases to come forward.

DISTINCTIVE ATTRIBUTES OF THE NEW SURVEILLANCE

All these efforts represent new opportunities for some citizens to learn about the activities—illicit or otherwise—of fellow citizens and hence infringe on their privacy. Although these surveillance methods differ, most share seven characteristics that distinguish them from traditional forms of social control.

The new technologies conquer distance, darkness, and physical barriers. Surveillance was historically difficult simply because of the physical impossibility of seeing to the farthest regions of political jurisdiction, through closed doors, and into an individual's intellectual, emotional, and physical states. However, technical impossibility and, to some extent, inefficiency are losing their roles as the unplanned protectors of liberty. Sound and video can be transmitted over vast distances, infrared and light-amplifying technologies can pierce the dark, intrusive instruments can 'see' through doors, suitcases, and fog. Truth-seeking technologies claim to penetrate surface reality to uncover subterranean truths of the body and mind.

The new technologies transcend time, yielding records that can easily be stored, retrieved, combined, analyzed, and communicated.   Stored electronically, information can be available for instant analysis many years after it was accumulated and used in totally different contexts. Data can also easily migrate to places far removed from the original location.

The new technologies are capital-intensive rather than labor-intensive. Technical developments making information much less expensive to gather have dramatically altered the economics of surveillance. A few people can monitor a great many people and places. Economy is further enhanced because people have become voluntary participants in and consumers of much of this technology.

The new techniques broaden the base of surveillance.   Instead of targeting a specific suspect, today's instruments survey everyone and operate continuously and tirelessly. The new surveillance is decentralized in that data are available to widely dispersed users for many different purposes. The camera, the tape recorder, the magnetic identity card, the metal detector, the ubiquitous computerized form make all who come within their province reasonable targets for surveillance, pushing us toward a society where people feel constantly under suspicion. As the French social theorist Michel Foucault observed, the neverending threat of 'judgments, examinations, and observation' has superseded physical coercion as our society's major form of control.

The new surveillance technologies are chiefly concerned with preventing violations and reducing risk and uncertainty.   These are positive benefits, and proponents are likely to extensively promote the use of the techniques to deter violations, to catch violators in the act, and to obtain strong evidence of criminals' identity. These social benefits tend to make us indifferent to the negative effects of the technologies on individual freedom.

Those watched by the new surveillance techniques often become active partners in their own monitoring.   These systems may be self-activated and automatic, triggered when people move, talk on the telephone, turn on a television set, check a book out from the library, or enter or leave controlled areas.

The new surveillance techniques have low visibility or are invisible, and they are increasingly depersonalized. Ascertaining when or whether we are being watched, and who is doing the watching, becomes ever more difficult. Because much of the surveillance is covert, accountability is lessened and exploitation invited.

RETHINKING THE NATURE OF PRIVACY

Citizens' ability to evade all this surveillance is diminishing. To participate in the consumer society and the welfare state, we must provide personal information. To venture into a shopping mall, bank, or subway, sometimes even into a bathroom, is to perform before an unknown audience. To apply for a job, we may have to face lie-detector tests concerning intimate details of our lives.

To avoid such intrusions, people may decline needed services such as mental-health care, and avoid controversial actions such as filing grievances against landlords or governments. We may shun risks and experiments as the new technology exerts subtle pressure for conformity at the expense of diversity, innovation, and vitality.

In a society where everyone feels as if he or she is a target for investigation, trust—the most sacred and important element of the social bond—is damaged. Indeed, today's surveillance technologies may be creating a climate of suspicion from which there is no escape. Proving innocence in such a society may become vastly more difficult than inferring guilt.

Furthermore, the new surveillance is lessening the power of the individual relative to large organizations and government. Individuals and even public-interest groups clearly do not have the monitoring capabilities of credit-card companies and market-research firms, landlords' associations and real estate syndicates, police intelligence units, the National Security Agency, and banks and large corporations. Organizational memories extend over time and across space, making surveillance broader, deeper, and even routine.

Even if one denies the potential danger of our present situation, the possibility of future disasters remains. Social conditions may change: a more repressive government or a less tolerant public may gain sway in the United States—perhaps because of a severe economic downturn, immigration pressures, or a major foreign-policy or military defeat. Under such conditions, today's surveillance systems—and tomorrow's more powerful ones—could easily be used against those with the 'wrong' political beliefs, members of racial, ethnic, or religious minorities, and even those whose life-styles offend the majority. Attempts to prevent disorder could lead to vastly expanded use of surveillance systems to identify and persecute 'suspects,' with patriotic necessity the rationale for the gradual erosion of liberties.

We need to recognize that the potential for harm from certain surveillance systems may be so great that the risks outweigh their benefits. At least two widely discussed examples come to mind: the idea of creating linkages between all federal and state databanks, and the plan for a mandatory national identification system.

We could not turn the clock back even if we wanted to; the new technologies that both serve us well and threaten us all are here to stay. Our response must be to rethink the nature of privacy and create new ways to protect it. Some protection measures, ironically, will rely on the same technologies that we find threatening, such as encrypted communications and debugging devices. Legislation to protect privacy is also crucial. The 1984 Privacy Act—which requires that individuals be notified that personal records are being kept, affords them the right to see and correct such records, and prohibits information provided for one purpose from being used in an unrelated context—applies only to federal records. These restrictions must be better enforced and extended to state, local, and private-sector records. Less than 1 state in 5 now has standards for collecting and disseminating personal information. The public must also be informed about the power of surveillance devices and told when they are in use. 'Truth-detection' systems that rely primarily on trickery and intimidation to gain results should be strictly regulated. Greater attention must be paid to the accuracy and currency of the data collected by all these techniques and means of redress provided to persons whose rights are violated.

The first task of a society that would protect liberty and privacy is to prevent physical coercion on the part of the state and private parties. The second task is to limit the information on individuals that can be collected and the ways that it can be manipulated. This is clearly the more difficult task, as such control is often invisible, diffuse, and shrouded in benign justifications. As Justice Louis Brandeis warned a half-century ago, 'Experience should teach us to be most on our guard when the government's purposes are beneficent. Men born to freedom are naturally alert to repel invasion of their liberty by evil-minded rulers. The greatest dangers to liberty lurk in insidious encroachment by men of zeal, well-meaning but without understanding.'

2.3 *An analogue for freedom: new technology and disabled people*

• Gerald Hales

At the end of 1986, one of the presenters of the BBC Television Programme 'Tomorrow's World'[1] was asked about those things they had investigated which seemed at the time to be the most ridiculous or far-fetched. She replied that the item of which she was most sceptical at the time was a prediction that within a short period of time from the programme there would be computers in people's homes, not as a rarity but as something common, cheap and easy. This did not happen many years ago, but in the late 1970s, many of us can appreciate how accurate that prediction was simply by looking round our own sitting rooms and yet only a few years ago, it seemed ridiculous.

Those last few years have brought computer technology within the experience of the vast majority of people in the Western world. Of course there has been a substantial expansion of the use of computer technology in professional settings, and very many people now have experience of this type of technology in their work, from the statistician using large machines to the secretary using a word processor. Certainly many of the possibilities now available have revolutionized the modern office, making the storing, utilization, manipulation and finding of information a much quicker and easier process than it had ever been before. For many people, however, the real transformation in their relationship with computer technology has come about because of the prediction mentioned above: the introduction of computers into the home. Here computer technology is beginning to be able to fulfil many functions involving domestic life as well as occupational life, and systems are beginning to be available which permit people to do things which they can perceive as being useful in the home; many people have learned to use the new technology in ways which they had not experienced before.

In order to try and define precisely the way in which all these developments have become useful we must consider what is the purpose for which so many people have begun to use computers at home. Of course, the uses are many and various, but the area may be summed up with a high degree of accuracy by suggesting that generally speaking we are talking about a *control function*. This is important, for not only does this control function relate to the manipulation of equipment, in such situations as computers controlling burglar alarms and other security devices, but also to control in the sense of personal control, where people are able to take over some direct responsibility for handling various aspects of their lives. In this context the use of on-line facilities such as Prestel have played a great part, and this development of personal control is especially noticeable in the expansion of areas like home banking.

So to make this discussion concrete and realistic, we must ask ourselves what the computer actually does for the individual. For some people, the computer may do something which they could not do without it, but in the vast majority of cases it does something which was already done, but much faster and with a higher level of efficiency and/or accuracy. In many respects, this statement typifies the ways in which the introduction of computer technology into the normal life of most able-bodied people differs from the increasing introduction of new technology into the lives of disabled people. For the disabled person, the introduction of computer technology usually represents the dawn of the ability to do something which he could not do previously, but can do with the aid of the technology; for the rest of us it customarily heralds the dawn of the ability to do something new. Thus it will be seen that there is a substantial difference between the potential part that may be played by computers in the lives of disabled people as compared with non-disabled people; for disabled people the computer becomes very much *part* of the normal process of living, not an addition to it which may be put down when not required.

People with a relatively small degree of handicap may find that the total effect of the disability on their life is simply that they do things more slowly, or with more effort, than others. A great number of handicapped people, however, have a range of things that they either cannot do or can only do so inefficiently that they must have help. This raises two points: the first is that until recently such help was only available by means of a human agency: in other words a helper. This is one of the aspects that new computer technology has begun to change; even in the early days of electronic development it was possible to begin to build machines that would do some of the tasks which the disabled person could not carry out alone, such as dialling telephone calls and driving a wheel chair. However, it is still true that a great deal of the provision for disabled people is still often considered in terms of a human helper, and this may be seen in our society in a number of areas; an obvious example is the way that British Rail makes provision for a helper accompanying a disabled or blind person on a journey, making the assumption that this is the normal and adequate means of fulfilling the need.

All this raises the second point—which is that disabled people themselves frequently express a deeply-felt need for independence of their own: an autonomy over their own destinies and the way that their own lives may be led. This is important to the psychological well-being of the disabled individual, and in a way that may not immediately be obvious. Of course it is true that none of us are wholly independent of other people, for the whole business of human interaction relies on a degree of mutual co-operation and assistance between all manners of person. Not only is this accepted by most of us but it is also clear that (at least in present-day society) it would be actually impossible for a disabled person to be one hundred per cent independent and free of the need to involve himself with other people. The difference is that the able-bodied person is able to choose both the *extent* to which he relies on other people and *when* he does so and when he doesn't; the disabled person is not (or at least not always) in a position to make that choice and thus his own personal autonomy is eroded in that he is no longer as much master of his own destiny as everyone else.

A good deal of thought has been given in recent years to the question of 'access' for disabled people, and this is frequently interpreted as meaning the physical entry into buildings which are difficult for someone in a wheelchair or on crutches. Of course, this sort of access is quite vital, for if the disabled individual is not able to get into the building where something is taking place, clearly he cannot participate. However, there are two other levels of access function which may not be so readily obvious, but may be equally a total obstacle to the individual. One of these is what we might call the *physical function*, which involves the individual's ability to do many of the things that everyone else would normally be able to do on entering a building, such as opening and closing doors, turning on and off lights, using telephones, writing with a pencil, etc. The second aspect of this type of access involves what might be called the *communication function*, or the *personal expression function*. This involves the ability of the individual to participate in the information exchange and communication which goes on in the process upon which he is engaged, and the problems here will include those who have difficulties particularly in the areas of vision, hearing and speech.

All of the types of 'access' mentioned above may be regarded as routes by which the disabled individual may achieve more autonomy or independence. This independence is not only physical and practical, for as well as covering such items as using the toilet oneself, or being able to eat meals without assistance, as well as use equipment, the greater the level of autonomous independence which the individual can achieve, the more disabled people are in a position which enables them to make personal decisions on the basis on what they *wish* to do, and then carry those decisions out. Thus there is a fairly substantial psychological element to this independence which may be assisted by the new information technology, and this relates to the comment made earlier that the equipment and systems become part of the disabled individual's life, a partner in his pathway through normal living, rather than an addition to it. A few moments thought will make it quite clear, therefore, that already we have moved the developments of new computer technology far beyond the practical possibility of using them as (effectively) mechanical servants.

We have thus drawn a distinction between the things that may be done for able-bodied people by the new information technology and those things that may be done for disabled people. In the case of able-bodied people the new technology can expand horizons and do new things; in the case of disabled people also its most immediate and exciting possibilities will permit them to do things that they could not do. However, it must be remembered that these are things that everyone else can already do, so the utilization of computer technology in this way, however welcome and however sophisticated, only redresses the balance to the extent that the disabled individual is at the point that everyone else has reached already. Thus the disabled person still needs to be able to use the computer technology to do the new things that are new to everyone, and so therefore has two steps to take before any degree of equality can be approached. This concept is important, because it is vital that we do not use any system to place disabled people in a position which the rest of us have already left, however much this is an improvement for them on what went before. The possibilities of the new technology are exciting in the sense that they can genuinely begin to redress the imbalance experienced by the disabled person in society, but these very developments must not be allowed to create barriers of their own.

For many disabled people a major component of their disability in a wider society is that of difficulty in communication. Here the individual is faced with problems which surround not simply the ability to do certain things, or do them efficiently enough, but problems in the area of interface with the rest of human society.

> For many disabled people, communications problems are at the heart of their disablement and central to their personal struggle to learn to overcome their disabilities. This is true whether they are young or old, whether they are male or female, whether they are disabled from birth or become disabled later in life. They are often left isolated, powerless and dependent. They are deprived of important ways of expressing their individuality. (Hawkridge, Vincent and Hales, 1985)[2]

Thus the ability to participate arises at two levels: one is the physical ability to enter buildings and operate equipment, the other is the communicative level which enables interaction with human systems. There is a most important area, however, which is greatly affected by both these levels of 'access', and which may have a thoroughly major effect on the individuals future life. This is the process of education.

A disability experienced by the individual very early in life (or even from birth) will be a major factor in that person's educational experience. Some difficulties of this nature naturally interfere with the ability to acquire information and to learn, something which is particularly true (though not exclusively so) of those with communication difficulties. The outcome of the situation can be extremely profound, for it is possible that the disabled individual has a less adequate, or at least less complete, educational experience than his able-bodied peers, and therefore enters into his life with two handicaps not one: one handicap is the problem of the disability he suffers, and the other is the handicap of an educational experience which is less than adequate.

Some of the problems faced in education by disabled people relate to the ability to grasp complex concepts while having a disability which renders this difficult. Thus people with a visual impairment, particularly the totally blind, will have difficulty in conceptualizing some aspects of experience which are thoroughly visually-related; equally people who are profoundly deaf will have substantial difficulties in coping with aural concepts such as music. This is not just a question of saying that the individual is unable to *do* certain things. The deaf person may have no aspiration to become a musician because of the great difficulties placed in his way, but may still need to know something of the concept of what music is in order to enable him to comprehend certain things taking place in the artistic and historical spheres, for example. Thus the learning experience is affected at a very deep level by the disability, not just at the level of 'not being able to see' or 'not being able to hear'.

Some researchers feel that the educational experience of disabled children is altered in a quite profound way; many disabled children are affected by being unable to participate in many things, particularly those things which may well reinforce their skills and give them practice. Foulds[3] suggests that this is because they cannot do rough work, or are unable to work things out visually on paper.

This sort of effect is seen very clearly in educating children who are deaf or have partial hearing, where their acquisition of language concept and linguistic skills is at the best slow. A system called Project Video Language has developed computer programmes which link descriptive sentences with video tapes and other material in such a way that a series of syntactical patterns can be developed by the computer which are then made real by the other material. This enables the computer to work with the child in many different patterns of language permutation, enabling a great deal of practice to be generated in the variations of language usage. This has proved to be very successful and is one method of circumventing the difficulty known in the education of the deaf that their language becomes very rigid and literal because they are unable to make the switch from one style of syntax to another—for instance from a passive sentence to an active sentence. The computing technology here enables a degree and quantity of practice which would be impossible for a single teacher in a classroom.

The same sort of difficulty with access to the educational experience may be seen in those suffering from dyslexia. Early moves to develop procedures using computer technology to help dyslexics have been involved with programmes to assist teaching. 'Spellmaster' is a teaching programme which is specifically designed to give the teacher a great deal of flexibility. Rieth *et al*, report that their intention was to provide teachers with a structure 'from which they can build individualized student spelling lessons'.[5] The report on this system says that the data so far has indicated very high ratings of satisfaction among the teachers, and that many of the children have increased their scores on spelling tests by an average of 50%.

In the area of dyslexia, there is increasing understanding that the hardware as well as the software may well be of advantage, as evidence becomes available to show that many dyslexics are able to gain advantage from using word processors instead of pens[6]. Kerchner and Kistinger[7] have reported work which has approached this use of word processors with learning disabled students and has already found that the preliminary results are very positive and suggest not only that written language skills improve, but that these skills do transfer to pencil and paper; they have used as their measurement the *Test Of Written Language*[8]. Kerchner and Kistinger are fairly scathing of the fact that we recognize the many advantages given to those who work with language from the new developments in word processing, but we largely deny them to children in schools, and suggest that such facilities may be of value to all children and not just to those with learning problems.

Thus we see that one of the major difficulties for disabled people in education, whether they be children or adults, is the inability to participate fully in those structures which are necessary, leading to the double handicap situation mentioned at the beginning. Papert and Weir[9] asked very basic questions about the ways in which language structures might develop in people who have no experience of speech production. They make the problem of disabled people in education quite clear by talking of

> the restriction on their expressive power, so that such mental activity as does go on is packed within the individual's own head.

They have looked particularly at the problems of spatial conceptualization in people who cannot handle objects, and have used Logo Turtle Geometry. This is a system designed by Seymour Papert and allows people to construct drawings from the computer. The results are their conceptualizations, shown either on the screen or transferred to a robot which moves about on the floor drawing the results of the child's instructions. This is a very significant step along the road of providing autonomy for the disabled individual, as Weir *et al*. state:

a severe physical handicap imposes a dependent, passive role on its victim. The uncompromising way in which Logo places initiative and control in the hands of the users allow them to have a direct effect on their environment.[10]

Not all communication is at the face to face level, of course, involving human interaction. Some involves access of the stored data available in various forms; the most common is the traditional form of written material, which abounds in the world. In terms of his access to this sort of information, the blind person has much the same difficulty that the person with no speech or no hearing has in terms of human interaction. Within the context of this present discussion, the one factor which could not be introduced into systems used to enable blind people to 'read' was total autonomy. Various systems worked well, but required another person to assist in the process of making it available. Thus, if the blind person could read Braille then someone had to produce the Braille copy; if he could not, then someone had to read the material to him, or read it onto tape.

One development in the area of new technology which has helped here is that there now exist various systems to produce a Braille output from an ordinary typed input, such as the system developed at Warwick University.[11] However, although such a system makes the bulk output of Braille copies easier, faster and relatively cheaper, it still does not solve the problem of autonomy.

In the last few years we have seen the development of Optical Character Recognition systems; these are devices which are able to take the information straight from the printed page and produce an output that the blind person can understand. Details have been refined over the years, and it is now possible to read a number of different type faces and styles so that the blind person is not so limited in the choice of input material. These systems now utilize synthetic voice equipment, and this aspect of new technology is an area of development which has been of great assistance to many handicapped people. In particular, it has been a light in the darkness to many who have no speech, as it enables the individual disabled person to produce an output that approximates very closely to the speech of those of us who are not thus disabled. This brings the disabled individual closer still to the autonomous function in society—on the same terms as everyone else.

This particular area of development has led to many success stories, some of them emanating from Michigan State University in America, where John Eulenberg (Professor of Linguistics, African Languages and Computer Science) has developed Voice Output Communication Aids at the Michigan Artificial Language Laboratory. One clear example of the effect that such a device can have is contained in the story of Jim Brooks. Jim had spastic athetoid cerebral palsy from birth and could not communicate. His parents only realized that he was not mentally retarded (which everyone had claimed) when he began to use an electric typewriter, typing with his big toe. He now has a computer system mounted on his wheelchair, to enable him to speak and communicate, and as this equipment has come into use it is clear that Jim is far from retarded, but actually has a brilliant scientific mind.[12]

One of the most moving descriptions of the effects that new information technology systems can have on the individual is that reported by Michael Williams.[13] He has no speech, and yet made an address to the Rehabilitation Engineering conference at Stanford University in 1982. At that time, he said the following:

> If, when I was a little boy, someone had told me that I would grow up and make speeches to large groups, I would have called him either a fool or a mad man. Yet here I am. I can only say this; modern technology has allowed me to release my creative spirit where it can soar, free, high above the clouds. Without the fruits of modern technology I would probably be stuck in a room and counting the hours until my death. For some people, this synthesizer may be an ugly box with cables. To me, however, it is *an analogue for freedom*. Let freedom ring.

Earlier in this paper, we addressed the question of the differences in the part computer technology plays in the life of a disabled person, by comparison with the part it plays in the lives of others. This is particularly vital in making sure that the equipment or systems do match the needs of the individual disabled person. In the case of the able-bodied person interfacing with a new system, he or she is able to modify behaviour, or understanding, to take account of the idiosyncrasies of any particular device (at least to a reasonable extent). This is not necessarily at all true of the disabled individual. Duncan, in 1983, wrote

> Some (personal computers) are designed to be friendly, even helpful. If we have good eyesight, good fingers, and a fairly functional brain, we can hardly ask for more . . . the conventional computer terminal, or the personal computer with VDU and printer, makes, however, no concession to the operator who through physical disability cannot use a standard typewriting keyboard or read the characters on a screen.[14]

This question is vital: in a book called *Special Technology For Special Children*, Goldenberg[15] made it quite clear that we need to explore this question in great detail. Indeed, as developments have progressed the new technology has been able to help in the assessment of the interface between the individual and the new technology. At the children's hospital at Stanford, a kit has been developed which enables systematic assessment of individual needs and ability to control various parts of the technology, taking into account not only what the individual prefers and says he would like in the best possible situation, but also measuring the actual usage of the devices, including objective measures of such things as accuracy and speed as well as fatigue. Thus an interface may be built which maximises not only what the individual person wants to happen, but takes into account what he or she can actually do.[16]

One practical expression of the utilization of these sorts of systems, once they are right for the individual and working properly, is in the area of employment opportunities. Among those who have knowledge of the work position of disabled people there is a substantial expectation that the new technology will increase possibilities, because not only will many disabled people be able to carry out tasks which they could not do previously, but are also able to indulge in interactive situations which are important, both in the sense of communicating with other people and in the sense of working co-operatively with them. Certainly such an improvement would do a great deal for the psychological and social well-being of individual disabled people, but there is also the added advantage that it would do no harm to the commercial and the industrial scene. One of the most interesting pieces of information to become known from the 'Fit for Work' campaign which took place in the United Kingdom a few years ago was that, averaged across the country, disabled workers lost less time because of illness than able-bodied workers.

However, in this area we meet not only technological obstacles but also social factors involving a certain degree of prejudice. In the United States of America, where provision for the disabled is laid down in stronger legislation than in the United Kingdom, a federal investigation of a large manufacturer in 1983 showed a large number of obstacles for the disabled applicant, many of them having the actual effect of excluding disabled people from being appointed to jobs which they could adequately do.[17] There is, of course, something of a self-perpetuating prophecy in all this, in that the more disabled people are seen to be able to take up jobs and hold them down satisfactorily the more people will be prepared to appoint them, and it is most certainly true that already commercial and industrial experience is such that employers who have employed disabled people almost without exception report favourably on the quality of their work, their loyalty, etc. Thus the slogan of the 'Fit for Work' campaign, which was 'Disabled workers are good workers' has been brought to fruition in reality.

Thus we may see that many people, including disabled people themselves, have formed a view that the use of systems involving computers, such as those described here, enables the disabled person to achieve greater autonomy, greater independence and greater dignity. This has been the aim of many systems and developments to assist disabled people for many years, but in recent times the initiative is passing from the helpers to the individual. Nowadays, instead of working *for* disabled people, many organizations (including educational institutions) are trying to arrange that decisions can be made *by* disabled people. In this context the use of technological equipment greatly assists the development of this autonomy.

It is obvious that disabled people themselves must be involved in decisions made about using such systems and developing new versions of them. This view is made particularly clear by Janis Firminger,[18] who has emphasized the fact that those who know most about the technology, including what it can and cannot do, are the individual disabled people themselves. She sounds the very salutary warning that, in many cases during the early development of technological aids, they were greeted with much praise by the professionals who were not disabled, and not used (because of faults in the design) by the disabled people themselves.

Eventually, of course, the solutions to disability will lie in rectification, whether by therapy, surgery, or some other reparative technique. Until that day, it seems only reasonable that disabled people should have access to the various technological systems which will enable them to carry out the functions with which they have problems. As the work progresses, one advantage which becomes increasingly apparent is that less and less of the equipment has to be custom-built or specially designed, and hand-in-hand with this development has gone the realization and understanding that many of the systems which have been developed for use by disabled people are of great value to many others as well. Another advantage to later development is that the capacity and range of systems have become greater as the size has become smaller, and portability has increased, so that they are now not only more facilitative, but are less obtrusive.

We are not yet in a position to rehabilitate, in every sense of that word, the disabled person in society. Until that time comes, it is particularly important that we utilize every avenue to minimize the difficulties met by a disabled person in a non-disabled society. The development of new computer technology is a great step in this direction, and in particular in those crucial fields of communication and education. It is bad enough that the individual person should have to go through life coping with the difficulties of his handicap in the first place, but to allow him to go through life doubly handicapped because of inadequate educational experience arising from that handicap is quite unforgivable. It is in this latter context that the application of computer technology may help a great deal, so that at least we can minimise the obstacles arising from disability, until that day comes when we can actually dismantle the obstacles themselves.

REFERENCES

1. British Broadcasting Corporation (1986) *Tomorrows World*, December 1986.
2. Hawkridge, D. G., Vincent, T. and Hales, G. W. (1985) *New Information Technology in the Education of Disabled Children and Adults*, Beckenham, Croom Helm.
3. Foulds, R. A. (1982) Applications of microcomputers in the education of the physically disabled child, *Exceptional Children*, vol. 49, no. 2.
4. Kreis, M. (1979) Project Video Language: a succesful experiment, *American Annals of the Deaf*, vol. 24, 542–548.
5. Rieth, H. J., Polsgrove, L. and Eckert, R. (1984) *Academic Therapy*, 20, no. 1, 59–65.

6. Miles, T. R. and Gilroy, D. E. (1986) *Dyslexia at College*, Appendix II. London and New York, Methuen.
7. Kerchner, L. B. and Kistinger, B. (1984) Language Processing/Word Processing: Written expression, computers and learning disabled students, *Language Learning Quarterly*, 7 329–335.
8. Hammill, D. and Larsen, S. (1978) *Test of written language* (Revised edition). Austin, Pro-Ed.
9. Papert, S. A. and Weir, S. (1978) Information prosthetics for the handicapped, *Artificial Intelligence memo 496*; Institute of Technology Artificial Intelligence Laboratory, Cambridge, Massachusetts.
10. Weir, S., Russell, S. J. and Valente, J. (1982) Logo: an approach to educating disabled children, *Byte*, September.
11. Gill, J. M. (1983) Microcomputer aids for the blind, *Computer Education*, November.
12. Moses, J. F. (1983) Impressions of Eulenberg, *Rehabilitation/World*, summer.
13. Williams, M. B. (1982) Confessions of a closet technocrat, *Communication Outlook*, vol. 3, no. 4.
14. Duncan, F. E. (1983) Substitutes for speech: experience of applications of artificial voice production in micro-processor based systems for the disabled, Paper presented at *EUROMICRO* 83, Madrid, September.
15. Goldenberg, E. P. (1979) *Special Technology for Special children*, Baltimore, University Park Press.
16. Barker, M. (1983) The control evaluator and training kit: an assessment tool for comparative testing of controls to operate assistive devices, In *Proceedings of the 6th Annual Conference on Rehabilitation Engineering*, San Diego, California.
17. Pati, G. C. (1983) A philosophical and cultural approach to high technology in rehabilitation, In *Technology and Rehabilitation of Disabled Persons in the Information Age*, Alexandria, National Rehabilitation Association.
18. Firminger, J. (1983) Assessing IT for severely disabled students: new developments at Hereward College, *NATFHE Journal*, December.

2.4 *Against the imperialism of instrumental reason*

- J. Weizenbaum

The list of ways in which the computer has proved helpful is undoubtedly long. There are, however, two kinds of computer applications that either ought not be undertaken at all, or, if they are contemplated, should be approached with utmost caution.

The first kind I would call simply obscene. These are ones whose very contemplation ought to give rise to feelings of disgust in every civilized person. The proposal I have mentioned, that an animal's visual system and brain be coupled to computers, is an example. It represents an attack on life itself. One must wonder what must have happened to the proposers' perception of life, hence to their perceptions of themselves as part of the continuum of life, that they can even think of such a thing, let alone advocate it. On a much lesser level, one must wonder what conceivable need of man could be fulfilled by such a 'device' at all, let alone by only such a device.

I would put all projects that propose to substitute a computer system for a human function that involves interpersonal respect, understanding, and love in the same category. I therefore reject [the] proposal that computers be installed as psychotherapists, not on the grounds that such a project might be technically unfeasible, but on the grounds that it is immoral. I have heard the defense that a person may get some psychological help from conversing with a computer even if the computer admittedly does not 'understand' the person. One example given me was of a computer system designed to accept natural-language text via its typewriter console, and to respond to it with a randomized series of 'yes' and 'no.' A troubled patient 'conversed' with this system, and was allegedly led by it to think more deeply about his problems and to arrive at certain allegedly helpful conclusions. Until then he had just drifted in aimless worry. In principle, a set of Chinese fortune cookies or a deck of cards could have done the same job. The computer, however, contributed a certain aura—derived, of course, from science—that permitted the 'patient' to believe in it where he might have dismissed fortune cookies and playing cards as instruments of superstition. The question then arises, and it answers itself, do we wish to encourage people to lead their lives on the basis of patent fraud, charlatanism, and unreality? And, more importantly, do we really believe that it helps people living in our already overly machine-like world to prefer the therapy administered by machines to that given by other people? I have heard this latter question answered with the assertion that my position is nothing more than 'let them eat cake.' It is said to ignore the shortage of good human psychotherapists, and to deny to troubled people what little help computers can now give them merely because presently available computers don't 'yet' measure up to, say, the best psychoanalysis. But that objection misses the point entirely. The point is that there are some human functions for which computers *ought* not to be substituted. It has nothing to do with what computers can or cannot be made to do. Respect, understanding, and love are not technical problems.

The second kind of computer application that ought to be avoided, or at least not undertaken without very careful forethought, is that which can easily be seen to have irreversible and not entirely foreseeable side effects. If, in addition, such an application cannot be shown to meet a pressing human need that cannot readily be met in any other way, then it ought not to be pursued. The latter stricture follows directly from the argument I have already presented about the scarcity of human intelligence.

The example I wish to cite here is that of the automatic recognition of human speech. There are now three or four major projects in the USA devoted to enabling computers to understand human speech, that is, to programming them in such a way that verbal speech directed at them can be converted into the same internal representations that would result if what had been said to them had been typed into their consoles.

The problem, as can readily be seen, is very much more complicated than that of natural-language understanding as such, for in order to understand a stream of coherent speech, the language in which that speech is rendered must be understood in the first place. The solution of the 'speech-understanding problem' therefore presupposes the solution of the 'natural-language-understanding problem.' And we have seen that, for the latter, we have only 'the tiniest bit of relevant knowledge.' But I am not here concerned with the technical feasibility of the task, nor with any estimate of just how little or greatly optimistic we might be about its completion.

Why should we want to undertake this task at all? I have asked this question of many enthusiasts for the project. The most cheerful answer I have been able to get is that it will help physicians record their medical notes and then translate these notes into action more efficiently. Of course, anything that has any ostensible connection to medicine is automatically considered good. But here we have to remember that the problem is so enormous that only the largest possible computers will ever be able to manage it. In other words, even if the desired system were successfully designed, it would probably require a computer so large and therefore so expensive that only the largest and best-endowed hospitals could possibly afford it—but in fact the whole system might be so prohibitively expensive that even they could not afford it. The question then becomes, is this really what medicine needs most at this time? Would not the talent, not to mention the money and the resources it represents, be better spent on projects that attack more urgent and more fundamental problems of health care?

But then, this alleged justification of speech-recognition 'research' is merely a rationalization anyway. (I put the word 'research' in quotation marks because the work I am here discussing is mere tinkering. I have no objection to serious scientists studying the psycho-physiology of human speech recognition.) If one asks such questions of the principal sponsor of this work, the Advanced Research Projects Agency (ARPA) of the United States Department of Defense, as was recently done at an open meeting, the answer given is that the Navy hopes to control its ships, and the other services their weapons, by voice commands. This project then represents, in the eyes of its chief sponsor, a long step toward a fully automated battlefield. I see no reason to advise my students to lend their talents to that aim.

I have urged my students and colleagues to ask still another question about this project. Granted that a speech-recognition machine is bound to be enormously expensive, and that only governments and possibly a very few very large corporations will therefore be able to afford it, what will they use it for? What can it possibly be used for? There is no question in my mind that there is no pressing human problem that will more easily be solved because such machines exist. But such listening machines, could they be made, will make monitoring of voice communication very much easier than it now is. Perhaps the only reason that there is very little government surveillance of telephone conservations in many countries of the world is that such surveillance takes so much manpower. Each conversation on a tapped phone must eventually be listened to by a human agent. But speech-recognizing machines could delete all 'uninteresting' conservations and present transcripts of only the remaining ones to their masters. [. . .] I ask, why should a talented computer technologist lend his support to such a project? As a citizen I ask, why should my government spend approximately 2.5 million dollars a year (as it now does) on this project?

Surely such questions presented themselves to thoughtful people in earlier stages of science and technology. But until recently society could always meet the unwanted and dangerous effects of its new inventions by, in a sense, reorganizing itself to undo or to minimize these effects. The density of cities could be reduced by geographically expanding the city. An individual could avoid the terrible effects of the industrial revolution in England by moving to America. And America could escape many of the consequences of the increasing power of military weapons by retreating behind its two oceanic moats. But those days are gone. The scientist and the technologist can no longer avoid the responsibility for what he does by appealing to the infinite powers of society to transform itself in response to new realities and to heal the wounds he inflicts on it. Certain limits have been reached. The transformations the new technologies may call for may be impossible to achieve, and the failure to achieve them may mean the annihilation of all life. No one has the right to impose such a choice on mankind.

I have spoken here of what ought and ought not to be done, of what is morally repugnant, and of what is dangerous. I am, of course, aware of the fact that these judgments of mine have themselves no moral force except on myself. Nor, as I have already said, do I have any intention of telling other people what tasks they should and should not undertake. I urge them only to consider the consequences of what they do. And here I mean not only, not even primarily, the direct consequences of their actions on the world about them. I mean rather the consequences on themselves, as they construct their rationalizations, as they repress the truths that urge them to different courses, and as they chip away at their own autonomy. That so many people so often ask what they must do is a sign that the order of being and doing has become inverted. Those who know who and what they are do not need to ask what they should do. And those who must ask will not be able to stop asking until they begin to look inside themselves. But it is everyone's task to show by example what questions one can ask of oneself, and to show that one can live with what few answers there are.

But just as I have no licence to dictate the actions of others, neither do the constructors of the world in which I must live have a right to unconditionally impose their visions on me. Scientists and technologists have, because of their power, an especially heavy responsibility, one that is not to be sloughed off behind a facade of slogans such as that of technological inevitability. In a world in which man increasingly meets only himself, and then only in the form of the products he has made, the makers and designers of these products—the buildings, airplanes, foodstuffs, bombs, and so on—need to have the most profound awareness that their products are, after all, the results of human choices. Men could instead choose to have truly safe automobiles, decent television, decent housing for everyone, or comfortable, safe, and widely distributed mass transportation. The fact that these things do not exist, in a country that has the resources to produce them, is a consequence, not of technological inevitability, not of the fact that there is no longer anyone who makes choices, but of the fact that people have chosen to make and to have just exactly the things we have made and do have.

It is hard, when one sees a particularly offensive television commercial, to imagine that adult human beings sometime and somewhere sat around a table and decided to construct exactly that commercial and to have it broadcast hundreds of times. But that is what happens. These things are not products of anonymous forces. They are the products of groups of men who have agreed among themselves that this pollution of the consciousness of the people serves their purposes.

But, as has been true since the beginning of recorded history, decisions having the most evil consequences are often made in the service of some overriding good. For example, in the summer of 1966 there was considerable agitation in the United States over America's intensive bombing of North Vietnam. (The destruction rained on South Vietnam by American bombers was less of an issue in the public debate, because the public was still persuaded that America was 'helping' that unfortunate land.) Approximately forty American scientists who were high in the scientific estate decided to help stop the bombing by convening a summer study group under the auspices of the Institute of Defense Analyses, a prestigious consulting firm for the Department of Defense. They intended to demonstrate that the bombing was in fact ineffective.[1]

They made their demonstration using the best scientific tools, operations research and systems analysis and all that. But they felt they would not be heard by the Secretary of Defense unless they suggested an alternative to the bombing. They proposed that an 'electronic fence' be placed in the so-called demilitarized zone separating South from North Vietnam. This barrier was supposed to stop infiltrators from the North. It was to consist of, among other devices, small mines seeded into the earth, and specifically designed to blow off porters' feet but to be insensitive to a truck passing over them. Other devices were to interdict truck traffic. The various electronic sensors, their monitors, and so on, eventually became part of the so-called McNamara line. This was the beginning of what has since developed into the concept of the electronic battlefield.

The intention of most of these men was not to invent or recommend a new technology that would make warfare more terrible and, by the way, less costly to highly industrialized nations at the expense of 'underdeveloped' ones. Their intention was to stop the bombing. In this they were wholly on the side of the peace groups and of well-meaning citizens generally. And they actually accomplished their objective; the bombing of North Vietnam was stopped for a time and the McNamara fence was installed. However, these enormously visible and influential people could have instead simply announced that they believed the bombing, indeed the whole American Vietnam adventure, to be wrong, and that they would no longer 'help.' I know that at least some of the participants believed that the war was wrong; perhaps all of them did. But, as some of them explained to me later, they felt that if they made such an announcement, they would not be listened to, then or ever again. Yet, who can tell what effect it would have had if forty of America's leading scientists had, in the summer of 1966, joined the peace groups in coming out flatly against the war on moral grounds? Apart from the positive effect such a move might have had on world events, what negative effect did their compromise have on themselves and on their colleagues and students for whom they served as examples?

There are several lessons to be learned from this episode. The first is that it was not technological inevitability that invented the electronic battlefield, nor was it a set of anonymous forces. Men just like the ones who design television commercials sat around a table and chose. Yet the outcome of the debates of the 1966 Summer Study was in a sense foreordained. The range of answers one gets is determined by the domain of questions one asks. As soon as it was settled that the Summer Study was to concern itself with only technical questions, the solution to the problem of stopping the bombing of the North became essentially a matter of calculation. When the side condition was added that the group must at all costs maintain its credibility with its sponsors, that it must not imperil the participants' 'insider' status, then all degrees of freedom that its members might have had initially were effectively lost. Many of the participants have, I know, defended academic freedom, their own as well as that of colleagues whose careers were in jeopardy for political reasons. These men did not perceive themselves to be risking their scholarly or academic freedoms when they engaged in the kind of consulting characterized by the Summer Study. But the sacrifice of the degrees of freedom they might have had if they had not so thoroughly abandoned themselves to their sponsors, whether they made that sacrifice unwittingly or not, was a more potent form of censorship than any that could possibly have been imposed by officials of the state. This kind of intellectual self-mutilation, precisely because it is largely unconscious, is a principal source of the feeling of powerlessness experienced by so many people who appear, superficially at least, to occupy seats of power.

A second lesson is this. These men were able to give the counsel they gave because they were operating at an enormous psychological distance from the people who would be maimed and killed by the weapons systems that would result from the ideas they communicated to their sponsors. The lesson, therefore, is that the scientist and technologist must, by acts of will and of the imagination, actively strive to reduce such psychological distances, to counter the forces that tend to remove him from the consequences of his actions. He must—it is as simple as this—think of what he is actually doing. He must learn to listen to his own inner voice. He must learn to say 'No!'

Finally, it is the act itself that matters. When instrumental reason is the sole guide to action, the acts it justifies are robbed of their inherent meanings and thus exist in an ethical vacuum. I recently heard an officer of a great university publicly defend an important policy decision he had made, one that many of the university's students and faculty opposed on moral grounds, with the words: 'We could have taken a moral stand, but what good would that have done?' But the good of a moral act inheres in the act itself. That is why an act can itself ennoble or corrupt the person who performs it. The victory of instrumental reason in our time has brought about the virtual disappearance of this insight and thus perforce the delegitimation of the very idea of nobility.

I am aware, of course, that hardly anyone who reads these lines will feel himself addressed by them—so deep has the conviction that we are all governed by anonymous forces beyond our control penetrated into the shared consciousness of our time. And accompanying this conviction is a debasement of the idea of civil courage.

It is a widely held but a grievously mistaken belief that civil courage finds exercise only in the context of world-shaking events. To the contrary, its most arduous exercise is often in those small contexts in which the challenge is to overcome the fears induced by petty concerns over career, over our relationships to those who appear to have power over us, over whatever may disturb the tranquility of our mundane existence.

If this [paper] is to be seen as advocating anything, then let it be a call to this simple kind of courage. And, because this [paper] is, after all, about computers, let that call be heard mainly by teachers of computer science.

I want them to have heard me affirm that the computer is a powerful new metaphor for helping us to understand many aspects of the world, but that it enslaves the mind that has no other metaphors and few other resources to call on. The world is many things, and no single framework is large enough to contain them all, neither that of man's science nor that of his poetry, neither that of calculating reason nor that of pure intuition. And just as a love of music does not suffice to enable one to play the violin—one must also master the craft of the instrument and of music itself—so is it not enough to love humanity in order to help it survive. The teacher's calling to teach his craft is therefore an honorable one. But he must do more than that: he must teach more than one metaphor, and he must teach more by the example of his conduct than by what he writes on the blackboard. He must teach the limitations of his tools as well as their power.

It happens that programming is a relatively easy craft to learn. Almost anyone with a reasonably orderly mind can become a fairly good programmer with just a little instruction and practice. And because programming is almost immediately rewarding, that is, because a computer very quickly begins to behave somewhat in the way the programmer intends it to, programming is very seductive, especially for beginners. Moreover, it appeals most to precisely those who do not yet have sufficient maturity to tolerate long delays between an effort to achieve something and the appearance of concrete evidence of success. Immature students are therefore easily misled into believing that they have truly mastered a craft of immense power and of great importance when, in fact, they have learned only its rudiments and nothing substantive at all. A student's quick climb from a state of complete ignorance about computers to what appears to be a mastery of programming, but is in reality only a very minor plateau, may leave him with a euphoric sense of achievement and a conviction that he has discovered his true calling. The teacher, of course, also tends to feel rewarded by such students' obvious enthusiasm, and therefore to encourage it, perhaps unconsciously and against his better judgment. But for the student this may well be a trap. He may so thoroughly commit himself to what he naively perceives to be computer science, that is, to the mere polishing of his programming skills, that he may effectively preclude studying anything substantive.

Unfortunately, many universities have 'computer science' programs at the undergraduate level that permit and even encourage students to take this course. When such students have completed their studies, they are rather like people who have somehow become eloquent in some foreign language, but who, when they attempt to write something in that language, find they have literally nothing of their own to say.

The lesson in this is that, although the learning of a craft is important, it cannot be everything.

The function of a university cannot be to simply offer prospective students a catalogue of 'skills' from which to choose. For, were that its function, then the university would have to assume that the students who come to it have already become whatever it is they are to become. The university would then be quite correct in seeing the student as a sort of market basket, to be filled with goods from among the university's intellectual inventory. It would be correct, in other words, in seeing the student as an object very much like a computer whose storage banks are forever hungry for more 'data.' But surely that cannot be a proper characterization of what a university is or ought to be all about. Surely the university should look upon each of its citizens, students and faculty alike, first of all as human beings in search of—what else to call it?—truth, and hence in search of themselves. Something should constantly be happening to every citizen of the university; each should leave its halls having become someone other than he who entered in the morning. The mere teaching of craft cannot fulfill this high function of the university.

Just because so much of a computer-science curriculum is concerned with the craft of computation, it is perhaps easy for the teacher of computer science to fall into the habit of merely training. But, were he to do that, he would surely diminish himself and his profession. He would also detach himself from the rest of the intellectual and moral life of the university. The university should hold, before each of its citizens, and before the world at large as well, a vision of what it is possible for a man or a woman to become. It does this by giving ever-fresh life to the ideas of men and women who, by virtue of their own achievements, have contributed to the house we live in. And it does this, for better or for worse, by means of the example each of the university's citizens is for every other. The teacher of computer science, no more nor less than any other faculty member, is in effect constantly inviting his students to become what he himself is. If he views himself as a mere trainer, as a mere applier of 'methods' for achieving ends determined by others, then he does his students two disservices. First, he invites them to become less than fully autonomous persons. He invites them to become mere followers of other people's orders, and finally no better than the machines that might someday replace them in that function. Second, he robs them of the glimpse of the ideas that alone purchase for computer science a place in the university's curriculum at all. And in doing that, he blinds them to the examples that computer scientists as creative human beings might have provided for them, hence of their very best chance to become truly good computer scientists themselves.[2]

Finally, the teacher of computer science is himself subject to the enormous temptation to be arrogant because his knowledge is somehow 'harder' than that of his humanist colleagues. But the hardness of the knowledge available to him is of no advantage at all. His knowledge is merely less ambiguous and therefore, like his computer languages, less expressive of reality. The humanities particularly

> have a greater familiarity with an ambiguous, intractable, sometimes unreachable [moral] world that won't reduce itself to any correspondence with the symbols by means of which one might try to measure it. There is a world that stands apart from all efforts of historians to reduce [it] to the laws of history, a world which defies all efforts of artists to understand its basic laws of beauty. [Man's] practice should involve itself with softer than scientific knowledge. . . . that is not a retreat but an advance.[3]

The teacher of computer science must have the courage to resist the temptation to arrogance and to teach, again mainly by his own example, the validity and the legitimacy of softer knowledge. Why courage in this connection? For two reasons. The first and least important is that the more he succeeds in so teaching, the more he risks the censure of colleagues who, with less courage than his own, have succumbed to the simplistic world-views inherent in granting imperial rights to science. The second is that, if he is to teach these things by his own example, he must have the courage to acknowledge, in Jerome Bruner's words, the products of his subjectivity.

Earlier I likened the unconscious to a turbulent sea, and the border dividing the conscious, logical mind from the unconscious to a stormy coastline. That analogy is useful here too. For the courage required to explore a dangerous coast is like the courage one must muster in order to probe one's unconscious, to take into one's heart and mind what it washes up on the shore of consciousness, and to examine it in spite of one's fears. For the unconscious washes up not only the material of creativity, not only pearls that need only be polished before being strung into structures of which one may then proudly speak, but also the darkest truths about one's self. These too must be examined, understood, and somehow incorporated into one's life.

If the teacher, if anyone, is to be an example of a whole person to others, he must first strive to be a whole person. Without the courage to confront one's inner as well as one's outer worlds, such wholeness is impossible to achieve.

Instrumental reason alone cannot lead to it. And there precisely is a crucial difference between man and machine: Man, in order to become whole, must be forever an explorer of both his inner and his outer realities. His life is full of risks, but risks he has the courage to accept, because, like the explorer, he learns to trust his own capacities to endure, to overcome. What could it mean to speak of risk, courage, trust, endurance, and overcoming when one speaks of machines?

NOTES AND REFERENCES

1. See the Gravel Edition of *The Pentagon Papers* (Boston, MA, Beacon Press, 1971), volume IV, especially p. 115.
2. Almost immediately after writing the last few paragraphs, I received a paper entitled 'Methodology and the Study of Religion, Some Misgivings' from Wilfred Cantwell Smith, McCulloch Professor of Religion at Dahousie University, Halifax, Nova Scotia. His paper expresses, among many other important ideas, many of the same points I have mentioned here. Since I had read some earlier papers by Prof. Smith, I cannot help but believe that I owe some of the ideas expressed here to him.
3. C. Oglesby, 'A Juanist Way of Knowledge,' lecture given to the M. I. T. Technology and Culture Seminar, Oct. 26, 1971. Copies are available from the Rev. John Crocker, Jr., 312 Memorial Drive, Cambridge, MA 02139.

2.5 *A metaphor upside down*

- D. Michie and R. Johnston

In the public mind the notion of creativity is associated first and foremost with the arts. So, when considering computer creativity it is natural to ask, 'Is it possible for computers to produce new works of art?' Of course in some ways art seems antithetical to modern technology. We still tend to think of the artist in his garret, too preoccupied with matters of the spirit to concern himself with nuts and bolts. But in fact artists throughout history have embraced new technology whenever it has offered them tangible benefits: new colours, new alloys, new methods of print-making, new musical instruments. On top of that, art is in its essence information, so we would expect the new information-handling technology to be relevant to it. Indeed since quite early in the history of computers, scattered individuals have braved the mutual suspicion of artists and technologists to explore how these machines could be used in such fields of aesthetic creativity as painting, sculpture, music and poetry. The results have been uneven, and surrounded by controversy. In what can only be a cursory review, we aim by citing some representative examples to give readers an idea of what is going on and of the issues involved.

PAINTING

Probably the field in which most work has been done, and in which the issues are most clear-cut, is painting and drawing. Here there are two distinct, indeed antagonistic, approaches to the use of computers. In one, the computer is being used simply as a tool—a very elaborate palette and canvas on which the artist 'paints' by a variety of methods. In the other way of working, the artist supplies a program for the machine to follow, without himself necessarily having any idea what the end-result will be. It is in this latter technique that we can begin to see the possibility of a computer actually creating art.

One follower of the 'computer as tool' approach is the American David Em, who has the improbable job of Artist-in-Residence at the Jet Propulsion Laboratory in Pasadena, California. This is the control centre for the US unmanned space probes to Jupiter, Saturn and beyond, and in the course of planning these probes the staff at JPL developed a very powerful computer graphics system for simulating what would be seen as the Voyager spacecraft flew past the giant planets in the outer reaches of the solar system. It was essential to make sure Voyager would get its pictures right the first time— there would be no chance of turning around and trying again.

Not only does the graphics system provide much higher colour definition than is normally available on computers, but James Blinn's software can generate solid figures and surfaces in perspective and manipulate the image in sundry ways: enlarging, shrinking, moving it around, copying, reflecting and so on. When he can find time on the machine in between scientific projects, David Em uses it to produce abstract 'paintings' of startling originality and vividness, of a dreamlike, almost nightmarish quality (Fig. 1).

He starts by drawing lines with a stylus on an electronic tablet, directing the computer to convert these into a range of thick or thin lines or 'sprays' in a choice of 256 colours, in the same way that a traditional artist chooses his

Figure 1   David Em: 'Persepol'. Software by James Blinn at Jet Propulsion Laboratory

paints and brushes. The results are shown on a very high-resolution colour screen. He can then manipulate the pictures by various geometrical operations—transforming images, shifting them about, combining them with others, adding surface patterns and 'textures' and experimenting with different types of 'space'. The whole process is one of trial and error. If the colour or texture of one feature seems not quite right, it can be changed at the touch of a few buttons. A painting can be stored away and recalled later for further work.

The finished pictures are best viewed on the actual colour screen, which gives brilliant, almost scintillating, images. Em describes himself as 'fascinated by the nature of electronic light'. For exhibitions where the computer equipment is not available, Em photographs the images from the screen and makes thirty-inch by forty-inch colour prints. He has also made some into lithographs, and is aiming to produce prints ten feet long.

Em's visions are literally fantastic. Some have a flavour of science fiction, no doubt stimulated by his environment. As he says himself, 'They are imagery that could not exist in reality.' People often tell him that the pictures remind them of things they have seen in their dreams, and this seems to stem from the curious mixture of purely abstract and vaguely natural forms they contain. Achitectural features, valleys and rudimentary landscapes seem to be visible in many of the paintings, as Em himself points out. In some surprise he tells us, 'It is forms found in nature that the computer likes to deal with on its own most of all.' Although the picture is entirely under Em's control, he is certain that the end-results are quite different from what he would be producing in a conventional medium. 'The computer leads me into trains of thought that would never have occurred to me without it,' he asserts. In a way, the medium does tell him what to do, and it is possible for him not to know at the beginning of a painting where it will end up. But that was true of classical painters too, he reminds us. The trial-and-error process has turned painting into a kind of exploration: Em can move about in the structures he has created and find out what is there, something painters have never been able to do before. 'It's a different mental process,' he says.

One thing of which he is certain is that he could never exhaust the possibilities of his new medium. 'I feel I have an infinite machine here,' he says. He is carrying on working with it to find new visions, new relationships between colours, new spaces. 'The medium is only at the Neanderthal stage,' he declares. It need not be confined to use with abstract art, he points out—others have used it to produce highly naturalistic, almost photo-realistic, pictures.

It was at a California plastics factory that Em was first lured away from conventional art by the aesthetic potential of technology. The firm's owner was interested in art and had the idea that his moulding machines could be used for creative ends. Em was hired as artist-in-residence and spent some time producing room-sized plastic sculptures. This led him into an environment completely foreign to him as a solitary artist—he had to learn to organize helpers to operate the machines with him, and he had to learn to deal with management. These continue to be sizeable preoccupations at JPL.

Outside the studio, or rather computer room, Em has a passionate interest in theatre. Scattered around Hollywood are a host of ambitious small play-houses which provide a creative outlet for talented people in the film indus-try who have to spend their working days producing pap. For these Em writes and directs extraordinary multi-media performances, using projec-tions of his own paintings as scenery, as well as lasers, synthetic music and bizarre insect-like costumes likewise designed by him. As yet the computer cannot control the projections directly, but this is the next logical step. An on-line video projector would open up the fascinating possibility of varying the visual effects in accordance with the action on the stage, as it happens.

For other events Em has generated huge moving displays, ten feet high and eighty feet long, using more conventional analogue electronics and pro-jectors. 'Scale makes a lot of difference psychologically,' he says. 'The effect of that display was overwhelming.'

How do people react to his work? 'The public for this sort of thing is still very small,' Em says, 'and people tend to spend a lot of time wondering how it is done rather than looking at the pictures.' He also has few peers to share his ideas with. Other artists he meets tend to be suspicious of technology, finding it cold and hostile, and he often finds more sympathy among scien-tists. Paul Brown, late of the Slade School, has had similar experiences. He once showed some drawings to a supposedly learned critic, who was very excited by them and praised them profusely. He asked Brown how they were drawn and, on hearing that a computer was involved, immediately changed his mind about the pictures. 'I thought there was something cold and calcu-lated about them,' he commented. Brown adds that while technologists may not be prejudiced in that way, they are often disinclined to regard art as a serious activity.

DRAWING BY EXPERT SYSTEM

Quite the opposite approach to Em's is taken by Harold Cohen, an English artist based at the University of California, San Diego. While working as a conventional painter in the late 1960s, Cohen became interested in seeing whether computers could be used to shed some light on the nature of visual experience—why it was that he could make some marks on paper and some-one else would say, 'That's a face.' Friends, notably Ed Feigenbaum, taught him programming, and the outcome of this was a system called Aaron, which produced drawings under the control of a PDP—11/34 minicomputer. The actual drawing was done by a little electric cart, about four inches long and carrying a pen, which trundled around a large sheet of paper stretched out on the floor. The computer kept track of where the cart was by means of sonar.[1]

The machine drew entirely on its own and Cohen took no part in the process. The program consisted of about 300 rules worked out in advance by Cohen, which gave the system an understanding of such concepts as lines, closures and shading. As the drawing proceeded, the program would make choices about what to do at various points by in effect 'rolling a die'—that is, it would activate a special routine that generated random (or almost random) numbers in a given range. As the picture filled up, the program would be more and more constrained in what it could do, by what was already on the paper interacting with the rules.

Rules would specify what kinds of features would be desirable, such as, 'If there is such-and-such a feature here, don't put another feature close to it' or 'If you are drawing a form and you run up against another form, lift the pen to let the earlier form overlap the new one.' Objects the program handled fell into a strict hierarchy:

pictures
   groups
      figures
         'systems' (parts of figures)
            lines (curved)
               straight-line segments

Figure 2   Harold Cohen: drawing by Aaron

Figure 3   Aaron in action (photograph: Becky Cohen)

Particularly important concepts that the program was given included the difference between open and closed forms, and occlusion.

The results were pictures containing plenty of zigzag lines and arbitrary shapes, but also what often appeared to be rocks, clouds, birds, fish and sometimes lines of hills. Each picture was different, and Cohen had no way of knowing what was going to come out each time. In building his program out of rules Cohen had in fact produced an expert system, albeit an unusual one. The human expert and the knowledge engineer in this case were the same person—himself. Cohen had also made a deliberate attempt to model the process by which a human artist draws, not as one smooth movement but by a series of short strokes with continuous feedback. Hence the cart did not move directly to point (x, y) like a computer plotter. Instead, the computer would say to the cart in effect, 'Turn the wheels by so much and tell me by the sonar where it has taken you,' and this was repeated over and over. There was slippage of the wheels on the paper, and adjusting the length of the axle and the rate and sensitivity of the feedback system would given considerable variation in the 'style' of the drawings.

Out of Aaron, Cohen has now developed Aaron2, which apart from having greater knowledge is intended to be much further down the road to genuine intelligence by being able to learn from experience.[2] Cohen sees it as dealing with *representations*, rather than images, which were what Aaron worked with. An image, Cohen explains, is 'a collection of marks implying ordering', while a representation is 'a collection of marks implying intention with respect to the outside world'. Again, the program's concepts are held in hierarchies: for example, the set 'representations of solid objects' is included in the set 'closed forms'. Aaron2 is designed to give much more of an illusion of three dimensions than its predecessor. Cohen has also dispensed with the drawing cart, because it was too difficult to keep the sonar working properly, and because the drawings were unmanageably large and slow to produce. He now uses a conventional computer plotter in which a pen is moved around on paper by a mechanical arm.

Even in its infancy Aaron2's drawings show a distinct 'maturity' compared to those of its progenitor. It remembers previous drawings so it can relate its current work to them, and eventually it is intended to be self-modifying so that, like a human artist, it can learn from its experience. That will require, as Cohen says, some means of giving it criteria by which to judge its own performance. We will then have the first expert-system art critic.

Looking further into the nature of representations, Cohen at one point devised another program called Anims, which produced figures with random variations around the basic structure of body, head and four legs. This was prompted by the work of David Marr into the question of how humans 'package' information in their brains. It transpired that remarkably little information has to be stored away in order for it to be possible to reconstruct images with a very real appearance. The figures from the program turned out to be surprisingly similar to prehistoric cave drawings of animals. However,

Figure 4   Harold Cohen: drawing by Aaron2

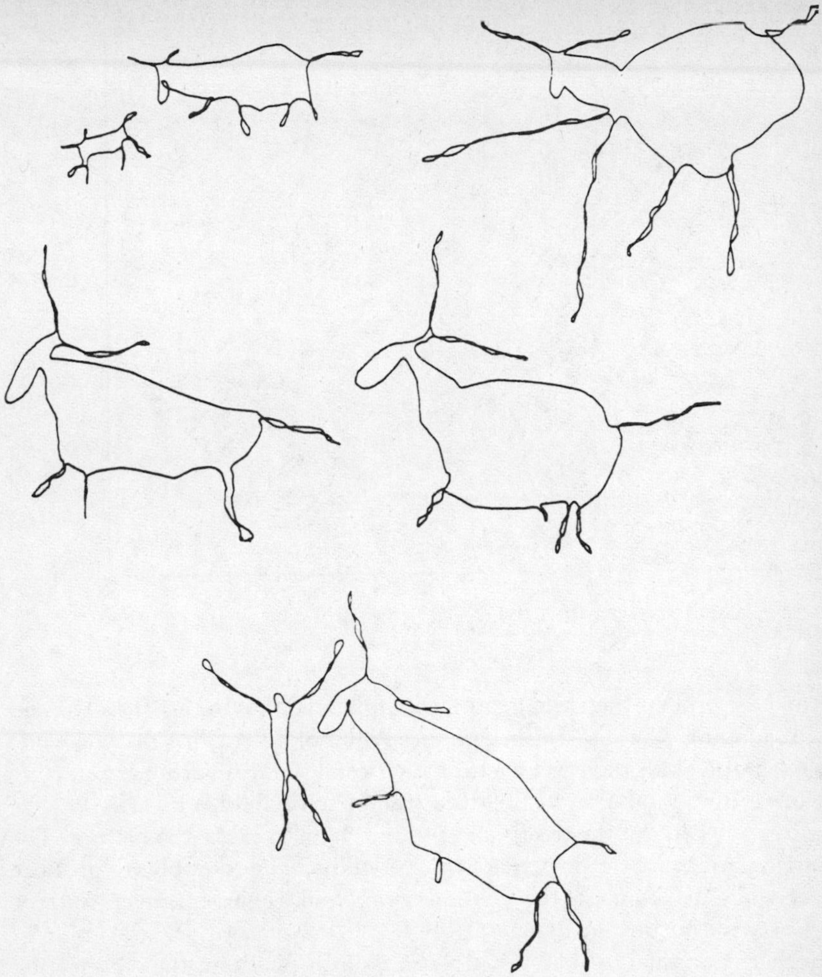

Figure 5   Harold Cohen: drawing by Anims

Cohen felt his work was too limited to be viewed as art-making and so has not taken it any further.[3]

THROWING AWAY THE DICE

Other computer artists tend to follow one or the other of the two approaches we have described, usually producing their work on an ordinary computer pen-plotter. Sometimes they take the pen out and substitute a paint brush. In contrast to the 'dice-throwing' technique of Cohen, it is possible to construct a drawing program in which there is no random element but in which the

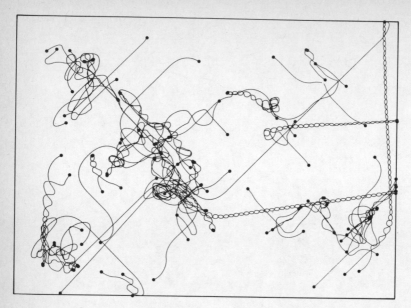

Figure 6   Chris Briscoe: untitled

rules and the process they lead to are so complicated that the artist still has no way of knowing what the finished picture will look like. Chris Briscoe while working at the Slade did this by letting a series of points in arbitrary starting positions move as if they were objects attracted to each other by gravity. The computer worked out the tracks and plotted them to make the picture. The Canadian Chris Crabtree in his 'story pieces' allows the computer to produce a linear sequence of images that look very much like people, flowers and the like, giving the impression of a narrative.[4]

Another Canadian, Theo Goldberg, is interested in the connection between painting and music, and has devised a graphics system and a music synthesizer which both work from initial sets of numeric data. He feeds the same data into both systems and from one gets pictures with large areas of soft colours overlaid with geometrical patterns of lines, and from the other gets electronic music in a modern cacophonous style. The music is played from tape while slides of the pictures are projected, and the viewer is invited by the artist to see how the picture represents the music and vice versa, as different manifestations of the same thing.

SHARPENING THE PALETTE KNIVES

The two approaches to computer art have led to a schism in the field every bit as vehement as the rivalry between painters and sculptors in Titian's day.

Figure 7 The creatures in Chris Crabtree's 'Story Pieces' move about, eat, grow, fight and reproduce in a manner reminiscent of John Conway's celebrated simulation of biological growth and competition, the Life Game

The 'tool' approach as exemplified by David Em tends to be dismissed by those in the other camp as trivial—as 'painting by numbers'—its products scorned as banal. Harold Cohen was presented some years ago with the idea for an 'electronic paint box' and responded thus:

> [The] image of the artist of the future painting with a paintless brush on a television tube with one hand—because it is after all an artist's touch that counts—while twiddling knobs with the other: dressed, presumably, in smock and beret, and cracking walnuts with his left foot: this image is as silly as misguided.[5]

Cohen's work in its turn is described by some of his opponents as 'chicken scratchings'. Analysing the principles at issue, the English artist Dominic Boreham maintains that the way a computer enables him to paint by an iterative process, trying out something, judging, changing what is not quite right, is entirely valid as art and produces pieces that could not possibly be made without a computer. The judgements he makes in accepting or adjusting aspects of a picture could not be embodied in rules, yet rules are what Cohen's system consists of in its entirety. 'You can't produce art with an algorithm,' Boreham declares.

The schism in David Em's case is accentuated by his determination not to learn the engineering skills involved in his art, but rather to rely on the experts around him. Otherwise, he feels, it is all too easy to dissipate all one's energy in just getting the equipment to work. Too many artists he knows have learnt programming and now spend all their time writing software and never producing any art. Cohen in contrast is heavily involved in the technology down to the smallest detail. He even builds all his circuit boards and plotting mechanisms himself. Artists are 'enabled', he insists, by the technology they use:

> Devices are what we seem to use: but the truth is that, unless we have a clear view of what they are, unless we are sensitive to their functions within the economic hierarchy which generated them, *they* will almost certainly end up using *us*. Technologies constrain their users. The more powerfully a technology serves its designed-in purpose, the more the individual is constrained by its use: not simply in the sense that an etching will always look like an etching and not like a watercolour: but that the individual is constrained intellectually from conceiving of any possibility other than what is given him by the technology . . .
>
> Just as the artist finds himself offered a whole toyshop full of new toys, he finds that a century of preparation has gone into ensuring that he asks no questions about what they are and how they work. They do what they do, and they are designed to require no participation of him more intellectually challenging than button-pushing.
>
> It must surely be the case that technological resources which do not challenge the artist's intelligence will not *enable* his intelligence, and through it the production of powerful and original work . . .

We know already that no one makes art by finding some tame programmer to write a few graphic subroutines. In the years that that game has been going on, not one single art-work of major importance has resulted from it. When you consider that the parallel case in printmaking would be that of a painter who has no idea what art is, working for an artist who knows nothing about printing technology and doesn't want to have to find out, there is absolutely no reason to assume that one will.[6]

Brian Reffin Smith of the Royal College of Art suggests there is a third category of use of computers in art, in which the machine helps the artist to develop his concepts and perceptions:

It arises out of the observation that (certainly at the Computer Studio of the Royal College of Art) one of the most frequent modes of interaction between artists and computers is as follows. A person comes in, with a problem that they might normally try to solve using pen and paper, paint, film or any other medium. They then use the computer to 'worry at' their problem, using graphics on the computer screen, or other, more conceptual representations of the problem. The person then, as often as not, goes away and carries on using the old materials—but their *perception* of the problem has changed. It has been externalized between the person and the computer screen a few inches away.[7]

Artists are constantly being influenced by the work of other artists, by the plays and films they see and so on, and experience with a computer can be just as valid, in Smith's view. This could be taken even further, with highly elaborate computer techniques of exploring art and perception. For example, one of the most important things computers can do for makers of animated films is 'in-betweening'—taking two drawings of a figure in different positions provided by the artist and working out all the intermediate frames to give the illusion of smooth motion in the finished film. 'What would happen', Smith asks, 'if you tried to "in-between" a Rembrandt and a Jackson Pollock?' Many other fascinating insights into art are waiting to be found through the use of computers, Smith is convinced.

ANIMATION

In addition to taking over 'in-betweening' and many of the other tedious processes of hand animation, computers open up substantial new possibilities in this medium. They can generate surface textures, shadows, reflections and shines all automatically, giving a realism and an illusion of three dimensions that are quite impractical in hand animation. [. . .] The principal problem involved is the computing power needed: each frame of a high-definition film can take up to one or two hours of processor time to produce because it contains so much detail.

As is the way with techniques of this sort, the first people in the outside world to take up computer animation enthusiastically have been television advertisers.

[. . .] Most of the objects depicted in films of this genre are artificial—spaceships and the like—and so can be generated as an assemblage of regular geometric shapes such as spheres and cylinders. The computer can handle these quite easily. On the other hand if the film maker wants to include natural elements such as landscapes, he has a problem in that to seem realistic the scene has to be irregular and contain large amounts of detail. A picture of a lawn, for instance, must comprise many thousands of blades of grass, but they cannot all be the same. If one image of a blade were repeated over and over in the usual computer technique, the lawn would look utterly unreal. Each blade needs to be slightly different, but for an artist to specify every one separately would be a colossal task. On top of that, the vast amount of information thus compiled would have to be held in a large data-base, unmanageable and costly. To overcome this problem, Benoît Mandelbrot of IBM and others following on from his work have devised the technique of 'fractals', whereby the irregularity of natural objects is simulated by the computer adding random variations to features supplied by the artist, making smooth lines crooked and so on (Figure 8). Using this method, surprisingly realistic mountains, rock-strewn valleys, coast-lines and star clusters can be generated, with the artist only having to specify a few points.[8] Indeed, fractals are now being used to produce still paintings and sculptures as well as animation (Figure 9). This raises the interesting question of whether fractal landscapes should be judged by the same criteria as the works of conventional landscape painters. Paul Brown thinks that up to a point they should, but other artists disagree strongly.

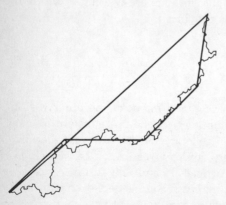

Figure 8   '. . . And the straight shall be made crooked . . .' Irregular curve obtained from four straight segments through the technique of fractals

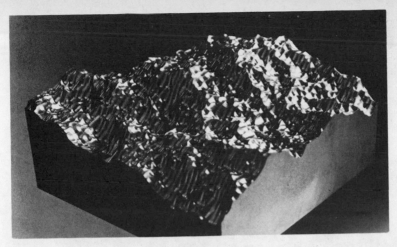

Figure 9 '. . . and the plain places rough.' Sculpture of a mountain range produced by Benoît Mandelbrot using fractals and a computer-driven machine-tool (photograph: IMB)

SCULPTURE

Some work has been done in producing sculpture by computer, with the processor connected to a machine-tool which carves a block of metal or other material. However, the principal interest computers have aroused in this field is to do with kinetic sculpture. An early example of this was Seek, put together in 1970 by Nicholas Negroponte and his colleagues at MIT. This consisted of a model overhead crane driven by a minicomputer, which would stack up 500 two-inch cubes in a random arrangement with plenty of nooks and crannies, remembering where all the cubes were. Into this 'environment' would be released a colony of gerbils, who would run around knocking the cubes every which way, and the computer would try to put them back into some semblance of order.[9] What started as a demonstration of a computer observably dealing with unpredictable events turned into a metaphor of interaction between an animate and an inanimate world. Opportunities for misinterpretation by the public (at the Jewish Museum in New York where Seek was on show) were rife. Negroponte comments:

> Reviews of the show failed to keep Seek intact, to see its animate and inanimate aspects as equally purposeful. *The New York Times* (September 18, 1970) reported that '. . . a mechanical grappler rearranges them [the blocks] to wall the furry creatures in'; *Art News* (December 1970, in a snide editorial entitled 'Gerbil ex Machina') wrote, 'The gerbils could use their blocks to achieve positive, socially meaningful ends, but not just mess around with them'; and

Figure 10   Edward Ihnatowicz: 'The Senster', on show at the Evoluon exhibition in the Netherlands. The computer is at the right rear

the *Wall Street Journal* simply found it and computer art in general ideologically 'kinky'.[10]

Many of the gerbils died; legend has it that this was from frustration.

Edward Ihnatowicz is a Polish-born sculptor living in England whose interest in the kinetic stems from his conviction that the behaviour of something tells us far more about it than its appearance. This led him to build the Senster (Figure 10), one of the most influential kinetic sculptures ever made. It consisted of a fifteen-foot-long steel frame articulated in six different places, with the joints all powered by hydraulics, the whole vaguely reminiscent of a giraffe made of tubular lattice. On the Senster's 'head' were carried an array of microphones and a Doppler radar system. The Honeywell minicomputer controlling the mechanism was programmed to make it react to three things: moderate and low sounds, loud sounds, and fast motion. Moderate sounds the head would move towards, loud sounds it would pull back from, and fast motion it would track. The result was an uncanny resemblance to a living thing, and the crowds at the Evoluon in Eindhoven, Holland, where it was on show reacted with enormous excitement. Children would shout and wave at it, call it names, and even throw things. Ihnatowicz explains that its movements seemed to stem from situations that people recognized.

In the quiet of the early morning the machine would be found with its head down, listening to the faint noise of its own hydraulic pumps. Then if a girl walked by the head would follow her, looking at her legs. Ihnatowicz describes his own first stomach-turning experience of the machine when he had just got it working: he unconsciously cleared his throat, and the head came right up to him as if to ask, 'Are you all right?' He also noticed a curious aspect of the effect the Senster had on people. When he was testing it he gave it various random patterns of motion to go through. Children who saw it operating in this mode found it very frightening, but no one was ever frightened when it was working in the museum with its proper software, responding to sounds and movement.

Although the Senster was dismantled some years ago, many people who saw it still remember vividly what a strong impression it made on them. Ihnatowicz has various ideas for further developments, including an investigation of how motion and perception are interdependent, an important topic for artificial intelligence. Unfortunately, the mechanisms are necessarily expensive, and the resources to build them are not easy to come by.[11]

I KNOW WHAT I LIKE

All this can seem puzzling to the outsider. We think of the art that impresses us most and recall the enormous mental effort and anguish that went into its creation. What can be the value of art that is produced without a clear idea of a desired end-result on the part of the artist? Intuitively we think of art as negative entropy, and as a general rule the better the art, the more negative the entropy, with every single detail contributing to the overall effect. The process of laboriously selecting the attributes of each detail so that they will contribute to the overall effect is the very reverse of entropy. Surely anything that is random or unpredictable will almost never turn out to contribute in this way, to have any value? After all, Stravinsky, no reactionary himself, said: 'I hold that music is given to us to create order.'[12]

In reply some computer artists put forward the view that what goes on in the human creative process is no different in kind from what happens in their machines. An artist has an algorithm in his head just as much as a computer does. They go on to dismiss free will as an illusion, no different from random choice, so the chance element in their programs should complete the equivalence of human and computer artistic creation.[13]

The central question then is, what are the algorithms that humans use? It is the search for an answer to this question that is the main preoccupation of many computer artists. Harold Cohen sets out deliberately to model human creative behaviour, to externalize the process which would otherwise be going on inside him. Lawrence Mazlack, at the University of Cincinnati, is trying 'to develop an aesthetic perception in a computer' in order 'to investigate the codification and specification of aesthetic judgement'.[14] This leads inevitably to the question, what is art? Some artists insist that art is nothing more than the process of asking, 'What is art?' This has prompted Marshall

McLuhan to comment, 'Art is anything you can get away with.'[15] Other artists are more positive. Edward Ihnatowicz asserts that art is the process of 'modifying the environment so that some aspect of nature, otherwise not discernible, can be revealed—to attract people's attention to an aspect of reality'. Robin Shirley suggests that basically 'art involves the human faculty of discerning order', and that the essential interaction is with the perceiver, not the creator. In its most general sense art is the process of making meta-phors, Negroponte maintains in a passage wryly headed 'A metaphor cannot be hung upside down'.[16]

Throughout all this we see continuing the argument between classicism and romanticism that has been going on in art for hundreds of years, with classicists trying to find order in nature while romanticists prefer to take nature as it is. Earlier in this century the dispute took the form of Deter-minism versus Indeterminism, with obvious pertinence to the use of randomness in computer art. Perhaps this art is not as revolutionary as it seems.

THIS IS JUST LIKE ART

So how successful have these artists been in their metaphor-making with machines? It is widely agreed that, taken as a whole, art with computers has not lived up to its potential. Negroponte is blunt about this: 'Rarely have two disciplines joined forces seemingly to bring out the worst in each other as have computers and art.'[17] Those who entered the field early have been disappointed at the low level of interest that has developed. Certainly this is due in part to the bad reputation computer art has acquired, deterring people with talent who might have contributed to raising the standard. Brian Reffin Smith puts foward his explanation of this:

> Traditionally the computer has been used to produce what you might call 'pretty pictures'. In a sense it's a kind of chocolate box art of information technology, which in some ways has given computing in art a bad name, because people have produced random number squiggles and spirals and so on—maybe they have been mathematicians or computer scientists. They've said, 'Hey! This is just like art!' and put it on their walls and so on. This drives artists and designers mad because if you had done it with a pencil or with string on nails or whatever, people wouldn't look at it twice. Certainly they wouldn't consider it worthy of having an exhibition.[18]

Harold Cohen sees the failure of computer art thus:

> For an artist proposing to make images with a computer, the body of know-ledge we should be considering is that which binds the nature of a program to the nature of an image, not simply programming skills, even though he can't do without them. 'Computer art' has never accomplished that binding, because it has always accepted the characteristic 20th-century definition of the computer

as a transformation device. To get an image out you have to put an image in. The binding of program to image is impossible, since a transformation process is indifferent to what is being transformed.

To use the computer as a transformation device is to use it on a trivial level. It is a completely general symbol-manipulating device, and allows the writer of a program essentially to define what the machine is any way he or she chooses. That generality gives the computer a very special significance as the first modern device which allows itself to be used as a sort of do-it-yourself design kit, rather than as a single fixed-function tool.[19]

The problem as far as the layman is concerned is that most computer art is highly abstract, and abstract art is hard enough for him to appreciate and judge, superficially or deeply, even when there is no computer involved. Then the aspect of computer creativity is introduced to complicate matters yet further. It is often pointed out that the pictures produced by Harold Cohen's program look very much like the ones he used to paint himself. What then is the point of going to all that trouble with the computer? Cohen remarks that 'The art-sceptic's three-year-old daughter really can *not* do as well as Picasso,'[20] and we agree, but can she do as well as Aaron? The exercise may be interesting intellectually but artistically . . .? Many people watch with fascination as Aaron draws its pictures in the museum, and happily buy the finished pieces, but it is hard to know how much of this is aesthetic appreciation and how much is novelty value.

Then there is the issue of randomness. Presumably, the bemused onlooker concludes, if Jackson Pollock could throw paint at his canvases, the computer might as well too, but the rhyme or reason can seem elusive. Then Cohen puts forward his view of randomness: 'Primarily, I believe its function is to produce proliferation of the decision space without requiring the artist to "invent" constantly.'[21] But surely the whole business of an artist is to invent! He should hardly regard this as a chore to be evaded! It is easy to reach the conclusion, as Negroponte puts it, that the technology is the whole point: like a burlesque of Marshall McLuhan's ideas, the medium is the message.

Alan Sutcliffe enters the fray at this juncture and insists that computer art has not yet been given a fair chance to prove itself. All art involves the production of a great deal of mediocre work before anything exceptional comes along, and computer art simply needs a longer trial. The public also has a lot of learning to do before it can really appreciate these new media, because the ideas involved are strange and new.

THE SUNDAY PAINTER

Negroponte sees computer art developing in two particular ways. One is an extension of kinetic art of which the Senster was a notable example:

Imagine more moody pieces. Simple extrapolations of interactive art can embellish the behavioural model to include inputs from the weather, time of day, Dow-Jones Average, and the results of sports events, elections, or film ratings. In some sense, this could be the art form of off-track betting. Or, with more fantasy, we can imagine a future of the visual arts populated with patronizing pieces of sculpture and caustic canvases that recognize the viewer to be male or female, rich or poor, bewildered or blasé, you or me. In this fiction, the artist runs a kennel for cuddly art forms that get to know their future owners, who in turn get to know and love them.[22]

Even before Negroponte had written that, Edward Ihnatowicz had built a sculpture with an arm that the viewer pulled as on a one-armed bandit, while the machine tried to make inferences about the puller's sex and temperament.[23] He must beware who prophesies in jest.

The other development Negroponte foresees is in the direction of personal, as opposed to public, art. He points to all the metaphors we treasure as individuals, but which are of no interest to anyone else: a drawing by one of our children, a stone brought back from an idyllic holiday years ago. Computers provide a whole new set of opportunities for self-expression:

Think of our Sunday painter reincarnated with an easel of electronics and a palette of computer graphics. His work is as invigorating as a game of tennis, his challenge is that of chess, his product is as ephemeral as a child's drawing. In this fantasy lies the potential for the major impact of computers on the visual arts of the future.[24]

Not everyone is happy with this vision. Harold Cohen relates a visit to Xerox's Palo Alto Research Center:

There was also a music program at Xerox, which, I was told, would enable people to compose music even if they didn't know anything about music. Didn't I think that was marvellous, I was asked? No, I said, I thought it was appalling. Why would anyone want to compose music without knowing anything about music? And why—as if I didn't have my suspicions already—would Xerox's well-meaning technologists want to encourage that particular form of lunacy? Well, they said, it was a beginning: I would surely have to admit it was a step in the right direction. No, I said, I was quite sure it was a step in the *wrong* direction.[25]

In the last analysis, if computers produce works of art that are original and interesting, by whatever process, then we have every reason to rejoice and accept the exercise as worthwhile. The problem must be fundamentally that art that says much to us is nearly always based on a great deal of knowledge about the world. The significant artist needs, above all, experience, both of his trade and of life. Up to now computer art programs have incorporated little knowledge, except perhaps for Harold Cohen's Aarons. Cohen even refers to the work of his Anims program as 'Drawings of a know-nothing, almost', although it is surprising how much knowledge of animals these pictures appear to contain. There is, as Robin Shirley puts it, 'an immense problem of putting a useful model of the world into a computer, and the task has only just started'. As we have said, Harold Cohen has embarked on the process of using the techniques of knowledge-based systems to make pictures, and other artists are certain to follow suit.

A really serious contribution by computers to the arts is still a long way off. Whether computers will ever create great works of art autonomously is hard to say. Negroponte declares that, for that to happen, the machine would have to *want* to create the work of art—and that raises any number of philosophical questions. But even if computers only provide a useful augmentation of the human artist's mind they will have added in an important way to creativity. There is no doubt that machines will play an increasingly prominent role in the arts.

NOTES AND REFERENCES

General

Jonathan Benthall, *Science and Technology in Art Today*, London, Thames and Hudson, 1972.
Cybernetic Serendipity, ICA exhibition catalogue (ed. Jasia Reichardt), London, Studio International, 1968.
Jasia Reichardt, *The Computer in Art*, London, Studio Vista, 1971.
Donald Greenberg et al., *The Computer Image*, Reading, MA, Addison-Wesley, 1982. This volume includes numerous colour illustrations but is more about computer graphics than art.
Joseph Deken, *Computer Images*, London, Thames and Hudson, 1983.

References

1. Cohen, H. (1979) 'What is an Image?', in *Proceedings of the Sixth International Joint Conference on Artificial Intelligence*, Tokyo, pp. 1028–57; Cohen, H. and Cohen, Becky, Catalogue of Harold Cohen Exhibition, Stedelijk Museum, Amsterdam, 25 November 1977–8 January 1978, reprinted in *Page*, bulletin of the Computer Arts Society, No. 41, November 1978.
2. Cohen, H. (1982) 'How to Make a Drawing', paper presented at Science Colloquium, National Bureau of Standards, Washington DC, 17 December; Cohen, H. (1983), Catalogue of exhibition, Tate Gallery, London, June–July.
3. Cohen, H. (1981) *On the Modelling of Creative Behaviour*, Rand Paper P-6681, Santa Monica, Rand Corporation.
4. Reffin Smith, B. (1982) Catalogue of the exhibition *Artists, Computers, Art* Canada House, London, 24 March–20 April.
5. Cohen, H. (1982), letter in *Art in America*, September/October.
6. Cohen, H. (1982), 'When Machines Can Generate Images Faster than You Can

Pull an Edition, Who Will Belong to the World Print Council?', invited paper at conference of the World Print Council, San Francisco, 15 May, p. 3 ff.

7. Smith, op. cit.

8. Alain Fournier, Don Fussell and Loren Carpenter, 'Computer Rendering of Stochastic Models', *Communications of the Association for Computing Machinery*, Vol. 25, No. 6, June 1982, pp. 371–84; Benoît Mandelbrot, *The Fractal Geometry of Nature*, Oxford and San Francisco, W. H. Freeman, 1982.

9. Benthall, Jonathan, *Science and Technology in Art Today*, London, Thamas and Hudson, 1972, pp. 75–8, 166–7.

10. Negroponte, N. (1979) 'The Return of the Sunday Painter', in *The Computer Age: A Twenty-Year View* (ed. Michael Dertouzos and Joel Moses), Cambridge, MA, MIT Press, p. 27.

11. Benthall, op. cit., pp. 78–83; Edward Ihnatowicz, 'The Relevance of Manipulation to the Process of Perception', *Bulletin of the Institute of Mathematics and its Applications*, May 1977, pp. 133–5.

12. In Nat Shapiro, *Encyclopedia of Quotations about Music*, Newton Abbot, David and Charles, 1978.

13. Marvin Minsky, 'Matter, Mind, and Models', in *Semantic Information Processing* (ed. Marvin Minsky), Cambridge, MA, MIT Press, 1968, p. 431.

14. In Smith, op. cit.

15. McLuhan, M. and Fiore, Q: (1967) *The Medium is the Massage*, London, Allen Lane, pp. 132–6.

16. Negroponte, op. cit., p. 22.

17. Negroponte, op. cit., p. 21.

18. Interview on LBC Radio, 1 April 1982.

19. Cohen, Stedelijk Museum Catalogue (see above).

20. Cohen, *On the Modelling of Creative Behaviour* (see above), p. 14.

21. Cohen, 'What is an Image?' (see above), p. 1045.

22. Negroponte, op. cit., p. 31.

23. Jonathan Benthall, 'Computer Arts at Edinburgh', *Studio International*, October 1973, p. 120.

24. Negroponte, op. cit., p. 37.

25. Cohen, '. . . World Print Council' (see above), p. 5.

3 COMPUTERS IN A TECHNOLOGICAL CULTURE: THE PRESENT SCENE

This section looks at how computers are used at work, and whether the skills fostered at school continue to be useful. Are computers enabling to all sectors of society or are some people unable to develop their full potential because they belong to a certain group (for example class or gender), which as a group has less access to new technology?

Section 2 presented an optimistic view of new technology, allowing, or indeed demanding, the use of the skills we have discussed. But these optimistic predictions have not come to fruition. In the industries discussed here we might expect to find the use of co-operation, decision-making skills, independent learning strategies, information handling and perhaps problem-solving skills. In fact the papers suggest that such skills are not widely required, and where they are required they are not needed by everyone.

Feickert describes how the introduction of new technology in mining led to higher productivity with a smaller workforce. The jointly agreed plan was open to different interpretations by management and unions: and the increased output could either be seen as a way of running a pit with fewer workers or the same number of workers could work less hours. Whilst the introduction of new technology improved physical working conditions it has also led to the de-skilling of jobs and reduced autonomy.

By contrast, the second paper argues for a more optimistic view. It describes UTOPIA: a joint project between unions and researchers, on developing new printing technology, which has enabled workers to participate in company decisions. However, some problems still remain. The introduction of new technology has reduced the number of workers in the printing industry; those that are left have experienced a reduction in their 'autonomy and creativity', and as in the coal pits, jobs have been de-skilled.

Finally, Cockburn describes the effect of new technology on women in each of three workplaces she studied. The optimists might predict that as 'old technology' is perceived as inappropriate for women because it is dirty and requires strength, that new technology would relax such barriers. This is not, however, the case. Here then, women emerge as another group for which computers are not necessarily enabling.

3.1   *Britain's miners and new technology*

●   Dave Feickert

What has the 1984–85 miners' strike got to do with new technology? A great deal. Indeed, the government's plan for mass redundancies follows inexorably from automated equipment installed in recent years and from the new high-tech capacity to be installed over the next few years. This brief article will sketch the origins of today's battles in the miners' 1974 victory, particularly in the resulting 'Plan for Coal', which has come to be manipulated by capital against labour.

For all of us 1974 was a crucial year. It was one of those turning points around which history revolves. Although we did not realize it at the time, it was effectively the last year of the long postwar economic boom. But as such it was also the door opening into a quite new period of profound restructuring of the international economy. One of the levers of this restructuring would quickly become apparent—information technology, based on the revolution in microelectronics.

The year 1974 was also the moment when the long wave of post-war working-class struggles reached its highest point. In Britain this was revealed in the 1974 miners' strike, the three-day week and the fall of Edward Heath's Conservative Government. Parallel struggles had been fought out in all other developed capitalist countries as the international cycle of struggle circulated. The heart of the fight was the wage offensive that caught up almost all major groups of workers in those countries.

At the same time Third World movements were experiencing reinvigoration, perhaps mostly seen in the struggle of the Vietnamese people, already near victory, against the technological might of the most powerful nation on earth. In the Middle East the dispossessed Palestinians were at the centre of an unfolding political process which launched not only the Arab–Israeli war but also an exceptional fight for the redistribution of wealth, oil wealth, to the Arab producer nations of the Middle East. In 1973 they unleashed the world oil crisis that then began rocketing through the world economy in

1974, thereby providing the incentive for the massive restructuring which we now witness.

The multinational oil companies, together with local Arab elites, surfed in on this huge wave of underemployed and peasant struggle, yet the struggle itself found a material, if not political, unity in Britain. This was no more clearly seen than during the 1974 miners' strike when Welsh miners demonstrating for the strike outside the National Union of Mineworkers HQ in London dressed themselves in Arab clothing.

'PLAN FOR COAL' 1974[1]

As these two powerful struggles intermingled, the new crisis became particularly acute for Britain. Oil prices were going through the roof, which for an energy-intensive nation was a terrifying experience. At the same time it became all too apparent that the only viable alternative to oil—British coal—had been run down to an almost disastrous degree. Miners' leaders had been warning of the dangers throughout the period of rundown, to both Conservative and Labour governments alike, but to no avail.

It was in this context that the long-standing 'Plan for Coal' was pulled out of a drawer at Hobart House, HQ of the National Coal Board (NCB), dusted off and laid on the table of a specially set up Tripartite group of government, employers and trade unions. Although some of the proposals had been sitting on various tables for some time, the final text of the 1974 Plan was written with the recent triumph of the miners' union behind the pen.

The new version of 'Plan for Coal' became the second victory scored by miners within the same year, the first being over wages. But like so many working-class victories, the Plan contained several elements that were open to manipulation and recuperation. Ten years later, the many hours of negotiations between the NUM and the NCB have arisen from this problem. The Plan, together with its 1977 update, agreed on four aims:

- to modernize the coal industry, investing substantial sums where neglect once ruled;
- to replace exhausting pits with brand new ones, like Selby in North Yorkshire, and bring in 42 million tonnes of new capacity;
- to expand the market for coal to 135 million tonnes at least by 1985;
- to bring the industry's finances up to date, taking into account the social costs of the past.

During negotiations between the two sides in 1984, the argument revolved around the interpretation of 'Plan for Coal'. That, at least, was the public projection of it. The NCB insisted on negotiating on what it called the 'principles of Plan for Coal', while the NUM insisted on holding to the 'Plan for Coal' itself. In its briefing package to the TUC, the NCB went some way towards outlining the principles of the Plan as it saw them. Of the above four points, it entirely left out expansion of the market and vigorously interpreted clauses relating to the closure of exhausting capacity as a carte blanche to close pits on economic grounds, even if they still had coal reserves.

The Coal Board felt justified in thereby screening out of existence one of the Plan's two most important principles—expansion of the market—because the energy market as a whole had contracted sharply since 1973, particularly after 1979. On the other hand they pointed out that they had made the promised commitment to invest substantial sums in the industry and to modernize it. All the new capacity, agreed under the Plan, was being introduced.

INVESTMENT AND RESTRUCTURING

While the NCB took few new marketing initiatives in the face of the declining energy market, they maintained high levels of investment both in new capacity and in reconstructing older coalfields, albeit all within the central coalfield. In this way it can be seen that the NCB have played off the growing contradiction between falling demand and an ever-increasingly productive supply of coal. Miners' jobs, caught in this vice, have been squeezed out in their thousands.

Moreover, the Plan for Coal had envisaged the maintenance of mining employment, as miners transferred from the old exhausting pits to the new ones or retired. In retrospect this assumption was misplaced, though understandably at the time. What was not realized at the time, especially by miners' leaders, was that the investment they had demanded for so many years would itself be used to cut thousands of jobs.

'Plan for Coal' was drafted in 1974 and redrafted in 1977. In 1974 the world's first commercially available microchip had only just appeared, and while engineers at the NCB's Mining Research and Development Establishment (MRDE) will have understood the potential use of microelectronics at that time, no one else did. Since then, however, investment in microelectronics has been used to transform mining operations both underground and on the surface, in collieries, offices and workshops, *in the central coalfield*.

Miners' leaders assumed the investment would be made in new pits, creating new jobs, and in the infrastructure of existing pits, to make them safer and guarantee their continued production. They had not bargained on the second focus of investment, in electronic control systems. Infrastructure investment—investment in new roadways underground, new face developments, and more up-to-date mechanical and electrical equipment—was essential in mines facing geological difficulties and years of underinvestment, as in South Wales, Scotland and the North East.

Even so, there still remains a contradiction within this investment. On the one side, the technology can help guarantee that a pit will stay open, producing coal. On the other side, the technology reduces substantially the number of jobs at the pit where it is applied; by hugely increasing productivity, it contributes towards the closure of collieries far away in other coalfields. It is this contradiction that the NUM finds so difficult to deal with today.

The clearest illustration of this problem can be seen in the Coal Board's intentions to use the remaining 25 million tonnes of high technology new capacity, agreed under 'Plan for Coal', to close 70 pits and cut 70,000 jobs, while maintaining the same deep-mined output of 100 million tonnes per year. Norman Siddall, caretaker Chairman of the Board for 1983, made this point at the industry's Consultative Committee in June 1983. As the new capacity was introduced over the next four to five years 25 million tonnes of older capacity would have to be phased out. And the new capacity will create many fewer jobs than it replaces; for example, at Selby less than 4,000 miners, deputies and management will produce nearly half of the new capacity output.

MICROCHIP MINING

In September 1983, when Ian MacGregor was installed as Board Chairman, he inherited the most technologically advanced underground coal industry in the world. Not even the German industry can rival the diffusion of computer-controlled machinery and processes that can be found in half of Britain's 174 pits. And NCB automated equipment is being exported to the USA for installation in American mines, against the dominant flow of the electronics trade.

While on-line computer control systems have been and are being developed for every section of the coal industry, it is at colliery level that most effort has been made. Learning from a series of near-disastrous experiences with analogue electronics in the 1960s, Coal Board engineers were quick to adapt the newly available microelectronics to every major mining operation, both underground and surface. [. . .]

The process of de-skilling mining jobs, to a large degree assumed by the systems design adopted by the Board's engineers, is taking place throughout the subsystems. One area of colliery work that many miners originally thought would be immune from this process is electrical and mechanical maintenance. However, the IMPACT—Inbuilt Machine Performance and Condition Testing system, so far a separate system—is already starting to lead to the same polarization in skilled/unskilled. Small teams of specialized technical craftsmen, recruited from among mechanics and electricians, carry out the specialized technician level work associated with the new systems, while other craftsmen are finding their jobs being de-skilled or are faced with the possibility that even under existing stringent mining safety regulations the NCB may be able to use unskilled workers to do their former work.

Of concern to the NUM, too, is a deterioration in the mental aspects of the working environment. While, as a rule, new mining technology does improve physical working conditions, the reduced autonomy of the de-skilled jobs results in increased levels of stress. This has even been studied and is now recognized by NCB ergonomists.

However, by far and away the main threat to miners from new technology is the threat to their jobs. If the Board's intention is to reduce the industry to 100 pits, with 100,000 miners producing 100 million tonnes, over the next few years, it is conceivable that mining employment could be reduced further to 79,000, for only a slightly reduced output.[2] This is a figure also quoted by Tory MP Ian Lloyd, Chairman of the House of Commons Select Committee on Energy, a strong Board supporter. Curiously, it is one that the Coal Board reject as utter nonsense when it is made by NUM supporters or academics who have studied the issue independently.

The automation of deep mining in Britain, as one weapon to be used in battle with the miners, was not part of the original 1978 Ridley plan, but at management level inside the Coal Board it has been seen in that way for some time. While the drive to develop automated mining goes back to the Robens period, now it is much closer to fruition. At the same time the majority of people in Britain have been led to believe that coal mining—that first of all major industries, and the power behind the industrial revolution—is outdated, traditional and dying. Nothing could be further from the truth. Few TV cameras have made the journey from the deliberate dereliction of South Wales pits to the shopping complex look-a-like superpits in the Selby countryside. But unless they do, the fiction of a lame duck industry is maintained. This issue was partly raised in a 'World in Action' programme, 'Miners and the Microchip', when Professor John Ashworth was parachuted into the Scottish mining community of Polkemmet. The NCB Scottish Area wants to close Polkemmet Colliery, a move fiercely resisted by the local NUM, even though they are in the middle of Scotland's 'Silicon Glen'. In spite of the geography there are no jobs in the burgeoning Scottish electronics industry for redundant miners. For several years now it has become obvious that, apart from university-trained systems staff, the only production jobs that exist have been restricted to young female school leavers. By the age of 21 even these young women are considered too old.

Ashworth has admitted this reality. As the National Economic Development Council's Information Technology expert, he has been pressing the Government hard over pursuing a more vigorous development of the UK microtech industry. He has suggested lamely that the miners get into university, train as systems engineers and move to London! Perhaps even more significant, Ashworth himself appeared to be totally ignorant of developments taking place in the British coal industry and how the automation of new and existing mines in the central coalfields is being used to close pits like Polkemmet.

The NUM has been becoming increasingly aware of these problems, but, like all other unions so affected, is finding it very difficult to deal with the contradictions involved. From a traditional position of demanding more investment to stop colliery closures, thus preventing neglected pits slipping down the low productivity spiral into an 'uneconomic' status, it is having to face the fact that Selby will make all other pits appear uneconomic by comparison. Projected net profits from the Selby complex, when on full stream in five years, will be £17/tonne in 1983 prices. The total annual *net* profit will therefore fall within the range of £170–£212.5 million, based on an annual output of 10–12.5 million tonnes. In crude terms Selby's 3,500–4,000 miners are to be used to replace 38,000 miners and the six-pit complex to close 45 of the 'least profitable' existing mines.

On the other hand, using a strategy which uses *free disposable time* as a measure of wealth, rather than labour time, Selby's profits could be used to pay for a four-day week for 125,000 miners. Kept in employment would be at least 25,000 of those to be displaced by Selby. (This calculation is based on a miners' average wage in 1983 of £164 per week.)

Accordingly, the central demand in the Draft Technology Agreement drawn up by the Union is for a four-day week, with no loss of pay. It would be practicable, when all other developments are taken into account. It also connects with the vision of a totally new form of society in which the employed are increasingly liberated from work and the unemployed are liberated from poverty and despair. Radical reductions in working time of this kind have been discussed in a theoretical way by socialists like Rudolf Bahro and André Gorz. In the context of the British mining industry, but with another eye fixed on the experience of the German Metalworkers' strike for a 35-hour week in 1984, we can see the practical shape such reductions might take.

In the meantime the forces arrayed against such a solution have steadily grown more determined and perhaps even stronger. However, with the strike over, the war itself remains to be won. Although 70 pits are threatened by automation and by the Government's refusal to allow British coal the market justified by its price and quality, they cannot be closed overnight. Within the next five years this battle over new technology in mining will continue, and an alternative marketing strategy is likely to be developed. These two issues can be more fully developed and linked strongly to the traditional struggle to defend mining communities.

REFERENCES

1. Ferrymoor Ridings NUM. 'Plan for Coal—With the NUM', 1985. NUM, 'New Technology in Mining' (Briefing Booklet No. 6), available from St. James House, Vicar Lane, Sheffield, S. Yorks.
2. A. Burns *et al.*, 'Second Report on MINOS', Working Environment Research Group, Bradford University, 1984.

3.2 *UTOPIA: Where workers craft new technology*

- Robert Howard

The sign on the door reads 'technical laboratory.' The walls are festooned with elaborate diagrams. In one corner a slide carousel projects images onto a small, VDT-sized screen, simulating a computerized work station in operation. In another corner, an individual puts together the photographs, headlines, and text of a newspaper page on the screen of a real terminal. At his side an observer jots down a few notes and asks an occasional question about the quality of the 'interface' and the 'feel' of the machine.

It could be a scene from the research department at any high-tech computer manufacturer. But this lab is in the government-funded Swedish Centre for Working Life in Stockholm. The individual using the terminal belongs to the Swedish Graphics Workers Union, while his partner is a computer scientist from Sweden's Royal Institute of Technology. Both worker and scientist are participants in an intriguing experiment in technology development known as the UTOPIA Project.

UTOPIA is a Swedish acronym for 'training, technology, and products from a skilled worker's perspective.' It is a three-year, $400,000 research effort, funded primarily by public sources, that has brought together two quite different social groups: on the one hand, systems designers, computer scientists, and work-efficiency experts at institutions in Sweden and Denmark; and on the other, activists and officials from unions representing some 120,000 printers, typographers, lithographers, and other skilled workers in the newspaper and printing industries of the five Nordic countries.

Since 1981, UTOPIA participants have worked to define a role for trade unions in the design of new workplace technology. The goal is to help unions translate their social values regarding job skills, quality of work, and quality of products into new computer hardware and software for the printing industry. In this way, participants hope to shape the impacts of new technology on workers before it ever reaches the shop floor.

Few Americans would expect unions to play an active role in developing new technology. The most common stereotype is that workers oppose it through restrictive work rules, feather-bedding, and even a Luddite resistance to the very idea of technological change. But the reality is considerably more complicated. While unions have often tried to cushion their members from the negative impacts of new technology, few have flatly opposed it. Especially since the end of the Second World War, most U.S. unions have chosen to accept management's plans for new technology, and then bargain over their share of the productivity gains that technology can make possible.

This attitude may now be changing for two basic reasons. The computer has transformed work on a scale not seen since the mass-production assembly line was introduced at the turn of the century. What's more, this technological change is occurring as a profound restructuring of the world economy has brought increased international competition and higher levels of unemployment to most advanced industrial economies.

As a result, trade unions—primarily in Europe, and to a lesser degree in the United States—have begun to ask several fundamental questions: What is the impact of the microelectronics revolution on employment? How does the ongoing computerization of work affect employees' skills and job quality? What are the potential health effects of the new technology? How can workers acquire the training to ensure that the computer revolution does not pass them by? And, perhaps most important, how is rapid technological and economic change reshaping the traditional balance of power between corporations and unions?

Nowhere has union activism on these issues gone further than in Scandinavia. Beginning in Norway in the late 1960s, and extending to Denmark and Sweden over the next decade, technical specialists from government-funded institutions such as the Norwegian Computing Center in Oslo and the Swedish Center for Working Life joined unionists to study the effects of new technology on work and to formulate realistic union strategies to address them.

These 'action research' projects spread throughout Scandinavia in metalworking shops, chemical refineries, railroad repair shops, insurance offices, retail stores, and newspaper offices. They quickly took on the form of a popular-education movement. Workers began to understand technology as something they might be able to influence—just like other aspects of working life. And technologists began to see some of the implications for people on the shop floor of the technologies they designed. They began to question some of the assumptions and methods of their profession.

Perhaps most important, action research has enabled workers to participate in company decisions about technological change. In Norway, for example, the projects have led to a new kind of collective bargaining mechanism known as 'technology agreements,' These give local unions the right to receive advance notice of all company plans for purchasing or designing new technical systems, and to appoint a union staff member to represent workers' interests in all technological matters. UTOPIA represents the most recent effort by Scandinavian unions to deal with new technology: building union influence over the design of technology itself. UTOPIA focused on the printing industry.

HOW COMPUTERS TRANSFORMED PRINTING

Printing has traditionally been considered the archetypal craft industry. In his sociological classic *Alienation and Freedom*, written in 1964, Robert Blaunder described how the combination of 'craft technology, favorable economic conditions, and powerful work organization and traditions' gave printers 'the highest levels of freedom and control in the work process among industrial workers today.' Yet in the past two decades, the introduction of computerized text-entry, typesetting, and layout have transformed both the industry and workers' roles within it. At the same time, newspapers, in particular, have faced intense competition from alternative advertising outlets, including television and the new mass-circulation 'daily shoppers.'

The most visible impact of such technological change has been on the number of jobs. Employment of production workers in the U.S. printing industry declined by perhaps 50,000 through the 1970s. Computer and telecommunications technology has also made it easier for companies to shift work from heavily unionized and relatively high-wage urban centres in the Northeast to non-union printing shops in other parts of the country.

Those printers who remain have experienced far-reaching changes in their autonomy and creativity. Obviously, the keyboards, terminal screens, and software of computerized systems require altogether new skills. Workers have suddenly found themselves dependent on their employers and computer companies for new training in the tools of what, for generations, they had considered 'their' trade. Computerization has also created conflicts over job definitions in what Scandinavian printers, borrowing a metaphor from soccer, like to call 'the struggle for the mid-field.'

Such changes sometimes result from the capabilities of the technology itself. Reporters can now type their stories directly into the computer system, which automatically typesets them and eliminates the need for many skilled typographers. In other cases, the technology provides a smokescreen to disguise what are really managerial decisions about how to organize work. For example, computerized layout systems have allowed several newspapers to shift work from union printers to other company employees.

Computerization has also brought more subtle changes to printers' work. In the days of lead, skilled craftspeople made up an entire page of articles, headlines, photo-engraving, and advertisements in metal, according to a rough sketch, provided by the editorial department. Because they could 'put their hands on it,' makeup workers could easily judge the quality of their design.

Lead was succeeded by paper, with workers pasting columns of text onto page boards. Although pages lose a certain crispness of detail during this process, makeup workers can more readily rearrange and evaluate the elements of the page.

With computerization, makeup workers' relationship with the page has changed drastically. Early systems made layout extremely abstract, and some still do not show the page on the terminal screen. They require the workers to retain a mental image of the page while they feed codes into the computer that instruct it to create certain shapes and spaces on the page. More recent systems do show empty boxes on the screen representing headlines, articles, and photographs. But makeup workers still have difficulty judging page design because they do not work with the actual pictures or text. 'It's almost as if you were working blind,' says Malte Ericsson, a Swedish lithographer and participant in UTOPIA.

The new computer technologies, Scandinavian printers argue, have diminished the quality of the product as well as that of their work experience. European newspapers have traditionally been far more design conscious than their American counterparts. They use higher-quality newsprint, a greater variety of typefaces, and more color, graphics, and special photography. Computerization, unions claim, has brought standardization—a trend toward a more boxy 'American' style based on uniformity of typeface and monotony of design. The ultimate result is visually less interesting.

This change is not the inevitable outcome of computerization. One need only look at a newspaper such as *USA Today* to see how state-of-the-art technology can allow newspapers to explore new frontiers in design. However, according to the Scandinavian printers' unions, many papers in the rush to automate seem to have eliminated not only workers' craft autonomy but also some fundamental principles of graphics design.

THE UNIONS' ALTERNATIVES

Such concerns have made technological change in the printing industry a divisive process in a number of countries. The New York City newspaper strike of 1963 and the *Washington Post* conflict in 1975 stemmed from the advent of new technology. Many unions have also resorted to less aggressive measures to protect their members from the negative consequences of technological change. In Britain, for example, labor has negotiated a ban on 'single key stroking—the automatic typesetting of text that journalists enter into the computer. Thus, after writers compose their stories at a terminal, a paper copy must be made. A union typographer then retypes the copy into the computerized typesetting system.

In the Nordic countries, the conflict has taken a different course. While print unions have negotiated protective measures similar to those in other countries, their participation in the action research projects taught them that such an approach can, at best, be a holding action. 'The real issue,' says Malte Ericsson, 'is determining how we can make sure that no single occupational group is totally expelled from the profession. To do that, we have to suggest alternatives.'

That is where the design of technology becomes important. 'We saw the big printing companies and newspapers doing their own research,' says Gunnar Kokaas, secretary of the Norwegian Graphics Workers Union. 'They were giving money to vendors to develop new equipment that we felt would undermine our traditional labour agreements. So we thought it was important for us to get into R & D as well, to support technology that would lead to the kind of skills and working conditions that *we* were interested in. Maybe that way we could influence the vendors.'

Scandinavian unions had already tried this approach in a more limited way. During the 1970s, they were among the first to urge VDT manufacturers to apply strict 'ergonomic' criteria to reduce strain on the human body caused by prolonged VDT work. By the early 1980s, Nordic computer companies were making some of the world's most ergonomic terminals. They had also become the most vocal proponents of adhering to such design standards, seeing in them a potential competitive advantage akin to the rigorous safety features of Volvo automobiles.

In effect, the unions were able to establish a set of standards for the entire VDT marketplace. UTOPIA set out to do the same for the technology of the entire printing industry.

UTOPIA's computer scientists were convinced that recent technological advances could benefit skilled printers. For example, powerful new software could create an accurate facsimile of the printed page directly on the terminal screen. This made it possible to create electronically the immediate feedback that makeup workers previously enjoyed using manual methods. Such capabilities could begin to restore printers' traditional autonomy and control. Instead of simply 'automating' work previously done by people, the computer could augment printers' design skills, becoming, in the words of UTOPIA director Pelle Ehn, 'an advanced tool for skilled graphics workers.'

Seeing the computer as a tool also implies a different understanding of the process by which new technical systems are developed. Most designers create a highly abstract model of a work process, and then try to incorporate that model into new computer hardware and software. Often, workers using the system end up as little more than passive objects of automation. UTOPIA's goal was to put the centuries-old traditions and occupational knowledge of printers at the center of the design process. Workers would play an active role in determining what kind of technology they needed and how it could support them in their work.

This did not mean preserving activities performed by printers in the past. As Pelle Ehn says, 'When a worker used lead he had to have the skill of reading upside down and backwards. Is that a skill one should want to protect? Probably not.' However, UTOPIA would maintain printers' ability to create an attractive page design. 'That is the kind of skill you have to make sure not to destroy when you shift to new technologies,' says Ehn.

The group discovered early on that the best way to articulate printers' demands for new technology was to give them direct experience using it. Since UTOPIA had no money to set up its own computerized printing shop, the project team opted for the next best thing—ever more sophisticated simulations of the page makeup process.

At first, participants used crude styrofoam and plywood mockups and paper diagrams to map out the steps of page makeup. Later, the team rigged up a slide projector that flashed makeup images onto a screen representing a computer terminal. By rearranging the order of the slides, the team could experiment with different ways of organizing the makeup process. Ultimately, the lab acquired a real computer work station, programmed with a few sample layout functions, that helped the team refine its ideas for hardware, software, and organization of work. As printers discussed the pros and cons of different approaches, the technical staff advised them on their feasibility.

DEVELOPING THE TECHNICAL COMPROMISES

Had this been the extent of the UTOPIA Project's work, it would have remained an interesting but somewhat abstract research project. However, in 1982, Sven Holmberg, the president of Liber Systems, made a proposal that helped turn UTOPIA into a concrete exercise in technological development. Liber was the chief participant in a $10 million Nordic project to develop a fully integrated text-and-image processing computer system known as TIPS. Based on technology developed at Sweden's University of Linköping, TIPS was to be one of the most sophisticated computer systems available in the printing and publishing industry. It would combine text entry, image enhancement, pagination, and layout in a single work station.

Holmberg offered UTOPIA a role in the Liber development process. Project participants agreed to produce a set of 'applications specifications' recommending how the Liber system should be used in printing. In exchange, the project acquired access to the TIPS technical staff and R & D labs. For Liber, co-operation with UTOPIA offered a way to incorporate users' ideas into the new system, although the company was not required to do so. For UTOPIA co-operation offered an opportunity to influence a specific technical system soon to reach the market.

Completed last year, the UTOPIA specifications try to strike a balance between workers' demands and technical capabilities. For example, one of the printers' top priorities is gaining the capacity to work with an entire newspaper page directly on the terminal screen. However, even the largest screens are too small to present a newspaper page in its normal size. Either the page must be reduced, making the text and the images too small to be seen clearly, or only a portion of the page can be projected on the screen, disrupting workers' sense of the whole.

The technical compromise developed by UTOPIA and TIPS engineers recommends software that provides makeup workers with 'lenses,' or 'viewports,' through which they can see different portions of the newspaper page. Different lenses allow scale reduction, magnification, or natural size. If workers want to change some text, they might use the lens that presents that portion in its natural size. But if they are assembling articles, headlines, and photographs into an overall design, they can chose the lens that reduces the whole page to fit on the screen. Makeup workers can also use different lenses simultaneously. They might enhance a photograph or drawing to full scale in one corner of the screen while watching the impact of this operation at a reduced scale on another part of the screen. Or they could compare different versions of the same page on the screen simultaneously.

The UTOPIA specifications also call for workers to have access to high-speed laser printers. These create hard-copy prints of layouts that allow the workers and their editors to check the design created with the computer in terms of how it will look on the printed page.

The specifications further touch on organization and training. The 'scanner station,' where a worker feeds photographs and graphics material into the computer, provides an example. UTOPIA recommends that the system allow workers to begin preparing photographs for layout in addition to simply feeding the information to the computer. This makes the job more varied and helps to avoid bottlenecks at later stages of production.

Finally, whereas most vendors train users to operate only their particular system, UTOPIA recommends that training include general education in what Pelle Ehn calls 'computer science for graphics workers.' Such training can yield dividends for management. When printers are more broadly trained, an organization can adapt more easily to fresh technology. And the more understanding workers have of the concepts underlying the systems they work with, the more they will be able to exploit the systems' versatility to create high-quality products. Pelle Ehn even foresees a not-too-distant time when powerful new software packages will enable printers to program systems themselves in order to maintain, upgrade, and adapt their technology to new uses.

PRACTICAL PROBLEMS

Liber unveiled its TIPS technology last spring. Six out of nine systems ordered so far are being installed, including two at newspapers in Finland and Sweden. Not surprisingly, in the move from technical lab to newspaper shop floor, UTOPIA's ideas have encountered some obstacles. How they are met will determine UTOPIA's ultimate impact. Indeed, the most important period of the UTOPIA Project may still lie ahead. [. . .]

UTOPIA's model of skilled workers using high technology to create high-quality products may also encounter problems with general trends in the newspaper industry. While the UTOPIA team was refining its concepts in the technical laboratory, U.S. manufacturers were perfecting a different approach to computerized pagination known as 'free-flow page makeup.' This allows editors to perform both page layout and copy editing. To remain competitive, especially in the U.S. market, Liber has had to include this feature in TIPS.

But how TIPS or any computerized pagination system is used in the Scandinavian printing industry will ultimately depend, at least in part, on how well the graphics workers' unions argue for their own model of technology and work. Perhaps UTOPIA's greatest accomplishment has been its contribution to workers' expertise about technology and its impacts. This knowledge is already affecting the outcome of labour-management negotiations in the printing industry. Malte Ericsson tells of entering negotiations with the managers of a Stockholm printing firm who wanted to introduce a new Xerox laser printer. Because of his involvement with UTOPIA, Ericsson found that he knew far more than his counterparts across the bargaining table about the system's labour requirements, the kind of skills workers would need to operate it effectively, and the type of training they would require. 'We feel we are stronger in negotiations now,' says Ericsson, 'because we have more knowledge than the employers.'

Last November, the UTOPIA specifications were used in national negotiations for the first time, forming the basis for proposals by the Danish Graphics Worker Union on new technology. And so seriously does Sweden's newspaper-industry trade association take the new union proposals that it is developing its own 'system specifications.'

Moreover, the idea of putting a union label on new workplace technology has spread to other Nordic unions. Those representing office workers have recently announced an effort to create their own organizational model for the 'office of the future.' According to project director Arne Pape of the Norwegian Computing Center, the model will emphasize the use of new technology to break down the traditionally rigid sexual division of labour in office work. Another project is exploring how to involve unions and professional associations in the design of 'expert systems'—programs that enable a computer to make judgments. A preliminary field experiment with nurses is currently underway at a major Oslo hospital. Other unions and researchers are considering similar projects in computer-aided design and manufacturing, retail sales, and warehousing.

One particularly interested observer of these developments is the small but dynamic Nordic computer industry. 'They are taking the discussion within the labour movement very seriously, because it may provide a signal of future trends in the market,' says Arne Pape. 'They are beginning to realize that trade unions can point things out to them that they aren't likely to hear from anyone else.'

The discussion within the Scandinavian labour movement has even produced an echo on this side of the Atlantic. As they begin to confront the issues that Nordic unions have been addressing for years, some American unions are turning to the Scandinavian labour movement for models and advice. For example, last September, leaders of the Communications Workers of America (CWA) went to Scandinavia with executives from AT & T to examine the way the unions and companies are addressing technology and its effects on work. Explains Lorel Foged of the CWA's Development and Research Department, speaking of UTOPIA, 'We'd love to be able to do something along those lines.'

So the impact of UTOPIA is continuing to expand, and the idea that workers and their unions have an important role to play in the design of new technology is reaching a wider and wider audience. Today, Scandinavia. Tomorrow, perhaps, the rest of the world.

3.3 Women and technology: opportunity is not enough[1]

• Cynthia Cockburn

When we raise the question of women and technology however it is nearly always within one of a limited range of contexts. The most common is a concern with 'the impact of new technology on women's employment'. This theme encompasses some substantial work on both technological redundancy and new openings created for women by new technology.[2,3,4,5,6] The genre also includes work on the exploited position of women in the supposedly unskilled, and certainly low paid, work of chip manufacture and electronic assembly.[7,8] The second context is one in which the focus is women's domestic or sexual existence. Research examines the effect of technological change on domestic work[9,10] and of medical and genetic technology on reproduction and health.[11,12] Finally, more geared to positive action for women and therefore more pragmatic in its treatment, has been work on the theme of 'getting women into technology', usually conceived as engineering. The Engineering Industry Training Board has undertaken initiatives to draw women into technician and professional engineering training and jobs, and some of these have been monitored by researchers.[13,14,15] In this same spirit, the EOC and the engineering industry sponsored a 'Women into Science and Engineering' Year during 1984.[16] Related research has focussed on the preparation of girls in school for technical and scientific careers[17,18] and on the attitudes of girls and women that predispose them to particular career choices. Holland[19] reviews this literature.

In setting up the research described in this chapter I [. . .] chose to focus on the relations surrounding technology, particularly the relations of work, to see what they could show about women's relative lack of power, our actual work situations and our absence from some occupations. In looking at the relations of work one is inevitably looking at class relations—what employers and employees expect and get from each other—and at relations of gender—how men and women interact.

The terrain I chose for examining these processes is that created by the advent of micro-electronic technology. A commonplace assertion establishes a starting point. In the old regime of electrical and mechanical technologies, women's hands seldom lifted or used a tool. They used domestic utensils and appliances, and they operated productive machinery but they were seldom craftspeople, technicians or engineers. It was often observed however that these technologies required physical strength and a tolerance of dirt that put them outside the sphere of women. Now, say these same observers, micro-electronics being light and clean, must surely lead to an entry of women into technical training and employment. Yet it has become increasingly clear that this is not happening. The technical division of labour appears to be persisting little changed.

I looked at the relations of technological work in three situations of change. They did not include office technology or the use of the computer as such, which are often taken to be the sum total of what the phrase 'new technology' means. Instead I chose to look at some less publicised applications of technological change where the possibilities inherent in electronics and the computer have transformed quite other labour processes. One of these is in production; one is in distribution; and one in a public sector service. In all of them, women have been involved both before and after the change.

In each instance I made a case study of one workplace using relatively unchanged technology and one with the new. In each I examined the causes of investment in new technology, employment practices and sexual segregation, the changing nature of the technology and its impact on employment and on labour processes and management practices. In all I interviewed around two hundred people, including management, trade union representatives and both male and female employees in the occupations most closely involved with the technology in question—whether operating it, maintaining it or managing it.

To these 'old' and 'new' workplaces in each case I added a third study, of an 'upstream' firm designing, manufacturing, importing, selling or servicing the new items of equipment. The necessity for this upstream component of the research will be obvious. Whatever happens in the firms in which new technology is applied, i.e. whether jobs in those sectors grow or decline in number, whether they are upgraded or deskilled, whether they become more or less prestigious and rewarding, one thing is sure. New, interesting and well-paid technical jobs are certainly being generated among those other business enterprises that are stimulated by and thrive upon technological advance. Skills and opportunities migrate from one kind of enterprise to another with the hazards of economic competition. Where they are lost and where they are gained also depends on the relative strength of different fractions of the workforce *vis à vis* employers. Only within this context does it make sense to ask, over all, what is happening to women.

By this research design I hoped to obtain a detailed understanding of the relationship that men and women have to machinery and to their employment, the way their technological persona carries over into their personal lives outside work, and the ways in which the relationship between men and women is mediated by technology.

In this brief presentation I can only sketch the three technologies in question and their significance to those who work on them.

AUTOMATION IN MAIL ORDER WAREHOUSING

The mail order business is that part of the retail trade that markets its goods and supplies its customers not through shops but by means of a printed catalogue and parcel post. The heart of the operation of a mail order firm is an enormous warehouse or system of warehouses, in which the problems of storage, stock control, retrieval, collating and packing of goods are considerable. Conventionally, goods are stored by a kind of logical spatial 'filing system' in which shoes will be stored in this rack, underwear in that. Orders are filled by a very labour intensive process. Women 'pickers', among the lowest paid and least regarded of workers, walk the racks in response to order forms, locating the goods, collecting them together in plastic bags carried on the arm or on a trolley, and sending them onwards to the packing room by wheeled bin or conveyor.

The new technology in such warehouses comprises a combination of computerisation of stock data with the acquisition of advanced materials handling equipment: trucks, moving belts, gondola systems. Goods can now be inserted randomly into the storage racks, to make best use of warehouse 'cube' and reduce journeys, because the computer memory represents a sufficient record of each item's whereabouts. Order slips are produced by computer, and indicate not only the type but the nearest location of goods required and the quickest order of search. The work of the pickers comes to be paced by the conveyors, greatly increasing the pressure and unpleasantness of the job. In the case I studied, a logical further step, the goods were stored in mobile carousels so that the pickers remained stationary, turned into a 'production line' under the eye of the supervisor.

This innovation is thus at one level a simple and belated mechanisation of the movement of goods. But at another it is a total reorganisation of work by means of the computer. Women, now, in a sense, work inside a big machine, as though they are some of its moving parts. Their autonomy, mobility and decision-making power, little as it was, has gone altogether and there has been no compensatory gain in technological know-how. If women 'control' the machinery by pushing buttons it is in the most rudimentary sense.

Meanwhile, new kinds of employee have come to pre-eminence in the ware-house: systems specialists, technological managers and maintenance techni-cians. They are men. In so far as employees can be said to control capital's technology, it is men who here control it. Meanwhile, productivity has greatly increased and, where not compensated by growth of output, has led to a loss of jobs, mainly by women. More use of temporary employees with inferior security is noticeable.

FRONT-END TECHNOLOGY IN CLOTHING MANUFACTURE

The second technology studied is that which is transforming the occupations of pattern-making, pattern-grading, lay-making and marker production in the clothing industry's leading firms. These jobs were all gradations within an inclusive apprenticed craft that included cloth cutting, and it was once an entirely male world. Clothing workers are organised by the National Union of Tailors and Garment Workers who helped define the craft and its standards. In earlier decades of this century, women on sewing machines took over from male tailors in garment manufacture.[20,21] For a while the cut-ting and pattern rooms remained a male stronghold, but today women are creeping in even here. They do not of course have either the actual status nor the self-identity of the craftsman. Nonetheless, many belong to the union and the occupations are still a little better paid and less routinised than that of the sewing machinists.

In the old regime, the jobs of pattern construction, grading, lay and marker making all comprised visualisation, calculation and working with pencil and eraser, paper and scissors. The cloth cutting job involved use of both an Eastman knife (an electric mobile knife with reciprocating blade that can be lifted and manoeuvred by hand) and the band-knife (a more danger-ous, stationary piece of equipment, used for cutting more intricate parts).

The new technology, which has entered fifty of sixty clothing firms in recent years, involves by contrast more sedentary work at a VDU. It is the CAD/CAM of clothing. Pattern pieces are digitised and so fed into the computer memory, whence they can be reproduced at will as images on a screen. Alterations from basic pattern 'blocks' to create new styles can then be made by reference to the screen, using a stylus and tablet combined with keyboard. Variations in dimensions needed to produce properly graded sizes from small to outsize, can also be coded and tapped in for the computer to calculate. The computer drives a plotter, which automatically prints out the individual pattern pieces or 'nests' of sizes. The pieces of several patterns then have to be organised along a notional length of cloth, preparatory to cutting. This too can now be done on screen.

While prior experience in cutting or pattern room helps, in fact the new processes can be taught in a couple of weeks. There has been considerable de-skilling, in that mental calculation and the knack with paper, pencil and knife or scissors are now redundant. On the other hand, this part in the production process is still a key factor in quality and speed of manufacture further down the line and it is not a job for the slow-witted.

Loss of employment has certainly occurred in the clothing industry as a whole where firms that have NOT taken the risk of investing in new technology or not succeeded in making it pay off, have gone to the wall. In the firm I studied, throughput had compensated for increased productivity and there had been no redundancies due to CAD/CAM technology. Numbers had in fact steadily increased, since more sewing units could be kept busy by the more productive pattern and cutting rooms.

What is interesting, however, from the gender point of view is that the new technology has confirmed and encouraged a trend away from male craftsmen towards female operators. Sometimes the women put to work on the CAD scopes are the ex-hand cutters, lay-makers or graders, but often they are fresh to the industry. Some men also do the job. But the dominant character of the pattern room in the CAD/CAM regime has subtly changed from masculine to sex-neutral. When that happens men, it seems, tend to withdraw, or to cease to push for employment openings in what is seen as a degraded industry. The jobs that are unambiguously masculine are ones to which neither the old craftsman nor the new female operator can aspire. They are the positions from which the new technology is controlled—those of systems manager. In these, it seems, the industry has yet to see a woman.

COMPUTED TOMOGRAPHY COMES TO THE X-RAY DEPARTMENT

The third technology is to be found in the very different world of the hospital. Radiography is strongly sex-stereotyped as female. Only latterly have men begun to enter the Society of Radiographers in greater numbers. As they enter however they are tending to percolate to the senior jobs. Radiographers are formally designated a 'profession supplementary to medicine'. Some would say they were para-professionals, others that their work is essentially that of a high-level technician. It is certainly one of very few occupations in which women have been enabled to acquire technological knowledge and competence.

In conventional X-ray, a beam of ionising radiation is passed through a human body, and differing attenuations of the beam are recorded in the form of a radiograph. The radiographer's training and expertise combines a knowledge of anatomy and positioning techniques with an understanding of and competence on the machinery—the X-ray generator, couch, stand etc. Normally she is required to make calculations and decisions concerning perhaps six or seven variables (kilovoltage, amperage etc.) governing exposures. She has to relate to and care for the patient while she or he is in the X-ray Department.

Computed tomography scanning was invented in the late sixties and has spread rapidly into clinical use, so that it is now available in around 90 hospitals in the UK. The unique capabilities of the CT scanner are that it can produce a cross-sectional image of the body and that it can differentiate between different forms of soft tissue. CT is one of several new diagnostic modalities in which the data are digitised and displayed on a screen where they can be manipulated and enhanced by colour and contrast. The main components of the scanner are a travelling couch for the patient; a gantry with a cylinder containing a rotating X-ray source and an array of X-ray detectors; a computer, console and video screen.

The effect of CT on the radiographer is contradictory. On the one hand it has removed from the job the need to calculate exposure time and other variables. In this sense it has become more of a push-button job than conventional X-ray. [. . .] However, it adds a whole new dimension literally, to anatomical imaging and, though there is no sign of a relaxing of the distinction between doctor and radiographer, nonetheless the latter may develop new skills of 'pattern recognition'.

Often the investment in such massively costly items of equipment, questioned by many critics of NHS policy, leads to pressure for greater throughput of patients. Indeed the advent of CT makes work, because new kinds of disease and condition become amenable to imaging.

CT is therefore potentially both a threat and a promise to the radiographer and the outcome depends in part on the deployment of the profession's organised strength. It is worth noting however that the radiographer has a legally defined role. The doctor alone may diagnose and report on a patient. The radiographer alone may operate the X-ray generator or scanner. On the other hand, only the hospital medical physicist or the maintenance technicians may make adjustments and repairs to the equipment. These latter are the ones with the growing and in-depth knowledge of principles and processes inherent in the new technology, and with the power to *intervene* in its operation. My study showed that, while radiographers are still predominantly female, the maintenance technicians and those physicists mainly involved with the equipment (as opposed to the patients) were almost entirely male. In interview they showed themselves to be dismissive of radiographers and their skills.

These three technology studies all show women, at varying levels of technical know-how and status, being retrained, brief though that retraining may be, and keeping their jobs in the advent of new technology. It is unlikely that most men would tolerate, let alone seek, the picking job in a mail order warehouse. Computerised pattern work seems to be arriving alongside a feminisation of the related occupations in clothing. And there is no significant change in the sex-typing of radiography related to technological change.

In other words, women are acceptable as *operators* of equipment, now as before.

On the other hand, the role of the operator or operative, however elevated this may appear in new technology, is one which is essentially vulnerable to further technological change. It may become yet more routinised or even wiped out by further advances in the technology. The invention of a robot hand will replace the mail order picker. The most modern clothing factories run their lay-making systems in 'automatic' mode, making the scope operator redundant.

One further thing is clear. Whatever opportunities the new technologies offer the operator they *never* enable her to cross a certain invisible, impenetrable barrier. This is the barrier that exists between operating the controls that put a machine to work and taking the casing off it in order to meddle with what goes on inside. This is the difference between an operator and a technician or engineer. For an operator there is always someone who is assumed to know better than she about the technology of the machine on which she is working. That someone is invariably a man.

THE TECHNICAL JOBS: DOWNSTREAM AND UPSTREAM

The systems manager jobs in these firms required an initial engineering training, acquired computer and electronic know-how and a career in the relevant industry of a kind that few women, if any, could be expected to have clocked up. Though senior managers expressed themselves open to a woman in this kind of job, where would such a paragon be found?

At the lower level, we have seen that in each of the work places studied there were teams of maintenance craftsworkers and technicians. Their jobs were represented to me as demanding 'good all-rounders', people capable of the imagination and flair to diagnose tricky faults, the dexterity to fiddle about with transistors and other tiny components, and the nerve and strength to clean out a boiler or unblock a sewer. The jobs were consistently represented to me as masculine jobs—since men alone could offer this range of abilities. A single woman (an Amazon as she was jokingly portrayed) should she present herself for the work would in any case not fit socially into an existing all-male team. Among the forty maintenance engineers in the six workplace case studies, covering old and new technology, there was but a single woman. I encountered her in the Medical Physics Department of one of the hospitals, a relatively sheltered environment for a woman to try out the technician role, and here she was being trained to put together replacement circuit boards for X-ray equipment. She was greatly over-qualified for this rather simple job, having a degree in physics. She represents women's sole gain due to new technology on the maintenance front. None of my informants anticipated a rapid feminisation of maintenance engineering.

Let's shift briefly to the upstream level. I will take as a not uncharacteristic example the technical personnel of a large firm that supplies CT scanners to British hospitals. It imports parts from its parent organisation abroad, assembles the scanners here, markets them to the UK and abroad, instals and services them. It also runs a repair workshop for recycling parts. I obtained details of the sexual division of labour in five of the departments—those most likely to employ technically qualified personnel.

In UK Service, of a total of 76 persons, only five—four secretaries and one administrator—were female. The remainder, which included 63 technician engineers and engineers, were all male. In Overseas Service, of 37 people, seven were female. They were junior administrators, secretaries, a statistical analyst and a computer operator. The remainder, including 16 technician engineers and engineers, were men. In the third department, Production, there were 289 employees. Fifty were women in the lowest grade of manual work: assembly and wiring. A somewhat more complex form of assembly work was split: 17 men, 7 women, but their work was differently specified, with that of the men requiring greater 'skill'. All inspectors and testers (fifteen) were men. Women were also present as clerks, secretaries and in junior management grades. All middle and senior management and all but one of the 92 hardware and software technician engineers and professional engineers were male. The one exception was a young woman design software engineer who had a degree in physics and had been trained in computer electronics and programming by her employers.

The fourth department, Sales, was rather more interesting. The six secretaries of course were female. But one salesperson among the many men, was female. And a curious section called Clinical Support also revealed some women. In this section of ten, seven 'training specialists' were women. The job of training specialist involves a follow-up to the installation of a CT scanner in a hospital, at home or overseas, by spending a couple of weeks introducing hospital personnel to its use. These training specialists were all radiographers by initial training, with experience in hospitals. They had sought to use their skills in the business world, where they could obtain more pay, develop their technical understanding of radiographic equipment, and relinquish responsibility for patients. These are quite remarkable and rare posts for women—involving in-house training, a fair degree of interaction with (male) engineers and, very unusually for women, extensive travel abroad.

Two factors concerning training specialists should be noted however. First, the job still does not require or allow the operator to penetrate the mysteries of the interior functioning of the machinery. It is an operator job writ large. Secondly, women are employed first because more women than men exist in the radiographer labour market, but secondly because women are considered more 'charming' and acceptable to the consultants and other senior hospital personnel whom they have to introduce to the new equipment. In other words, these women are not achieving access to a man's job in new technology—rather a woman's job has taken on certain interesting characteristics due to technical change.

My study showed a similar story in other 'upstream' firms. [. . .] The fifty per cent of technicians and engineers who notionally should be women, if all was fair in an equal world, are simply not there.

THE GENDERED RELATIONS OF TECHNOLOGY

But why are they not there? Most of my informants, personnel managers, trade unionists, individuals in different occupations, put the blame on parental advice, school, careers advisers. They also put a measure of blame firmly on women themselves, who 'are their own worst enemies'. All the firms I encountered claimed to have equal opportunities employment and promotion policies and open minds regarding women in technical posts. But they said they were continually disappointed by the fact that 'women just don't put themselves forward'. If they were offered a job 'they turned it down'. If they got the job they 'left after a few months to have a baby'.

All the factors pointed to above are real. We should however also suppose that firms do, for all their fine words, sometimes discriminate against women, knowingly or unknowingly. Yet there has to be a further factor at work. I believe it is hidden in the *consistency of women's refusal*. It comes to light in the subjective, personal interviews I obtained with men and women in a range of jobs, from unskilled manual work through to high level engineering and top management. The relations of technology and technological careers are gendered; they repel women; and they help to make men of men.

The overwhelming impression I gained in interview in men's accounts of their technical occupations, from the hands-on fitter/welder to the conceptual professional engineer, is one of an energetic commitment to their own know-how and competence and career. This relationship has all the absorption and enthusiasm of a love affair for many of the men.[22] Men in technical jobs are characteristically part of a team, a maintenance workshop perhaps, or a design and development outfit. The team is a social clique as well as a working group of colleagues, it involves camaraderie, rivalry, humour and much talk about technology and technical problems and solutions. In some situations the competitive nature of capitalist business adds a zest and an overdrive to these masculine relationships. Some men don't survive in this environment, some go to the wall, some have coronaries. But those that stay with it have a secure status in the eyes of other men.

Often I sat and listened for two or three hours to a man talking about his work. When I tried to imagine a woman sitting there telling me a similar tale, it seemed, to say the least, unlikely. The fact is that no ordinary woman with an ordinary woman's values and interests can join this club and fit in and survive in it. It is only a woman who is prepared to sacrifice, or greatly attenuate, her woman's identity and those responsibilities normally designated as hers, who can do so. For these jobs are not neutral, waiting innocently to be filled by either men or women. They are deep into partitioned, gendered terrain. This is something that is increasingly being recognised in research in other countries.[23,24,25,26,27]

My interviews with women showed a contrasting reality however. Of course the great majority were far lower down the scale of pay and 'skill' than the men. And many were self-deprecating, in the conventional way, about their technical abilities. But a substantial proportion showed self-respect, an interest in technology and in some cases an enthusiasm and flair for it. They expressed an appetite to learn more, and do more. But—and this is the important point—they would not do so at just any cost. And the costs they perceived to be considerable.

First, they knew that to be the only woman in an all male training course or an all male workplace was going to be uncomfortable. They were getting the message (it is hard to miss it): women don't fit here. Men's interaction with each other, the things they say about their jobs, and imply less directly about women, make it clear that a woman has to choose: if she is competent she will be considered unfeminine and unlovable. She will be resented. If she is incompetent she will be scorned. And she will still be resented.

Besides, these technological jobs require a career commitment and a single-mindedness that are predicated on a wife in the home to care for children and elderly and to keep things going. What woman has such a wife? The women showed that their jobs mattered to them, they were committed to them. But it was always with a proviso: family responsibilities might at any point intervene and have to take priority. None of these work places were providing the smallest token of contribution towards the very extensive support systems that are needed to help women combine a responsibility for home life and a technological career. Nor were they expecting men to carry such responsibilities and supporting them in doing so. On the contrary they expected their male employees to show commitment to the firm by large amounts of overtime.

We should, then, be conscious of the high social and emotional costs paid by the few pioneering women who do enter and stay the course in such environments; and, second, the possibility that the great majority of women, the absent thousands, who do not set themselves on the technological course at all, are not misguided, ill-informed or simply 'don't know what's good for them'. They may as I have suggested elsewhere,[28] be consciously refusing a course of action that seems to them likely to waste their energies, prove a false start and not deliver what it promises. In other words, much as they may like to work in technology, women may be boycotting it.

Women need a grasp of technology. Men's control of it is one source of their power to control women.[29] It is only if women get a grip on technology that they can make a constructive social critique of its uses. And it is only if they get a grip on technology that women will escape from the physical constraints and passivities to which male power has condemned them. For us to enter the technological sphere however more is needed than 'equality of opportunity'. Positive action for women, including many women-only initiatives and a massive development of employer and state support systems, from nurseries to changed hours and conditions of work, are needed.

More than this, however: we are not simply in a situation where men fall into some occupational niches, women into others like balls on a pin-ball table. Work and occupations are gendered environments. Technological occupations are particularly gender-skewed. This association of occupations with gender, and the exaggerated polarity of gender itself, more than the simple exclusion of women from technology, are what has to be melted away. So long as technological training and work have a function in building and burnishing masculinity it cannot be accessible to women. 'Equal opportunities' will mean no more than the masculinizing of women, if it does not also mean as a first step the feminizing of some men and as a second the creation of common human ground. So far, while official policies on equal opportunities have sometimes focussed on urging women (regardless of the cost) onto male terrain, they have not included a campaign to help men learn the skills required for domestic responsibilities, caring and social jobs, support and service jobs, located on female-gendered terrain. The uncoupling of occupation and gender has not yet seriously been attempted.

NOTES AND REFERENCES

1. Paper presented at the Annual Conference of the British Sociological Association, University of Bradford, April 1984. The research referred to was funded by the Economic and Social Research Council and the Equal Opportunities Commission and carried out at the Department of Social Science and Humanities, The City University, London, where the author is a research fellow.
2. Bird, E. *Information technology in the office: the impact on women's jobs*, Equal Opportunities Commission, September 1980.
3. Arnold, E. 'Microelectronics and women's employment', *Employment Gazette*, September 1982.
4. Huws, U. *Your job in the eighties: a woman's guide to new technology*, Pluto Press, 1982.
5. Science Policy Research Unit, *Micro-electronics and women's employment in Britain*, a report to the Department of Employment and the Manpower Services Commission, 1982.
6. Equal Opportunities Commission, *Working with computers, the opportunities for girls and women*, 1983(a).
7. Lin, L. 'Women workers in multinational corporations in developing countries, the case of the electronics industry in Malaysia and Singapore', *Women's Studies*

Programme, Occasional Paper No. 9, University of Michigan, 1978.

8. Grossman, R. 'Women's place in the integrated circuit', *S.E. Asia Chronicle* No. 66, joint issue with *Pacific Research,* Vol. 9, No. 506, 1979.

9. Rothschild, J. 'Technology, housework and women's liberation: a theoretical analysis', in J. Rothschild (ed) *Machina ex dea: feminist perspectives on technology,* Pergamon USA, 1983.

10. Schwarz Cowan, R., *More work for mother,* Forthcoming.

11. Winters, B. 'Engineered conception: the new parenthood', in J. Zimmerman (ed) *The Technological Woman,* Praeger, 1983.

12. Parker, A. 'Juggling health care technology and women's needs', in J. Zimmerman (ed) *The technological woman,* Praeger, 1983.

13. Engineering Industry Training Board, *The technician in engineering, Part 4, Women,* Research Report 9, Helen Connor, 1983.

14. Newton P. and Brocklesby, J. *Getting on in engineering: becoming a woman technician,* Department of Behavioural Science, Huddersfield Polytechnic, 1983.

15. Weinbreich-Haste, H. and Newton, P. 'A profile of the intending woman engineer', in *Women in engineering,* Research Bulletin No. 7, Equal Opportunities Commission, 1983.

16. Equal Opportunities Commission, *'WISE—1984', Women into Science and Engineering,* 1984.

17. Walden, R. and Walkerdine, V. *Girls and mathematics: the early years,* Bedford Way Papers No. 8, University of London, Institute of Education.

18. Kelly, A. et al, *Girls into science and technology,* Final report of a research project, Department of Sociology, University of Manchester, 1984.

19. Holland, J. *Work and women,* Bedford Way Papers No.6, University of London Institute of Education, 1981.

20. Coyle, A. 'Sex and skill in the organisation of the clothing industry' in J. West (ed) *Work, Women and the labour market,* Routledge and Kegan Paul, 1982.

21. Coyle, A. *Redundant Women,* The Women's Press, 1984.

22. Cockburn, C. *Brothers: male dominance and technological change,* Pluto Press, 1983(a).

23. Game A. and Poringle, R. *Gender at work,* Pluto Press, 1984.

24. Wagner, I. 'New work experiences for women', Mss, Vienna, 1983.

25. Berner, B. 'Technical knowledge and vocational identity' and 'Women, power and ideology in technical education and work', Mss, Lund University, 1983.

26. Hacker, S. L. 'The culture of engineering: woman, workplace and machine', *Women's Studies International Quarterly,* Vol. 4, No. 3, 1981.

27. Walshok, M. L. *Blue collar women: pioneers on the male frontier,* Anchor Books, NY, 1981.

28. Cockburn, C. 'Caught in the wheels', *Marxism Today,* November 1983.

29. Cockburn, C. 'The material of male power' *Feminist Review* No. 9, 1981.

4 COMPUTERS ACROSS THE CURRICULUM

This section opens with a contribution from Seymour Papert. He challenges teachers directly, claiming that computers can facilitate learner-centred education but that schools are too conservative to allow this to happen. This view is partly echoed by Sharples in his conclusion, but other contributors assume that the school curriculum can (and does) allow for innovation. Between them the authors discuss a wide range of learner-centred aims, and how they might be pursued in various subject areas. It is interesting to see how in the articles by Papert, Scrimshaw and Sharples a two-dimensional categorization of aims emerges, content defining one of these dimensions and process aims the other.

The complexity of curriculum aims even within a single curriculum area emerges clearly in the paper by Scrimshaw, raising the question of how CAL programmes can contribute to achieving these. Here the authors identify a range of different strategies. Ball looks to a diversity of programmes that will fit piecemeal into the Maths curriculum, each being exploited by the teacher for its particular strengths. The art packages described by Scrimshaw, like word processor or music composition packages, offer a different approach. They allow the learner to attempt a variety of tasks with one programme. However, the child needs some help in their use, and the usual assumption is that it is the teacher who will provide this. Sharples suggests instead the provision of a set of related but separate tool programmes, to be used unaided by children. These are then supported by written material to structure the children's learning.

4.1 *Computers and computer cultures*

• S. Papert

[. . .] Consider an activity which may not occur to most people when they
think of computers and children: the use of a computer as a writing instrument. For me, writing means making a rough draft and refining it over a
considerable period of time. My image of myself as a writer includes the
expectation of an 'unacceptable' first draft that will develop with successive
editing into presentable form. But I would not be able to afford this image if I
were a third grader. The physical act of writing would be slow and laborious.
I would have no secretary. For most children rewriting a text is so laborious
that the first draft is the final copy, and the skill or re-reading with a critical
eye is never acquired. This changes dramatically when children have access
to computers capable of manipulating text. The first draft is composed at the
keyboard. Corrections are made easily. The current copy is always neat and
tidy. I have seen a child move from total rejection of writing to an intense
involvement (accompanied by rapid improvement of quality) within a few
weeks of beginning to write with a computer. Even more dramatic changes
are seen when the child has physical handicaps that make writing by hand
more than usually difficult or even impossible.

This use of computers is rapidly becoming adopted wherever adults write
for a living. Most newspapers now provide their staff with 'word processing'
computer systems. Many writers who work at home are acquiring their own
computers, and the computer terminal is steadily displacing the typewriter
as the secretary's basic tool. The image of children using the computer as a
writing instrument is a particularly good example of my general thesis that
what is good for professionals is good for children. But this image of how the
computer might contribute to children's mastery of language is dramatically
opposed to the one that is taking root in most elementary schools. There the
computer is seen as a teaching instrument. It gives children practice in
distinguishing between verbs and nouns, in spelling, and in answering
multiple-choice questions about the meaning of pieces of text. As I see it,
this difference is not a matter of a small and technical choice between two

ching strategies. It reflects a fundamental difference in educational philo-
phies. More to the point, it reflects a difference in views on the nature of
ildhood. I believe that the computer as writing instrument offers children
 opportunity to become more like adults, indeed like advanced profes-
nals, in their relationship to their intellectual products and to themselves.
 doing so, it comes into head-on collision with the many aspects of school
hose effect, if not whose intention, is to 'infantilize' the child.

Word processors *can* make a child's experience of writing more like that of
eal writer. But this can be undermined if the adults surrounding that child
il to appreciate what it is like to be a writer. For example, it is only too easy
 imagine adults, including teachers, expressing the view that editing and
e-editing a text is a waste of time ('Why don't you get on to something new?'
or 'You aren't making it any better, why don't you fix your spelling?').

As with writing, so with music-making, games of skill, complex graphics,
whatever: The computer is not a culture unto itself but it can serve to
advance very different cultural and philosophical outlooks. For example,
one could think of the Turtle as a device to teach elements of the traditional
curriculum, such as notions of angle, shape, and coordinate systems. And in
fact, most teachers who consult me about its use are, quite understandably,
trying to use it in this way. Their questions are about classroom organization,
scheduling problems, pedagogical issues raised by the Turtle's introduction,
and especially, about how it relates conceptually to the rest of the curriculum.
Of course the Turtle can help in the teaching of traditional curriculum, but I
ave thought of it as a vehicle for Piagetian learning, which to me is learning
ithout curriculum.

There are those who think about creating a 'Piagetian curriculum' or
'iagetian teaching methods.' But to my mind these phrases and the activities
ey represent are contradictions in terms. I see Piaget as the theorist of
earning without curriculum and the theorist of the kind of learning that
appens without deliberate teaching. To turn him into the theorist of a new
urriculum is to stand him on his head.

But 'teaching without curriculum' does not mean spontaneous, free-form
classrooms or simply 'leaving the child alone.' It means supporting children
as they build their own intellectual structures with materials drawn from the
surrounding culture. In this model, educational intervention means changing the culture, planting new constructive elements in it and eliminating
noxious ones. This is a more ambitious undertaking than introducing a
curriculum change, but one which is feasible under conditions now
emerging.

Suppose that thirty years ago an educator had decided that the way to
solve the problem of mathematics education was to arrange for a significant
fraction of the population to become fluent in (and enthusiastic about) a new
mathematical language. The idea might have been good in principle, but in
practice it would have been absurd. No one had the power to implement it.

Now things are different. Many millions of people are learning programming languages for reasons that have nothing to do with the education of children. Therefore, it becomes a practical proposition to influence the form of the languages they learn and the likelihood that their children will pick up these languages.

The educator must be an anthropologist. The educator as anthropologist must work to understand which cultural materials are relevant to intellectual development. Then, he or she needs to understand which trends are taking place in the culture. Meaningful intervention must take the form of working with these trends. In my role of educator as anthropologist I see new needs being generated by the penetration of the computer into personal lives. People who have computers at home or who use them at work will want to be able to talk about them to their children. They will want to be able to teach their children to use the machines. Thus there could be a cultural demand for something like Turtle graphics in a way there never was, and perhaps never could be, a cultural demand for the New Math.

Throughout the course of this chapter I have been talking about the ways in which choices made by educators, foundations, governments, and private individuals can affect the potentially revolutionary changes in how children learn. But making good choices is not always easy, in part because past choices can often haunt us. There is a tendency for the first usable, but still primitive, product of a new technology to dig itself in. I have called this phenomenon the QWERTY phenomenon.

The top row of alphabetic keys of the standard typewriter reads QWERTY. For me this symbolizes the way in which technology can all too often serve not as a force for progress but for keeping things stuck. The QWERTY arrangement has no rational explanation, only a historical one. It was introduced in response to a problem in the early days of the typewriter: The keys used to jam. The idea was to minimize the collision problem by separating those keys that followed one another frequently. Just a few years later, general improvements in the technology removed the jamming problem, but QWERTY stuck. Once adopted, it resulted in many millions of typewriters and a method (indeed a full-blown curriculum) for learning typing. The social cost of change (for example, putting the most used keys *together* on the keyboard) mounted with the vested interest created by the fact that so many fingers now knew how to follow the QWERTY keyboard. QWERTY has stayed on despite the existence of other, more 'rational' systems. On the other hand, if you talk to people about the QWERTY arrangement they will justify it by 'objective' criteria. They will tell you that it 'optimizes this' or it 'minimizes that.' Although these justifications have no rational foundation, they illustrate a process, a social process, of myth construction that allows us to build a justification for primitivity into any system. And I think that we are well on the road to doing exactly the same thing with the computer. We are in the process of digging ourselves into an anachronism by preserving practices that have no rational basis beyond their historical roots in an earlier period of technological and theoretical development.

The use of computers for drill and practice is only one example of the QWERTY phenomenon in the computer domain. Another example occurs even when attempts are made to allow students to learn to program the computer. As we shall see in later chapters, learning to program a computer involves learning a 'programming language.' There are many such languages —for example, FORTRAN, PASCAL, BASIC, SMALLTALK, and LISP, and the lesser known language LOGO, which our group has used in most of our experiments with computers and children. A powerful QWERTY phenomenon is to be expected when we choose the language in which children are to learn to program computers. I shall argue in detail that the issue is consequential. A programming language is like a natural, human language in that it favours certain metaphors, images, and ways of thinking. The language used strongly colours the computer culture. It would seem to follow that educators interested in using computers and sensitive to cultural influences would pay particular attention to the choice of language. But nothing of the sort has happened. On the contrary, educators, too timid in technological matters or too ignorant to attempt to influence the languages offered by computer manufacturers, have accepted certain programming languages in much the same way as they accepted the QWERTY keyboard. An informative example is the way in which the programming language BASIC[3] has established itself as the obvious language to use in teaching American children how to program computers. The relevant technical information is this: A very small computer can be made to understand BASIC, while other languages demand more from the computer. Thus, in the early days when computer power was extremely expensive, there was a genuine technical reason for the use of BASIC, particularly in schools where budgets were always tight. Today, and in fact for several years now, the cost of computer memory has fallen to the point where any remaining economic advantages of using BASIC are insignificant. Yet in most high schools, the language remains almost synonymous with programming, despite the existence of other computer languages that are demonstrably easier to learn and are richer in the intellectual benefits that can come from learning them. The situation is paradoxical. The computer revolution has scarcely begun, but is already breeding its own conservatism. Looking more closely at BASIC provides a window on how a conservative social system appropriates and tries to neutralize a potentially revolutionary instrument.

BASIC is to computation what QWERTY is to typing. Many teachers have learned BASIC, many books have been written about it, many computers have been built in such a way that BASIC is 'hardwired' into them. In the case of the typewriter, we noted how people invent 'rationalizations' to justify the status quo. In the case of BASIC, the phenomenon has gone much further, to the point where it resembles ideology formation. Complex arguments are invented to justify features of BASIC that were originally included because the primitive technology demanded them or because alternatives were not well enough known at the time the language was designed.

An example of BASIC ideology is the argument that BASIC is easy to learn because it has a very small vocabulary. The surface validity of the argument is immediately called into question if we apply it to the context of how children learn natural languages. Imagine a suggestion that we invent a special language to help children learn to speak. This language would have a small vocabulary of just fifty words, but fifty words so well chosen that all ideas could be expressed using them. Would this language be easier to learn? Perhaps the vocabulary might be easy to learn, but the use of the vocabulary to express what one wanted to say would be so contorted that only the most motivated and brilliant children would learn to say more than 'hi.' This is close to the situation with BASIC. Its small vocabulary can be learned quickly enough. But using it is a different matter. Programs in BASIC acquire so labyrinthine a structure that in fact only the most motivated and brilliant ('mathematical') children do learn to use it for more than trivial ends.

One might ask why the teachers do not notice the difficulty children have in learning BASIC. The answer is simple: Most teachers do not expect high performance from most students, especially in a domain of work that appears to be as 'mathematical' and 'formal' as programming. Thus the culture's general perception of mathematics as inaccessible bolsters the maintenance of BASIC, which in turn confirms these perceptions. Moreover, the teachers are not the only people whose assumptions and prejudices feed into the circuit that perpetuates BASIC. There are also the computerists, the people in the computer world who make decisions about what languages their computers will speak. These people, generally engineers, find BASIC quite easy to learn, partly because they are accustomed to learning such very technical systems and partly because BASIC's sort of simplicity appeals to their system of values. Thus, a particular subculture, one dominated by computer engineers, is influencing the world of education to favour those school students who are most like that subculture. The process is tacit, unintentional: It has never been publicly articulated, let alone evaluated. In all of these ways, the social embedding of BASIC has far more serious consequences than the 'digging in' of QWERTY.

There are many other ways in which the attributes of the subcultures involved with computers are being projected onto the world of education. For example, the idea of the computer as an instrument for drill and practice that appeals to teachers because it resembles traditional teaching methods also appeals to the engineers who design computer systems: Drill and practice applications are predictable, simple to describe, efficient in use of the machine's resources. So the best engineering talent goes into the development of computer systems that are biased to favor this kind of application. The bias operates subtly. The machine designers do not actually decide what will be done in the classrooms. That is done by teachers and occasionally even by carefully controlled comparative research experiments. But there is an irony in these controlled experiments. They are very good at telling whether the small effects seen in best scores are real or due to chance. But they have no way to measure the undoubtedly real (and probably more massive) effects of the biases built into the machines.

We have already noted that the conservative bias being built into the use of computers in education has also been built into other new technologies. The first use of the new technology is quite naturally to do in a slightly different way what had been done before without it. It took years before designers of automobiles accepted the idea that they were cars, not 'horseless carriages,' and the precursors of modern motion pictures were plays acted as if before a live audience but actually in front of a camera. A whole generation was needed for the new art of motion pictures to emerge as something quite different from a linear mix of theater plus photography. Most of what has been done up to now under the name of 'educational technology' or 'computers in education' is still at the stage of the linear mix of old instructional methods with new technologies. The topics I shall be discussing are some of the first probings toward a more organic interaction of fundamental educational principles and new methods for translating them into reality.

We are at a point in the history of education when radical change is possible, and the possibility for that change is directly tied to the impact of the computer. Today what is offered in the education 'market' is largely determined by what is acceptable to a sluggish and conservative system. But this is where the computer presence is in the process of creating an environment for change. Consider the conditions under which a new educational idea can be put into practice today and in the near future. Let us suppose that today I have an idea about how children could learn mathematics more effectively and more humanely. And let us suppose that I have been able to persuade a million people that the idea is a good one. For many products such a potential market would guarantee success. Yet in the world of education today this would have little clout: A million people across the nation would still mean a minority in every town's school system, so there might be no effective channel for the million voices to be expressed. Thus, not only do good educational ideas sit on the shelves, but the process of invention is itself stymied. This inhibition of invention in turn influences the selection of people who get involved in education. Very few with the imagination, creativity, and drive to make great new inventions enter the field. Most of those who do are soon driven out in frustration. Conservatism in the world of education has become a self-perpetuating *social* phenomenon.

Fortunately, there is a weak link in the vicious circle. Increasingly, the computers of the very near future will be the private property of individuals, and this will gradually return to the individual the power to determine patterns of education. Education will become more of a private act, and people with good ideas, different ideas, exciting ideas will no longer be faced with a dilemma where they either have to 'sell' their ideas to a conservative bureaucracy or shelve them. They will be able to offer them in an open market-place directly to consumers. There will be new opportunities for imagination and originality. There might be a renaissance of thinking about education.

4.2 The use of micro-computers to support mathematical investigatons

• Derek Ball

INTRODUCTION

Computers are increasingly being used to support the teaching of mathematics, and many teachers and educationalists now see the use of computers as a way of introducing new styles of teaching and learning. Teachers have not, on the whole, found it easy to implement the advice of Para. 243 of the Cockcroft Report[1] and to include discussion, problem-solving and investigation into their teaching of mathematics. But computers appear to encourage pupils to discuss mathematics and also seem able to provide situations which lead them to solve problems and investigate mathematics for themselves. This article considers some of the ways in which computers can be used to support investigations.

PROGRAMS THAT CONTROL AN INVESTIGATION

Software writers, aware of the increasing emphasis being placed on mathematical investigations, have not been slow to produce investigation programs. Some of these appear designed to provide all that is necessary for introducing and completing an investigation within a single program.

Programs designed to help pupils investigate the 'Frogs' problem provide a good example. 'Frogs' is a pegboard problem which was often introduced to pupils by more adventurous teachers as a 'people game'. Seven chairs are lined up at the front of the classroom. Three girls sit on the three chairs at the left-hand end, and three boys on the three chairs at the right-hand end.

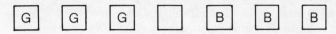

Figure 1   Layout for acting out the 'Frogs' problem

Boys and girls may then move either by sliding on to an adjacent vacant chair or by 'hopping' over one other person on to a vacant chair. The object is for the girls and boys to change places. This situation can be investigated by posing and answering questions. Here are a few such questions:

(a) How many moves did they take?
(b) Could they have done it in fewer moves?
(c) Was it easy to count the moves?
(d) On which moves did they 'hop'?
(e) How many moves would they need if there were only two girls and two boys?
(f) What happens if the number of girls is not equal to the number of boys?
(g) What patterns do you get if the number of boys and girls are kept equal, but that number is varied?
(h) What pattern do you get if there are always two more girls than boys?
(i) What if there are 60 girls and 60 boys?
(j) What if there are two spare chairs in the middle?
(k) What if you have to 'hop' over two people instead of one?

Teachers may not always want to investigate 'Frogs' by using people: they may decide that the people concerned would behave badly, or they may want individuals or small groups to investigate the problem at some length. The problem can obviously be investigated using pegboard or counters or any objects that can be conveniently moved around.

There are several reasons why teachers may want to use one of the 'Frogs' computer programs to help pupils investigate the problem. Firstly, the programs are often attractively produced, with good graphics and amusing sounds, and may encourage pupils to take an interest in the investigation. Secondly, they may make it easy for teachers to encourage small groups of pupils to investigate the problem. (Such small-group work is often considered desirable in mathematics learning but many teachers find it very difficult to manage successfully.) Also use of the programs may make the initial stages of the investigation easy for pupils: the programs may ensure that pupils follow the rules of the problem properly, they may remove from pupils the need to count the moves, and so on.

Removing the need to count the moves may, alternatively, be considered to be one of the disadvantages of all the 'Frogs' programs currently on the market. When pupils investigate mathematics they are gaining the opportunity to be mathematicians, researching into their own problems. Mathematicians researching situations such as the 'Frogs' problem need to be systematic, they need to be careful and accurate, and they need to be able to spot their own errors. If pupils are using programs which force them to be systematic, which take away the need to be careful and which point their errors out to them, they do not themselves develop these qualities.

Another disadvantage of the 'Frogs' programs available is that none of them allows many of the questions listed above to be investigated; in other words, the programs are only of any use if pupils want to investigate those problems considered interesting by the program's designer. The Cockcroft report suggests that one of the main benefits to be gained from investigating is encouraging pupils to ask 'what would happen if?' It is precisely this question that they are unable to ask when they use the 'Frogs' programs.

Another disadvantage of some of the 'Frogs' programs is that they are concerned at too early a stage with answers. One program, for example, asks pupils how many moves they think are required long before they are in a position to know. Other programs present answers already obtained in the form of a table displayed on the screen. This may be useful (although recording systematically on paper the data you have obtained is an important skill to learn) but the information is sometimes presented in a way intended to provide clues for those using the program. This has two disadvantages: it prevents pupils from having the satisfaction of trying to make sense of patterns of numbers without help; and it once again focuses attention on those aspects of the patterns that the program designer thinks are interesting and effectively prevents users from considering other aspects.

A fuller discussion of the 'Frogs' problem and of the advantages and disadvantages of particular programs is given in *Micromath* 1, 2.[2]

Other programs that provide different investigations for pupils may have similar advantages and, more particularly, disadvantages. A program is likely to have the same advantages and disadvantages as the 'Frogs' programs described in this section if it poses the problem for students. In this case, the chances are that the program forces students to tackle only certain aspects of the problem and to tackle those aspects in ways considered appropriate by the designer of the program.

PROGRAMS THAT SET THE SCENE FOR AN INVESTIGATION

Some computer programs provide mathematical games for pupils to play. Others provide tools for pupils to use; such tools may, for example, help pupils draw pictures or graphs, or save information systematically. Programs of either of these types may provide a suitable context for teachers, or for pupils themselves, to pose problems for investigation.

The SMILE program, FACTORS[3], provides a game for a pupil or for a group of pupils to play against the computer. This game provides an interesting starting point for an investigation, which can be set by a teacher to pupils who have just played the game. No attempt will be made here to describe the game, it is difficult to describe briefly in words, but easy to grasp when presented in the form of a computer program.

Games for electronic calculators can similarly provide starting points for investigations. The SMILE booklet, *Calculating*[4], contains a problem called '1000 up'.

Can you make your calculator display the number 1000 by using only the keys below?

2   7   ×   −   =

Many different questions can be asked following a successful solution of this problem. Here are some of them.

(a) What is the least number of key-presses needed to get 1000? How do you know?
(b) Does 999 take fewer or more key-presses?
(c) If you can choose which five keys you are allowed to press, what choice would you make in order to obtain the numbers 987, 654 and 321 with as few key-presses as possible?

The calculator does not play a major role in the solution of such subsidiary problems, but it plays an indispensable role in posing them.

Adventure games are computer games on a grand scale, and can provide the means for posing situations for investigation. *L—a Mathemagical Adventure*[5] contains numerous situations which must be successfully investigated if Runia is to be rescued. Here, as before, the computer offers little help in the investigation of the problems but provides an indispensable context for posing some of them and an interesting context for posing others.

BRANCH and SEEK are programs which allow users to structure information. The motivation for structuring it is a guessing game which the computer is taught to play. Here the program motivates pupils to find appropriate or interesting ways of structuring mathematical (or other) information. *Micromath* 1, 2,[6] contains an article describing how BRANCH was used in this way with a class of infants.

TURTLES is a program that permits two or more turtles to be moved simultaneously round the computer's screen. The use of TURTLES in a middle school to instigate class investigations into transformation geometry is described in an article in *Micromath* 1, 2.[7]

CIRCLE PATTERNS[8] is a program that enables its users to draw on the computer's screen the patterns obtained when equally spaced, numbered, dots on the circumference of a circle are joined according to a particular rule. The diagram shows the result of joining twelve dots according to the rule $n \rightarrow n + 3$.

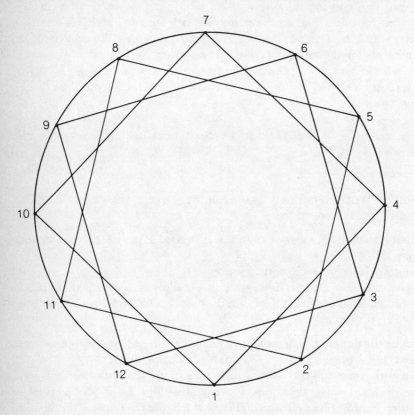

Figure 2   Diagram illustrating 'CIRCLE PATTERNS'

The program provides the context in which teachers can pose a number of problems for investigation. Here are a few of them.

(a) The example given above produces a pattern consisting of three squares. In what other ways can squares be obtained? In what other ways can three squares be obtained?

(b) When the rule $n \rightarrow 3n$ is used, patterns produced have one line of symmetry. Which numbers of dots must be used if the patterns are to have more symmetry than this? why?

(c) Investigate geometrically the patterns obtained using the rule $n \rightarrow -2n$.

A useful comparison can be made between the SMILE program CIRCLE[9] and the program CIRCLE PATTERNS. The latter enables the user to do much more than the former. The former can, however, be used by teachers without preparation, because it poses the problem for pupils to investigate. CIRCLE is therefore a program of the type described in the previous section, and has all the strengths and weaknesses of programs of this type.

PROGRAMS THAT SUPPORT INVESTIGATIONS

The previous section described how problems could be posed by the teacher, using the program CIRCLE PATTERNS. The program can also be used to support pupils when they begin investigating the problems. Pupils can save a considerable amount of time and labour by getting the computer to draw the diagrams required to test their hypotheses. The only diagrams they need draw for themselves are the key diagrams which are required to explain clearly the conclusions they arrive at.

Other programs may not be indispensable for explaining the situation to be investigated (although teachers may sometimes find that they provide a handy 'electronic blackboard'), but they may, like CIRCLE PATTERNS, make it considerably quicker and less tedious for pupils to investigate that situation. TILEKIT[9] helps pupils decide which regular shapes, and which combination of regular shapes, can be used to cover a plane surface. It also helps them explore some of the patterns which can be made by arranging shapes systematically, or by overlapping them.

FUNCTION GRAPH PLOTTER[10] and other graph-plotting programs enable pupils to explore, with or without the help of teachers, the Cartesian graphs of polynomial, trigonometric and other functions. Here are some of the many problems that can be investigated.

(a) What does the graph of $y = 2x + 3$ look like? What is the effect of changing the 2? What is the effect of changing the 3?
(b) What does the graph of $y = 12 - 4x - x^2$ look like? What is the effect of changing the 12? What is the effect of changing the 4?
(c) What is the relationship between the graphs of $y = \sin x$ and $y = \sin 2x$? Explore the effect of other ways of complicating $y = \sin x$.
(d) Which polynomials' graphs are symmetrical?

None of these questions are particularly difficult to pose without a micro-computer. Some of them (and particularly the last) would be tedious to investigate in depth if all the graphs had to be drawn by hand.

A small minority of teachers has for some time used films to encourage pupils to investigate geometrical situations. Rather more teachers seem happier about using 'films' in the form of microcomputer programs, probably because most programs of this type are interactive and allow teachers and groups of pupils to ask questions which begin 'what would happen if?' ARMS and CIRCLES[10] are two programs of this type which allow users to explore properties of loci. One of the problems with film programs on eight-bit computers, such as the BBC microcomputer, is that the animation is usually slow and therefore the pictures have to be rather crude. The advent of sixteen-bit machines will make such programs far easier to write and may make it possible for geometrical investigations to play a greater part in the school mathematics curriculum.

WRITING YOUR OWN PROGRAM TO HELP YOU INVESTIGATE A PROBLEM

In some mathematics classrooms teachers encourage pupils to write their own programs to help them learn mathematics. Such programs may be written in LOGO, in BASIC, or in another computer language. Frequently the purpose of these programs is to help pupils to investigate a mathematical topic.

Pupils in some primary schools make extensive use of LOGO, and of floor turtles in particular. Many of the tasks they set themselves, such as getting the turtle to draw pictures of particular objects of interest to them, are in effect mathematical investigations. Pupils can use LOGO to investigate more obviously geometrical problems. An article in *Micromath*, 1[13] described in detail how two girls carried out such a self-determined investigation of this kind. The inexpensive booklet, *Creative Geometry*[14], provides several excellent ideas for geometrical investigations which involve pupils writing LOGO programs. Here is one of their problems.

Can you make a five-pointed star? How short can you make the procedure? Try making stars with other numbers of points.

Pupils also write BASIC programs to help them investigate mathematical problems. Sometimes such programs are suggested by teachers; at other times a pupil who has his or her own computer at home uses it naturally to help with homework? Among the problems which pupils have used computers to investigate in this way are Pythagorean triples, and the numbers that have exactly 15 factors. But a BASIC program is likely to be of help in any situation in which something has to be counted or a table of results has to be produced. Pupils may, for example, use a program to draw up the table of values required to draw a graph.

Other languages may also be useful. *Micromath* 1, 2, contains an article describing how PROLOG can be used to help solve a variant of the 'Frogs' problem, but PROLOG is a language which has so far been little used in mathematics classrooms, partly because few teachers have had access to the language. Spreadsheet programs may also have uses in mathematics classrooms in connection with investigations, and teachers are beginning to experiment with their use.

PROGRAMMING AS MATHEMATICAL INVESTIGATION

Before pupils can write a BASIC program to draw a house on the screen they need a working knowledge of coordinates, pupils who write a program to produce a number sequence or a table of numbers will almost inevitably learn some algebra or will come to understand better the algebra they know already. Pupils who want to write a BASIC program to draw a circle must first learn some elementary trigonometry. Pupils who write a LOGO program are incidentally building up their knowledge of angles, and of the angle properties of polygons, and may also be becoming aware, at an intuitive level, of important ideas in connection with limits or curvature. Thus almost any programming task undertaken by pupils can be thought of as a mathematical investigation.

Above all, pupils writing programs are learning from their mistakes. They are trying out ideas and finding that they do not work. They are then making hypotheses: what would happen if we changed that bit? Creating your own mathematics, learning to analyse what you have already done, learning from your mistakes and hypothesising are all activities which pupils engage in when they investigate mathematics. Pupils also inevitably become involved in all these activities when they write a program to make the computer do something.

COLLABORATIVE INVESTIGATIONS

Teachers who watch pupils using computers in classrooms are constantly amazed by the length of time for which a group of pupils is prepared to concentrate on the task in hand and by the amount of purposeful conversation which takes place. Thus, one use to which computers can be put in mathematics classrooms is the support of group investigations. The advantages of encouraging a group of pupils, rather than an individual pupil, to engage with a mathematical problem are many. Pupils learn to hypothesize by listening to one another's hypotheses; they learn to reason by arguing against these hypotheses; they become more confident as they watch themselves and others publicly making mistakes which do not really matter because they can be corrected 'at the press of a button'.

With the help of computers, a teacher may find it easier to allow a class to explore a situation to which a pupil has drawn attention in the middle of expository teaching. For example, a teacher who is using a graph-plotting program to explain some aspects of graphs of a particular kind of function is more likely to respond favourably to 'what would happen if' questions asked by pupils, if the questions can be answered by a graph drawn by the computer on the screen rather than a graph drawn by the teacher on the blackboard.

With the help of computers, groups of children may also engage in group projects, or in individual projects where much of the initial work is done collaboratively. There is no reason why any of the programs described in this article should not be used by a group of pupils, indeed, an educational opportunity is likely to be lost whenever pupils are told to use such programs on their own.

CONCLUSION

Many mathematical investigations do not require a computer. Some investigations can make profitable use of a computer. For some investigations a computer is more or less indispensable. Computers may help some teachers more than others to present topics in an 'open' way and may provide for some pupils more than others the confidence to respond to such 'open' challenges. The question 'what will happen if?' is one of the commonest questions asked by the mathematician; it is also one of the commonest responses to an interactive computer program. It would therefore be surprising if computers did not make a major contribution to the quality of mathematics investigated in classrooms.

NOTES AND REFERENCES

1. *Mathematics Counts*, Her Majesty's Stationery Office, 1982.
2. This issue of *Micromath* contains three articles about this problem, and also a review of available software. *Micromath* is a journal of the Association of Teachers of Mathematics, and is published by Basil Blackwell.
3. FACTORS is one of the programs in *MICROSMILE 1*, available from the Centre for Learning Resources, 275 Kensington Lane, London SE 11 5QZ.
4. *Calculating* is a booklet of activities for pupils using calculators, and is also available from the Centre for Learning Resources.
5. Published by the Association of Teachers of Mathematics, Kings Chambers, Queen Street, Derby DE1 3DA.
6. This is one of the software reviews.
7. *A School of Turtles* by Barrie Galpin, *Micromath*, 1, 2, 1985.
8. An unpublished program, available from the author.
9. Another of the programs in *MICROSMILE 1*.
10. One of the programs in *Some More Lessons in Mathematics with a Microcomputer*, published by the Association of Teachers of Mathematics (address above).
11. FUNCTION GRAPH PLOTTER is one of the programs in *Some Lessons in Mathematics with a Microcomputer*, published by ATM. It is also one of the programs in *Micros in the Mathematics Classroom*, published by Longman.
12. These are both available in *Some Lessons in Mathematics with a Micro-*

computer, published by the Association of Teachers of Mathematics (address above).

13. *Two Children and Logo* by Celia Hoyles, Rosamund Sutherland and Joan Evans, *Micromath*, 1, 1, 1985.
14. *Creative Geometry: investigations on the microcomputer* is by Alan Bell, David Rooke and Alan Wigley. It is published by the Shell Centre for Mathematical Education, University of Nottingham.

4.3 Computers in art education: threat or promise?

• P. Scrimshaw

The starting point for this article was the chance to read evaluations by a number of teachers of the recently published art package IMAGE.[1] This was designed specifically for schools and colleges, but is just one example of a type of package that is becoming widely available to schools. Consequently while the points made below largely arise from reflecting upon the specific program and the reaction of teachers to it, most of the conclusions have a far wider relevance for art teaching in primary and middle schools.[2] These art packages (as I will call them) are open-ended graphics programs with supporting documentation designed to enable children to produce, modify, store and print out artwork created on the computer. While they are not the only type of software relevant to art education[3] they offer the obvious starting point for most teachers. Consequently just as the arrival of suitable word processor packages has brought the computer into the language curriculum, so too the advent of art packages may do the same for the art curriculum. The question is whether this development is desirable.

At its simplest an art package is designed to enable the user to colour each pixel or small block of pixels on a screen in any one of the colours available, and if required, to store, retrieve and reproduce the resulting image. As single pixel colouring is time-consuming and difficult, each art package provides ways of speeding up the process. In doing so the designer tacitly channels the user's energies in a specific way, by making some kinds of use easier and more visible than others. These 'speeding up' features may mimic processes used within traditional media (such as freehand drawing) or those easily achieved by using the computer's distinctive capacities (such as procedures to draw a circle where the user is required only to mark in the centre and any point on the circumference).

The conventional processes that all packages cover are methods of creating lines, points and shapes, all in a variety of colours. Lines of different lengths and widths can be drawn, by choosing a 'brush width' and either drawing freehand or by specifying a starting and finishing point. In the latter case a choice of curved or straight lines may be available. Dots of varying dimensions are also usually provided, and these can often be placed semi-randomly to create a simple 'air spray' effect. Solid shapes are created by drawing a closed figure and then filling it with the chosen colour or pattern. The figure can be drawn freehand or by using whatever procedures the package offers for making up common shapes such as circles, arcs and triangles. The range of colours that can be provided on the screen by an art package obviously depends upon the range of colours initially provided, but with most packages a pattern of pixels of different basic colours can be built up to provide other colour effects. Where the tones of the basic colours used are similar, such patterns can give the impression of a new intermediate colour, especially if viewed from a distance. Where the tones are very different a textured effect is produced within which the colour elements remain distinguishable.

Art packages are notable for the ease with which the images created can be manipulated. Usually, any part of the screen image can be rotated, reversed, altered in size vertically and/or horizontally and repeated on another part of the screen. Any basic colour in the image can be changed to any other, to see the different effects possible. In some packages flashing colours can be used, alternating regularly between any two basic colours. There may also be a simple text creation facility, in which letters can be manipulated and modified in the same way as any other shapes.

Finally some art packages allow the user to load in and manipulate video images, provided suitable video equipment is available.

It is clear that art packages differ strikingly from traditional art media (such as pencil, pen, water colour, pastels and oils) in several respects. This difference is more than that which exists between any two of the traditional media, because art packages characteristically stand at the extreme position on any major dimension of comparison with conventional media.

The following four respects are particularly distinctive:

- The computer connection. Art packages provoke the same range of conflicting emotions as any other unfamiliar computer related equipment, while the other media do not.
- Crudity. Line, shape and colour can all be handled with more subtlety and delicacy in traditional media.
- Flexibility. Art packages are more flexible in the sense that effects can be changed, repeated or reversed more easily than in the traditional media.
- Ease of use. The effective use of art packages requires less physical dexterity than any traditional medium.

Clearly a comparative evaluation of an art package and traditional media is not straightforward, even if the technical quality and user friendliness of the package is taken as given. The difficulty is increased by the multiplicity of aims that teachers have when using such packages, and the need to take other factors into account in any evaluation.

One such factor is the diversity in people's emotional responses to any use of computers in art at all, independently of its actual effects on learning. For some people investing art with the high-tech aura of the computer is a sign of modernity and progress; for others it is a source of resentment and perhaps anxiety. On one level both reactions might be dismissed as irrelevant; what matters is whether in fact computers or any other new tools help or hinder learning, regardless of social attitudes towards them. On the other hand there is a very realistic practical point hidden here; the use in art lessons of what parents, children and other teachers see as high status equipment does to some extent increase the prestige of the subject. But this in itself is largely irrelevant, unless the use of computers also genuinely improves art education. This takes us back once more to aims.

For some teachers the main value of art packages lies in their general effects rather than in their relevance to art education as such. Most children are interested by such packages and teachers may value this interest in its own right. Any open-ended art package provides opportunities for exploration and experimentation, with immediate feedback on the effects. These are naturally welcome features to teachers interested in strengthening general problem solving skills and openmindedness. Furthermore, computer images can be evolved by a small group of children and this allows for co-operative working and group discussion. As the images can be modified as well as discussed, the group has both the opportunity and obligation to come to definite decisions, the emerging picture being both a record of the choices made and a focus for further debate. Here again the specifically aesthetic aspect of the activity may not be the most salient, either for teachers or children. Indeed for some teachers it is precisely the aesthetic aspect that raises doubts about the value of computer use.

One source of their concern is the fact that art packages make it possible for children to achieve quite complex visual effects without needing to develop much dexterity or delicacy of touch. In other curriculum areas this feature is widely welcomed. The role of computers in reducing the need for motor skills or good eye–hand co-ordination in such tasks as writing or the production of graphs or bar charts is generally welcomed. However in the case of art the matter is less clear cut. Some teachers take the view that the learning of craft skills is only a necessary and rather tedious means to the production of work of an acceptable quality. From this perspective an art package releases children from the frustration of being able to envisage a result that they lack the motor control or the patience to achieve with paint or pencil. This could be particularly important for physically handicapped or emotionally disturbed children.

However other teachers value the development of the craft skills involved in art in themselves, or believe that they are an essential element in developing a deep visual appreciation of works of art. For these teachers the use of such packages is naturally less attractive, and may indeed be seen as educationally counterproductive. The value of craft skills in increasing visual awareness could be argued for on two grounds. One is that the direct experience of the tactile and motor features of painting is an integral element in developing a visual appreciation of them; paintings simply look different if one has had that experience from the way that they do otherwise. Alternatively it could be claimed that the activity of working carefully at the task, with less possibility of recovering from any error, in practice encourages closer attention to the work, and hence greater awareness of it. Both arguments assume that the children involved have the manual capacity and sufficient eye–hand co-ordination to achieve a higher level of skill than is required by the art package. This may well not be the case for some handicapped learners, or for young children. For these groups at least the objective may not apply.

Very fine detail and gradations of colour and hue cannot be achieved with current art packages and equipment. Consequently the images produced are inferior to virtually all those that can be produced in the traditional media in fineness and precision of line and in subtlety of colour. This is partly to do with the input devices used, which include keyboards, mice, graphics pads and lightpens. Most of these cannot give very fine line control if used at a reasonable speed, and none are responsive to changes in pressure in the way that a brush, crayon or pencil is. More fundamentally the power and sensitivity of current classroom computers and monitors limits the number of basic colours available and the resolution of the images that can be created, whether we are thinking of screen or printer generated versions of the picture. While some trade-offs are often possible between colour range and resolution, the fundamental difficulty remains. This weakness will undoubtedly be reduced as computers, monitors and printers become more powerful and sophisticated, but for the forseeable future it is hard to imagine that computer-generated graphics created in schools will be able to achieve the quality possible in other media.

The point about the relative crudity of computer-based artwork is that it presumably limits the potential level of visual awareness that children can develop through the creation and study of such work. However the word 'potential' is important here. What children actually produce using traditional media may be below the level of complexity that even the computer can handle, either by the child's choice or because of limited skills. If so, it is irrelevant whether they are working in paint, pencil or light, as far as the potential for raising visual awareness goes. Here again the situation with very young children may be different from that of older learners.

Can art packages encourage children to be creative? Woods and Barrow[4] argue that:

If our intention is to promote creativity then clearly we have to meet the following requirements: (1) We have to avoid instilling in children the idea that everything is known and determined, and that they must subserve the acknowledged experts in any field and cannot follow their own distinctive way of looking at things. (2) We have to promote ingenuity and imagination so that individuals are capable of making the imaginative leaps necessary for breaking new ground in any sphere. (3) We have to produce skill and understanding in any given sphere, for without these how, except by chance, is the individual going to be a good scientist, artist or whatever: how is he going to have the excellence that is part of creativity?

How do art packages measure up to these requirements? Firstly, it is hard to guess what effects (if any) computer use might have. Secondly, there is some cause for optimism; the modifiability of computer-based art should provide a concrete and readily intelligible way for children, particularly the less confident, to try out ideas and see the results for themselves. While this will not guarantee imagination and ingenuity it could at least reduce some of the psychological obstacles to their exercise. The computer may also help with developing aesthetic understanding, but not with craft skills, for the reasons discussed earlier. Overall then it seems probable that the use of the computer can reduce some of the obstacles to creativity in art. Whether that amounts to the same thing as enabling all children to become creative artists is a further question.

So far I have discussed art packages purely as an alternative to the traditional media. Seen in this way they display a distinctive pattern of comparative strengths and weaknesses. Clearly one approach then is to use the computer as a new but separate medium alongside the established ones. However some teachers have evolved ways of integrating the use of the computer with other media.

In the discussion above it was assumed that the final product of the use of an art package was the screen image or computer printout that it helps the child to produce. Alternatively the teacher can try to evade the limitations of an art package by using it in combination with other media to create the final work. Examples of this would be the hand colouring of monochrome printouts, the use of colour printer output as material for a collage, or the incorporation of acetate prints of images in light and sound shows. Such uses offer ways of incorporating manual skills and greater delicacy of line and colour into the creative process, while still making good use of the computer. The relevant question in each specific case is whether the resultant activity is more educative than going directly to traditional approaches from the start.

A second way of using computers and traditional media together is to use the computer purely as a planning and design tool, for instance to make quick preliminary sketches for traditional design work or fabric printing. The image or printout in this case does not form an actual part of the final creation, but it allows children to separate the planning of a piece from its actual execution, and to consider several different patterns, colour combinations or designs with relative ease. As the images created can be saved at any point the packages also allow for serial or alternative lines of development to be saved and compared. This enables both child and teacher to trace and discuss the way in which a problem in conceiving or representing an image has been formulated, partially solved and then redefined by the child. Here then is another important if partial role for the computer.

So is the arrival of the computer in the art class desirable or not? Although practical issues about cost and reliability of equipment and so on are very important they are bound to become steadily less of a problem as time goes on. What strikes me as the more fundamental point is that what teachers make of art packages depends very much upon their different underlying philosophies of education and of art. However it is clear that the programs available are generally open-ended enough to allow teachers with very different perspectives to try out a wide variety of approaches to art education.

Consequently one important result of using such art packages can be to help teachers make explicit the complexity and underlying structure of what they personally hope children will gain from art lessons. Like all important curriculum innovations, the use of art packages is likely to change a teacher's approach to art as well as that of the children. For the non-specialist teacher in particular that interesting prospect alone may make an art package worth trying.

NOTES AND REFERENCES

1. Most of these evaluations are now available in 'The Homerton IMAGE Papers' ed. Daly, F. and Spence, D. published by Homerton College, Cambridge, 1987. (Available for approximately £3.50 from Homerton College, Hills Road, Cambridge).
2. IMAGE itself together with Picture Craft, AMX Super Art and Grafpad 2 exemplify the main kinds of packages available for school use with 8-bit computers. The points made in the paper are relevant to all of these packages, and most of them are also broadly applicable to art packages designed for 16-bit machines.
3. Two related kinds of packages already available are those that help with typographic layouts, font design and computer-aided design packages that assist with various kinds of technical drawing. Several other quite different lines of development in computer art will undoubtedly have educational consequences in the longer term. These are discussed in paper 2.5 in this collection, and in Reffin Smith, B., *Soft Computing: Art and Design*, Wokingham, Addison-Wesley, 1984.
4. See Paper 1.2 in this collection.

4.4 The use of computers to aid the teaching of creative writing

● Mike Sharples

The teaching scheme for language arts and creative writing described in this paper is based upon three elements which are believed essential if a child is to develop an understanding and control of creative writing: (a) a well-defined theory of the writing process; (b) tools, which may be used by children, unaided, to plan, compose, transform and explore language: (c) written material, including games, exercises and project work, which provides structured teaching.

It is designed to expose a child's intuitive knowledge of language and, by addressing issues of style rather than correctness, extend the child's skills of creative writing.

THEORY

The scheme is based on a cognitive theory of the writing process[1,2] in which writing is seen not as a simple extension of speaking, but as a major reconstruction. The theory provides an analysis of writing as a three-stage process, comprising concept formation, text production and text revision. Thus a writer first produces a complex network of ideas and concepts, which constitute a story-form. The story form is then turned into a visible text, which is finally revised and polished. The process is subject to constraints: of purpose (whom am I writing for, and why?), content (what ideas are to be expressed and how are they related?) and structure (what are good text forms, word choices?). In order to write successfully, for a variety of functions and audiences, the child must understand the writing process and learn to produce language without the aid of conversational cues, to communicate with an unknown audience, and to create text with a well-turned form and elegant style.

Thus, mature composition demands an ability to divorce language from its immediate context, so that it becomes an object to be shaped and revised. Such metalinguistic knowledge is very different from the intuitive awareness of language needed for conversation. This has clear implications for the teaching of writing. It suggests that:

1. As a prerequisite to effective writing, the child should develop the ability to conceive and manipulate language as an object.
2. The child should progress from 'spilling thoughts onto paper' towards an understanding of the process of writing. Story planning and text revision should be as important to the process as text production.
3. The child should have a clear understanding of the audience and function of her writing, in order to choose an appropriate form and style.
4. The child should come to view writing as an act of communication to an unseen audience, and not merely as a classroom exercise abstracted from reality.

TOOLS

Computer programs are integral components of the scheme. They provide representations of two abstract systems—a generative grammar and an associative network—which the child may manipulate to investigate language structure. Further programs provide a medium for story creation and revision and offer easy reference aids.

The programs, developed at the Artificial Intelligence Department of Edinburgh University, are intended for use by people with no previous computer experience and are written in the POP2 language for a DEC 11/60 computer.

The first three programs are a series of text generators with increasing constraints, which lead a child into an exploration of the structure and function of language. By specifying first an appropriate vocabulary, then syntactic structure and then agreement of meaning the child can use the computer to generate interesting and increasingly refined sentences, poems and stories.

GRAM1

GRAM1 is a random word generator. As a preparatory exercise to using the computer a child writes words on blank slips of paper—one word per slip— and puts them into an empty 'word box'. The slips are drawn out blind-fold and the words copied onto paper.

The child can then carry out the same process with the computer, using simple commands (PUT, GET, CLEAR) and guided by prompts (the W prompt signifies that the computer is waiting for a command). The child's responses in the following dialogue are in italics and comments are enclosed in square brackets.

W: *put*   [add words to the word box]
WORDS: *the love birds my fly free moving*

W: *get*   [generate word strings]
NUMBER OF WORDS IN A LINE: 3
NUMBER OF LINES: 4

birds love my
loving moving love
birds the fly
free birds the

GRAM1 accustoms the child to using a computer, provides simple metaphors for linguistic terms (for example: a 'vocabulary' is the 'box that holds words') and demonstrates that language consists of more than a random string of words. By choosing words on a single theme the child also builds functional vocabularies which can be used later to develop creative writings.

GRAM2

GRAM2 allows the user to generate word strings from a grammar and is used first by the student in its simplest form. The child sorts the word slips from the 'word box' into new boxes according to part of speech. These provide the grammar for the GRAM2 program. The child then uses the PUT command to specify this grammar to the program:

W: *put*   [put words into the grammar]
PART OF SPEECH: *name*
WORDS: *Muldoon/Sproggs/Jones*   [words to be generated from
                                                                    the part of speech. Alternatives
                                                                    are separated by '/']

PART OF SPEECH: *noun*
WORDS: *igloo/telephone/bicycle/lampshade/cat/banana*

PART OF SPEECH: *verb*
WORDS: *looked/walked/roller-skated/pushed*

PART OF SPEECH: *adverb*
WORDS: *sadly/stupidly/grandly/nastily*

PART OF SPEECH: *adjective*
WORDS: *bold/sad/dangerous/wise/stupid/round/square*

PART OF SPEECH: [finish PUT by a blank line]
PUT FINISHED

The next stage is for the child to form patterns, using the GET command, for 'silly sentences' which the program completes by substituting, at random, a word for each part of speech.

> W: *get*   [generate from story pattern]
> PATTERN: *One day Mrs name verb out of her noun*
> PATTERN: *and shouted 'noun!' adverb to a adjective*
> PATTERN: *noun near her noun.*
> PATTERN:
>
> One day Mrs Sproggs roller-skated out of her lampshade and shouted 'Igloos!' stupidly to a dangerous banana near her cat.

GRAM2 offers more than simple word substitution; it is an implementation of a context-free grammar. The GET procedure scans the pattern repeatedly, substituting words for recognized parts of speech until no names of parts of speech are found. Thus, in a more advanced exercise, a child might add 'nounphrase' or 'sentence' to the GRAM2 grammar:

> W: *put*
>
> PART OF SPEECH: *nounphrase*
> WORDS: *the adjective noun/the noun*
>
> PART OF SPEECH: *sentence*
> WORDS: *nounphrase verb/nounphrase verb nounphrase*

or, by a judicious selection of grammar rules and vocabulary, produce a grammar for an entire poem.

A context free grammar is not restricted to generating English words: one can just as easily be written to produce French phrases, arithmetic expressions, or random computer programs. Further commands in the GRAM2 program allow a user to save a grammar on disk and retrieve it at a later session and to access a library of grammars which provide language games and exercises. Of course GRAM2 does not always produce meaningful sentences or poems, even when given a plausible-looking grammar. This does not invalidate the program—it is not a teaching machine but a tool to probe the structure and constraints of language—but an intelligent child will soon realize that GRAM2 has a clear limitation, it contains no representation of meaning.

GRAM3

GRAM3 allows the user to specify meaning words and phrases, semantic markers, which constrain the generated text. Restriction of the choice of adjectives to those that agree with the previous noun. This is done in GRAM3 by (a) associating meanings with grammar rules, and (b) specifying the parts of speech to be matched. Thus, GRAM3 accepts rules, such as:

W: *put*

PART OF SPEECH: *sentence*

WORDS: *a [noun 1] is [adjective 1]*

(a number following a part of speech indicates that it is to be matched for meaning with a similarly numbered part of speech; the sentence itself has no prescribed meaning)

MEANING:

PART OF SPEECH: *noun*
WORDS: *lion/tiger*
MEANING: *animal big*

[meaning words for 'lion' and 'tiger']

PART OF SPEECH: *noun*
WORDS: *mouse/rat*
MEANING: *animal small*

PART OF SPEECH: *adjective*
WORDS: *huge/large/big*
MEANING: *big*

PART OF SPEECH: *adjective*
WORDS: *tiny/small/little*
MEANING: *small*

The GET command, given the pattern sentence will always generate a sentence in which the adjective agrees with the noun in meaning, for example: 'A tiger is huge' or 'a mouse is little.'

GRAM3 contains a few more sophistications which, while not making the program more difficult for a child to operate, offer the possibility of specifying more complex grammars with greater semantic constraints. For example, the semantic markers can propagate up and down levels of grammar rules, as illustrated by the poem generated below, in which each entire poem is constrained by the marker 'sad'. Below is a fragment of a poem grammar for the GRAM3 program (not devised by a school child!) and a poem generated from the grammar.

PART OF SPEECH: *line*
WORDS: *why [sent 11] ∧ [sent 11]*
MEANING:

(the '∧' is a 'new line' symbol)
(no prescribed meaning)

PART OF SPEECH: *sent*
WORDS: *[np 15] [vt 15 16] [np 16]*
MEANING:

PART OF SPEECH: *vt*
WORDS: *hates/despises/dislikes*
MEANING: *human sad bad*

PART OF SPEECH: *vt*
WORDS: *loves/likes*
MEANING: *human happy good*

.

.

.

W: *get*
PATTERN: *poem*
PATTERN:
MEANING: *sad*

A lonely boy

Wait!
A boy still hates you.
Weeps beside a stream.

The poem grammar was designed to produce a 'deep structure' representation of a sentence.[3] Each generated line is stored on disk as a list of words with their associated parts of speech and meaning descriptors. The second line of the first poem, for example, is stored as:

[article a] [noun human boy] [vt human bad sad hates]
[adverb human bad sad still] [pronoun human you]

This deep structure representation can be given as input to the WALTER program, a text transformer, described below—which transforms the sentence structure, tidying up the grammar and producing a 'surface structure': 'a boy still hates you' for the example above.

An additional poem, generated for the same grammar with the meaning description 'hear' follows:

You

Hear a cheerful boy.
While you wants to hear a voice
A busy woman does not work quickly with you.
Listen!
You fade.

A fifteen year old boy designed a poem generating grammar for a prototype version of GRAM3[4] which produced many poems, of which the following is an example:

Dry path
Lonely moon fades subtly
In cold plains
Black clouds
Frost fades by wish

We feed slowly
Black path fades to red rocks
I feed.

The GRAM programs can be likened to a child's engineering construction kit, such as a Meccano or Erector set. The child starts by following construction plans, or by building his own simple and unwieldy structures from a small set of parts. Then, as he learns about the properties of the parts and the constraints of the system, he can create more sophisticated models. Finally, he can combine the simple parts into sub-assemblies (with Meccano, a pulley system or trolley, with GRAM a phrase or sentence) which can then be used as the building units for complex and realistic structures.

WALTER

WALTER (Word ALTERER) is a general purpose text transformer. At its simplest WALTER acts as a two command word processor. The child types 'new' to create a story and 'change' to modify the text.

W: *new*   [type in a new story to WALTER]

STORY: *Once there was a pretty princess. The princess lived*
STORY: *in a big house in a forest. The forest was drak. She*
STORY: *was very lonely because she had no friends to play with. . . . . .*
STORY:
NEW FINISHED

W: *change*   [alter text]

OLD WORDS: *drak*
NEW WORDS: *dark*   [correct spelling]

OLD WORDS: *house*
NEW WORDS: *castle*   [substitute words]

OLD WORDS:

Once there was a pretty princess. The princess lived in a big castle in a forest. The forest was dark. She was very lonely because she had no friends to play with.
CHANGE FINISHED

WALTER automatically carries out a surface structure on the input text associating a part of speech (plus optional meaning descriptors) with each word. The child can discover the effect of transforming (deleting, rearranging) selected parts of speech. In the example below the child used the 'try' command, which shows the effect of a transformation, but does not permanently alter the text:

W: *try*
OLD WORDS: *adjective1*
NEW WORDS: [remove all the adjectives from the story—a number appended to a word indicates that it is be matched with a part of speech)

OLD WORDS: *noun1 words1 noun2*   ['words1' matches any text]
NEW WORDS: *noun2 words1 noun1*   [swap pairs of nouns in each sentence]

OLD words:

Once there was a princess. The castle lived in a princess in a forest. The forest was. She was very lonely because she had no friends to play with.

Normally a child would not create his own grammatical transformations, but would refer to a prewritten library of transformation rules. With the 'combine' rule, for example, the student can discover the effect of combining sentences using relative clauses:

Once there was a pretty princess. The lived princess in a big castle in a forest. The forest was dark. She was very lonely because she had no friends to play with.

W: *change*
OLD WORDS: [if there is no input for 'OLD WORDS' the 'RULES' prompt is given]
RULES: *combine*   [use the prewritten rules for sentence combining]

Once there was a pretty princess who lived in a big castle in a dark forest. She was very lonely because she had no friends to play with.

'Combine' applies three transformation rules: a 'reduced relative rule' (to produce 'Once there was a pretty princess. The princess lived in a big castle in a dark forest'): a 'relative rule' to produce 'Once there was a pretty princess which lived in a big castle in a dark forest') and a 'who' rule (which alters the 'which' following a 'human' noun, to produce the final transformed sentence).

Using WALTER a child can focus on the parts of a story needing revision, rather than laboriously copying and recopying the entire text. An automated thesaurus is available, within WALTER, to offer suggestions for word substitution:

W: *thesaurus*
WORD TO BE LOOKED UP: *pretty*
pretty (adjective): beautiful, elegant, lovely, attractive
pretty (adverb): fairly, rather, somewhat

A further program, FANTASY, has been used by children to plan stories as a focus for discussion on alternative methods of story construction. FANTASY allows a child to create simulation games, similar to the popular 'Adventure' computer game and will be described in more detail later.

WRITTEN MATERIAL

By themselves the computer programs are insufficient as a teaching aid—a tool without an application—and so they are accompanied by written work, sheets containing games, exercises, questions, projects and instructions for the use of the computer. These provide a self-study course on language arts and creative writing. A draft version of the course has been tested with six pupils (average age 11.7) of an Edinburgh school, who visited the Edinburgh University Department of Artificial Intelligence for 2–4 hours per week over two school terms. The course was in two sections. The first part developed a child's understanding and manipulation of language, through games—such as a sentence version of SCRABBLE and a grammar crossword which provided practice in word substitution and sentence construction. The worksheets also introduced the GRAM programs and suggested 'patterns' for generating sentences and poems. This gave the children a foundation for the second part of the course in which they explored and developed their written style.

The second section of the course covered two functional forms of composition—composition and narration—and, for each, the children were first introduced to the purpose of the form of writing and then encouraged to develop an appropriate language style and vocabulary. They generally wrote for a newsletter, designed and edited by themselves, which was circulated around the school. They were encouraged to create the articles and stories in discrete stages: by producing a plan, transforming the plan into prose and typing it into the computer, and then revising the draft text. The section below describes in detail a series of worksheets from the second part of the course, concerned with descriptive writing.

DESCRIPTIVE WRITING

The children began the section by playing language games designed to expand their range of descriptive words and phrases. One game made use of rules for the GRAM2 program which substituted an asterisk for an adjective and an exclamation mark for an adverb. As the computer only recognized some 200 words, the purpose of the game was to outwit the machine by inventing sentences with unusual modifiers, which would not be substituted by the program. The pupils were provided with core sentences, which they then embellished, for example, 'The man sat on the bench.'

W: *get*
PATTERN: *The old grey-haired man sat sadly on the uneven*
PATTERN: *green bench.*
PATTERN:

The * grey-haired man sat ! on the uneven * bench.

To break the children from their normal clutch of uninspired modifiers, such as, big, nasty, horrible, the on-line thesaurus provided them with up to eight synonyms of a common word.

The children then were introduced to the constraints and conventions of story content, again through games and exercises. In one game a group of children wrote a description of an unusual picture: the description was passed to another group who attempted to redraw the picture, guided only by the written description. This proved to be a useful exercise of descriptive completeness. One group's description, for instance, omitted any mention of colour; the second team complained that they could not draw the picture as they had no idea which coloured crayons to use. From the exercises the children formed a strategy and checklist for descriptive composition. They were then encouraged to break down the process of descriptive writing into manageable stages—planning, draft writing, revision—with the aid of a computer-based game. The children were split into two groups. Each group drew up a plan of the rooms of a haunted house and then wrote descriptions of each room, plus details of treasure and the occupants of the house. The descriptions were incorporated into a game, similar to the 'Adventure' computer game and the opposing group then explored the house, fought off the inhabitants and found the treasure, by typing commands to the program. Below is the start of a game session. The descriptions of rooms, characters and treasure were written entirely by one group of the children (game commands are in italics).

Welcome to FANTASY

You are in a long straight hallway with brown oak walls, hanging on the walls are old victorian pictures. On the ground is a telephone table and chair.

a wooden door leads south
a front door leads east

south

You are in a blue colored bedroom, with a mysterious atmosphere there is a strange rattling noise coming from the window. In the bedroom there is a toilet which is at the left hand corner. There is a chest of drawers and a wardrobe to match. In front of the bed there is a grey, wet mist.

a wooden door leads north
a wooden door leads west

a chef has just arrived through a wooden door (west)

objects

you can see
1—a gold bracelet and earrings to match
2—a bottle of wine

The role of FANTASY was to aid the children in moving from static descriptions into dynamic narrative. After playing the game the children discussed their experiences and this led them to an examination of goals (the goal of the explorer is to find the hidden treasure and the goal of the inhabitants is to attack the intruder) and strategies (one way to play the game is to stay in a room, wait until people arrive in it with treasure and then attack them!) in narrative writing and of interaction between description and plot (houses with secret passages and hidden treasure demand more complex exploration strategies and so increase suspense). The children then wrote an adventure story, using the TRAN program as a simple text editor, based on their experiences of playing FANTASY.

RESULTS

In terms of performance during the entire pilot scheme the children can be divided into 3 pairs. One pair seemed unable to view written text as an object for manipulation and improvement, and they gained little benefit from the first section of the course. Initially they showed no enthusiasm for writing and their early written products were terse and unco-ordinated. These children were not taken through the second section, but instead used a computer text processor to compose, modify and print short, descriptive pieces. Once they discovered that the computer could aid the tedious process of revision and presentation, their interest in writing increased and they produced articles for a class newsletter and items for the children's page of the local Edinburgh newspaper.

By contrast, two other children showed a strong enthusiasm for language and writing. During the course their ability to manipulate language and revise text improved markedly. One girl in particular, described by her teacher as having 'no exposure to books, except through school,' developed an interest in language and literature and showed a marked improvement in language understanding and manipulation during classroom English language exercises. Of the two remaining children one, whom the teacher described as 'showing no interest in literature, except when forced,' completed the course and his later essays showed gleams of imagination. The other, mid-way through the course, began to experiment with prose style and, according to her class teacher, 'became dramatically addicted to literature during the year and progressed through Enid Blyton to good teenage books.'

In summary, the course required some prior ability from the children to view language as an object for experiment and revision. Of the six children, four initially displayed such skills and profited from the opportunity to develop their written style in a conscious and systematic manner. For the two remaining children, the games, exercises and chance to use a computer as a creative tool, revived a flagging interest in creative writing.

CONCLUSION

The GRAM and TRAN programs have already been squeezed onto a TERAK personal computer and versions are being written in PASCAL for other microcomputers.

Given the instruments, who will call the tune? Some home computer manufacturers already offer drill and practice programs in arithmetic or spelling. Programs which teach prescriptive grammar or, with speech output, present spelling lists and dictation exercises, will find a ready market of 'back to basics' English teachers.

A computer-based language workshop is more troublesome. The pilot project indicated no single method of use—some children tired of the computer after five minutes, others worked happily for an hour or more: some preferred to work alone, others used the computer in pairs or groups; some worked smoothly without help, others demanded constant attention and advice. This was expected. The workshop is not intended to replace or relieve the teacher, nor to fit neatly into a school curriculum. It does not present a well defined and examinable set of facts. It was designed to give a child the experience of a research worker, with control over the content and structure of his learning, tools to carry out worthwhile experiments and equipment to draft and revise the results.

The best location for such a language workshop would be a resource centre, with books and audio-visual material, as well as computers, where children can plan their own study and adults would be available as advisers— more like a children's library than a classroom.

The pilot project suggests that children can learn to control and extend their written language in such an environment, and enjoy the experience: for example, two children volunteered to write descriptions of the haunted house rooms as a home exercise and arrived the following week with five pages of imaginatively written text, ready to be added to the computer game.

Home and school computer users of the future will, we hope, take a break from Space Invaders to generate poems, compose essays and play word games.

Acknowledgement

I should like to thank the children of class Primary 7, South Bridge School, Edinburgh, and their teacher Mrs. Finlayson, for all their cooperation. I am grateful also to Dr. Jim Howe and Dr. Ben DuBoulay for their supervision of the project, to Dr. Peter Ross, Dr. Tim O'Shea and Ms Helen Pain for comments on the text and to the Social Science Research Council for financial support.

NOTES AND REFERENCES

1. Bereiter, C. and Seardamalia, M. (1982). From conversation to composition: The role of instruction in a developmental process, in R. Glaser (Ed.) *Advances in instructional psychology*, Vol. 2, Hillsdale, New Jersey, Lawrence Erlbaum Associates.
2. Bruce, B. C., Collins, A., Rubin, A. D. and Genter, D. G. (1982) A cognitive science approach to writing, in *Writing: The nature, development and teaching of written communication*, Hillsdale, New Jersey, Lawrence Erlbaum.
3. Chomsky, N. (1965) *Aspects of the theory of syntax*, Cambridge, Massachusetts, MIT Press.
4. Sharples, M. (1979) *A computer-based language workshop*, (D.A.I. Research Paper No. 135). Edinburgh University Department of Artificial Intelligence.

5 LEARNING WITH COMPUTERS

What happens when computers are used with the aim of developing skills such as problem-solving and effective co-operation? The aims of the authors in this section are to facilitate the kinds of learning which, traditionally, may not be found as often as we would wish, and one of the authors, Cummings, refers to a commissioned report (Bullock) which supports this view. In discussing language work, he quotes Rosen's advocacy of 'small groups which can use their talk to move towards understanding by means which are not present in the normal teacher-directed classroom.' Cummings has used the computer with groups of children who control the discussion and use their collective experience to solve problems. His analysis of the children's conversation indicated logical thought, hypothetico-deductive, and co-operative behaviour.

Huber uses Piaget's stage theory to relate the levels which children have reached with educational software and points out that some of our target aims (hypothesis seeking, for example) are not achievable by children until they are at the appropriate stage. However, programs such as LOGO can help children make the transition to the next stage.

Johnson *et al.* found that computer-assisted co-operative instruction was superior to competitive or individual learning, both in terms of achievement and also in skills such as problem-solving. Interestingly, girls were adversely affected in the competitive condition.

Much research suggests that girls may not benefit as much as they could from the introduction of microcomputers. Turkle outlines two styles of dealing with computers: hard and soft mastery—where hard mastery is the imposition of skill over the machine through implementation of a plan—whereas soft mastery is more interactive. Not surprisingly, girls tend to be soft masters and boys tend to be hard. Her main contribution is in offering a different model for how women may wish to relate to computers, which has implications for educational development and evaluation.

5.1 Small-group discussions and the microcomputer

- R. Cummings

INTRODUCTION

So loud each tongue, so empty was each head.
So much they talked, so very little said.

Charles Churchill (1731–64), *The Rosciad*.

In a recent investigation of 10–16 year olds engaged in group discussions during a CAL simulation game,[1,2] an attempt was made to discover to what extent the micro was a quiet catalyst in the learning environment. The cognitive strategies employed by children discussing concepts essential to the program (vectors and co-ordinates) were analysed in addition to aspects of their discourse related less directly to the software. Social allusions, asides and talk irrelevant to the task in hand were also monitored in order to compile as broad an inventory of the components of their conversations as possible. The contribution of the computer in a pedagogically prominent role in specialist subjects has been more fully documented than has its potential as an instrument for discursive work. This would seem an opportune time to present to those teachers still hesitant of adopting the technology some of its merits in a wider context. The results of the investigation suggest that the micro may be able, in some measure, to satisfy the 'urgent need' cited in *Language as Educator*:[3]

> So much masquerades under the disguise of 'discussion' which has no resemblance at all to human beings genuinely thrashing out a problem, pooling experience and speculating. Classrooms of 30–33 pupils putting their hands up (or not!) to edge in a word or two do not lend themselves to mastery of new forms of the spoken language. There is an urgent need to explore new ways of working which will permit real talk.

Further, the *London Association for Teaching English*,[4] following Bullock,[5] avers that 'Many school activities should be carried out by small groups which can use their talk to move towards understanding by means which are not present in the normal teacher-directed classrooms.'

It is hoped to demonstrate in this paper that the computer can contribute significantly to language across the curriculum.

While some of the inadequacies of the teacher-directed classroom elaborated below are incontrovertible, one must say that the precise function of the micro in this particular project, involving a total of 40 boys and girls from two primary and three secondary classes, is indicative rather than prescriptive. It suggests, however, that the micro has a positive influence. As with many empirical studies which eschew *a priori* theories, several hypotheses (Fig. 1) sprang from the data. This inductive method was applied to almost 100,000 words transcribed from recordings which were taped in the course of 10 individual group discussions. Group size was restricted to four pupils which Barnes & Todd[6] found to be the optimum for effective groupwork. The left-hand column in Fig. 1 shows the sources of evidence and the tests applied to verify the hypotheses viz: videotape, readability formulae, pre- and post-written tests, word count, audiotapes, conversation components, transcripts and checklist.

This paper concentrates on the analysis and results of some of the nine categories of conversation components listed below which incorporate a wealth of words which would not normally reach the teacher's ears. The letters on the left are used on the segments in Figs. 2 and 3 which indicate both the global picture across the 10–16 age ranges, in a 5% sample, and a case study of 12 year old boys and girls in a selected 8-min discussion 'Captain's Cabin' which was also videotaped.

A References to tactics, or moves of the .... ADVERSARY
C Specific mention of .... CO-ORDINATES
D Comments not relevant to the game .... DIGRESSIONS
M Reference to 'authority' e.g. Rules, Teacher or .... MICRO
R Logical thought or hypothetico-deductive .... REASONING
*S Co-operative behaviour, friendly or .... SOCIAL
T Direct allusions to strategy or .... TACTICS
V Idiomatic, interesting or colourful .... VOCABULARY
W Specific reference to the .... WIND

At the outset a check was made to see whether the micro was a distraction or an aid to concentration. Segment 'M' on the global pie-chart (Fig. 2) indicates that only 3% of all utterances in pupil discussions were direct references to the micro itself. As the limited sum-totals in Table 1 indicate, the technology

---

* This category also shaded on pie-charts in Figs. 2 and 3.

Figure 1.   The research hypotheses

Source of evidence	All the below to be prefixed by; 'That pupils, discussing in groups . . .'	Outcome
A R W	'. . . did not show differences in forms of language with age.'	False
Cc	'. . . did not show differences in conversation content with age.'	False
Cc	'. . . did not show differences in conversation content with gender.'	False
Cc	'. . . did not spend less than half the available time on problem-solving activities.'	True
Cc U	'. . . were not preoccupied with the technology.'	True
Cc V	'. . . did not spend a high proportion of the time discussing irrelevancies.'	True
Cc	'. . . did not make a high proportion of social comments.'	False
V W	'. . . did not learn anything.'	False
R V X	'. . . did not use different forms of language when the teacher is present.'	False
% V X	'. . . did not individually get a fair share of talking time.'	False
' X	'. . . did not use a full range of cognitive strategies.'	False
A V W	'. . . did not communicate in words alone.'	True

V = Videotape, X = First-year group exclusively, R = Readability, W = Written post/test, X = Word count, A = Audiotapes, Cc = Conversation components, U = Universal transcripts, ' = Checklists.

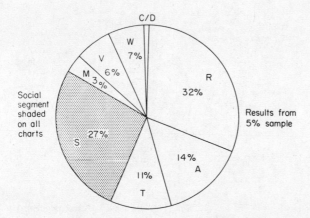

Figure 2   Conversation components: global. Global total 566 utterances in approx. 5000 words. Percent = combined global total utterances. See text for key to symbols

was by no means obtrusive in the learning situation. Notable among the value judgements of these children, all unfamiliar with CAL lessons, were that the computer was 'silent and sophisticated' and that it 'didn't talk back' (Fig. 4). The machine was accepted by the pupils as an adjunct, no more prominent in their learning than apparatus used in science lessons or weather instruments in environmental studies. In all cases it became a means to an end rather than an end in itself. Whether the remaining 97% of 'bons mots' generated by the pupils' involvement with the particular program were a direct result of the use of a computer as such is conjectural. The similar pencil-and-paper game 'Battleships' has engrossed many an otherwise disruptive class, albeit with an excess of convergent thinking, but those verbal exchanges have not been monitored hitherto. That a pleasingly high proportion of conversation related to logical reasoning (57% by combining

Table 1. Comments related directly to the micro (M) across the age ranges

Type of comment	Age/years				
	10	11	12	14	16
	Number of comments				
(a) General qualitative	4	2	0	0	2
(b) Reference to graphics	1	2	0	3	3
(c) Precision of micro	1	3	1	2	5
(d) Infallibility of micro	1	3	2	0	1
(e) Limitations of micro	0	0	1	4	7
Total	7	10	4	9	18

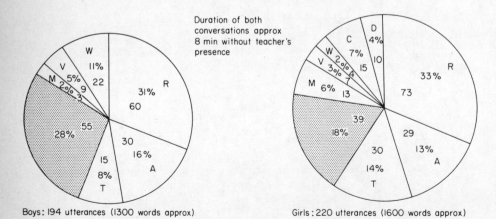

Boys: 194 utterances (1300 words approx)   Girls: 220 utterances (1600 words approx)

Figure 3 Conversation study: case study. 'Captain's Cabin': conversation components. Bold figures show total utterances in category given. % = proportion of a single discussion. See text for key to symbols

Figure 4. Spontaneous comments on the micro (M). * Related to the software specifically

Age

(a) General qualitative

10   This game's really good.
     I hope we carry on after dinner.
     This is a good game . . . I always guess for others.
     I hate it; I'd rather be doing Maths.

16   This program's pretty crummy.
 * It's nothing without playing the hazard rules.

(b) Graphics

11 * If we touch that circle we have to pick up the treasure.
     The dot is appearing where we've already travelled.

14 * I think the islands look funny.
     I quite like the ships.
     The graphic letters are quite good but not quite clear.

16   I like the italic writing.
 * I counted the blips from the bottom . . . not enough.
 * The islands are rather low resolution.

(c) Micro precision

10   It must be 22,17 Justine, it said it on the computer.

11   We're one out, one out . . . 18,4.
 * They're not numbered beside the screen.
     It takes some time to show . . . memory.

14   Can we go diagonally?
 * 360, this computer only understands that, not 000.

16 * You have to put 0 (zero) and not O.
 * Do we have to put O before 45?
 * I expect it's been rigged so we won't land right next to . . .
     Perhaps it was a dud island—no jewels on it.
 * There's some weird thing whereby you terminate your go if you go into a port. It's not reasonable to go wrong.

(d) Micro infallibility

10   The computer would have told us.

11   Dear God computer please help us, change the wind to South.
 * Well has it lied to put us off course? We've done something wrong.
     They're not there because it doesn't say on the computer.

12   What if it goes more . . . no but there's only eight points.
     Don't betray us, Computer!

16   Is this right? Of course it's right, it's a computer.

(e) Micro limitations

14   There must be a bug in the program.
     Stupid computer went and got rid of two of our hours.
     We don't seem to have much of that old variable wind.
     Maybe some hazards weren't selected.

16 * Pythagoras gets ignored in this game which is a bit annoying.
     There's something wrong with the program.
     It's taken a disliking to us.
     I think it's time we cracked this program.
     It's a bit complicated, I don't credit it with that much intelligence.

categories R, A and T) was, however, a promising aspect. The children, motivated by the micro, were undoubtedly occupied during their group discussion with thought *processes* rather than preoccupied with the written *products* of their task.

The lesson structure and the stimulus from the micro provided an opportunity to set out their thinking in preference to setting down their thoughts. In some ways this was reminiscent of working with LOGO. Laurillard[7] has cautioned that no proof as yet exists that the computer is a 'mathemagenic' agency whereby learning is an inevitable outcome. While not a deterministic element, the computer appears from this project to be a highly influential factor in kindling group discussions of meaningful nature. An in-depth analysis of two 8-min sections of 11 year olds conversing indicated that they engaged in a remarkably high number of cognitive strategies in so short a time. These are incorporated in the 'R' segment in Fig. 3. In this particular sample the boys did not attempt to 'project into the feelings of others'; the only item from the checklists (Fig. 5), derived from the work of Tough[8] and Barnes & Todd, evading identification. That all the other items listed were represented (some more than once) in both boys' and girls' discussions, indicated a breadth of logical thinking remarkable in so short a time and at such a young age.

TREASURE ISLANDS, the program used—tried and tested elsewhere[9]—has all the ingredients which ensure that a simulation is a stimulation: gamefulness, randomness, conjecture and motivation. An irresistible recipe was provided (familiar by now to many teachers) when a class clamours to continue after the final lesson bell. The combination of the following four elements in the group-learning scenario appears to have been both sufficient and necessary to cause the pupils to treat each other as resources:

1 a program with a minimal screen output of words,
2 relegation of the micro to a passive role,
3 withdrawal of the teacher from the discussions,
4 efficient management of a single micro and privacy in discussion.

Aided in this manner, the children exploited such opportunities by:

(i)   completing their peers' unfinished sentences,
(ii) encouraging others to continue,
(iii) inviting others to contribute,
(iv) modifying another's statement,
(v)   offering evidence to support the foregoing.

Such collaborative moves in discussion were, quite possibly, unique to a situation where the teacher was absent from his conventional role as interlocutor. His gestures and intonations were not available to the class for the customary scrutiny for signals. The children were talking to clarify their

Figure 5. Checklists

---

1 Use of language and supporting strategies, Tough[8]

Towards logical reasoning:
(i) Explaining a process.
(ii) Recognizing causal and dependent relationships.
(iii) Recognizing problems and their solutions.
(iv) Justifying judgements and actions.
(v) Reflecting on events and drawing conclusions; deducing.

Predicting:
(i) Anticipating and forecasting events.
(ii) Anticipating the detail of events.
(iii) Anticipating a sequence of events.
(iv) Anticipating problems and possible solutions.
(v) Anticipating and recognizing alternative courses of action.
(vi) Predicting the consequences of actions or events.

Projecting:
(i) Projecting into the experience of others.
(ii) Projecting into the feelings of others.
(iii) Projecting into the reactions of others.
(iv) Projecting into situations never experienced.

2 Social and cognitive functions of conversation, Barnes & Todd[6]

Logical process:
(a) Proposes a cause.
(b) Proposes a result.
(c) Expands loosely (e.g., descriptive details).
(d) Applies a principle to a case.
(e) Categorizes.
(f) States conditions under which statement is valid or invalid.
(g) Advances evidence.
(h) Negates.
(i) Evaluates.
(j) Puts alternative view.
(k) Suggests a method.
(l) Restates in different terms.

---

understanding as well as to communicate and collaborate with others. They seemed inspired by the freedom to use 'expressive' and spontaneous speech. Full rein was given to language in its 'exploratory, hesitant, experimental, pause-peppered, 'er-um' phase—an essential building block as learning in transition moves to learning as understanding'.[10] Language in school had become a medium to inform rather than to conform.

In the 'palaeotechnic' era[11] oracy in schools was not so rosy as in 'Granny's Garden'! Flanders,[12] demonstrated that in the traditional lesson, two-thirds of the time is occupied with talk, two-thirds of which is teacher-talk and two-thirds of that is lecturing. Twenty seconds is the average ration of time available for each pupil to speak. Teachers' questions occur every 10 sec, the more complex ones eliciting just single word replies. The teacher often appears to be the only person using language to organize thoughts. Richards[13] has shown that a single 15 year old pupil spoke in class for only 12 sec in a whole day and that a 14 year old wrote 10,000 words (16 sides). It was found that, one primary child talked only to two friends in a full day and not once to the teacher.

The microcomputer is able to provide a productive medium for inquiry learning if it enables children to turn the tables and become more accustomed to asking questions rather than answering them. Cognitive bridges between the teacher and the taught are more likely where pupils are permitted exercise in language as a vehicle for learning in preference to an instrument for teaching. This is especially so in joint word-processing activities or with content-free programs like TRAY. As with a regrettably large number of skills-and-drills programs, rote-learning or in transmission-reception style of teaching, the name of the game has been 'hunt the label' in place of 'discover the meaning'. Discovery methods increase the need for a pupil to record, define and hypothesize. Listeners in exploratory talk are a stimulus since they are likely to *mis*understand, to *dis*agree or to suggest an alternative idea. Speakers must, therefore, clarify or modify their views in response. The 'neutrality' of the computer obviates inhibition in thinking aloud. By verbalizing we alert our perceptual expectations and talking ideas through in debate is more likely to achieve this than passive listening. The more aids or resources that are available in school to promote conjecture the better. In short, we observe not with our eyes but with our hypotheses.

Considerable scope for the 'What if . . .' approach, characteristic of much of the more powerful educational software, is provided by *TREASURE ISLANDS*. The need to locate the opponent's ship and navigate a collision course creates a competitive context which promotes hypothetico-deductive reasoning. The substantial number of direct references to the adversary ('A' in Figs. 2 and 3) in all the age groups bears witness to this, while a close examination of the statements indicates both the increasing ability with age to 'decentrate' and a developing complexity of reasoning approaches. The primary children were barely out of the stage of concrete operations, often expressing themselves in eloquent body language. As illustrated by the videotape, their position was frequently indicated by jabbing a finger on the map. The secondary pupils, on the other hand, showed higher order skills and used more abstract, symbolic or formal modes of communication.

As would be expected, much time was spent on social, chiefly behaviour-shaping, or other non-cognitive elements in conversation. This is represented by the shaded segments on the pie-charts. The amount varied from 45% in the 10 year olds total discussion to only 15% in the 16 year olds. The youngest pupils had less developed skills of inter-personal communication and devoted much time to negative dispute compared with constructive discourse. It is not suggested, however, that this finding negates the value of the program with the youngest children. The lowest class spent an inordinate amount of time attributing the vicissitudes of their voyage to any number and type of factors apart from the variability of the wind: the true cause. In this group, unlike the older ones, there was not a single child (and often only one voice of persuasion is needed in simulations to sway the rest) who could enlighten the others with the fact that a wind is named according to the direction *from* which it is blowing. While the game for the youngsters may have been less conclusive, the processes of thinking it demanded in considering possibilities were nonetheless beneficial. Both literally and metaphorically, making the journey was more important than reaching a destination.

By segregating the groups it was possible to ascertain any significant gender differences. The only category (a mere 1% of the global total) in which any bias was evident was the one where irrelevancies intruded. As much as four times this percentage (still a small proportion of the whole discussion) registered in the girls' 'Captain's Cabin' conference (Fig. 3) yet none in the boys' equivalent. While not wishing to adopt a chauvinist stance nor to detract from the girls' competitiveness or application to the exercise, both of which matched the boys, it must be admitted that across all age ranges it was found that not only did the girls utter more words than the boys (see numbers in Fig. 3) but that their talking tended to incorporate a range of issues which were, albeit interesting, not altogether relevant. The remarkable ability to depart temporarily from a reasoned argument, and shortly to return to it with equal facility, seems to be an exclusively female phenomenon. Boys, from a certain social class, according to Bernstein,[14] tend to pause more frequently and thereby give themselves more thinking time. Girls, it would appear, have less need of silence to develop their inner thoughts and are not distracted if they all talk at the same time or overlap, as happened occasionally. The average rate of speech was 10 utterances per minute, but the girls spoke faster. The average length of an utterance was nine words. For both boys and girls it is well-known that there is considerable redundancy in speech and their meanings were generally satisfactorily conveyed by as little as one-third of the words spoken.

CONCLUSION

From examination of the conversations chronicled in this study, it is suggested that the microcomputer can be an effective motivator in groupwork. The assertion: 'This is happening here, now', should justify its validity through observation. Readers are able to replicate the exercise and draw their own conclusions by scanning transcribed data from their own classes and to judge to what extent the medium may help children think aloud and communicate their messages. The teacher is becoming, new technology notwithstanding, more manager than mentor. As with any pedagogic prop, responsibilities are increased not diminished. Software must be tailored to be used as courseware. With increasing application of IT in the curriculum teachers' time and energy can easily be freed for the fuller exercise of the pupils' skills in oracy which are so often relegated by over-attention to the written word. Language has a triple function in education: for communication, as a thinking tool and as a shaper of meanings. It is to be regretted that teachers dwell disproportionately on the first of these in the conventional classroom for the sake of a permanent record. Talk is evanescent but writing leaves footprints. This dichotomy, hopefully, may be bridged by a wider adoption of the microcomputer as a learning aid in school and an acknowledgment that listening and talking skills are of growing importance out of school where the printer is fast ousting the pen. Further research into the applications of the technology is to be recommended if it will redress the balance between our understanding of learning *with* rather than *about* the machine.

REFERENCES

1. Cummings, R. (1984) Pupil-talk in groups during a CAL simulation game. Unpublished MA (Ed.) Dissertation, University of London.
2. Holmes, B. and Whittington, J. (1981) *Spanish Main/Treasure Islands Disk*. Aylesbury, Ginn & Co.
3. Britton, J. (1979) *Language as Educator*, London, Macmillan.
4. Rosen, H. (1975) *Language and Literacy in Our Schools*, University of London Institute of Education.
5. Bullock, A. (1975) *A Language for Life*, London, H.M.S.O.
6. Barnes, D. and Todd, F. (1977) *Communication and Learning in Small Groups*, London, Routledge and Kegan Paul.
7. Laurillard, D. (1980) The promotion of learning using CAL. University of Surrey, IET Occasional Paper.
8. Tough, J. (1976) *Communication skills project*. London, Schools Council/Ward Lock.
9. Rawle, N. (1982) Case study—The Spanish Main. In *Five of the Best* (Ed R. Jones), MEP/CET, London.
10. Slater, F. (1982) *Learning Through Geography*, London, Heinemann.
11. Kent, A., Hall, D. and Wiegand, P. (1982) Geography teaching and computers, in *Teaching Geography* Vol. 7 No. 3. Jan. 1982, Sheffield, Geographical Association.
12. Flanders, N. (1970) *Analyzing Teacher Behaviour*, London, Addison Wesley.
13. Richards, J. (1978) *Classroom Language: What Sort?* London, Allen and Unwin.
14. Bernstein, B. (1971) *Class, Codes and Control*, London, Routledge and Kegan Paul.

5.2 Computer learning, through Piaget's eyes

- Leonard Huber

What's so different about a computer? To a child, nothing. It's just another playground to explore, to manipulate, and even to get bored with. Children working or playing with computers use the same intellectual patterns as when they play with blocks or crayons or tackle their homework.

For the teacher, it is important to recognize how children's intellectual patterns develop, and for the teacher using computers in the classroom, it is important to recognize how this connects with various computer activities. On one hand, the developmental level of children in a certain grade determines the computer literacy activities and concepts appropriate for that grade. On the other hand, appropriate computer experience can stimulate development in children's mental patterns.

But what is 'appropriate computer experience'? Jean Piaget devised hundreds of experiments to explain intellectual growth. One of his classics examined the way children think about a game of billiards. He asked the children to shoot a ball from a plunger so it bounced off the side wall of the billiard table and hit a target. Their behaviour fell into three stages Piaget called *pre-operational*, *concrete operational*, and *formal operational*.

PRE-OPERATIONAL BEHAVIOUR

The youngest children in the experiment were four and five years old. They were rarely able to shoot the ball to hit the target. This inability was not due to a deficit in physical co-ordination. Rather, the youngsters lacked the mental apparatus to predict accurately the path of the ball. Piaget proved this by interviewing each child after a successful shot, asking the child to trace the path of the ball with his or her finger. Invariably, the child traced a curved line from the starting point to the target. As far as the child was concerned, the ball never bounced off the wall!

How could a child with normal vision and intellect ignore the obvious trajectory of a rolling billiard ball? According to Piaget, children at this stage do not really understand actions. Their thinking is dominated by static images rather than mental representations of change. They can see where the ball begins and where it ends, but they cannot reason through the transition.

The four- and five-year-olds' emphasis on end-states instead of actions is the hallmark of 'pre-operational' thinking. 'Operations' are the mental representations of actions—and young children don't have them. This kind of pre-operational thinking explains some common problems such children encounter with computers.

For example, four- and five-year-olds often have a related problem trying to use *Bank Street Writer*. In this elementary word process, children must press a particular key to change from the 'writing' to the 'cursor-movement' mode. Kindergarten teachers can testify that this is difficult for young children to remember. When they are in a particular mode, they fail to see the possibility of changing to another mode. Logo also requires the child to change from an 'editing mode' to a 'turtle graphics' mode; and predictably, when young children are using one mode, they have a hard time recalling the other.

The static images that dominate the thoughts of four- and five-year-olds do not let them think of more than one thing at a time. Piaget showed this in a simple experiment which you can perform with a child just learning to count. Lay some coins on a table—say, five pennies and three nickels. Ask a five-year-old how many pennies there are, how many nickels, and how many coins all together. After you are convinced she can answer these questions, try another: 'Are there more pennies or more coins?' A pre-operational child will answer, 'More pennies.'

How can a child who clearly can count claim that five pennies are more than eight coins? Here is Piaget's explanation: In order to count up the pennies, the child divides the coins into two groups, pennies and nickels. Now the only comparison the child can make is between pennies and nickels, and there are indeed more pennies. If you now ask the child to count all the coins, she will look at the group as a whole and correctly count to eight. What pre-operational children cannot do is see the whole group and its parts *at the same time*.

For a child who thinks this way, instructing the Logo turtle to perform certain manoeuvres on the screen is difficult. He must envision not only the shape he wants to draw, but also its components. (These are usually some combination of turtle actions such as FORWARD, RIGHT TURN, and LEFT TURN). But this is exactly what he cannot yet do—co-ordinate the whole and its parts. Piaget's description of pre-operational youngsters in his studies fits perfectly the young Logo beginner: 'We are inevitably struck by the fact that the child is taking each step as he comes to it, forgetting what went before, and not foreseeing what must follow.'

For a pre-operational child beginning Logo, one of the hardest things to understand is that the turning commands do not draw lines. Why is this difficult? Because pre-operational children confuse the 'part' with the 'whole'. It's the flip side of the coin from their inability to see the whole and its parts at the same time. In this instance, the 'part' is the turning command and 'whole' is the line.

Confusion between parts and wholes is also quite evident when youngsters at this stage edit what they have typed, whether in Logo, BASIC, or on a word processor. They will invariably erase an entire word when only one letter is incorrect. For example, a child who types CATT instead of CAT will backspace over the whole word and type it again from scratch, instead of erasing only the last letter.

Does all this mean that wide open computer environments like Logo, BASIC, and word processing are inappropriate for preschoolers? Not at all. Young children do learn to use Logo, albeit in a fashion peculiar to their stage of mental development. Pre-operational children, who think in terms of one-to-one correspondences, can learn rules like 'FD always needs a number' and 'RT always needs a number.' (RT is the Logo abbreviation for 'right turn'; FD stands for 'forward.') Then they can learn something like 'RT and a number, then FD and a number, make a line.' They can go on to learn that LT (for 'left turn') works much like RT. BK works like FD. And so on. These simple relationships can add up to a comprehensive repertoire of Logo skills. And they can nurture a more mature understanding of the turtle's 'behaviour.'

There are also several ways of introducing Logo concepts that make them more accessible. One is to write a Logo program that lets children move the turtle by typing a single letter. Such a program need be only a few lines long, as in the following program written in Terrapin Logo:

```
TO ONEKEY
MAKE "COMMAND READCHARACTER
IF :COMMAND = "F THEN FD 10
IF :COMMAND = "R THEN RT 30
IF :COMMAND = "L THEN LT 30
IF :COMMAND = "D THEN DRAW
ONEKEY
```

If you use Apple Logo, substitute the program on page 162.

```
TO ONEKEY
MAKE "COMMAND READCHAR
IF :COMMAND = "F [FD 10]
IF :COMMAND = "R [RT 30]
IF :COMMAND = "L [LT 30]
IF :COMMAND = "C [CLEARSCREEN]
ONEKEY
END
```

In *Delta Drawing*, published by Spinnaker, children use one-key commands to draw pictures. There is also a one-key command to fill parts of a picture with bright colours. This is quite thrilling to pre-operational children, with their emphasis on immediate perception.

After pre-operational children learn a few commands in Logo, they should be encouraged to use them without trying to accomplish any particular result. In this way they can see the effects of the commands without being dominated by the mental image of what they are trying to draw. Then they can begin to anticipate the results of their actions.

In general, any computer program in which a single key press produces a change of state on the computer screen is satisfying to pre-operational children. Of course, it is nice if there is also some educational content. Software that offers both includes the *Early Games* Series from Springboard and *Spellicopter* from Designware. Bear in mind that these programs, as well as *Delta Drawing* and the Logo ONEKEY program, are quite boring to children much older than 6.

CONCRETE OPERATIONS

Experience with Logo can be a valuable doorway to the next level of intellectual development, which Piaget labeled 'concrete operations.' Concrete operations usually emerge around age seven or eight. Children at this stage can form mental representations of the actions they observe, but they cannot extend these images to examine the realm of the possible. They are limited to the concrete world they see around them, and their inability to hypothesize prevents them from thinking scientifically.

On the surface, concrete operational children give a good show of adult thinking. They can solve Piaget's problem of the billiard game. They consistently shoot the ball at the proper angle to bounce off the wall and hit the target. And they can accurately trace with their finger the ball's trajectory.

Their mastery of the mental representation of action is evident in their comprehension of Logo 'reversibility.' They understand that any Logo action has an opposite that will 'undo' it. (For instance, RT 90 is undone by LT 90.) They also understand the 'additivity' of Logo actions. (RT 40 followed by LT 50 adds up to LT 10.)

But they are not perfect and they are not adults. Although they see what is, they are blind to what might be. Because they do not consider the hypothetical, they are unable to invent rules which cover all possibilities. That's why Piaget labelled their mental operations 'concrete.' They stick close to reality as they see it.

Here is an imaginary interview with a concrete operational child taking part in the billiard experiment:

> 'How did you get the ball to hit the target?'
> 'It hits here, then it goes there.'
> 'Why does it go there?'
> 'It just does.'
> 'And what if you shot the ball more to the right?'
> 'Then it would bounce off more to the right.'
> 'Why?'
> 'Because that's the way it works.'
> 'And what if I moved the target more to the left?'
> 'You would have to aim the ball more to the left.'
> 'Why?'
> 'If you didn't, it wouldn't hit the target.'

Would you have answered any of these questions differently? Perhaps you remember from high school physics the rule that says 'the angle of incidence equals the angle of reflection.' That is, the angle at which the ball hits the wall is the same as the angle at which it rebounds. Teenagers and adults discover this rule when they try the experiment. They say things like 'the rebound depends on the angle of the plunger in relation to the wall.' That is, they recognize the key variables.

Here's another example of the concrete operational approach. Jamie (age 9) created a graphics program in BASIC that produced stripes on the screen changing colours randomly and rapidly. Then he haphazardly changed words or numbers in his program in order to change the graphic display. There was no method to his madness, just curiosity about the effect. He was totally stymied when his teacher challenged him to produce rectangles on the screen, instead of stripes. He did not know which variables to change.

Similarly, concrete operational children love to doodle in Logo. It provides just the experience they need—seeing how a perceptual whole, the drawing on the screen, is composed of separate elements, the turning and drawing commands. They are excited to learn about patterns—for instance, the way Logo commands can be repeated to produce geometrical figures.

But concrete operational thinking makes it difficult for children to solve a Logo problem such as drawing a triangle. Typically, they will have mastered—with the help of the teacher—the sentence to produce a square: REPEAT 4 [FD 30 RT 90]. But they will be unsettled and uncertain about what modifications might produce a triangle.

With some coaxing they may agree that to make a triangle the word

'REPEAT' should be followed by the number '3,' rather than '4.' And after some experimentation, they conclude that size of the angle (RT) must also be changed, but not the length of the sides (FD). But what size should the angle be? They try every number between 1 and 1,000 except the right one.

The teacher intervenes. 'Why don't you make a list,' she suggests, 'of each angle that you try, and whether it was too big or too small?' But the students can't quite follow the instructions. They want to find the *right* number. They don't see the point of writing down the *wrong* numbers. They lack a key element of scientific thought—appreciation for negative results. Negative results let a scientific thinker exclude all possibilities until only the correct answer remains.

Even more shocking is the 10-year-old student who submits to the teacher's guidance and makes a list, but doesn't know how to use it. He finds that RT 130 is too big and RT 115 is too small, and he wants to try RT 105 next. (The correct angle for a triangle is RT 120.)

Ah, well. What would be the point of school if nine-year-old children could solve problems like this? Fortunately, when it comes to teaching elementary classes how to organize information and reach logical conclusions, we have our work cut out for us. Piaget calls these skills of adulthood 'formal operations.' They are 'formal' in the sense that they reduce a problem to its underlying form, rather than relying on concrete appearances.

Another challenging computer activity for concrete operational children is the program *Factory* from Sunburst. In this game, players have a set of mock machines that they can use to stamp out imaginary metal plates. After they master the stamping procedure, their task is to create plates that match others created automatically by the software. Children are particularly intrigued—and it is important for them to learn—that the same pattern can result from different stamping procedures. In other words, this program teaches children that there are more ways than one to accomplish the goal.

FORMAL THINKING

Formal thinking generally first appears in the teen-age years. (It is not uncommon, however, to find 11- and 12-year-olds beginning to show the scientific skills of formal thought.) Formal thinking is characterized by attention to 'the essential constitution of a thing as distinguished from the matter composing it.'

Here's an example of how concrete and formal thinking might affect students' use of Logo. The students are taught the word RANDOM. (The command produces some unpredictable number.) Then they are told to produce a drawing using RANDOM in conjunction with the word REPEAT. Compare these typical sentences:

concrete: REPEAT 50 [FD RANDOM 100 RT 90 FD 29 RT 70 FD 90]
formal: REPEAT 50 [FD RANDOM 100 RT RANDOM 360]

Concrete operational children can make it work, but formal operational children get the point! They recognize the key components and discard the rest.

Snooper Troops from Spinnaker, is a great activity for children making the transition from concrete to formal operational thinking. In this game, players must solve a mystery by organizing a number of clues and carefully excluding suspects. They must take notes and make maps. A concrete operational child can't possibly do it. An older teen-ager may find it pointless. But a 13-year-old will stick with it for hours. They love their newly developed ability to consider possibilities and reason by a process of exclusion.

Tribbles, from Conduit, is an excellent challenge in scientific thinking for older children and adults. Tribbles are little creatures that appear on a grid. Their arrangement on the grid changes 'daily.' (A new day begins whenever the user presses the space bar.) The job of the student scientists is to determine if the arrangement of tribbles follows a pattern from day to day. Students can test their hypotheses by placing the tribbles in a particular arrangement and following their appearance in subsequent days.

At first, students—even at the graduate level—often find the process frustrating. They don't know where to begin. Sometimes they make a good formal operational thrust by trying to establish whether the daily change in tribble arrangement is random. (It is not.) This step correctly summarizes *all* possibilities into two: random or predictable. By concluding that the change is not random, students implicitly discover some pattern. Their next step is to make that intuition explicit—that is, to come up with a more specific hypothesis. This requires them to isolate particular aspects of the patterns to see if they are predictive of the observed changes. Usually, it takes quite a few such steps to get the picture right. The whole process is one of imagining and testing possibilities.

Formal operational children can learn to program like professionals. (Obviously. We read in the paper every week about some teen-ager earning $100,000 by writing computer programs.) Professional programmers work with 'modules.' They divide their programming task into the smallest possible sub-problems, solving each one in turn. Then they fit the pieces together. In other words, they isolate the key components.

Still, it takes practice to develop formal operations and apply them to the world of problems in the worlds of childhood and adolescence. Computer projects provide a good opportunity because the computer is easier to control than most other facets of school life. The teacher's challenge, as always, is to invent projects that motivate children to stretch their minds.

SO, WHAT'S SO DIFFERENT ABOUT COMPUTERS?

Nothing much, except that they may change the basis of human thought. Normal children march through the stages of mental development in a predictable order at predictable ages. But these stages are not exactly innate. They are the result of a particular environment interacting with a particular set of sensory organs connected to a particular brain. Theoretically, if the environment were radically changed, the stages of development would differ—say, in the mind of a dolphin.

How much will computers change the environment for today's children? In the past, children learned the principles of reality by playing with sticks and stones and blocks. That's why their mental operations are so concrete. Now they can learn by manipulating symbols on a computer screen. They can compare the effects of hugely different numbers, such as 5 and 5,000. They can create new words and combine them into sentences that the computer understands.

Here's a more specific example. According to Piaget, as children begin to grow out of concrete thinking, around age 11, they begin to understand the random fluctuation of natural events. They see that if they roll a ball down a hill it will not always stop on the same dime, but it will always stop in a certain range. This is an important cornerstone of scientific thought. With Logo, eight-year-olds using the word RANDOM can reach the same conclusion. Does this mean that they will reach formal operations at age 10? Or, will they create a new version of concrete operations which incorporates the random component of life on earth?

As they say in formal operations, 'Anything is possible.' Before the invention of the printing press probably few people even reached the formal operational stage. They simply lacked the intellectual stimulation. Our new revolution in technology may promote a new stage of mental development *more* advanced than formal operations. Perhaps we will even discover a way of thinking that can solve the monumental problems of our modern world.

5.3 Effects of cooperative, competitive and individualistic goal structures on computer-assisted instruction

- Roger T. Johnson, David W. Johnson and Mary Beth Stanne

[. . .] The growth of computer technology presents education with several challenges. One is promoting computers' effective instructional use without increasing the isolation and alienation of students. Computer-assisted instruction brings with it the possibility that student interaction with computers may result in less interaction with teachers and classmates. An individualistic assumption has dominated the instructional use of computers, [. . .] and the possible use of computer-assisted co-operative or competitive instruction is largely ignored. Because interpersonal interaction is an important influence on instructional effectiveness and classroom climate[1], computer-assisted instruction may have a detrimental effect on educational practice. Whether computer-assisted co-operative, competitive, or individualistic instruction is most effective in promoting desired learning outcomes is an empirical issue.

Given that in almost all schools the number of students far exceeds the number of computers, it is inevitable that students work with computers in small groups. In such learning groups students may work individualistically and take turns using the computer, they may compete to see who is best, or they may co-operate. Like any academic task, tasks presented by computers may be structured co-operatively, competitively, or individualistically. The purpose of the present study was to compare the relative efficacy of computer-assisted co-operative, competitive, and individualistic learning.

In a *co-operative* learning situation, students' goal achievements are positively correlated; when one student achieves his or her goal, all others with whom he or she is competitively linked achieve their goals.[2,3] In a *competitive* learning situation, students' goal achievements are negatively correlated; when one student achieves his or her goal, all others with whom he or she is competitively linked fail to achieve their goals. In an *individualistic* learning situation, students' goal achievements are independent; the goal achievement of one student is unrelated to the goal achievement of others. Each of these goal structures may be used with learning tasks involving the use of computers.

There is an absence of research comparing the relative effectiveness of computer-assisted co-operative, competitive, and indivdualistic learning in promoting achievement, task-related interaction among students, positive attitudes toward the subject area and instructional experience, and relationships among students. Of special interest is the relative performance of male and female students in computer-assisted instructional situations. The specific questions addressed in the present study were as follows: What is the relative efficacy of computer-assisted co-operative, competitive, and individualistic learning on

- quantity and quality of daily achievement, problem-solving success, and test performance of male and female students?
- task-related oral interaction patterns of male and female students?
- attitudes of male and female students toward the subject being studied and the instructional experience?
- relationships among students?

Some controversy exists about whether the instructional use of computers affects students' achievement. Whereas some researchers have concluded that the use of computers does raise student achievement,[4] others have concluded that a computer is a vehicle that delivers instruction but does not itself affect student achievement.[5] Although computer-assisted instruction is most often used within drill and practice situations aimed at memorizing basic facts and increasing the quantity of production, there is hope that an increased use of computer-assisted instruction in more complex learning situations will increase students' ability to apply their knowledge and solve problems. It is of interest, therefore, to investigate the impact of computer-assisted co-operative, competitive, and individualistic learning on quantity and quality of daily performance, problem-solving success, and test questions requiring different levels of cognitive functioning. Given indication from previous research that co-operative learning situations generally promote higher achievement than do competitive or individualistic learning,[6,7] it may be hypothesized that higher performance on all the achievement measures will be found in the co-operative condition. [. . .] There is a need to extend the previous research on achievement, however, to computer-assisted instruction situations.

Almost no systematic investigation has been made of the nature of the interaction among students working in groups with a microcomputer. Anecdotal descriptions have been written of students sharing ideas when writing stories with a computer,[8-10] producing publications such as class newsletters,[11] and writing a program,[12] but planned observations of students working in groups at computers have rarely been conducted. There are at least three types of statements that students may make while working at a microcomputer: task statements involving presenting and elaborating on the information being learned, management statements involving informing other students on the procedures being used to accomplish the group's work, and social statements unrelated to the task or the working procedures of the group. These statements may be addressed to other students or to the teacher. In the present study the frequency of task, management, and social statements was observed to determine the impact of the microcomputer on interaction among students and between the students and the teacher.

Some evidence exists that co-operative learning situations promote more positive attitudes toward the subject area and the instructional experience than do competitive or individualistic experiences. The use of computers within the instructional situation, however, often produces high interest in the class, which may result in positive attitudes toward working with computers and toward the subject area being studied. It is of some interest to determine if the positive views of computer-assisted instruction extend to competitive and individualistic learning situations.

In computer-assisted instruction boys may achieve higher, have more positive attitudes toward computers and science classes, and feel more confident in their ability in learning with computers than may girls. At three different age levels (9, 13, and 17 years), the achievement level of boys was higher than that of girls in three national assessments of science (1969, 1973, and 1977; National Assessment of Educational Progress, 1978). In the 1977 national assessment, at all three age levels boys were more likely than girls to have favorable attitudes towards science classes and science-related careers. Johnson, Johnson, Scott, and Ramolae[13] found that in science classes boys achieved higher and liked science better than did girls and were more confident of their ability to achieve in science than were girls. Johnson *et al.* found no significant differences between boys and girls on perceiving science as a male domain. Steinkamp[14] found that in general, girls did *not* view science as a male domain but did have more negative attitudes toward science and science classes. At every level, from kindergarten through graduate school, women are underrepresented in computer studies.[15] The gap in computer skills between girls and boys starts in elementary school and grows through high school. The ratio of boys to girls involved with computers appears to increase the more advanced, effortful, or costly the level of involvement.[16,17] A number of studies have found no difference between boys and girls in attitudes toward learning with computers,[18] although girls may be more apprehensive about computer-assisted instruction than boys. Another purpose of the present study, therefore, was to compare the results of computer-assisted co-operative, competitive, and individualistic learning on male and female students.

Girls have been shown to have more negative attitudes toward competition than do boys, especially during junior high school years.[19,20] The combination of competition and computer-assisted instruction may create different reactions from male and female students. The performance and attitudes of male and female students in the competitive computer-assisted instruction condition, therefore, are of special interest.

Fewer studies have been performed on the use of the microcomputer on problem-solving tasks than have been performed on its use on drill-review tasks. In this study, therefore, a problem-solving task was used.

METHOD

Sample

Subjects were 71 eighth-grade students (ages 11–13) from a midwestern, suburban, middle-class school district. Three separate English classes, selected on the basis of teacher interest in using computer-assisted instruction, were used in the study. All subjects were assigned to three conditions stratified for sex and ability level. Twenty-four students (13 boys and 11 girls) were assigned to the co-operative condition, 22 students (11 boys and 11 girls) were assigned to the competitive condition, and 25 students (14 boys and 11 girls) were assigned to the individualistic condition.

Procedure

In all conditions, students were involved in a 10-day instructional unit that paired a computer simulation with written materials on the fundamentals of map reading and navigation. The computer simulation required students to sail an ancient ship to the new world and back in search of gold, using the sun, stars, ocean depth, climate, and trade winds to navigate. The daily instructional sessions lasted 45 min. Each condition was assigned a separate classroom and given access to six computers. The amount of computer time available to each student was balanced across conditions. Three certified teachers (with more than 90 hr each of training in how to structure co-operative, competitive, and individualistic learning) worked from prepared scripts, giving directions and supervising daily activities. Each day the teachers would explain the day's task to the students, distribute the appropriate materials, and review the condition's goal structure. At the end of the instructional session the completed work and all materials were collected. To control for possible teacher effects, the teachers rotated among conditions so that each teacher taught each condition approximately one third of the time.

Six research assistants observed student oral interaction on a daily basis in all conditions. Each observer received 25 hr of training on the observation instruments. There were at least two observers in each condition each day. Observers rotated so that they observed each condition an approximately equal number of times. The research assistants observed the groups in random order for 2 min each. The interrater reliability was more than 80% (using the percentage method of agreement and disagreement for occurrence, quality, and direction.)

Curriculum

A modification of a computer simulation named *Geography Search* was used in the study. The computer simulation was supplemented with written materials on the fundamentals of map reading and navigation. All students were initially trained in how to get on file with the program on the computer. The computer simulation required students to sail an ancient ship to the new world and back in search of gold, using the sun, stars, ocean depth, climate, and trade winds to navigate. The basic role of the computer was to be an adjunct to students' decision making and problem solving and the written technical materials by providing information and giving feedback on the consequences of the actions taken. The students' role was to master the relevant technical information and apply their knowledge in deciding what actions to take to successfully solve the problem, using the computer to record their decisions and give feedback on the consequences. [. . .]

Each class session, students were given materials to read. Typical reading assignments included how to determine latitude from the position of the stars, how to determine longitude from the position of the sun, and how wind direction and speed affect sailing. After planning what to do, students would go to the computer and enter their decisions, the computer would determine the results of the action taken and give additional information such as wind direction and speed and the position of the stars, the students would record the results and the information, and then the students left the computer to plan their next series of actions.

Independent variables

The independent variables were (a) co-operative vs competitive vs individualistic learning and (b) male vs female students. In the co-operative learning condition, students were randomly assigned to computers in groups of 4
(stratified for sex and ability) and were instructed to work together as a
group in completing the computer simulation task. The group's goal was to
sail to the new world and back, accumulating as much gold as possible. In
doing so they were to ensure that all group members learned the map reading
and navigational skills taught in the simulation. Students were informed that
(a) they would individually complete daily worksheets and take a final test,
(b) their unit grade would be based on the average of the scores of their group
members on the final test and the daily worksheets, and (c) they would be
awarded bonus points on the basis of how much gold the total class accumulated (10% of the gold all co-operative groups accumulated). Three times
during the unit a subgoal was given and bonus points awarded. Subgoals
included (a) how fast can your ship reach land and (b) how fast can all the
ships in the class reach land. Groups received daily feedback on how well
they were performing. Group members were assigned specific roles (captain,
navigator, meteorologist, and quartermaster), which were rotated among
group members daily. These roles focused on task (learning the material,
recording information from computer, completing the work, making sailing
decisions by consensus, checking members' understanding) and maintenance
(encouraging participation by all group members) behaviours. The teacher's
role was to structure each day's work and monitor the learning groups to
ensure that appropriate collaborative and role behaviours were taking place.

In the competitive learning condition, students were randomly assigned to
computers in groups of 4 stratified for sex and ability and were instructed to
compete to see who was best. Students were informed that they would
(a) individually complete daily worksheets and take a final test; (b) be
graded on whether their performance was first, second, third, or fourth in
their group; and (c) receive bonus points if they were the first student in the
class to complete the voyage. Three subgoals (for example, who can reach
land first, who is the first to collect gold) were given and bonus points
awarded during the unit. A class chart was used to show which students were
winning. Students were told to play fair by observing the time limits on the
computer, to try to be first in completing the computer search and the daily
worksheets, to compare their performance with that of the other three members of the group, and to do their own work without interacting with the
other students. The teacher's role was to structure each day's work and
monitor the competitive groups to ensure that appropriate behaviour was
taking place.

In the individualistic learning condition, students were assigned randomly to computers in groups of 4 (there was one group of 5) stratified for sex and ability. Students were informed that they would (a) individually complete daily worksheets and take a final exam, (b) be graded on the basis of how their performance compared with a preset criteria of excellence, and (c) receive bonus points on the amount of gold they accumulated individually. Three subgoals were presented during the unit. The subgoals included who could reach land within a certain time period and who could obtain some gold within a certain time period. Students received daily feedback in a folder available only to the individual student and the teacher. Students were told to observe the time limits on the computer to work hard to achieve up to the preset criteria of excellence, to keep track of their progress, and to do their own work without interacting with classmates. The teacher's role was to structure each day's work and monitor the students to ensure that appropriate behaviour was taking place.

Dependent variables

The achievement measures consisted of daily worksheets, the final examination, and students' success in accumulating gold. The six 8-item worksheets tested students' comprehension of and ability to apply the reading material assigned that day. The final examination consisted of 46 multiple choice items of which 16 measured factual recognition, 16 measured application, and 14 measured *problem solving*. The test was constructed by the teachers and research staff involved in the study. Finally, the amount of gold accumulated by the student was used as an index of problem-solving success.

The oral interaction measure consisted of observing students' task, management, and social interactions. Task interactions were defined as those involving repetition of information, presenting new information, elaborating on information being learned, asking task-related questions, replying, giving support for others' learning and indicating understanding of what is being learned. Management interactions were defined as those informing group members on procedures being used to accomplish the group's work, asking questions about group procedures, and replying. Social interactions were defined as informing group members about topics unrelated to the group's work and procedures, asking questions about such topics, and replying. This instrument has been validated in previous studies[22] and has a reliability of more than .90. The frequency of task, management, and social interaction was determined for each condition.

Students' perceptions of each other were measured by a sociometric nomination instrument in which students were asked to list the names of the boys and girls in their class who (a) were most able to get other people to do things, (b) were best at games or sport, (c) had the most trouble with reading, and (d) were best at computers.

The *attitude scales* included the six-item Liking for Computers (α = .86; Johnson *et al.*, 1985), four-item Liking for Geography (α = .81; Johnson *et al.*, 1985), three-item Confidence With Using Computers (α = .71; Johnson *et al.*, 1985), four-item Computers Are A Male Domain (α = .76; Johnson *et al.*, 1985), seven-item Achievement Motivation Goal Orientation (α = .67; Johnson & Johnson, 1983a), nine-item Achievement Motivation Persistence (α = .70; Johnson & Johnson, 1983a), four-item Teacher Academic Support (α = .79; Johnson & Johnson, 1983a), four-item Teacher Personal Support (α = .75; Johnson & Johnson, 1983a), four-item Co-operation (α = .82; Johnson & Johnson, 1983a), four-item Individualistic (α = .87; Johnson & Johnson, 1983a), and eight-item Competition (α = .81; Johnson & Johnson, 1983a) scales.

Analyses

The multivariate analysis of variance (MANOVA) for the co-operative–competitive–individualistic variable was 2.50 (p < .01), and the multivariate MANOVA for the male–female variable was 4.52 (p < .01). On the basis of the significant multivariate analysis, a 3×2 ANOVA was used to analyze differences between the three conditions and boys and girls. The least significant difference (LSD) post hoc comparisons were conducted to test specific differences between conditions. In the competitive condition, *t* tests were conducted to determine the degree of difference between boys and girls.

Experimental check

Each classroom was observed daily to verify that the conditions were being taught appropriately. The results of these observations verified that the conditions were being implemented appropriately.

RESULTS

The MANOVA results appear in Table 1, with specific *F* ratios. For each dependent variable the LSD post hoc comparisons were computed and are discussed below. The first dependent variable was achievement. From Table 1 it may be seen that the LSD post hoc comparisons among conditions indicate that students in the co-operative condition completed more worksheet items and had more worksheet items correct than did the students in the competitive or individualistic conditions (p < .05). Students in the individualistic condition had more worksheet items correct than did the students in the competitive condition ($p < .05$). The final exam contained three types of questions: factual recognition, application, and problem solving. Students in the co-operative condition performed higher than did the students in the other two conditions on the factual recognition and application questions ($p < .05$), and on the problem solving questions students in the co-operative condition performed higher than did the students in the individualistic condition ($p < .05$). The students in the co-operative condition accumulated significantly more gold than did the students in the competitive and individualistic conditions ($p < .05$). Boys performed higher than did girls on test questions requiring factual recognition and problem solving.

The LSD comparisons for the interpersonal interaction variables indicate that students in the co-operative condition made more task statements, more management statements, fewer social statements, and fewer talks to the teacher than did the students in the competitive condition ($p < .05$) and more task statements, more management statements, and fewer talks to the teacher than did the students in the individualistic condition ($p < .05$). Students in the co-operative condition tended to make fewer social statements than did those in the individualistic condition ($p < 10$). Boys made more task statements than did girls. In the co-operative condition, less than 1% of students' statements were addressed to the teacher; in the competitive condition, 19% of the statements were addressed to the teacher; and in the individualistic condition, 12% of students' statements were addressed to the teacher. The sociometric data indicate that students in the competitive condition perceived more peers as being poor readers ($p < .05$) than did students in the co-operative condition.

Compared with girls, boys were perceived in all conditions as more able to influence other group members, as best at sports, as tending to have more trouble reading, and as best at using computers.

Students in the co-operative condition indicated higher goal orientation ($p < .05$) and tended to have more task persistence ($p < .10$) than did those in the other two conditions. The girls in the co-operative and individualistic conditions expressed higher persistence in trying to achieve than did the boys, whereas just the opposite was true in the competitive condition. The students in the co-operative condition were more co-operatively oriented ($p < .05$) and tended to be less individualistically oriented ($p < .10$) than were the students in the other two conditions. Students in the individualistic condition were somewhat less competitive than were students in the co-operative condition ($p < .10$). Compared with boys, girls were somewhat more individualistic, had more negative attitudes toward competition, perceived less teacher academic support, tended to like computers less (true for only the competitive condition), and perceived computers to be less of a male domain.

Given previous evidence that girls are less comfortable with competition

Table 1. Means for dependent measures

Measure	Co-operative		Competitive		Individualistic		MS_e		F ratio
	Boys	Girls	Boys	Girls	Boys	Girls			
Achievement									
Questions completed	45.82	43.56	33.00	26.10	36.93	30.55	1,071.47	CCI	8.11***
Questions correct	20.73	17.56	7.46	8.00	12.71	10.73	604.78	CCI	13.24***
Factual recognition test	11.44	8.86	9.10	7.11	8.64	6.55	32.92	CCI	3.00**
							70.98	MF	6.47***
Application test	8.78	7.86	6.40	5.44	5.50	5.73	38.71	CCI	4.48**
Problem-solving test	10.67	6.71	8.80	7.11	6.86	6.46	21.54	CCI	2.46*
							58.22	MF	6.66***
Gold accumulated	71.64	84.11	30.64	6.30	13.14	6.91	27,490.88	CCI	31.20***
Verbal Interaction									
Task statements	2.78	2.00	.78	.44	.64	.53	23.59	CCI	35.62***
							3.15	MF	4.76**
Management statements	.20	.21	.07	.06	.08	.07	.11	CCI	5.31***
Social statements	.10	.06	.53	.17	.25	.25	.30	CCI	5.17***
Statements to teacher	.03	.01	.11	.07	.12	.13	.07	CCI	4.98***
Sociometric Data									
Nominated most able	6.58	3.73	3.90	2.83	5.23	2.92	75.12	MF	8.05***
Nominated best at sports	6.75	1.82	4.00	1.83	6.62	1.42	292.03	MF	18.59***
Nominated most trouble reading	1.42	1.18	3.40	2.42	2.54	1.25	14.77	CCI	3.46**
							12.13	MF	2.84*
Nominated best at computers	4.25	1.55	6.10	.92	4.15	3.08	14.98	MF	18.74***
Attitudes									
Goal orientation	22.92	24.70	22.10	20.30	21.86	21.91	38.06	CCI	4.21**

Task persistence	28.85	31.10	31.67	25.10	27.57	30.45	139.00	INT	5.71***
Co-operative	3.43	3.67	2.75	2.65	2.66	2.82	4.74	CCI	8.85****
Individualistic	2.82	3.19	3.32	3.58	3.23	3.68	1.37	CCI	2.37*
							2.11	MF	3.65*
Competitive	3.77	2.65	3.53	2.73	3.10	2.46	1.37	CCI	2.46*
							11.92	MF	23.94***
Teacher academic support	4.27	4.03	4.07	3.28	3.98	3.86	2.41	MF	4.11**
Teacher personal support	3.71	3.58	3.64	2.80	3.34	3.39			
Liking for geography	3.21	3.47	3.48	2.78	3.15	3.32			
Liked computers	3.68	4.06	4.20	3.13	3.89	3.96	1.88	MF	2.96*
							4.01	INT	6.32***
Computer confidence	3.82	4.00	4.15	3.20	3.74	3.70			
Computers male domain	2.14	1.69	2.09	1.81	2.27	1.32	3.76	MF	5.79**

Note. CCI = condition (co-operative, competitive, individualistic); INT = interaction; MF = male–female.
$df = 66$.
* $p < .10$. ** $p < .05$. *** $p < .01$. **** $p < .001$.

and computers than are boys, a specific comparison of the male and female students in the competitive condition was conducted. In the competitive condition, girls completed fewer worksheet items than did boys, accumulated less gold, expressed lower persistence, were less competitive, liked geography less, perceived less academic support from the teacher, perceived less personal support from the teacher, liked computers less, and had less confidence in their ability to work with computers (see Table 2).

Table 2.   Comparison between boys and girls on dependent measures in competitive condition

Measure	Boys		Girls		
	m	se_m	m	se_m	t
Worksheets completed	33.00	3.20	26.10	6.23	3.44*
Gold accumulated	30.64	10.31	6.30	3.49	2.21*
Achievement motivation	3.41	.17	2.86	.20	2.13*
Competitive	3.53	.21	2.73	.23	2.61*
Liked geography	3.48	.24	2.78	.23	2.10*
Teacher academic support	4.07	.16	3.28	.32	2.30*
Teacher personal support	3.63	.22	2.80	.27	2.43*
Liked computers	4.20	.25	3.13	.37	2.43*
Computer confidence	4.15	.26	3.20	.37	2.15*

Note. $df = 21$ for each variable.
*$p \leq .05$ **$p \leq .01$.

DISCUSSION

[. . .] The achievement results of this study parallel the findings of the previous research on co-operative, competitive, and individualistic learning situations and provide empirical confirmation of Clark's conclusion that computers are a vehicle that do not per se change the consequences of instruction. [. . .]

The results of this study clearly indicate that when computer-assisted co-operative, competitive, and individualistic learning were compared, computer-assisted co-operative learning promoted higher quantity and quality of daily achievement, greater mastery of factual information, greater ability to apply one's factual knowledge, and greater ability to use factual information to answer problem-solving questions. Students in the co-operative condition were far more successful in problem solving than were students in the competitive and individualistic conditions. Co-operation also promoted greater motivation to persist in striving to accomplish learning goals than did competitive and individualistic efforts. Given the complex problem solving required by the task, the conceptual material on mapping and navigation to be learned, and the additional problem of learning how to operate the computer program successfully, students co-operating with one another outperformed those competing with one another or working individualistically. These results corroborate the previous research comparing the impact of the three goal structures on students' achievement on tasks that did not require the use of the computer. The discussion, co-ordination, and joint actions taken by the students in the co-operative condition promoted greater conceptual understanding of the material by all students and greater retention of what they learned. The finding that students in the co-operative condition daily worked faster and more accurately than did the students in the competitive and individualistic conditions should reassure educators who worry that group discussion slows down the progress of students' learning.

The second issue examined in this study was the oral statements made by students while working with computers. All students were placed in groups of four, which were structured co-operatively, competitively, or individualistically. How learning goals were structured greatly influenced who students interacted with and what they tended to say. Within the competitive and individualistic learning situations, relatively few comments took place. [. . .] In the co-operative and individualistic conditions, no significant differences occurred in the oral interaction patterns of male and female students: in the competitive condition, the boys engaged in more off-task socializing than did the girls. Within the co-operative learning situation, students engaged in relatively frequent exchange of task-related information with almost no interaction with the teacher. The student–student interaction within the co-operative condition was almost entirely learning oriented, consisting of statements concerning the completion of the assigned work and the ways in which the group could best work to maximize their success. Such oral interchange has been related to use of higher level reasoning strategies, conceptual understanding, and long-term retention of information being learned. A number of researchers have concluded that the cognitive processes most necessary for deeper level understanding and the implanting of information into memory, such as elaboration and metacognition, occur only through dialogue and interaction with other people.[23-25] Co-operative learning promoted more of such interaction than did competitive and individualistic learning.

The third issue examined in this study was the attitudes toward computer-assisted instruction and the subject area being studied. There were no differences among conditions on these attitudes. These findings corroborated the previous research that boys and girls do not differ significantly in attitudes toward computers and girls do not perceive science to be a male domain. In this study the positive views of computer-assisted instruction seemed to extend to competitive and individualistic learning situations.

The fourth issue examined was the difference between male and female students in the three types of computer-assisted instruction situations. There were a number of interesting differences between the male and female students in the study. Boys performed higher on the recognition and problem-solving questions on the final examination, were less individualistic and more competitive, perceived more academic support from teachers, and perceived the computer to be more of a male domain. In the co-operative condition, girls liked working with computers more than did boys, whereas the opposite was true in the competitive condition. If educators wish to promote girls' success in using computers and positive attitudes toward working with computers, computer-assisted co-operative learning situations should be emphasized.

Competition among students over who was most successful in the computer-assisted instruction seemed to have an especially debilitating effect on the female students. Within the competitive condition, girls completed fewer worksheet items than did boys, performed less well on the problem-solving task (i.e., accumulated less gold), were less motivated to achieve (were less goal-oriented and persistent), felt less confident in their ability to work with computers, liked computers less, liked geography less, and felt less supported personally and academically by the teacher. The lower level of success girls had using the computer within the competitive condition and the negative attitudes toward computers they developed is of some concern. Social scientists warn that those who avoid computers will shut themselves out of a wide range of careers and opportunities.

Computers are reputed to be becoming indispensable in business, government, the sciences, and communication. If girls go through school feeling they cannot cope with technology, they will limit their career choices and will eliminate themselves from many higher level positions. It may be that the mixture of technology, science, and competition is especially detrimental to female achievement and attitudes.

When the comparative status of male and female students was examined, boys were nominated more frequently than were girls as being most able to influence other group members, as best as sports, as having trouble reading, and as best at using computers. Within the computer-assisted instructional situation, both boys and girls perceived the former to be of higher status.

The present study was one of the first to compare the effectiveness of co-operative, competitive, and individualistic goal structures in computer-assisted instruction. The results indicate that when teachers wish to maximize achievement in computer-assisted learning tasks they will be well-advised to structure the lesson co-operatively rather than competitively and individualistically. Girls will especially be adversely affected by competitively structured computer-assisted lessons. The combination of co-operative learning and computer-assisted instruction seems like a productive one for classroom learning.

REFERENCES

1. Johnson, D. W., and Johnson, R. (1983b) The socialization and achievement crisis: Are co-operative learning experiences the solution? in L. Bickman (Ed.), *Applied Social Psychology Annual 4*. Beverly Hills, CA, Sage.

2. Deutsch, M. (1962) Co-operation and trust: Some theoretical notes, in M. R. Jones (Ed.), *Nebraska Symposium on Motivation* (pp. 275–319), Lincoln, University of Nebraska Press.

3. Johnson, D. W., and Johnson, R. (1975) *Learning together and alone: Co-operation, competition, and individualization*, Englewood Cliffs, NJ, Prentice-Hall.

4. Kulik, J., Bangert, R., and Williams, G. (1983) Effects of computer-based teaching on secondary school students, *Journal of Educational Psychology*, 75, 19–26.

5. Clark, R. (1983) Reconsidering research on learning from media, *Review of Educational Research*, 53, 445–459.

6. Johnson, D. W., Maruyama, G., Johnson R., Nelson, C., and Skon, L. (1981) The effects of co-operative, competitive, and individualistic goal structures on achievement: A meta-analysis, *Psychological Bulletin*, 89, 47–62.

7. Sharan, S. (1980) Co-operative learning in teams: Recent methods and effects on achievement, attitudes, and ethnic relations, *Review of Educational Research*, 50, 241–272.

8. Rubin, A. (1980) Making stores, making sense, *Language Arts*, 57, 258–298.

9. Rubin, A. (1982) The computer confronts language arts: Cans and shoulds for education, in A. Wilkinson (Ed.), *Classroom computers and cognitive science*, New York, Academic Press.

10. Zacchei, D. (1982) The adventures and exploits of the dynamic storymaker and textman, *Classroom Computer News*, 2, 28–30.

11. Collins, A., Bruce, B., and Rubin, A. (1982) Microcomputer-based writing activities for the upper elementary grades, *Proceedings of the International Learning Technology Congress and Exposition*, Warrenton, VA, Society for Applied Learning Technology.

12. Jabs, C. (1981) Game playing allowed, *Electronic Learning*, 1, 5–6.

13. Johnson, R. T., Johnson, D., Scott, L. and Ramolae, B. (1985) Effects of single-sex and mixed sex co-operative interaction on science achievement and attitudes and cross-handicap and cross-sex relationships, *Journal of Research in Science Teaching*, 22, 207–220.

14. Steinkamp, M. (1982 April) *Sex-related differences in science attitude and achievement: A quantitative synthesis of research*. Paper presented at the annual meeting of the American Educational Research Association, New York.

15. Kolata, G. (1984, January) Equal time for women, *Discover*, pp. 24–27.

16. Hess, R., and Mjura, I. (in press) Gender and socioeconomic differences in enrolment in computer camps and classes, *Sex Roles*.

17. Kiesler, S., Sproull, L., and Eccles, J. (1983, March) Second-class citizens? *Psychology Today*, pp. 19–26.

18. Castleberry, S., Montague, E., and Lagowski, J. (1970) Computer-based

teaching techniques in general chemistry, *Journal of Research in Science Teaching, 7,* 197–208.

19. Johnson, D. W., and Ahlgren, A. (1976) Relationship between students' attitudes about co-operative learning and competition and attitudes toward schooling, *Journal of Educational Psychology, 68,* 29–102.

20. Johnson, D. W., Johnson, R., and Anderson, D. (1978) Relationship between student co-operative, competitive, and individualistic attitudes toward schooling, *Journal of Psychology, 100,* 183–199.

21. Snyder, T. (1982) *Geography search,* New York, Webster Division of McGraw-Hill.

22. Johnson, D. W., and Johnson, R. (1983a) Social interdependence and perceived academic and personal support in the classroom, *Journal of Social Psychology, 120,* 77–82.

23. Baker, L. (1979) *Comprehension monitoring: Identifying and coping with text confusions* (Tech. Rep. No. 145). Urbana, University of Illinois, Center for the Study of Reading.

24. Markman, E. (1979) Realizing that you don't understand: Elementary school children's awareness on inconsistencies, *Child Development, 50,* 643–655.

. Schallet, D. L., and Kleinman, G. (1979) *Some reasons why the teacher is easier to understand than the textbook* (Reading Education Rep. No. 9). Urbana, University of Illinois, Center for the Study of Reading. (ERIC Document Reproduction Service No. ED 172 189.

5.4 Child programmers: the first generation

- Sherry Turkle

[. . .] Do computers change the way children think? Do they open children's minds or do they dangerously narrow their experience, making their thinking more linear and less intuitive? There is a temptation to look for a universal, isolable effect, the sort that still eludes experts on the effect of television.

The problem here is the search for a universal effect. I have found that different children are touched in remarkably different ways by their experience with the computer. However, by looking closely at how individual children appropriate the computer we can build ways to think about how the computer enters into development, and we begin to get some answers to our questions. In a sense, I turn the usual question around: instead of asking what the computer does to children I ask what children, and more important, what different kinds of children make of the computer.

A SETTING FOR DIVERSITY

I observed child programmers in a variety of school settings [. . .] A private school that I shall call Austen, with children from preschool through fourth grade, was the site of a broadly conceived research project involving the design of a special computer, the training of a group of teachers, and a research program to study the children's progress. All the children at Austen had access to computers, and a group of about fifty third- and fourth-graders were offered a more intensive experience. Fifteen of them, chosen for the diversity of their backgrounds, interests and talents, were studied in depth. The school itself had a long tradition of open classrooms and flexible scheduling, which facilitated the integration of computers into classroom life. At almost any time of the day I saw children, working alone or in groups, at small personal computers scattered throughout the school.

At Austen, programming was not treated as a 'school subject.' The children had liberal access to the machines, to program as they wished. The general ferment of activity that resulted was so great that teachers could not closely monitor the children or impose an 'official' way of doing things even if they had wanted to. And in this case, there was also an explicit commitment to encouraging the children to appropriate the project as their own.

This is not a school that 'brought in some computers,' but a school that created conditions for the growth of a computer culture. The intention was to simulate a future where computers would be everyday objects in the life of the child.

The Austen School used the Logo computer language and [. . .] one of the most striking things about the Austen project was the way in which the creation of a child programming culture created new relationships between students, teachers, and curriculum.[1]

Commonplace assumptions about what happens in schools did not hold true for the computer-rich Austen classrooms: that teachers know more than students, that teachers are more interested than students, and that it is the teacher's job to design artful ways to motivate children to learn things that would not come naturally to them. [. . .]

At Austen we are faced with the growth of an intellectual community that we do not normally see among schoolchildren. What makes the community most special is that it includes children with a wide range of personalities, interests, and learning styles who express their differences through their styles of programming.

JEFF AND KEVIN

Jeff, a fourth grader, has a reputation as one of the school's computer experts. He is meticulous in his study habits, does superlative work in all subjects. His teachers were not surprised to see him excelling in programming. Jeff approaches the machine with determination and the need to be in control, the way he approaches both his schoolwork and his extracurricular activities. He likes to be, and often is, chairman of student committees. At the moment, his preoccupation with computers is intense: 'They're the biggest thing in my life right now.' He speaks very fast, and when he talks about his programs he speaks even faster, tending to monologue. He answers a question about what his program does by tossing off lines of computer code that for him seem to come as naturally as English. His typing is expert—he does not look at the code as it appears on the screen. He conveys the feeling that he is speaking directly to an entity inside. 'When I program I put myself in the place of the sprite. And I make it do things.'

Jeff is the author of one of the first space-shuttle programs. He does it, as he does most other things, by making a plan. There will be a rocket, boosters, a trip through the stars, a landing. He conceives the program globally; then he breaks it up into manageable pieces. 'I wrote out the parts on a big piece of cardboard. I saw the whole thing in my mind just in one night, and I couldn't wait to come to school to make it work.' Computer scientists will recognize this global 'top-down,' 'divide-and-conquer' strategy as 'good programming style.' And we all recognize in Jeff someone who conforms to our stereotype of a 'computer person' or an engineer—someone who would be good with machines, good at science, someone organized, who approaches the world of things with confidence and sure intent, with the determination to make it work.

Kevin is a very different sort of child. Where Jeff is precise in all of his actions, Kevin is dreamy and impressionistic. Where Jeff tends to try to impose his ideas on other children, Kevin's warmth, easygoing nature, and interest in others make him popular. Meetings with Kevin were often interrupted by his being called out to rehearse for a school play. The play was *Cinderella*, and he had been given the role of Prince Charming. Kevin comes from a military family; his father and grandfather were both in the Air Force. But Kevin has no intention of following in their footsteps. 'I don't want to be an army man. I don't want to be a fighting man. You can get killed.' Kevin doesn't like fighting or competition in general. 'You can avoid fights. I never get anybody mad—I mean, I try not to.'

Jeff has been playing with machines all his life—Tinkertoys, motors, bikes—but Kevin has never played with machines. He likes stories, he likes to read, he is proud of knowing the names of 'a lot of different trees.' He is artistic and introspective. When Jeff is asked questions about his activities, about what he thinks is fun, he answers in terms of how to do them right and how well he does them. He talks about video games by describing his strategy breakthroughs on the new version of Space Invaders: 'Much harder, much trickier than the first one.' By contrast, Kevin talks about experiences in terms of how they make him feel. Video games make him feel nervous, he says. The computer is better,' he adds. 'It's easier. You get more relaxed. You're not being bombarded with stuff all the time.'

Kevin too is making a space scene. But the way he goes about it is not at all like Jeff's approach. Jeff doesn't care too much about the detail of the form of his rocket ship; what is important is getting a complex system to work together as a whole. But Kevin cares more about the aesthetics of the graphics. He spends a lot of time on the shape of his rocket. He abandons his original idea ('It didn't look right against the stars') but continues to 'doodle' with the scratchpad shape-maker. He works without plan, experimenting, throwing different shapes onto the screen. He frequently stands back to inspect his work, looking at it from different angles, finally settling on a red shape against a black night—a streamlined, futuristic design. He is excited and calls over two friends. One admires the red on the black. The other says that the red shape 'looks like fire.' Jeff happens to pass Kevin's machine on the way to lunch and automatically checks out its screen, since he is always looking for new tricks to add to his toolkit for building programs. He shrugs.

'That's been done.' Nothing new there, nothing technically different, just a red blob.

Everyone goes away and Kevin continues, now completely taken up by the idea that the red looks like fire. He decides to make the ship white so that a red shape can be red fire 'at the bottom.' A long time is spent making the new red fireball, finding ways to give it spikes. And a long time is spent adding detail to the now white ship. With the change of colour, new possibilities emerge: 'More things will show up on it.' Insignias, stripes, windows, and the project about which Kevin is most enthusiastic: 'It can have a little seat for the astronaut.' When Jeff programs he puts himself in the place of the sprite; he thinks of himself as an abstract computational object. Kevin says that, as he works, 'I think of myself as the man inside the rocket ship. I daydream about it. I'd like to go to the moon.'

By the next day Kevin has a rocket with red fire at the bottom. 'Now I guess I should make it move . . . moving and wings . . . it should have moving and wings.' The wings turn out to be easy, just some more experimenting with the scratchpad. But he is less certain about how to get the moving right.

Kevin knows how to write programs, but his programs emerge—he is not concerned with imposing his will on the machine. He is concerned primarily with creating exciting visual effects and allows himself to be led by the effects he produces. Since he lets his plans change as new ideas turn up, his work has not been systematic. And he often loses track of things. Kevin has lovingly worked on creating the rocket, the flare, and a background of twinkling stars. Now he wants the stars to stay in place and the rocket and the flare to move through them together.

It is easy to set sprites in motion: just command them to an initial position and give them a speed and a direction. But Kevin's rocket and red flare are two separate objects (each shape is carried by a different sprite) and they have to be commanded to move together at the same speed, even though they will be starting from different places. To do this successfully, you have to think about co-ordinates and you have to make sure that the objects are identified differently so that code for commanding their movement can be addressed to each of them independently. Without a master plan Kevin gets confused about the code numbers he has assigned to the different parts of his program, and the flare doesn't stay with the rocket but flies off with the stars. It takes a lot of time to get the flare and the ship back together. When Jeff makes a mistake, he is annoyed, calls himself 'stupid,' and rushes to correct his technical error. But when Kevin makes an error, although it frustrates him he doesn't seem to resent it. He sometimes throws his arms up in exasperation: 'Oh no, oh no. What did I do?' His fascination with his effect keeps him at it.

In correcting his error, Kevin explores the system, discovering new special effects as he goes along. In fact, the 'mistake' leads him to a new idea: the flare shouldn't go off with the stars but should drop off the rocket, 'and then the rocket could float in the stars.' More experimenting, trying out of different colours, with different placements of the ship and the flare. He adds the moon, some planets. He tries out different trajectories for the rocket ship, different headings, and different speeds; more mistakes, more standing back and admiring his evolving canvas. By the end of the week Kevin too has programmed a space scene.

STYLES OF MASTERY

Jeff and Kevin represent cultural extremes. Some children are at home with the manipulation of formal objects, while others develop their ideas more impressionistically, with language or visual images, with attention to such hard-to-formalize aspects of the world as feeling, colour, sound, and personal rapport. Scientific and technical fields are usually seen as the natural home for people like Jeff; the arts and humanities seem to belong to the Kevins.

Watching Kevin and Jeff programming the same computer shows us two very different children succeeding at the same thing—and here it must be said that Kevin not only succeeded in creating a space scene, but, like Jeff, he learned a great deal about computer programming and mathematics, about manipulating angles, shapes, rates, and coordinates. But although succeeding at the same thing, they are not doing it the same way. Each child developed a distinctive style of mastery—styles that can be called hard and soft mastery.[2]

Hard mastery is the imposition of will over the machine through the implementation of a plan. A program is the instrument of premeditated control. Getting the program to work is more like getting 'to say one's piece' than allowing ideas to emerge in the give-and-take of conversation. The details of the specific program obviously need to be 'debugged'—there has to be room for change, for some degree of flexibility in order to get it right—but the goal is always getting the program to realize the plan.

Soft mastery is more interactive. Kevin is like a painter who stands back between brushstrokes, looks at the canvas, and only from this contemplation decides what to do next. Hard mastery is the mastery of the planner, the engineer, soft mastery is the mastery of the artist: try this, wait for a response, try something else, let the overall shape emerge from an interaction with the medium. It is more like a conversation than a monologue. [. . .]

MASTERY AND PERSONALITY

Computer programming is usually thought of as an activity that imposes its style on the programmer. And that style is usually presumed to be closer to Jeff and his structured, 'planner's' approach than to Kevin and his open, interactive one. In practice, computer programming allows for radical differences in style. And looking more closely at Jeff and Kevin makes it apparent that a style of dealing with the computer is of a piece with other things about the person—his or her way of facing the world, of coping with problems, of defending against what is felt as dangerous.[3] Programming style is an expression of personality style.

For example, the hard masters tend to see the world as something to be brought under control. [. . .] Jeff is popular and sociable, but he likes to be committee chairman, the one who controls the meeting. From the earliest ages most of these children have preferred to operate on the manipulable—on blocks, on Tinkertoys, on mechanisms. It is not surprising that the 'hards' sometimes have more difficulty with the give-and-take of the playground. When your needs for control are too great, relationships with people become tense and strained. The computer offers a 'next-best' gratification. The Tinkertoy is inert. The computer is responsive. Some children even feel that when they master it they are dominating something that 'fights back.' It is not surprising that hard masters take avidly to the computer. It is also not surprising that their style of working with the computer emphasizes the imposition of will.

The soft masters are more likely to see the world as something they need to accommodate to, something beyond their direct control. In general, these children have played not with model trains and Erector sets but with toy soldiers or with dolls. They have taken the props (cowboy hats, guns, and grownup clothes for dress-up) from the adult world and used them in fantasy play with other children. In doing so, they have learned how to negotiate, compromise, emphathize. They tend to feel more impinged upon, more reactive. As we have seen, this accommodating style is expressed in their relational attitude toward programming as well as in their relationships with people.

Very young children find the computer evocative because it seems to stand betwixt and between the world of alive and not alive. The sprite, the computational object that is there to command on the screen, is also evocative. It stands between the world of physical objects and the world of abstract ideas. Ambivalent in its nature, it is taken up differently by the hard and soft masters, the hard masters treating it more like an abstract entity—a Newtonian particle—the soft masters treating it more as a physical object: a dab of paint, a building block, a cardboard cut-out.

Jeff sees the system of Logo sprites as a formal system, something apart from his everyday life. He identifies with an abstract piece of it. He objectified the sprite, saw it as a thing apart, and then put himself in its place in order to command its actions. Jeff said, 'I'm a sprite in there.' The soft master identifies differently. Kevin did not objectify the sprite, he did not become the abstract thing—he took who he feels himself to be and entered a new world of make-believe. He said, 'I'm me in there, driving the spaceship.'

Identification is not for an instrumental purpose, but in the service of fantasy.

[. . .] MASTERY AND GENDER

I have used boys as examples in order to describe hard and soft mastery without reference to gender. But now it is time to state what might be anticipated by many readers: girls tend to be soft masters, while the hard masters are overwhelmingly male. At Austen, girls are trying to forge relationships with the computer that bypass objectivity altogether. They tend to see computational objects as sensuous and tactile and relate to the computer's formal system not as a set of unforgiving 'rules,' but as a language for communicating with, negotiating with, a behaving, psychological entity.

There are many reasons why we are not surprised that girls tend to be soft masters. In our culture girls are taught the characteristics of soft mastery—negotiation, compromise, give-and-take—as psychological virtues, while models of male behavior stress decisiveness and the imposition of will. Boys and girls are encouraged to adopt these stances in the world of people. It is not surprising that they show up when children deal with the world of things. The girl child plays with dolls, imagined not as objects to command but as children to nurture. When the boy unwraps his birthday presents they are most likely to be Tinkertoys, blocks, Erector sets—all of which put him in the role of builder.

Thinking in terms of dolls and Erector sets, like talking about teaching negotiation and control, suggests that gender differentiation is a product of the social construction that determines what toys and what models of correct behavior are given to children of each sex. Psychoanalytic thought suggests many ways in which far earlier processes could have their role to play; styles of mastery may also be rooted in the child's earliest experiences. One school of thought, usually referred to as 'object relations theory,' is particularly rich in images that suggest a relation between styles of mastery and gender differences.

It portrays the infant beginning life in a closely bonded relationship with the mother, one in which boundaries between self and other are not clear. Nor does the child experience a separation between the self and the outer world.[4] The gradual development of a consciousness of separate existence begins with a separation from the mother. It is fraught with conflict. On the one hand, there is a desire to return to the comfort of the lost state of oneness. On the other hand, there is the pleasure of autonomy, of acting on independent desire. Slowly the infant develops the sense of an 'objective' reality 'out there' and separate from the self. Recently, there has been serious consideration of the ways in which this process may take on a sense of gender. Since our earliest and most compelling experiences of merging are with the mother, experiences where boundaries are not clear become something 'female.' Differentiation and delineation, first worked through in a separation from the mother, are marked as 'not-mother,' not-female.

Up to this point the experiences are common to girls and boys. But at the Oedipal stage, there is a fork in the road. The boy is involved in a fantasized romance with the mother. The father steps in to break it up and, in doing so, strikes another blow against fusional relationships. It is also another chance to see the pressure for separation as male. This is reinforced by the fact that this time the boy gives up the idea of a romance with the mother through identifying himself with his father. Thus, for the boy, a separation from the mother is more brutal, because in a certain sense it happens twice: first in the loss of the original bonded relationship, then again at the point of the Oedipal struggle.

Since separation from the mother made possible the first experiences of the world as 'out there,' we might call it the discovery of the 'objective.' Because the boy goes through this separation twice, for him objectivity becomes more highly charged. Boys feel a greater desire for it: the objective, distanced relationship feels like safe, approved ground. There is more of a taboo on the fusional, along with a correspondingly greater fear of giving in to its forbidden pleasures. According to this theory the girl is less driven to objectivity because she is allowed to maintain more elements of the old fusional relationship with the mother, and, correspondingly, it is easier for her to play with the pleasures of closeness with other objects as well.[5]

ANNE AND MARY

In the eyes of a true hard programmer like Jeff, his classmate Anne, also nine, is an enigma. On the one hand, she hardly seems serious about the computer. She is willing to spend days creating shimmering patterns on the screen in a kind of 'moiré effect' and she doesn't seem to care whether she gets her visual effects with what Jeff would classify as technically uninteresting 'tricks' or with what he would see as 'really interesting' methods. Jeff knows that all the children anthropomorphize the computer to a certain extent; everyone says things like 'My program knows how to do this' or 'You have to tell the computer what speed you want the sprites to go,' but Anne carries anthropomorphizing to what, to Jeff, seems like extreme lengths. For example, she insists on calling the computer 'he,' with the explanation 'It doesn't seem right to call it an it.' All the same, this doesn't keep her from getting down to serious programming. She has made some technical inventions, and Jeff and the other male hard masters recognize that if they want to keep abreast of the state of the art at Austen they must pay attention to what Anne is doing. And Anne knows how to take advantage of her achievements. She analogizes the spread of programming ideas to the game of telephone and enjoys seeing versions of her ideas on half a dozen screens. 'They didn't copy me exactly, but I can recognize my idea.' Jeff's grudging acknowledgement of Anne's 'not quite serious' accomplishments seems almost a microcosm of reactions to competent women in society as a whole. There, as at Austen, there is appreciation, incomprehension, and ambivalence.

When Jeff talks with the other male experts about the computer, they usually talk 'shop' about technical details. Anne, on the other hand, likes to discuss her strong views about the machine's psychology. She has no doubt that computers have psychologies: they 'think,' as people do, although they 'can't really have emotions.' Nevertheless, the computer might have preferences. 'He would like it if you did a pretty program.' When it comes to technical things, she assumes the computer has an aesthetic: 'I don't know if he would rather have the program be very complicated or very simple.'

Anne thinks about whether the computer is alive. She says that the computer is 'certainly not alive like a cat,' but it is 'sort of alive,' it has 'alive things.' Her evidence comes from the machine's responsive behaviour. As she types her instructions into the machine, she comments, 'You see, this computer is close to being alive because he does what you are saying.'

This remark is reminiscent of the talk among the somewhat younger children who were preoccupied with sorting out the computer's status as a living or a not living thing. There is, however, a difference. For the younger children, these questions have a certain theoretical urgency. For Anne, they are both less urgent and part of a practical philosophy: she has woven this way of seeing the computer into her style of technical mastery.

Anne wants to know how her programs work and to understand her failures when they don't. But she draws the line between understanding and not understanding in a way that is different from most of the hard master boys at a similar degree of competence. For them, a program (like anything else built out of the elements of a formal system) is either right or wrong. Programs that are correct in their general structure are not 'really correct' until the small errors, the bugs, are removed. For a hard programmer like Jeff, the bugs are there to ferret out. Anne, on the other hand, makes no demand that her programs be perfect. To a certain degree, although to put it too flatly would be an exaggeration, when she programs the computer she treats it as a person. People can be understood only incompletely: because of their complexity, you can expect to understand them only enough to get along, as well as possible for maintaining the kind of relationship you want. And when you want people to do something, you don't insist that it be done exactly as you want it, but only 'near enough.' Anne allows a certain amount of negotiation with the computer about just what should be an acceptable program. For her, the machine is enough alive to deserve a compromise.

This 'negotiating' and 'relational' style is pervasive in Anne's work but is more easily described by an example from her classmate Mary, another soft-mastery programmer and an even stauncher lobbyist for the use of personal pronouns to refer to computers. Mary differs strikingly from Anne in having a soft style that is verbal where Anne's is consistently visual.

Mary wanted to add a few lines of dialogue to the end of a game program. Her original idea was that the computer would ask the player, 'Do you want to play another game?' If the player typed 'Yes,' a new game would start. If the player typed 'No,' the machine would print out the final score and 'exit' the program—that is, put the machine back into a state where it is ready for anything, back to 'top level.' She writes a program that has two steps, captured in the following English-language rendition of the relevant Logo instructions:

> If what-the-user-types is 'Yes,' start a new game.
> If what-the-user-types is 'No,' print score and stop.

As instructions to an intelligent person, these two statements are unambiguous. Not so as instructions to a computer. The program 'runs,' but not quite as Mary originally planned. The answer 'Yes' produces the 'right' behaviour, a new game. But in order to get the final score and exit, it is necessary to type 'No' twice. Mary knew this meant there was an 'error,' but she liked this bug. She saw the behaviour as a humanlike quirk.

What was behind the quirk? The computer is a serial machine; it executes each instruction independently. It gets up to the first instruction that tells it to wait until the user types something. If this something is 'Yes,' a new game is started up. If the user doesn't type 'Yes,' if, for example, he or she types 'No,' the computer does nothing except pass on to the next instruction without 'remembering' what has come before. The second instruction, like the first, tells the computer to wait until the user has typed something. And if this something is 'No,' to print the score and stop.

Now the role of the two 'Nos' is clear. A single 'No' will leave the computer trying to obey the second instruction—that is, waiting for the user to type something. There are ways of fixing this bug, but what is important here is the difference in attitude between a programmer like Jeff, who would not rest until he fixed it, and a programmer like Mary, who could figure out how to fix it but decides not to. Mary *likes* this bug because it makes the machine appear to have more of a personality. It lets you feel closer to it. As Mary puts it, 'He will not take no for an answer' unless you really insist. She allows the computer its idiosyncrasies and happily goes on to another program.

Mary's work is marked by her interest in language. Anne's is equally marked by her hobby, painting. She uses visual materials to create strategies for feeling 'close to the machine.'

Anne has become an expert at writing programs to produce visual effects of appearance and disappearance. In one, a flock of birds flies through the sky, disappears at the horizon and reappears some other place and time. If all the birds are the same colour, such as red, then disappearance and appearance could be produced by the commands 'SETCOLOUR :INVISIBLE' to get rid of them and 'SETCOLOUR :RED' to make them appear. But since Anne wants the birds to have different colours, the problem of the birds reappearing with their original colour is more complicated.

There is a classical method for getting this done: get the program to 'store away' each bird's original colour before changing that colour to 'invisible,' and then to recall the colour when the birds are to reappear. This method calls for an algebraic style of thinking. You have to think about variables and use a variable for each bird—for example, letting A equal the colour of the first bird, B the colour of the second bird, and so on. Anne will use this kind of method when she has to, but she prefers another kind, a method of her own invention that has a different feel.

She likes to feel that she is there among her birds, manipulating them much in the way she can manipulate physical materials. When you want to hide something on a canvas, you paint it out, you cover it with something that looks like the background. This is Anne's solution. She lets each bird keep its colour, but she makes her program 'hide it' by placing a screen over it. She designs a sprite that will screen the bird when she doesn't want it seen, a sky-coloured screen that makes it disappear. Just as the computer can be programmed to make a bird-shaped object on the screen, it can be programmed to make an opaque sky-coloured square act as a screen.

Anne is programming a computer, but she is thinking like a painter. She is not thinking about sprites and variables. She is thinking about birds and screens. Anne's way of making birds appear and disappear doesn't make things technically easy. On the contrary, to maintain her programming aesthetic requires technical sophistication and ingenuity.[6]

For example, how does the program 'know' where the bird is so as to place the screen on it? Anne attaches the screen to the bird when the bird is created, instead of putting it on later. The screen is on top of the bird at all times and moves with the bird wherever it goes. Thus she has invented a new kind of object, a 'screened bird.' When Anne wants the bird to be seen, the screen is given the 'invisible' colour, so the bird, whatever its colour, shows right through it. When she wants the bird to disappear, the screen is given the colour of the sky. The problem of the multiplicity of bird colours is solved. A bird can have any colour. But the screens need only two colours, invisible or sky blue. A bird gets to keep its colour at all times. It is only the colour of its screen that changes. The problem of remembering the colour of a particular bird and reassigning it at a particular time has been bypassed.

Anne's bird program is particularly ingenious, but its programming style is characteristic of many of the girls in her class. Most of the boys seem driven by the pleasures of mastering and manipulating a formal system: for them, the operations, the programming instructions, are what it is all about. For Anne, pleasure comes from being able to put herself into the space of the birds. Her method of manipulating screens and birds allows her to feel that these objects are close, not distant and untouchable things that need designation by variables. The ambivalence of the computational sprite—an object at once physical and abstract—allows it to be picked up differently by hards and softs. Anne responds to the sprites as physical objects. Her work with them is intimate and direct. The formal operations need to be mastered, but they are not what drive her.

No one would find Anne's relation to the birds and the screens surprising if it were in the context of painting or making collages with scraps of this and that. There we expect to find 'closeness to the object.' But finding a sensual aesthetic in the development of a computer program surprises us. We tend to think of programming as the manipulation of a formal system which, like the objects for scientific inquiry, is 'out there' to be operated on as something radically split from the self.

GENDER AND SCIENCE

Evelyn Keller has coined the phrase 'the genderization of science.' She argues that what our culture defines as the scientific stance toward the world corresponds to the kind of relationships with the object world that most men (if we follow psychoanalytic theories of development) would be expected to find most comfortable.[7] It is a relationship that cuts off subject from object.

Scientific objects are placed in a 'space' psychologically far away from the world of everyday life, from the world of emotion and relationships. Men seem able, willing, and invested in constructing these separate 'objective' worlds, which they can visit as neutral observers. In this way the scientific tradition that takes objectivity as its hallmark is also defined as a male preserve. Taking it from the other side, we can see why men would be drawn to this construction of science. Men are highly invested in objective relationships with the world. Their earliest experiences have left them with a sense of the fusional as taboo, as something to be defended against. Science, which represents itself as revealing a reality in which subject and object are radically separated, is reassuring. We can also see why women might experience a conflict between this construction of science and what feels like 'their way' of dealing with the world, a way that leaves more room for continuous relationships between self and other. Keller adds that the presentation of science as an extreme form of objective thinking has been reinforced by the way in which male scientists traditionally write and speak about their work. A characterization of science that appears to 'gratify particular emotional needs' may 'give rise to a self-selection of scientists—a self-selection which would in turn lead to a perpetuation of that characterization.[8]

In Anne's classroom, nine- and ten-year-old girls are just beginning to program. The fact that they relate to computational objects differently from boys raises the question of whether with growing expertise they will maintain their style or whether we are simply seeing them at an early stage before they become 'recuperated' into a more objective computational culture. In my observation, with greater experience soft masters, male and female, reap the benefits of their long explorations, so that they appear more decisive and more like 'planners' when they program on familiar terrains. But the 'negotiating' and 'relational' style remains behind the appearance and resurfaces when they tackle something new.

Lorraine is the only woman on a large team working on the design of a new programming language. She expresses her sense of difference with some embarrassment.

> I know that the guys I work with think I'm crazy. But we will be working on a big program and I'll have a dream about what the program feels like inside and somehow the dream will help me through.
>
> When I work on the system I know that to everybody else it looks like I'm doing what everyone else is doing, but I'm doing that part with only a small part of my mind. The rest of me is imagining what the components feel like. It's like doing my pottery . . . Keep this anonymous. I know this sounds stupid.

Shelley is a graduate student in computer science who corrects me sharply when I ask her when she got interested in electronics and machines. 'Machines,' she responds, 'I am definitely not into machines.' And she is even less involved with electronics:

> My father was an electrician and he had all of these machines around. All of these wires, all of this stuff. And he taught my brothers all about it. But all I remember him telling me was, 'Don't touch it, you'll get a shock.' I hate machines. But I don't think of computers as machines. I think of moving pieces of language around. Not like making a poem, the way you would usually think of moving language around, more like making a piece of language sculpture.

These words are reminiscent of women in other scientific disciplines. Barbara McClintock, an eminent biologist, describes her work as an ongoing 'conversation' with her materials, and she speaks of frustration with the way science is usually done: 'If you'd only just let the materials speak to you . . .'[9] In an interview with her biographer, Evelyn Keller, McClintock described her studies of neurospora chromosomes (so small that others had been unable to identify them) in terms that recall Anne's relationship with the birds and the screens. 'The more she worked with the chromosomes, the bigger they got, until finally, "I wasn't outside, I was down there—I was part of the system." . . . As "part of the system" even the internal parts of the chromosomes become visible. "I actually felt as if I were down there and these were my friends." '[10]

Keller comments that McClintock's 'fusion' with her objects of study is something experienced by male scientists. But perhaps McClintock was able to exploit this less distanced model of scientific thought, far from the way science was discussed in the 1950s, more fully, visibly, and less self-consciously, because she is a woman. This is surely the case for the girls in the Austen classrooms. Their artistic, interactive style is culturally sanctioned. Of course, with children, as in the larger world, the lines of division are not rigid. Some girls are hard masters and I purposely took a boy as the first case of a soft master—Kevin, who did not see the sprites as 'outside' but who is right there with them, who imagines himself a traveler in the rocket ship, taking himself and his daydreams with him.

Children working with computers are a microcosm for the larger world of relations between gender and science. Jeff took the sprite as an object apart and in a world of its own. When he entered the sprite world, it was to command it better. Kevin used the sprite world to fantasize in. Anne does something more. She moves further in the direction I am calling 'feminine,' further in the direction of seeing herself as in the world of the sprite, further in the direction of seeing the sprite as sensuous rather than abstract. When Anne puts herself into the sprite world, she imagines herself to be a part of the system, playing with the birds and the screens as though they were tactile materials.

Science is usually defined in the terms of the hard masters: it is the place for the abstract, the domain for a clear and distinct separation between subject and object. If we accept this definition, the Austen classroom, with its male hard masters, is a microcosm of the male genderization of science. But what about Anne and Mary? What about the other girls like them who are exploring and mastering the computer? Should we not say that they too are 'little scientists'? If we do, then we see at Austen not only a model of the male model that characterizes 'official science,' but a model of how women, when given a chance, can find another way to think and talk about the mastery not simply of machines but of formal systems. And here the computer may have a special role. It provides an entry to formal systems that is more accessible to women. It can be negotiated with, it can be responded to, it can be psychologized.

The computer sits on many borders; it is a formal system that can be taken up in a way that is not separate from the experience of the self. As such, it may evoke unconscious memories of objects that lie for the child in the uncertain zone between self and not-self. These are the objects, like Linus' baby blanket, the tattered rag doll, or the bit of silk from a first pillow, to which children remain attached even as they embark on the exploration of the world beyond the nursery. Psychoanalytic theorists call these objects 'transitional' because they are thought to mediate between the child's closely bonded relationship with the mother and his or her capacity to develop relationships with other people who will be experienced as separate, autonomous beings.[11] They are experienced as an almost inseparable part of the infant and the first not-me possession. As the child grows, the actual objects are discarded, but the experience of them remains diffused in the intense experiencing throughout life of an intermediate space. Music and religious experience share with the early transitional objects the quality of being felt simultaneously from within and from without.[12] So do creative moments in science and mathematics.

The idea of 'formality' in scientific thought implies a separateness from the fuzzy, imprecise flow of the rest of reality. But using a formal system creatively, and still more, inventing it, requires it to be interwoven with the scientist's most intuitive and metaphorical thinking. In other words, it has to be mastered in a soft form.

So, in addition to suggesting a source of the computer's holding power, women's relationships with computational objects and the idea of the transitional object may illuminate the holding power of the formal systems for people who are in the closest contact with them. Even for the hard masters, the 'feminine' may be the glue that bonds.[13] [. . .]

NOTES AND REFERENCES

1. I followed the Austen project from its inception, spoke to the teachers during training, and then when the machines were in place observed and interviewed the students and had access to the results of the psychological tests—Rorschach, WISC (IQ), Locus of Control—that had been administered to the fifteen children selected for special study. The study of the Austen students was a collaborative effort with Seymour Papert and John Berlow.

2. The classification 'hard' and 'soft' is related to several other distinctions. Herman Witkin introduced an influential dichotomy by defining two basic cognitive styles: field independent and field dependent. The former implies firmer barriers between self and nonself and a greater tendency to rely on internal referents. Another related dichotomy is J. B. Rotter's concept of locus space of control. Individuals have internal locus of control when they tend to believe that they make events happen; they have external locus of control when they tend to see events as 'happening to them.' Internal locus of control is conceptually closer to hard than to soft. It is also empirically closer. Locus of control tests were administered to the children at Austen and the hards showed an internal and the softs an external locus. See Herman Witkin, *Cognitive Styles in Personal and Cultural Adaptation*, Worcester, Mass, Clark University Press, 1978; J. B. Rotter, *Social Learning and Clinical Psychology* New York, Prentice-Hall, 1954; and J. B. Rotter, 'Generalized Expectancies for Internal versus External Control of Reinforcement,' *Psychological Monographs* 80 (1966). Other dichotomies that suggest themselves for further correlative study include convergent/divergent, verbal/spatial, and 'left brain'/'right brain.'

   The concept of hard and soft had its roots in Papert, Watt, diSessa, and Weir, 'Final Report of the Brookline Logo Project.' The authors make a distinction between the cognitive styles of planners and tinkerers. In my work, hard and soft refers also to a quality of interaction with the computer and a quality of identification with computational objects.

3. Not all computer systems, not all computer languages offer a material that is

flexible enough for differences in style to be expressed. A language such as BASIC does not make it easy to achieve successful results through a variety of programming styles. This does not make BASIC any less adequate as a computer language. It means that it provides a less malleable material for different styles of use. In the Austen School the conditions were right for a wide variety of children to form very different relationships with programming. The environment allowed freedom to experiment, and the computer system was designed to go further than most in allowing for a diversity of approaches.

4. See D. W. Winnicott, *Playing and Reality*, New York, Basic Books, 1971.
5. See Evelyn Fox Keller, 'Gender and Science,' *Psychoanalysis and Contemporary Thought* 1 (1978), pp. 409–33. My studies of women were deeply influenced by the work of Nancy Chodorow; see *The Reproduction of Mothering: Psychoanalysis and the Sociology of Gender*, Berkeley, University of California Press, 1978, and Carol Gilligan; see In *a Different Voice: Psychological Theory and Women's Development*, Cambridge, Mass, Harvard University Press, 1982.
6. The idea of a screened bird makes unusual use of a feature of the LOGO system where moving objects are built out of screen sprites, each of which can be thought of as a mobile frame about half an inch square. On each sprite you can draw a picture. Large objects such as Jeff and Kevin's rocket ships are made by placing sprite side by side to make a large picture. Anne's birds are small enough to be drawn on a single sprite. Her innovation consisted of using two sprites (one for the screen, one for the bird) and placing them one on top of the other so that they occupy the same space, rather than side by side. To make them move together as a single object, she applied the techniques Jeff and Kevin used for keeping their compound objects together, but instead of thinking of the compound objects as a way of getting more size, Anne thinks of them as a way of getting more complexity of behaviour.
7. Keller, 'Gender and Science.'
8. Ibid, p. 427. In a classic work in the sociology science, Ian Mitroff studied the relationship of Apollo moon scientists to their work. He note the 'intense masculinity' and 'aggressiveness' of these scientists: 'It is an aggressiveness that not only deeply infuses their relationships with one another, but, as we have seen, their abstract concept of science . . . They were free and quick in displaying aggressive or harsh emotions; they were far less free, however, in displaying more affective or soft emotions. In this sense they do avoid complex human emotions. They displayed only one half of the sphere of human emotionality and that hemisphere with such an intensity that it tended to obliterate the other.' See Ian Mitroff, *The Subjective Side of Science*, New York and Amsterdam, Elsevier Scientific Publishing, 1974, pp. 144–145.
9. Keller, 'Women, Science, and Popular Mythology,' unpublished manuscript. See also Evelyn Keller, *A Feeling for the Organism: The Life and Work of Barbara McClintock*, San Francisco, W. H. Freeman, 1983.
10. Keller, 'Women, Science, and Popular Mythology.'
11. Winnicott, *Playing and Reality*, p. 2.
12. Ibid., p. 5.
13. Mitroff's study of the Apollo moon scientists showed that although the scientists were 'masculine' in their aggressivity and judged affective and inter-personal dimensions as irrelevant to their concept of the 'Ideal Scientists,' they also

'insisted that it was not an either/or between analysis and speculation, rationality and intuition, and so on.' The Subjective Side of Science, p. 143. Mitroff takes up this theme in 'Passionate Scientists,' Society (September-October 1976), pp. 51–57.

6 TEACHER AND COMPUTER, TEACHER OR COMPUTER?

In this section we look at various roles available to teachers, pupils and the computer—and how they may help in achieving our target aims. In the three papers the computer has quite different roles: as a resource (Fraser); as coach, (Lesgold), and as learner (Self).

Fraser *et al.* refer to the Cockroft report which calls for opportunities for (among others) discussion between teacher and pupil, between the pupils themselves, problem-solving and investigative work. These match some of our target aims: problem-solving skills, a capacity for systematic enquiry, information-handling ability, and decision-making skills. The authors point out that most lessons do not involve pupils in more open-ended higher level skills. They argue that teachers need to take on new roles in order for pupils to develop such skills. They suggest that the micro helps teachers to adopt different roles—for example counsellor, or consultant, by taking on some of the teacher's roles, and by having a distinct personality which enables teachers to distance themselves from it. This would suggest that another of our target aims might be achieved—effective co-operation between pupils, and pupils and teacher.

Lesgold discusses tutoring sytems in which the computer acts as problem setter, diagnoser and coach, taking up roles closer to those in the traditional teacher model. The aim here is consolidation and practice in arithmetic: the intelligence is in guiding that practice, and to do it effectively the computer must have some information about the student's present knowledge, be able to diagnose errors, and also know when to intervene.

Self argues that approaches such as Lesgold's embody a view of the learner conforming to some expert's pre-determined standard; not allowing the learner to have different methods or goals. The focus is on how to do the task, rather than what the learner does or knows. He suggests an alternative approach of guided discovery learning systems which puts the learner back in control. Again, this seems more likely to achieve aims that we have discussed.

6.1 Learning activities and classroom roles with and without the microcomputer

- Rosemary Fraser, Hugh Burkhardt, Jon Coupland, Richard Phillips, David Pimm and Jim Ridgway

This paper is concerned with the range and balance of learning activities in the classroom and with elucidating how the various roles assumed by those involved relate to these activities. The analysis is based on records of the detailed observation of 174 mathematics lessons; the use of the micro-computer as a teaching aid in parts of these lessons was a crucial element in the analysis, giving insight through its perturbation of the familiar pattern of roles and activities. This enabled us to develop a taxonomy relating observable classroom activities, inferred learning activities and the roles played by the teacher, the pupils and, when it was in use, the computer. Exemplar lessons are described; they have been chosen to illustrate the taxonomy and the shifting and sharing of roles that we most commonly observed. Among other results, it is shown that the micro is regarded by the pupils as an independent 'personality' and that, suitably programmed, it can temporarily take over some of the roles usually assumed by the teacher in such a way that the teacher adopts other roles, rarely found in the classroom, that are essential to the promotion of higher level learning activities.

1. INTRODUCTION

The problem

The range and balance of learning activities found in nearly every classroom is very much narrower than that recognised to be essential if the pupils are to acquire the skills and understanding sufficient for them to be effective performers in the various facets of the curriculum at anything like the level at which they are currently taught. Factual recall and skill exercises of an imitative kind predominate over activities which develop the other, higher level skills needed effectively to marshal the facts and employ the skills in tackling realistic tasks.

This is a serious problem at many levels. Historians look for balanced reasoned argument from facts but find only facts recalled in a narrative fashion. Physicists, chemists and biologists look for a scientific approach to phenomena and experimental design but find only factual recall or the application of given rules. In mathematics the situation has been crisply summarized by the Cockcroft Committee of Inquiry into the Teaching of Mathematics in Primary and Secondary Schools in its report 'Mathematics Counts'.[1]

243 Mathematics teaching at all levels should include opportunities for
- exposition by the teacher;
- discussion between teacher and pupils and between pupils themselves;
- appropriate practical work;
- consolidation and practice of fundamental skills and routines;
- problem solving, including the application of mathematics to everyday situations;
- investigational work.

In setting out this list we are aware that we are not saying anything which has not already been said many times and over many years. The list which we have given has appeared, by implication if not explicitly, in official reports, DES publications, HMI discussion papers and the journals and publications of the professional mathematical associations. Yet we are aware that although there are some classrooms in which the teaching includes, as a matter of course, all the elements which we have listed, there are still many in which the mathematics teaching does not include even a majority of these elements.

Based on a variety of evidence, particularly the HMI Secondary Survey[2] of over 50,000 hours of teaching in over 300 schools, this firm but tactful summary reflects the predominance of teacher exposition and pupil practice in imitative technical exercises and the virtual absence of practical work, problem solving, more open investigations and discussion as regular activities in classrooms.

It is not for lack of encouragement or exhortation that so many teachers have not widened the spectrum of learning activities in their classrooms—clearly it cannot be easy so to do. These difficulties have not been adequately faced; to understand them better, we need to know more about the dynamics of teaching and learning in the classroom and the demands and pressures on the teacher. This requires analysis based on a fairly fundamental look at the problems, to which this present study seeks to contribute.

The aim

In this paper we accept the position that such a restricted curriculum cannot expect to produce children and adults who can use what they have learnt outside the restricted frame in which they have met it and that a balanced spectrum of learning activities is thus a prime educational objective. We look for reasons for the general imbalance, paying particular attention to the various roles played by teacher and pupils in these classroom activities.

We show how the presence of a microcomputer, suitably programmed for use as a teaching aid, introduces a powerful new factor which, in taking on some of the roles enables the teacher naturally to assume others that are normally difficult to adopt or to sustain—particularly those associated with these missing, more 'open' classroom activities. This work has implications beyond the classroom which are discussed elsewhere.[3]

Although the microcomputer plays a central role in this work, perhaps the most important results, in particular the classification of roles and activities in Section 2, relate to the teaching and learning processes themselves which are re-examined in responding to this new stimulus.

The study

The analysis of the interrelation between visible classroom activities, the learning activities that can be inferred and the roles played at various times by teacher, micro and pupils, forms the content of this paper. This analysis and the resulting classification is primarily based on a systematic study of 174 mathematics lessons taught in the Autumn term of 1981 to 17 classes of 12–14 year old pupils by their teachers, whose individual styles and approaches together covered a wide range. The study is described in detail in a separate paper.[4] In summary, the teachers agreed to use a micro in the course of one mathematics lesson per week with the class concerned, choosing freely from a collection of 97 program teaching units supplied to them;

each of these lessons was observed and a detailed record compiled containing observational data of three different kinds:

1. A few facts recorded in a standard form,
2. A structured event-by-event description, using a Systematic Classroom Analysis Notation (SCAN) developed earlier,[5] which gives a rich and detailed picture of the pattern of teaching in the lesson,
3. Notes by the observer on any important aspects of the lesson not picked up by the more systematic elements 1. and 2.

Discussion with the teacher, and with individual pupils, during the lesson, material used and pupil work are other important elements in the total observation system.[6] Immediately after the lesson, following discussion with the teacher, the observer summarised the information in a lesson report of a few hundred words. The aim was to provide enough data to enable others not present to analyse the lesson in terms that would prove convincing to the observer; we found that this aim was achieved. Enough cross-observation was undertaken to indicate that disparity between observers was not a serious problem. [. . .]

While the range of normal teaching style encompassed by the 17 teachers was wide, in some other respects the coverage was narrow. Only a few had extensive experience of using the micro in their teaching; most were using it for the first time. By the end of the term all were accustomed to it and the practical handling problems did not generally seem to distort the pattern of classroom interactions seriously, though there are a number of important ergonomic implications that emerge.[7] In almost every case the teachers were using the individual teaching units for the first time so, with a few clearly identifiable exceptions, this was a study of the use of 'unfamiliar' material. It is therefore particularly notable that in their choice of programs to use, teachers mainly went for the richer more complex ones. [. . .] Substantial amounts of teaching *without* the micro were also observed for each teacher in the course of the term, largely in those parts of each observed lesson when it was not in action.

The micro as a 'personality'

The systematic use of computers in this way is a relatively new field. The overwhelming majority of computer assisted learning (CAL) material has been designed for use by an individual student at his own microcomputer or computer terminal, which takes on the complete teaching function for the period of use. (The difficulties of designing material that will be effective in this mode for anything but factual recall and routine exercising have gradually become clearer.) The use of a single microcomputer as a class teaching aid produces a quite different situation—the teacher remains fully involved and programs should be designed to help the teacher utilise the talents of the pupils, the micro and themselves appropriately; the situation is thus more complex, but equally more secure in that the micro need only take over those functions that it can effectively assume [. . .] The value of this approach has been confirmed by several qualitatively important factors that have emerged, some of which are surprising.

(a) The micro has an effective 'personality', and an associated independence, that are not displayed by other classroom resources. This allows teachers to distance themselves from the micro and, most importantly, to join with the pupils in relating to it, adopting a consultative, counselling role that seems to be excluded in practice for most teachers by their normal and necessary authoritative, didactic posture. This independence of the micro in the pupils' eyes is remarkable in view of its overall control by the teacher (just as with a blackboard or a textbook) but it seems to be a fact. It is enhanced by aspects of program design, such as the introduction of situations with a random element.

(b) Thus it is perhaps most helpful to view the micro as a 'teaching assistant', whose talents and personalities may (be programmed to) assume a wide variety of roles to match the teacher's intentions and style. It is because these last vary so much that the designer must build in flexibility and 'willingness'—an 'assistant' that does not fit in with your wishes can be worse than useless. It must thus support and enhance different teaching approaches and modes of use; if it allows teachers to make it more 'their own' by adding material, so much the better.

(c) From the pupils' viewpoint, however, the micro presents a very different image from that of another teacher—its various and varying attributes of behaviour and personality provide an unknown system to explore. This element of 'disguise' is a helpful contributing factor to the independence noted in (a).

Wider implications

Even from these brief introductory comments the possibility of application of this approach in other areas than the classroom can be seen. The difficulties in the introduction of computer systems to human organisations are well known. Though work has been done on the human problems involved at a sociological level, most studies of man-machine interactions have concentrated on one-one situations and on a concept of 'user-friendliness' that is both simple and rationally based. Two themes revealed in this work have not received general attention.

1. That conveying insight from the computer to members of the 'user

community' is an educational design task in which the planning of the active involvement of the learner may be crucial.

2. That the design of the 'personality' presented by the system may be as crucial as its function in promoting effectiveness.

This side of the work is discussed in more detail separately.

This paper

The structure of this paper is set out as follows. We have chosen to begin at the end, as it were—with the scheme of classification that opens Section 2; we then elucidate its provenance by alternating the description of particular lessons with discussion of the various facets of the taxonomy, before going on to pursue the implications for classroom dynamics in Section 3.

In the course of this we describe three lessons using the same program, PIRATES, so that the reader can get some feeling for the analysis given in Sections 2 and 3 of the learning activities, and for the roles that pupils, teacher and computer may play in them. The analysis itself is based on the detailed observation of all the lessons, but many of its features are sufficiently general to be seen in the small sample of lessons given [. . .]

Table A   Observable Pupil Classroom Activities

Passive		*Active*
Watching	*Writing*	note taking
Listening		recording
Reading		exercises
'Thinking'		symbolizing
		explaining
Off Task		
Dreaming	*Talking*	asking
Fooling		answering
Chatting		describing
		discussing
		explaining
		hypothesizing
		asserting

Mode of Classroom Activity
Competition
Experimenting
Testing
Imitating computer or teacher

2. ANALYSIS OF ROLES AND ACTIVITIES

A taxonomy

Out of the observations of this study has grown a classification of roles and activities that provides a framework within which we can discuss the relationship between the roles of the teacher, the pupils and other resources such as the micro, and the learning activities that take place in the classroom. The balance of roles is a crucial factor in the environment within which learning can occur. In this Section we explain the classification with lesson exemplars that show how it has arisen.

Table A1

	Passive	*Writing*			*Active*
* (1)	Watching		(1) (2)		note taking
(1)	Listening		(1) (2)		recording
(2)	Reading		(2)		exercises
(3) (4) (5) (6)	'Thinking'		(4) (5) (6)		symbolizing
			(4) (5) (6)		explaining

	Off Task	*Talking*			
(1) (3)	Dreaming		(1) (2) (3)		asking
(1) (2) (3)	Fooling		(1) (2) (3)		answering
(2) (3) (4) (5) (6)	Chatting		(3) (4) (5) (6)		describing
			(3)		discussing
			(3) (4) (5) (6)		explaining
			(3) (4) (5)		hypothesizing
			(3) (4) (5) (6)		asserting

Mode of Classroom Activity

(6)	Competition
(4)(5)(6)	Experimenting
(4)(5)(6)	Testing
(4)(5)(6)	Imitating computer or teacher

* The numbers indicate the most commonly observed 'Cockcroft' activities that were operational when the particular category shown was noted.

Key to Cockcroft Activities Paragraph 243 of the Cockcroft Report

(1) . Teacher exposition
(2) . Pupil exercise, consolidation and practice
(3) . Discussion
(4) . Investigation
(5) . Applied and or Practical Mathematics
(6) . Problem-Solving

We think it would be helpful to the reader to begin simply by tabulating the resultant taxonomy. The meaning of the terms used will become clearer through their appearance in the lesson descriptions. While there is an inevitable element of arbitrariness in the detail of any such classification scheme, we have found that this one is basically robust. (The reader may like to explore alternatives.)

Table A lists the observable 'surface' classroom activities, grouped in a fairly obvious fashion, while Table A1 shows them linked to those teaching activities, listed in paragraph 243 of the Cockcroft report[1], in which they commonly occurred. These six activities, reordered and numbered, are listed at the bottom of Tables A1 and B1. Thus, for example, when 'watching' was observed, the activity was frequently exposition. ①, with other categories appearing significantly less often. Conversely, we may conclude that exposition ① and practice ② promote the more commonly observed classroom activities, whereas when the more 'open' activities ④, ⑤, and ⑥ are present, higher level skills are likely to be in use.

Table B shows the learning activities that are taking place—some are directly observable (e.g. symbolizing) while others are inferred from the surface activity pattern. Here the clusterings are less obvious and will be discussed later. The links to the Cockcroft classification are shown in Table B1; again ① and ② support the more easily promoted learning activities of a more passive kind, whereas the high level activities are more frequent we found when ③, ④, ⑤ and ⑥ are present. This provides a strong objective indication

Table B   Pupil Learning Activities

d *didactic*	absorbing
	recalling
	rule following
s *symbolizing*	using
	translation skills
i *investigating*	guessing
	checking
	particularizing
p *problem-solving*	technical skills
	tactical skills
	strategic skills
	control skills
h *higher level skills*	image building
	analysing
	generalizing
	abstracting
	linking
	proving
	reflecting

of the reasons for the importance of ③, ④, ⑤ and ⑥, which are rarely found in normal mathematics classrooms[2]. The importance of looking for ways of creating a balance of learning activities follows from this; this paper provides a new approach to this problem.

Table C gives a corresponding taxonomy of the observed roles that are played at various times by the teacher, the micro and the pupils. The given role is often shared between them in varying proportions. Again the clustering into groups will be of importance in our detailed discussion in Section 2.5. Our central concern will be to link these roles with the learning activities of Table B which they help to promote. In the introduction, we indicated some of the features that emerge.

Table B1

d *didactic*	* ①② absorbing
	①② recalling
	② rule following
s *symbolizing*	(all) using
	③④⑤⑥ translation skills
i *investigating*	④⑥ guessing
	④⑤⑥ checking
	②④⑤⑥ particularizing
p *problem-solving*	④⑤⑥ technical skills
	④⑤⑥ tactical skills
	④⑥ strategic skills
	④⑥ control skills
h *higher level skills*	④⑤⑥ image building
	④⑤⑥ analysing
	④⑥ generalizing
	④⑥ abstracting
	②④⑥ linking
	②④⑥ proving
	④⑥ reflecting

* The numbers indicate the most commonly observed 'Cockcroft' activities when the particular category shown was noted.

Key to Cockcroft Activities Paragraph 243 of the Cockcroft Report

① . Teacher exposition
② . Pupil exercise, consolidation and practice
③ . Discussion
④ . Investigation
⑤ . Applied and or Practical Mathematics
⑥ . Problem-Solving

Lesson 1   *Joan with PIRATES*

This section gives a description of a lesson by Joan with the PIRATES program. PIRATES is a program about co-ordinates, set in the context of a problem solving game. The aim is to find the location of a buried treasure on a rectangular whole-number grid of predetermined size. Each suggestion promotes a clue from the computer, which may be given in the form of a compass direction, a bearing, a vector direction, a distance or as 'warmer–colder' clues, depending on the particular skills that the teacher wants to practise. Thus the teacher defines the type of problem and the type of clue and the program then accepts co-ordinate pair 'guesses' and responds with clues—all plotting of points is done by the children individually or in group discussion, with or without the teacher. At no time does the computer display the grid; the children are expected to plot their own points and keep a record of the information received. We comment on this aspect of the program design later.

The description is laid out in two columns, the first column describing the lesson as it progresses while the second column comments on the roles and activities involved. To link it to Tables A, B and C, the observable classroom activities are underlined, the learning activities are classified as *d s i p h* as in Table B and the roles are related to Ⓜ Ⓣ Ⓔ Ⓕ Ⓒ Ⓡ as in Table C. The roles are suffixed to indicate whether teacher t pupil p or computer c are playing that particular role at that stage—for example, Ⓣ^{c} indicates that the computer c is assuming the role of Tasksetter Ⓣ.

She has loaded and tried out PIRATES before the lesson. After a short managerial introduction, she starts straight in—explaining the program, the 0–9 grid, and the compass direction clues.

At this point the computer is a system to *explore* Ⓡ^{c}. The screen summarises the situation—the teacher is in overall control and is *explaining* Ⓔ^{t} what's what.

T   Who wants to make the first guess? Richard?

Rd (5,5)

T   We'll put in (5,5) and see what it says. 'Go South West', Put that down on your grids. What shall we try next, Susan?

Sn (2,2)

The teacher is simply *managing* Ⓜ^{t} tactical use of the program working in quite traditional roles with a computer providing *task setting* Ⓣ^{c} (and a system to *explore* possibly in more flexible ways later).

Table C   Classroom Roles

Ⓜ Manager (tactical)	Ⓣ Task setter
corrector	questioner
marker	example-setter
computer operator	strategy setter
Ⓔ Explainer	Ⓒ Counsellor
demonstrator	advisor
scene-setter	helper
image builder	devil's advocate
focuser	encourager
imitator	stimulator
rule giver	listener/supporter
coach	observer
	receiver
	diagnostician
	problem solver (C)
Ⓕ Fellow pupil	Ⓡ Resource
rule applier	system to explore
hypothesizer	giver of information
problem solver (F)	

T (2,2). It says 'Go North West'. Tony?	The learning activities here includes symbolising *s*, problem
Ty (1,3)	solving *p* and other higher level
T (1,3). Any other ideas? Gillian?	skills *h*.
Gn (1,4)	
T Which shall we try first? (1,3)? Well done, that's it!	

In this episode the children have been *watching* and *listening* and *thinking* about the problem, with little sign of off task activity. In drawing and using their grids they are *symbolising* (*s*) and *recording*; in playing the game they are *experimenting*, *testing* and *competing*, and probably *hypothesising* (*h*). Those who respond are certainly *hypothesising* and *answering*—a wide range of activities in one of the 'missing' classroom modes *discussion* ③.

T Shall we do another?	There followed two more similar
Ps Yes. . . .	successful episodes, with the
. . . . .	teacher providing less detailed
. . . . .	guidance leaving most of the *tactical managing* Ⓜ^{c} to the program as the pupils get familiar with it.
T Can any one say which they think is the best way to find the	The teacher here largely dissociates herself from the *task*

treasure?

(Pause)

What is the best first guess?
Tony?

Ty (5,5) Miss.

T Why?

Ty Because it's in the middle, so each
direction has the same size area
(*h*).

Pt (4½, 4½) is in the middle, Miss.

T Yes, but we can only have whole
numbers. Are there any others as
much in the middle as (5,5)?

Ps (4,4) (Pause) What about (4,5)?
(*p*) (*i*)

T Let's try that. It says 'Go east'.
What is the best thing to do next?

An Does it mean exactly East, Miss?

T I don't know. What do you
think? Does anybody remember
what happened before?

Rd Last time is said go South, it has
the same first co-ordinate in the
end. (*h*).

T Alright, shall we try that? Where
shall we go next?

Sn (5,6)

T It says 'Go East' again. Where
next?

Ty (5,7) (*p*)

Gn No. (5,8)

T Why?

Gn Well, it could be at (5,7) (5,8) or
(5,9). (Pause) If we try (5,8) we
either get it straight away or one
step after. If we try (5,7) it could
take two more steps if its at (5,9).
(*p*) (*i*) (*h*)

T Shall we do that then?

Ps Yes.

T (5,8) That's it.
Let's try a different sort of clue—

setting Ⓣ^{c} and become a
counsellor Ⓒ^{t} on the
strategy.

Some other teachers might
explain the strategy of 'binary
search', either immediately or
after the pupil's less than totally
lucid attempt. This would help
more pupils to understand the
strategy, but prevent their
working it out for themselves.

A controlling decision to leave

'Warm' clues tell you if you are getting closer to the treasure or not.
(Pause)
This is harder so we'll change the grid to (0,4) in each direction. Where shall we start?

Jn (2,2)

T (2,2). It says you are cold. Which way shall we go Paul?

P It doesn't tell you, Miss.

T No it doesn't. What shall we try?

P (3,3) Miss. (*i*)

T Why did you choose that one?

P (Pause) Don't know, Miss.

T (3,3) It says you are getting colder.

that strategic domain for a while at least and go on to another more challenging problem, again with an intuitive approach. Note teacher warns it will be harder, which is not obvious to the children at this stage. The teacher begins on a repetition of the search for a strategy for warmth clues (where the 'centre' is seldom the best place to start). More guidance as *counsellor* $©^t$ and *fellow pupil* $Ⓕ^t$, or much more patience may be needed here. The teacher can take these roles because the tactical *management* $Ⓜ^c$, *task setting* $Ⓣ^c$ and *correction* $Ⓜ^c$ are being handled by the computer.

The reader will have observed how, at times, some of the roles are assumed by the computer, and at other times, by the teacher or pupils. Roles can also be shared—the pupil roles throughout the lesson included Explaining $Ⓔ^p$ and Fellow Pupil $Ⓕ^p$ both of which were also shared by the teacher.

Classification of classroom activities and learning activities

Classroom activities. Table A lists major observable classroom activities —these are pupil activities grouped under the headings Passive and Active the latter being subdivided under Writing and Talking. There is also a separate group called Mode of Classroom Activity, with the headings Competition, Experimenting, Testing and Imitating. The group and subgroup headings were used in analysing lessons both in the lesson descriptions that appear in this paper on pp. 212, 217 and 221, and also in the Matrix representation of lessons that appear on pp. 224–5. The more detailed labels such as recording, note taking etc. are included to help the observer classify the large range of observable activities into the groups proposed in this particular taxonomy. We give brief descriptions of the major headings and subheadings and leave the reader to interpret the words describing particular activities, guided by their normal meaning and illustrated by their use in the lesson descriptions.

Passive. This includes all the activities where the child is receiving rather than actively using information. It links very much towards promoting the learning activities of recall, absorbing and rule following which come under the *didactic* heading in Table B. We include here also the off-task activities of fooling, chatting etc., though these don't appear in the Matrix analysis in Section 3.

Active.   This is subdivided into *writing* and *talking*, each with their list of detailed activities.

The following modes of activity have been included; they may also be observed and they are particularly relevant in this study:

Competition, where pupils are placed in some type of competition either amongst themselves or against the computer.

Experimenting where the children are actually experimenting with ideas or 'apparatus' in the broadest sense.

Testing where the children are testing out certain hypotheses on particular cases.

Imitating where the children are actually imitating the recent roles of computer or teacher. This last category is of special interest as will become apparent from the exemplars and the comments on them.

Learning activities.   The learning activities are clustered together in groups as shown in Table B. The headings in order, and in fact in the order that they most commonly occur are:

d didactic activities are those traditional in classrooms where children are absorbing, recalling, recording and rule following. These were the activities that tend to dominate in classroom according, for example, to the HMI Survey.[2]

s symbolizing—any activity where the child is employing symbols to represent information in the exercise or problem being studied; the subheadings 'using' and 'translation skills' are given but other headings could also be listed here—we have kept the list deliberately short and its main purpose is to indicate our understanding of this cluster as a group.

i investigating—this cluster has three subheadings, which could again be expanded, those included again being indicative of the activities that we classify under this heading.

p problem-solving—under this more general heading, the list has been expressed in terms of the skills employed; there is no clear division between this heading and the next one.

h higher level skills—a long list is given here to help identify activities that fall in this heading.

Tables A1 and B1 link the taxonomy developed here with paragraph 243 of the Cockcroft report. This is of interest in that it gives detailed support to the link between the dominance of exposition and practice and a heavy emphasis on the relatively passive learning activities of absorbing and imitative exercising which are characteristic of the didactic approach. In contrast, it shows how the ability both actively to understand mathematics and to use it effectively depend on activities related to higher level, more strategic skills. If this is indeed generally true, as seems likely, then it points to two possibilities:

1. The teacher is unaware of the need to promote these activities or
2. The teacher is aware but finds it too difficult.

There are related difficulties both for the pupil and for the teacher. The standard elements of the didactic approach—the absorption and recall of facts and techniques, and the repetitive practice of imitative exercises based on rule following—are relatively straightforward for teachers and pupils; the latter have clearly defined and unambiguous tasks, while the teacher can pursue a single pedagogical track, explaining, illustrating and, in coaching pupils' working, reiterating the standard technique. Most teachers experienced this approach as pupils and have no compelling reason to change, as the examination system also reflects and encourages a didactic approach to the acquisition of knowledge.

Almost all the other activities require more initiative from the pupil and a more flexible sensitive responsiveness from the teacher; we shall see that these require the teacher to play quite different roles, and in some conflict with, the traditional authoritarian ones of the didactic approach. A key strength of the micro seems to be in taking over some of the latter and liberating the teacher to establish a more consultative relationship with the pupil. Evidence of this is shown in the exemplars.

There are some exceptions to this general summary. The activities grouped under symbolizing, which are concerned with translating statements or information from one form to another, depend on skills which can be taught in a similarly didactic way. The separate and explicit teaching of such translation skills has not received much emphasis in English schools, but this and other research has shown that such teaching is, at least in part, relatively straightforward. Nonetheless, the micro is capable of providing significant assistance in it.

Lesson 2   Jack with PIRATES

In this section we describe a different teacher's lesson with PIRATES.

Jack is concerned with compass points, and the inequality constraints that define regions. Here the computer will set up the situation and produce a statement such as 'The treasure lies in the region $x < 8$ and $y > 2$'. The clues are then given in compass directions as in lesson 1.

He starts with revision; with a picture drawn on the blackboard, he *explains* Ⓔ^{t} the lines x = 4, y = 6 and so on. Pupils appear to *attend* (*d*) and *absorb* (*d*). (7 mins)

He explains Ⓔ^{t} the program, getting children to *draw* (*d*) several co-ordinate grids (0,9; 0,9) in preparation for the 'game'—a straightforward *exercise* (*d*) on their part. Similarly they draw compass directions (N, NE, E, . . .) on tracing paper. (10 mins)

Traditional *didactic* (*d*) teaching with its well-defined pattern of activities and roles—the teacher *explaining* Ⓔ^{t} *managing* Ⓜ^{t} and *task setting* Ⓣ^{t} while pupils *attend, absorb* (*d*) and exercise (*d*).

Setting the computer to produce inequality constraints, it chooses x < 8, y > 2. the pupils produced guesses (i) and follow clues; successively (3,4) 'Go NE', (6,7) 'Go SE', (5,6) 'Go E', (7,6) finds the treasure.

The computer is now the *task setter* Ⓣ^{c} and the encourager Ⓒ^{c}, while the teacher *manages* Ⓜ^{t} the class.

Three more search episodes follow in similar vein. The teacher *corrects* pupil suggestions not consistent with the constraints, filtering them out rather than letting the computer respond. The possibility of *strategy* is raised ('who can do it in the least number of times?') but not pursued except in the recognition of accumulating evidence ('that's got to be it'). (18 mins)

As the task becomes familiar the computer takes over more of the detailed *management* Ⓜ^{c}, leaving the teacher freer to take other roles. The teacher, however, does not move outside the usual explainer Ⓔ^{t}, task setting Ⓣ^{t} and managerial Ⓜ^{t} roles, while letting the computer take the major burden of task setting Ⓣ^{c} and detailed management Ⓜ^{c}. He is content simply to exercise overall control.

The teacher, who will be away for the two following class lessons, instructs children to play PIRATES in pairs, taking over in turn the computer role of *task setter* Ⓣ^{p} and *manager* Ⓜ^{p}

For the subsequent lessons, the teacher is handing over to the pupils, subject to the overall *control* consent of the stand-in teacher who will take care of the class.

The children are now asked to imitate the teacher's and computer's roles in their next lesson. They are used to doing initiative exercises but imitating the teacher's and computer's role is only possible because of the clear examples of these roles experienced in this lesson. However in imitating even this focused role, they are most likely to be drawn into developing high level skills (or something like them).

The classification of roles

We now turn to the classification of the roles which may be played by teacher, computer or pupils, and how they may serve the activity objectives. The grouping of these observed roles into the six larger categories is an important element in the construction of this taxonomy; we encourage the reader to consider it critically.

We do not think it would be helpful to attempt a definitional description of what we mean by each of the individual roles; we have tried to use words with their usual, informal meanings to illustrate our interpretation of the headings for the clusters and they are illustrated in our lesson descriptions. It may be worthwhile however, to comment on the six groups into which we see them as falling.

Ⓜ *Management group*—the more detailed tactical management of the lesson is again usually heavily teacher dominated. These are authoritative roles in the organisational sense and, in allowing the teacher to direct the pupils' learning activities at any level of detail, correspondingly removes responsibility from the pupils for that learning. In open investigative lessons pupils largely carry these roles themselves. Equally, they can be carried by the computer, liberating the teacher to do other things.

Ⓣ *Task setting group*—these roles are also related to tactical management but are of such central importance in mathematics (and in some other areas of the curriculum), that it has to form a group on its own. Similar comments apply as with M—normally teacher dominated, with few teachers transferring the responsibility for posing questions to pupils to any significant degree. The micro can easily and usefully assume these common roles (PIRATES, SUBGAME, etc), releasing the teacher for other more subtle ones including 'strategy setter' ('how may we *best* do this, or that?')

Ⓔ *Explanatory group*—these epitomise the teacher's *academic* authority as management does the organisational, with task setting bridging the two domains. The teacher *knows*, and gives knowledge which the pupils receive, and more or less absorb via explanation, demonstration and so on. This is a crucially necessary part of teaching and learning but, because it involves passive constricted learning by pupils, it is not a sufficient way of developing their skills and concepts.

The missing learning activities cannot develop while the teacher remains in the E, T and M roles. Pupils *can* explain to each other in groups of varying size or on paper—but they rarely do; the micro can help stimulate this (e.g.

EUREKA). The micro itself can contribute a useful explanation in a self-contained or supportive way (indeed, there are still those who talk of the class use of the micro as 'demonstration mode') but, because of its essential pupil-passivity, this is not a major contribution to its enhancing pupil learning activities. In can, however, again allow more teacher concentration on other roles including the broader more strategic explanatory ones we call 'scene setting' and 'focusing'.

Ⓒ *Counsellor group*—the consultative roles epitomise a different relationship between teacher and pupils. They are working *together* on common problems, the older more experienced giving *general* help on approaches to tackling them to the younger explorers. The pupils will be more motivated if the teacher, although more knowledgeable in applying skills to the problem, does not appear to know the problem in detail. With the micro as task setter, often using a random element in the particular tasks, this sort of situation can be achieved, apparently naturally. Because the teacher can know the program and thus the essence of the task it is setting, the demands on teacher confidence and competence remain much at the normal level of didactic teaching, and yet, because of the perceived independence of the micro in pupils' eyes, the teacher is able to establish a consultative relationship. This can provide a valuable bridge to the introduction of pupil investigations on more open problems, some of them unfamiliar to the teacher, which place greater demands on all concerned. These extra demands arise in all types of problem solving, including mathematical 'games', from a number of factors including the different stages and approaches of different pupils; the micro can reduce the total demand on the teacher to a tractable level in taking over the task setting and the tactical management of the task related activity leaving the teacher free for the more important consultative roles. The micro is (pace ELIZA)[8] not easily programmed to exercise the skills involved in these high level roles, which are normally best left to the teachers. Pupil–pupil discussion, which is strongly encouraged by the presence of the microcomputer, can allow pupils to help each other in this sort of way.

Ⓕ—in the *Fellow pupil* roles teacher and class are together facing the same challenge, of learning or problem solving say. The teacher is no longer an 'expert', even in a general advisory strategic sense, as in C, but is apparently searching, trying and competing on a more-or-less equal footing. This requires a lot of teacher confidence, which can apparently be built in the well defined context of a program without damaging credibility on either side.

These roles allow the pupil to see a credible model for themselves in action. The micro can also play or share such roles, when used as a computational device by the pupil in applying rules or models to work out consequences—it does the hard work leaving the pupil free from the technical load to work on the strategic considerations.

®—the computer's role as a *resource*, a system to explore, a data store needs little emphasis; indeed we believe it is more difficult to realise in the classroom the undoubted potential in this area than many optimists have implied, the value of the teachers taking on these roles, responding only to specific requests for information from the pupils, needs to be restated. Such roles are more and more accessible alongside those linked to open learning (C and F) than the traditional (M, T, E) didactic approach.

One role that is not listed in those in table C is that of *Controller* i.e. in overall command of the lesson, the topic of study, the general approach and organisation and the resources employed. This is and will be the teacher, except in those rare cases where they genuinely allow a class to choose or when control breaks down. Thus we have not considered it as a likely candidate in the discussion of role sharing and shifting.

Lesson 3   *Jan with PIRATES*

This is yet another PIRATES lesson, illustrating the variety of roles of activities that can occur.

Jan begins by revising compass directions (N, NE, E etc.) and plotting co-ordinate points, *explaining* E^t and *illustrating* E^t clearly on the blackboard to a partly attentive class; she uses a question-and-answer exposition technique but most pupils are essentially passive (*d*) and the demand is α (recall). (7 mins)

Traditional *didactic* teaching, with the *explanation* Ⓔ^{t} roles and *absorption* (*d*) pupil activities clear.

She *explains* E^t what PIRATES does and launches into two successive runs—pupils suggesting the next moves, teacher marking each on the blackboard. All are attentive. Some natural development of strategy (*p*) occurs but the teacher plays no part in it here. (8 mins)

After *scene setting* Ⓔ^{t}, the teacher hands over *tactical management* Ⓜ^{c} and *task setting* Ⓣ^{c} to the computer; by *marking* guesses on the blackboard herself, she removes a useful technical pupil activity, perhaps to be sure they understand it thoroughly for later.

She now firmly sets a *strategic task* T^t 'This time we must find it in the least possible number of guesses', and soon after, 'Where is the best place to start?' and she *manages* Ⓜ^{t} a discussion to ensure that all the

In all this, pupils use (recording) grids to mark points if they wish; the teacher still puts them on the blackboard. A high level of demand on the pupils, extending their previous knowledge (i.e. γ), class gets this new (i.e. γ in SCAN notation (5)) idea of dividing the possible region each time by guessing the middle ('binary search'), 'the middle' (5,5) gives clue 'Go South East'. 'Where next?' '(7,3)' 'Why' 'Because it's in the middle.' (p) (h)

Next the different nature of the clues is explored.
'Go North' (from (7,3)) leads into '(7,5)'
'Why?'
'Because it says go North.'
'What do we know from this clue?'
'That it should not be below three.' (h)
'Yes, but more than that.'
'It's obviously on the seven line.'

The teacher again *explains* E^t to reinforce the point—N, S, E, W clues define lines, while NE, SE etc define regions of points.

Pupils play PIRATES in pairs without the computer, *imitating its roles* without difficulty. Some pairs still show incorrect interpretation of (N, S, E, W) clues but most are good technically and strategically. (15 mins)

The teacher now sets a vaguely related exercise on co-ordinates from the textbook; all children get involved but with varying understanding of what is needed.

with guidance that is fairly close (10 mins)
Again, Jan is looking for *strategic skills* (h) (p), minimising the *technical* load; the computer is *managing* $\textcircled{M}^c$ and *task setting* $\textcircled{T}^c$ while she is *manager* $\textcircled{M}^t$, counsellor $\textcircled{C}^t$ and adviser $\textcircled{C}^t$ on the strategic issue which is established.

Pupils now take over from the computer in *management* $\textcircled{M}^p$ (though rather more weakly) and *task setting* $\textcircled{T}^p$ in turn, while the teacher retains the *counselling* $\textcircled{C}^t$ role—but most pairs lose contact with that. Technical and strategic consolidation takes place. It is notable that pupils, because of the competitive spirit, do not *counsel* each other on *strategies*, though they do play fair *technically* (p).

Teacher takes over *management* $\textcircled{M}^t$ and *task setting* $\textcircled{T}^t$ roles; *scene setting* is not clear to pupils. Vivid earlier scene setting $\textcircled{E}^c$ by the computer gives a better

Homework is set—'draw a map, mark on it the position of the treasure and of five separate pirates. Then give each pirate a compass direction to reach the treasure.' These instructions were clearly understood.

grasp of the task situation; the *pupils' imitation of the computer role* is easy. The pupils are now back to *exercises (d)* but with some interest in a 'real context'.

Notes on task setting

The flow of the task setting role in this lesson was interesting. As always under *overall control* of the teacher, the computer took the main initiative but teacher explanation was an integral part of this phase of *task setting*, extended by the teacher's marking all 'guesses' on the blackboard over the whole 18 min of class activity. Imitating this model, the pupils take over the *task setting role*.

ROLE SHIFTING AND THE BALANCE OF ACTIVITIES

Role sharing, role shifting and role imitation

We have developed in Section 2 a taxonomy of roles that the teacher, the pupils or the micro may assume in the classroom. We now examine the possibility of programs' promoting role shifts and whether it is possible to relate this to aspects of program design, its obviously being an aspect of program use.

We took all the lesson reports relating to a particular program and analysed each phase (or Activity in SCAN notation[5]) of each lesson, entering the results in a Matrix, (although only the PIRATES lessons are discussed here).

The object of the Matrix is to give us an overview of the use of the program by different teachers. In particular we are interested in identifying when the important but less common learning activities occur, and also when the teacher adopts the more demanding roles in an effective way.

The following diagram shows the Matrix completed for the second and third PIRATES lessons described in Section 2. These are shown in Table D.

You will notice that each lesson is divided into phases labelled E, W_2 etc. The time in minutes of each phase is given. This division is the SCAN[5] division of Activities—the Activity is the largest natural unit into which a lesson divides. E stands for teacher exposition, W_2 indicates pupils working in groups of 2.

In the Matrix, the first set of headings come directly from the observer's

Table D Program-in-Use Matrix

Pirates

	1	2	3 Next Lesson
Phase	E	E	(Next Lesson)
Time (mins)	16	14	40
Demand	αβ	αβ	—
Guidance	1	2	—
Interest/10	7	7	—
% on Task	100	100	—
Roles Analysis (Section 2) M Tactical Manager	t	t/c	p
T Task Setter	t	c	p
E Explainer	t	p	p
C Counsellor			
F Fellow Pupil			
R System to Explore			
Observable Activities (Section 2) Passive	•	•	•
Writing	•		
Talking	•	•	•
Learning Activities (Section 2) d Didactic	•	•	•
s Symbolizing			
i Investigating			
p Problem-Solving			
h High level Skills	•		

Pirates

	1	2	3	4
Phase	E	E	W₂	W₁
Time (mins)	7	15	15	15
Demand	α	β	αβ	β
Guidance	2	2	1.5	1.5
Interest/10	5	7	7	7
% on Task	70	95	100	95
Roles Analysis (Section 2) M Tactical Manager	t	t/c	p	t
T Task Setter	t	c	p	t
E Explainer	t	t		
C Counsellor	t			
F Fellow Pupil			(t)	
R System to Explore				
Observable Activities (Section 2) Passive	•			
Writing			•	•
Talking		•	•	•
Learning Activities (Section 2) d Didactic	•		•	•
s Symbolizing				
i Investigating				
p Problem-Solving		*	*	
h High level Skills		*	*	

Taken from Observation Records related to SCAN(5)

CONTENT
Possible Topics

Co-ordinates
Plot points
Shifts
Compass Direction
Vectors
Distances
Circles intersect
Angles
Bearings
Lines intersect
Pythagoras
Areas
Regions

Activity

Strategy
Competition
Abandon

Lesson 2

Lesson 3

record; they also relate to the SCAN notation.[5] 'Demand' is the demand on the pupils as perceived by the observer on the following basis:

α = recall of a single fact or carrying out of a single act

β = exercise of a straightforward nature, putting together several facts or acts and

γ = extension of previous work involving new ideas.

'Guidance' is the observer's perception of the level of guidance given to the pupils by the teacher

1 = close guidance, highly structured with a small number of choices

2 = some guidance offered but requires the connection of facts rather than mere selection

3 = minimum guidance in an 'open' style.

The Interest column is a score, out of ten, of the observer's perception of how highly involved the children appeared to be; finally in this section of the Matrix is an indication of the percentage of the class on task in this activity.

The next section of the Matrix concentrates on identifying the roles that are being taken on by the Teacher(t), the pupils(p) or the computer(c); it also recognises the importance of shared roles (t/c etc.). The headings are the major categories described in the taxonomy in Section 2. The more common roles are placed first so that the pattern of entries shows clearly when the less common roles are being observed.

In the next Section come three headings only, for the observable classroom activities—again these have been selected to cover the more detailed headings of the taxonomy in Section 2. The learning activities follow, categorized in the same way, and again with the more commonly observed activities given first. Thus the Matrix contains a Summary of the observation report of the lesson concerned, related to the classification developed in Section 2 which is based on the analysis of all the lesson reports.

The final section of the Matrix is peculiar to the particular program teaching unit being used, in that it lists the possible mathematical content or topic areas that the program could be used to support, together with specific classroom or learning activities that we might hope to see (e.g. competition, strategy); these also relate back to the taxonomy.

In the body of the Matrix the following notation is used. A cell that has a • records the occurrence of this item, a cell with * indicates a strong effective use for this category.

The Matrix can be examined for evidence of what happened in the lesson in the framework that we have established in Section 2. We are particularly interested when the teacher moves from the traditional authoritarian roles in the Ⓜ tactical management, Ⓣ Task setter and Ⓔ Explainer groups to the less often assumed roles of Ⓒ Counsellor, Ⓕ Fellow pupil or Ⓡ resource or system to explore. We are also interested when pupils appear to adopt roles that have been mainly teacher roles and, of course, to relate these role shifts to the roles that the computer has assumed.

Before commenting on our findings, based on all the lesson observations, we illustrate the line of argument in a discussion of the two records given on the Matrix grid in Table D.

In the first two phases of lesson 2 (which is described in detail in Section 2) the Matrix highlights the teacher role as it moves from tactical Manager and Task setter to a position of sharing Ⓜ with the computer, dropping Ⓣ and taking over a counselling role Ⓒ. This appears to have occurred because the computer is sharing Ⓜ and taking over Ⓣ. The pupil learning activities have moved to more open ones during this change with entries of *h* (higher level skills) and *strategy* appearing on the table in Phase 2. The third phase is unusual in this case, as it actually relates to the subsequent lesson. It is included as the children were explicitly asked to *imitate the roles* of both the computer and the teacher during the next lesson, when the teacher was to be absent.

This highlights the important idea of role-imitation, which appeared during these trials as a powerful aid for the teacher to encourage pupils into high level activities. With the computer program, together with the teacher, clearly defining an investigation, the children were often asked to imitate the exercise together in groups, taking it in turns to play the role of the computer; the computer so often appeared to provide the pupils with an effortlessly vivid model of what was intended, which contrasted sharply in its effectiveness with verbal descriptions. Of course, a very great deal of pupil activity in classrooms consists of 'imitative exercises', which aim to promote through practice, low level technical skills; the success of another, richer kind of imitation, involving greater 'transfer', in the promotion of higher level skills is that of imitation both of teacher roles and of computer roles. In this example, the pupils were asked to be in both Ⓜ and Ⓣ roles, but the task was slightly easier. The observer has not noted (*h*) in this session but strategy continues to be present. As the pupils were without teacher or computer support, this is an encouraging result.

In lesson 3, the higher level activity of pursuing a strategic approach occurs first when the teacher has moved into Ⓒ, is sharing Ⓜ with the computer and is also adopting Ⓔ. Secondly strategy occurs when the pupils are again role imitating and assume Ⓜ and Ⓣ, working in pairs. [. . .]

The overall qualitative evidence from the whole of these trials, of which the two above examples are but illustrations, is clear and strong. Programs can be designed which result in teacher's working with a potentially wider style range than they would otherwise employ in a way that does not appear to increase the pressure or demands on them; in particular they assume roles in the Ⓒ, Ⓕ and Ⓡ groups, and the more open learning activities tend to occur when this happens. The operational style range varied from teacher to teacher and program to program, but the qualitative shift was observed in a large number of lessons; the only exception was provided by 2 teachers whose style is habitually open, and even here there was a noticeable enhancement of pupil learning activities; indeed, one of these teachers is not surprisingly an exceptionally powerful user of the microcomputer as an aid to his teaching.

Another major outcome was that, when pupils assumed or 'imitated' teacher or computer roles, it led them to take greater responsibility for the learning activity and invariably to move into the higher level skills area.

Since the production of such style shifts has proved a quite intractable problem with all but a few teachers over at least thirty years of enthusiastic advocacy and energetic promotion, this result, if confirmed in general, is of great importance.

An explanation of why the micro can succeed, where other approaches, (printed material, for example) have no effect emerges from the observation and is implicit in our discussion so far. It appears that the micro can take on certain roles, particularly the traditional authoritarian teacher roles in the Ⓜ, Ⓣ and Ⓔ groups, lifting that demand from the teacher; furthermore, the opportunity to assume the less common roles in the Ⓒ, Ⓡ and Ⓕ groups is presented to the teacher in a way that is natural, supportive and unthreatening to their authority, and thus to their confidence—probably because the framework is less 'open' to the teacher than it appears to the pupils, due to the illusory independence of the micro.

Caution is essential in such a difficult area. Although the study was conducted in as realistic a way as possible, with the minimum of special attention to the teachers, circumstances were inevitably not normal in all aspects and there is some evidence that at least one teacher responded to the trial, as well as to the micro with exceptional efforts; we must check that similar results to those reported here pertain when teachers start using micros and material through normal school channels (some informal indications over the year since the trial give hope in this regard). Equally, it is important to see how far the style-broadening effects carry over into other teaching in which the micro is not involved; such transfer would greatly enhance the educational benefit of the very limited amount of good material currently or prospectively available, though it would be surprising if there were a large permanent effect from a restricted experience without follow up support— further effort and study in this direction are planned. [. . .]

POSTSCRIPT

Rather than repeating the conclusions given in each Section of this paper, we suggest that the interested reader-in-a-hurry who has read the abstract will be able to decide whether to read further from a look at the taxonomy of Section 2, and the classroom analysis of Section 3.

The work described here mirrors the general experience that the study of the effects of perturbation on a system is a powerful way to increase understanding of the system itself. The microcomputer suitably programmed, has shown itself a powerful perturbation showing promise of dual benefit—in better understanding of the dynamics of teaching and learning in classrooms, and in offering hopeful ways of making progress with some intractable problems.

We should like to thank Jim Eggleston and Alan Bell for help with many strategic questions, Maggie Anderşon, David Benzie, Graham Field, Marian Martin and Sue Sandle for their help with classroom observation, and Heather Brown for her contribution to the data analysis. We are grateful to all those who provided educational software, in many cases before its publication. Special thanks must go to the schools for their co-operation and to the teachers in whose classrooms this study took place—Patsy Freeman, John Godwood, Gordon Habbishaw, Roger Hatcher, Jan Jones, Bill Morrell, Gill Morris, Peter Rylatt, Chris Smith, Ian Smith, Karen Smith, Mike Smith, Tony Tomaney, Jack Trenery, Brian Tunbridge, Paddy Turpitt and Graham Winter.

We are grateful to the Science and Engineering Research Council for the financial support of this work.

REFERENCES

1. *Mathematics Counts* (1982) Report of the Committee of Inquiry into the Teaching of Mathematics in Schools under the Chairmanship of Dr. W. H. Cockcroft, HMSO, London.
2. *Aspects of Secondary Education* (1982) Report of the HMI Secondary Survey, HMSO, London.
3. Burkhardt, H., Fraser, R., Coupland, J., Pimm, D., Phillips, R. and Ridgway, J. (in preparation) *Human Interactions with Computers in Complex Situations*.
4. Burkhardt, H., Fraser, R., Coupland, J., Pimm, D., Phillips, R. and Ridgway, J. (in preparation) *Microcomputers in the Mathematics Classroom*.
5. Beeby, T., Burkhardt, H. and Fraser, R. (1979) *Systematic Classroom Analysis Notations*, Shell Centre for Mathematical Education, Nottingham.
6. Burkhardt, H., Fraser, R. with Clowes, M., Eggleston, J. and Wells, C. (1982) *Design and Development of Programs as Teaching Material*, Council for Educational Technology, London.
7. Phillips, R. J., Burkhardt, H., Coupland, J., Fraser, R., Pimm, D. and Ridgway J. (to be published) *Computer-aided Teaching*.
8. Weizenbaum, J. (1976) *Computer Power and Human Reasoning*, San Francisco, Freeman.

6.2 *Intelligent tutoring systems*

• Alan M. Lesgold

America's most significant invention, the computer, is a powerful tool that can help improve both teaching and learning. Computer tools, along with the contributions of cognitive instructional psychology, can help bring about some of the improvements needed in our schools. This paper describes one of the ways in which computers can be important learning resources: It reviews the special contributions that computers can make to education today and discusses capabilities expected in the future. [. . .]

EXPERT TUTORING METHODOLOGY

Several approaches to the task of building an intelligent tutor are being taken. All share the basic strategy of comparing student performance to some ideal and basing interactions with the student on a specific diagnosis. This section describes three general approaches and gives an example of each. These are (1) coaching of performance in a game; (2) an object-oriented approach called the bite-sized tutor; and (3) fragmentary insertions of intelligence into traditional CAI systems.

Coached games. Perhaps the first significant effort to use artificial intelligence techniques in instruction was the WEST tutor developed by Richard Burton and John Seely Brown[1, 2] Burton and Brown started with a game called *The Old West*, which was written for the PLATO system by Bonnie Seiler. That game is, in my opinion, one of the finest examples of traditional computer-assisted instruction, so it is useful to see what Burton and Brown were able to add. *The Old West* is very similar to the board game called *Chutes and Ladders* or *Snakes and Ladders*. Players try to move their pieces along a track, hoping to be the first to get to the end. Various special situations exist. For example, if you land on a special space called a town, you get a free move to the next town, and if you land on the space occupied by an opponent, then he must move back two towns, unless he is currently on a town.

None of this sounds very educationally relevant—that had to be added by Seiler. In the standard board game, children move according to roll of the dice. Seiler decided that children could get useful arithmetic practice if they instead moved an amount determined by the solution to an arithmetic problem. To make the game more interesting, she developed problems that have many possible answers. Here's what happens on a child's move. Three spinner dials spin for a while and then stop, ending up pointed to randomly chosen numbers. The child must concoct an arithmetic expression from the three numbers. He can use parentheses and cannot use any operator more than once. So, for example, if the spinners came up with the numbers 2, 3, and 4, the child might produce an expression like $2 \times 3 - 4$ if he wanted a small result, or $4 \times (2 + 3)$ if he wanted a large value. The child must then tell the computer the value for his expression. If he has a valid expression and if he gives the correct value, then his piece moves that many squares on the game board display.

Seiler's work is a very imaginative way to give children practice manipulating numbers and expressions. In the WEST system, Burton and Brown added several other important components. One component is an ideal model of performance. Given any of several strategies for playing the game, the ideal model analyzes each move and shows how it ranks relative to other possible moves as an application of the selected strategy. For example, one good strategy is always to make an expression that will result in your piece being as far ahead or as little behind the opponent as possible. Given that strategy, all possible moves can be ranked according to the difference between the square on which you will end up and the square on which your opponent will end up.

Another component of the Burton–Brown system compares the student's actual moves to the ideal model and qualitatively analyzes this comparison by asking questions about various issues. For example, some students have trouble understanding when and how to use parentheses in arithmetic expressions. So, the student modeller part of the program asks whether the student could have produced better moves by using parentheses. If the answer is 'yes,' then a numerical score of the student's capabilities for parentheses is lowered. Similarly, one can ask whether the student would do better if he used division as an operator more often. One can also analyze the quality of game play independent of arithmetic skill, looking to see whether the student's moves exemplify any of a set of known strategies. The result of the student modelling process is a profile that tells the system what issues are candidates for coaching.

Another part of WEST observes the course of the student's play and occasionally interrupts with advice when attention to one of the issues on its list has high probability of improving the student's luck in the game. For example, suppose that the computer observes that the student seldom uses parentheses in his expressions. It then would wait for a move on which the student could do much better with an expression that involves parentheses. At that point, it interrupts play and asks the student if he would like some advice. If the student says 'yes,' then the coach points out the value of parentheses and offers the student a chance to take the turn over. The student can even ask the coach to elaborate with more specific advice. The coach has a number of strategies that govern its operation. For example, it limits the proportion of moves on which it interrupts and has knowledge that allows it to decide which issues to tutor first.

What is learned from such a game? WEST shows that intelligent diagnosis can lead to other outcomes besides didactic instruction. In this case, the diagnosis of the student is used to inform a coach that offers advice on the playing of a game. One could easily imagine coaches offering advice on the exploration of a physical phenomenon in a simulated laboratory, suggesting specific reading assignments, tailoring arithmetic problems assigned to a child as homework to that child's specific learning needs, and so on. WEST also demonstrates a basic property of intelligent tutors—they have separate pieces of program, each dealing with a different problem that requires intelligence. Ideal performance modelling, modelling the student, running the game, and providing coaching are the intelligent activities in WEST.

The bite-sized tutor.   The approach used in WEST is an organization based upon instructional roles that must be filled if a good learning environment is to be created. An alternative approach currently under development at the Learning Research and Development Center by Jeff Bonar and other colleagues is based upon the goal structure of the curriculum to be taught. For example, an intelligent system to teach subtraction has been built (a demonstration version) that matches current thoughts about the skill components that make up subtraction. For example, the easiest subtraction involves subtracting a single digit number from a larger single digit number. Then comes multi-digit numbers where the top digit is always greater than or equal to the bottom digit. Finally, there are cases where regrouping or borrowing is required. Those cases come in several varieties: simple borrowing, borrowing across a zero column, borrowing across two zero columns, and so forth. In this hierarchy of the curriculum for subtraction, each entry is represented by a piece of program called an object. The lowest level objects represent bites of knowledge small enough to be taught with a single lesson. That is why it is called the bite-sized tutor. Objects do their work either by carrying out instructions directly or by sending messages to other objects. So, for example, an object that is high in the hierarchy will accomplish its teaching goals by telling its subordinate objects to each 'do their thing.' Current object-oriented approaches have borrowed heavily from a programming language called Smalltalk.

What intelligence must each object have in order to carry out the teaching of its little piece of the curriculum? Exactly the kinds of things that the main components of WEST deal with: modelling the student, providing activities from which the student can learn, and providing advice. In fact, here's what each of the objects in one bite-sized tutor needs to know;

1. The object's relationship to the rest of the curriculum—that is, which objects are prerequisites to this one and which are enabled once this one is learned.
2. Other kinds of relationships to other parts of the curriculum: generalizations, exemplifications, part/whole relationships, and the like.
3. How to determine accurately what the student knows of the material covered by this bite.
4. How to generate instructional materials to teach this bite.
5. How to decide whether the knowledge this bite deals with was missing when a student failed to solve a problem assigned by a bite that is related to this one. For example, the student first learns that the bottom digit in a column should be subtracted from the top one. Later, faced with borrowing situations he can't handle, a student might 'forget' that constraint. The object in charge of the knowledge that the bottom digit always should be subtracted from the top one needs to be able to respond to a request from a related object to provide refresher training on that issue *if it is appropriate.*

To summarize, all expert or intelligent tutoring systems operate by having pieces of program that know how to carry out the essential steps of instruction for each little piece of a body of knowledge. They are effective only if they are able to diagnose student performance, to decide what to teach, and to do the teaching. The important work that must be done before good intelligent tutoring systems evolve is psychological work that fills gaps in our knowledge of how the basic academic skills are learned and what comprises those skills.

Fragmentary intelligence. So, what intelligent computer software are educators going to see in the near future? Probably *not* whole systems, but rather small insertions of intelligence into programs that follow fixed scenarios. For example, a program like Seiler's *The Old West* can be enhanced with snippets of intelligence. One possibility is to add a piece of program that understands something about precedence errors in evaluating expressions. For an expression that has a sequence of additions and multiplications in it, all multiplications are done *before* any additions—this precedence rule is a convention of mathematics. Students may not completely assimilate this rule, though. It is quite easy to add a little bit of intelligence to a program that will, when appropriate, type messages to the student such as the following:

You must have made a mistake. 3 + 2*4 is NOT 20. Without parentheses,

*multiplication is done before addition. 3 + 2*4 means we first multiply 2 by 4
and then add 3 to the result. In other words 3 + 2*4 is equal to 3 + (2*4) not
(3 + 2)*4. Would you like to change your expression?* (Sample tutor commentary from *West*.)

Educators can expect to see such programs increase in the future. It is important to understand that such feedback is based upon very little knowledge, so
it occasionally may be produced at less-than-optimal moments.

EVOLUTION OF CLASSROOM COMPUTERS

By 1990, some classrooms will have computers that are much more usable
and much more powerful than those now in the schools. Screen resolution
will be improved to the point where almost anything that can be printed in a
cheap book can also be shown clearly on a computer screen. Computers will
have perhaps 2,000,000 characters of primary memory instead of 16,000 to
64,000. The standard processor will be a 32 bit chip with the power of
computers like those that handle major business functions in large companies today. Students will have easy-to-use pointing devices that allow communication with the computer by selecting from menus and by pointing to
areas of interest on the screen; seldom will much typing be required, except
in composition classes. Among the capabilities that these computers can be
expected to have are as follows:

Summary of Possibilities for Computers
in Classrooms in 1990

- Intelligent tutors and coaches.
- Monitoring student performance in instructional games and exploratory
  environments and providing detailed diagnoses of student weaknesses
  and misconceptions.
- Exploratory microworlds with substantial animation and with intelligent
  coaching of the student.
- Advisors that detect language errors in written compositions and provide
  advice for making changes based upon what an individual student knows.
- Tools to help teachers design and print instructional materials for their
  classes.
- Integrated classroom computer systems in which the same conventions
  are used in all components and in which all components can interact.

As already discussed, substantial tutoring, coaching, and student diagnosis will be possible. In addition, realistic simulations will be the basis for
exploratory microworlds in which children can experiment with ideas, perhaps getting occasional advice from a coach. Experimentation with simulated science and math labs will be possible, but so will exploration with
words. Systems will emerge that can provide some amount of advice and

help to the student who, for example, knows that run-on sentences are bad but does not know how to apply the rule that each sentence should express a complete thought. Integrated tool kits will permit teachers to design and print (or program for screen presentation) homework assignments that are tailored to each student's needs. The vocabulary and style of such programs will help the less-trained teacher to better understand the underpinnings of the curriculum, too, since the structure of the knowledge being taught will be mirrored in the structure of the system. Finally, systems will have simple, integrated, coherent interfaces so that, for example, a student can copy a graph from a laboratory simulation into an essay he is writing. All of this sounds a bit fantastic, and perhaps it is. Each item just mentioned, however, is close to existence today, at least as a laboratory prototype.

But what is possible for schools that are buying computers now? Schools are often buying machines like the IBM PCjr. These machines usually have a better quality of display than standard television, perhaps 300×400 dot positions on the screen, give or take 50%. They have 64,000 to 512,000 characters worth of memory and a 16-bit processor of moderate speed. Some of the things that can be done with such machines are listed in the following summary.

Summary of Possibilities for Computers
About to be Purchased by Schools

- Diagnostic analyses of performance on arithmetic tests.
- Exploratory microworlds for science and math instruction.
- Word processing tools for writing instruction.
- Business graphics packages adapted for classroom use.
- Tools for computer-based art and music creation.

Given the pattern of answers on a set of arithmetic problems, these computers can determine whether a student has any serious misconceptions about arithmetic, simply needs more practice, or is already facile. These computers can present limited microworlds in which one or two specific scientific principles, such as *Force = Mass × Acceleration*, are demonstrated, but cannot do much coaching. Sophisticated word processing packages run on these computers. They allow students to write easily and revise essays and to present legible copies to their teachers for commentary. Such tools can also be used to combine the writing of many students into classroom newspapers. Business tools for summarizing data and graphing relationships run on these computers and can be important adjuncts to math and science instruction and to areas like economics that receive little attention in most schools today. Creative possibilities for generating graphic displays and music are also worth noting. Music theory can be taught much more easily with a computer-based music composition and editing system.

The last few remarks have been less exciting for those whose school systems bought Commodore PETs or TI 99/4's a couple of years ago and are not about to start over on a new set of machines. However, much can be done with these smaller computers. For instance, our children have learned more from writing LOGO programs for a small 8-bit computer than from some of the more sophisticated systems they have tried out. Some of the ways that an 8-bit computer with only 48,000 or 64,000 characters of memory space can be used are listed below:

Summary of Possibilities for Computers in Classrooms Today

- Game formats that provide monitored practice in basic skills.
- Simulated laboratory experiences.
- Tools to support simple classroom newspapers.
- Simple versions of many of the possibilities that intelligent computer-based analyses will provide in later versions.

Simpler, less flexible versions of the possibilities mentioned earlier are possible on these machines, especially if a good teacher is available to make creative use of them. For example, a few years ago, Harold Abelson and Andrea diSessa wrote a book which developed an entire geometry curriculum from grade school level to the theory of relativity using only the kinds of capability present in most LOGO systems. Wonderful classroom newspaper projects have been done on computers that used only a television screen for display. Many of the simpler demonstrations done in physics courses and chemistry courses can be done on a computer, with all the advantages mentioned earlier, though without any seriously tailored coaching element.

More computer power in the future will enable better displays, easier-to-use programs, and more potential for embedding intelligence in computer programs. Intelligent tutoring approaches, however, will require substantial cognitive research on subject-matter learning as well as more powerful computers. This research will pay off in better understanding of how to teach, with or without a computer. Indeed, it may turn out that the approach of deep diagnosis and highly individualized instruction is not very cost-effective—even if it leads the way toward better instructional approaches of other kinds.

Education shares with medicine the possibility of being approached from two viewpoints. For the most part, work on computer-based tutors has assumed a model similar to diagnostic medicine. The physician searches for a disease that will account for the patient's problems and then treats that disease. The tutor searches for missing knowledge or a misconception—an ignorance disease—and then attempts to teach what is missing.

Some physicians are now pursuing a different approach, preventive medicine, which focuses less on repairing specific pathologies and more on helping people find life styles that are health-preserving. It is possible to imagine intelligent systems on computers that do not overtly diagnose the student, but rather are 'pedagogically health-inducing' in that they promote learning among a wide range of students. The exploratory laboratory world seems to be a possibility of that sort. In the extreme, both the diagnostic approach and the attempt to teach generative skills of learning can be dangerous, but both viewpoints need to be preserved.

REFERENCES

1. Brown, J. S. (1974, April) *Structural models of a student's knowledge and inferential process.* (BBN Proposal No. P74–CSC–10). Cambridge, MA, Bolt Beranek and Newman.
2. Brown, J. S. and Burton, R. R. (1978) Diagnostic models for procedural bugs in basic mathematical skills, *Cognitive Science*, 2, 155–192.

6.3 A perspective on intelligent computer-assisted learning

- J. Self

INTRODUCTION

Intelligent computer-assisted learning (ICAL) has been identified as one of nine research themes in the Alvey programme for action on intelligent knowledge based systems (IKBS).[1] ICAL is described as 'an extremely important task area' with 'potential mass markets', and the ICAL theme is offered as a 'somewhat practically-oriented theme' compared to the other eight. The Alvey enthusiasm for ICAL, then, derives from its commercial potential rather than from the fact that it addresses fundamental research issues in IKBS design.

It is not clear why ICAL should be seen in this light. A handful of prototype ICAL systems do exist, but most are incomplete demonstrations and the others show that we lack the knowledge necessary to carry out successful implementations. Nonetheless, there is an emerging concensus on the methodology of ICAL system design. The purpose of this paper is to suggest that this methodology is mistaken, and to propose a 'Copernican shift' in the focus of attention in ICAL system design.

BACKGROUND

Existing ICAL systems fall into two classes: small-scale, 'paradigmatic' programs and large-scale, 'expert system based' programs. The former class of ICAL system, the 'paradigmatic', includes systems such as *BUGGY*[1], *WEST*,[2] *WUMPUS*[3] and *LMS*[4]. These programs concentrate on small, often idealized, domains such as arithmetic skills and games and attempt to establish paradigms for the implementation of larger-scale, realistic systems. Typically, a small set of about a dozen production rules models some problem-solving process. (A production rule is a rule defining an action to be performed when some set of conditions is satisfied, see Young, 1980[5]). The psychological validity of these rules is stressed. The main research enterprise is to model or explain student errors by modifying the problem-solving production system, by, for example, deleting individual rules or by introducing deformed rules (called 'mal-rules').

These 'toy' systems, with production rule knowledge bases much smaller than those developed for expert systems, are rarely developed into complete tutorial systems. For example, *BUGGY* has been used to give trainee teachers practice in diagnosing student errors but has not been used to support an 'intelligent' tutorial with students. The implication remains, however, that design strategies which it has not been possible to carry out for toy domains will be appropriate for real ones.

The two most significant members of the expert system based class are *SOPHIE*[6] and *GUIDON*.[7] The two key features of *SOPHIE* are:

1 that it was built on top of an analysis package for simulating electronic circuits,
2 that, over the years, it was found necessary to include a new inference scheme which 'mimics methods used by human electronics experts and therefore provides a better basis for tutorial assistance'.[8]

GUIDON was built around *MYCIN*, a prototypical expert system. An expert system is one designed to solve real world problems that would otherwise require specialized human expertise. Initially, the *MYCIN* designers emphasized that, unlike statistically-based medical diagnosis programs, their program followed the reasoning process of a human expert (forming judgements, evaluating alternatives, etc.), with the desired consequence that the program could explain its conclusions in comprehensible ways.

Clancey, the implementor of *GUIDON*, proposes that ICAL systems be designed as shown in Fig. 1. At the core is an expert system (like *MYCIN*), which, with teaching knowledge also expressed in a rule-based form, is enveloped in a tutoring system to integrate domain and pedagogical expertise. An intended virtue of this design is that different 'domain knowledge bases' can be plugged in, leaving the other components unchanged. In a

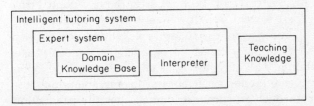

Figure 1 Components of an intelligent tutoring system (from Clancey, 1984)

similar vein, Fisher & Howe[9] identify 25 features that should be present in an ideal ICAL system, the first two of which are:

1 there should be an underlying expert system capable of solving a class of problems at expert level,
2 there should be an explicit overall educational strategy.

These correspond to the two main components in Clancey's design.

PROBLEMS

There are various problems with the methodology represented by Fig. 1. First, the existence of an expert system to solve problems in a certain domain does not necessarily mean that that domain is an appropriate one for ICAL. Indeed, the expert system itself may reduce the need for humans to develop the expertise embedded in it! It is somewhat contradictory to imagine that expert systems will be developed to perform certain tasks, thereby rendering that area of human expertise redundant, and will then be used to teach that expertise. Surely, if it is 'mass markets' we are after, ICAL systems should be oriented not to specialized expertise but to general skills which are widely sought (such as how to use a word-processor, how to design simple electronic circuits, how to play a reasonable game of chess, how to understand the basics of musical harmony).

Secondly, the proposed methodology focuses first on expertise and only as an afterthought on what learners actually do and know. 'The model of the student's knowledge, as built by the program, is a subset of the internal, idealised knowledge base', according to Clancey (1984). The implication is that the goal of ICAL is to lead the learner to conform to the image of perfection embodied in the expert system. This follows a tradition, begun by Carbonell,[10] of developing ICAL systems by adapting existing programs. But instead of treating student inputs as manifestations of errors to be eliminated, an alternative philosophy could emphasise the learner's present ability. The basic teaching strategy then would be to seek to extend this knowledge, but not necessarily towards some idealized goal (remembering that there is rarely a unique, 'correct' way to do anything significant).

Thirdly, present ICAL systems (of both classes) have adopted the predominant style of expert system design, namely, the production rule framework. The motivation for using production rules differs for the two classes of ICAL system. For the 'paradigmatic' programs, the main emphasis is on psychological validity. The outcome is usually a small production system which solves, say, subtraction or algebra problems, but which it is very difficult to reason through to convince oneself that the production system does indeed solve those problems. This is partly because the interpreter often makes use of concepts (such as 'refractoriness', that is, the idea that no rule is applied more than once with its conditions satisfied in the same way) for which there may be a rationale in psychological terms but for which there is no precise theoretical formalism. It is difficult to imagine such a system being able to explain in general terms how the program works. For expert systems, production systems provide a framework within which domain knowledge can be codified and maintained relatively easily. However, Clancey (1984) admits that 'rules are not written independently of the whole rule base: a rule author must think about how a given rule will fit'. Understanding comes more from seeing how the rules 'fit' than seeing what an individual rule accomplishes. Clancey found, then, that 'MYCIN's rules have to be restructured in order to be applied to teaching'.

Fourthly, and following on from this, is the realization that the emphasis with expert systems on cost-effective performance may not be appropriate for intelligent tutoring. Clancey writes that 'in expert systems, there is no attempt to simulate how human experts think'. This perhaps is a simplification since expert systems are designed in collaboration with human experts and are intended to be understandable by them, but it confirms that the orientation to develop a program with a high level of performance alone does not lead to the 'more explicit, psychologically valid model of problem solving', which Clancey now believes is necessary.

A DIFFERENT PERSPECTIVE

Despite these shortcomings, expert systems are still proposed as the core component of ICAL systems. However, the commercial success of expert systems does not necessarily mean that they are the best place from which to start designing ICAL systems. The remainder of this paper suggests that the focus should be on the learner rather than on subject expertise.

The prevailing methodology views learners as errorful experts. But a learner's activities are all meaningful to the learner, in his own terms. It may be more productive to attempt to represent a learner's view directly than to try to distort an expert's view. The central component of ICAL systems should be the student model; the program's representation of the learner's view at any time. In case this 'learner-centred' perspective on ICAL should seem evidently desirable it is perhaps worth noting that of Fisher & Howe's 25 features the only one considered unnecessary to support a tutorial is that 'the system should have a model of the student's factual and reasoning process knowledge' (but maybe this was an oversight!).

A program which determines the dynamically changing contents of a student model is a computer implementation of a theory of human learning. This suggests that the most promising source of insights for the design of ICAL systems is not expert systems but recent research on machine learning.[11] While much of this research is not directly addressed to modelling

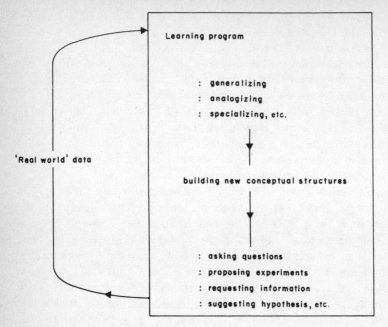

Figure 2   Machine learning

human learning, the programs do demonstrate how ICAL systems could maintain a realistic student model and could determine teaching actions to meet the learner's needs.

The overall design of a machine learning program is as shown in Fig. 2. The program accesses data (which may be directly from the real world, but is more usually provided by some other program such as a simulator or an information retrieval package or by human input) and attempts to organize this into some internal conceptual representation. Some programs rely on a human user to decide what data is useful but others are self-contained learners which have their own strategies for deciding what data to seek.

For example, concept learning programs indicate how instances appropriate to the contents of a student model could be generated, and what a competent learner could be expected to learn from them. In particular, *LEX*,[12] which learns by performing experiments to tune procedures for symbolic integration, suggests how ICAL systems could monitor learning in the absence of a teacher, and so could form the basis of ICAL systems which sought to understand a student's attempt to learn by experimentation. We could imagine such a system commenting upon an experiment proposed by a learner, asking him, for example, what he might expect to learn from the experiment. It is important to appreciate that this would be a 'shared experiment', for *LEX*-type programs do not themselves know what is to be learned. To the extent that *LEX* itself is a capable learner, we may expect a student to absorb good learning strategies from such a collaboration.

The most intriguing machine learning program is AM,[13] which also learns by itself. Again, we can picture a shared investigation, with the learner learning not only about the domain but also what it means to 'learn by discovery'. These programs remind us that most human learning occurs without the learner being explicitly directed towards some externally pre-scribed objective. The design of the programs suggests how this learning could be made more effective. The programs' representations of what is learned suggest what ICAL systems need to know about a learner if they wish to understand him, in order to direct his activities, to a greater or lesser extent.

In particular, student models need to be complex, containing many hun-dreds of frames defining relevant (and indeed irrelevant) concepts, pro-cedures and heuristics. (Frames are data structures consisting of collections of slots that describe aspects of objects, and with a great deal of internal structure designed to make them useful in specific kinds of problem-solving tasks.) The prospect of creating such complex student models is not too daunting for tools, such as *RLL*,[14] now exist for manipulating frames, and, in any case, most of the frames will be created automatically by the ICAL system itself. Learning heuristics (the desired meta-level of MYCIN) could also, in principle, be expressed as frames and so could be explained. These frames would enable the system to create, for example, new concepts from old ones, by, for example, generalization and specialization. Among these frames would be some which we might regard as erroneous. Such frames might enable the system to anticipate or understand misconceptions that a learner develops. Slots in lower-level frames could refer to such 'buggy' procedures to allow the system to identify the reasons for apparent mistakes. This could prove more effective than the present strategy which is, in essence, to introduce bugs into a working program until one is found which causes failures the same as those produced by the student. If the system is to play a directive role, then frames defining 'what is to be learned' could be specified and compared to frames within the student model to determine teaching actions (in a similar but more flexible way to that proposed for expert, system based ICAL).

We propose, therefore, that an attempt be made to implement a 'guided discovery learning' (GDL) style of ICAL, as outlined in Fig. 3. The learner would be trying to learn 'by discovery' about some domain. We imagine a system which has access to (or can generate) a large body of facts, e.g. biological data, but does not have rules and meta-rules organizing these facts. The learner will explore this database—asking questions, presenting hypotheses, occasionally answering questions—in an endeavour to under-stand the database (i.e. to form a conceptual structuring of it). The learner's learning program would be modelled by a machine learning program within the GDL system: the machine learning program would use the same data as accessed by the learner, and would use its own conclusions to lead a 'collabo-rative interaction'. This would be a genuine collaboration in that the GDL

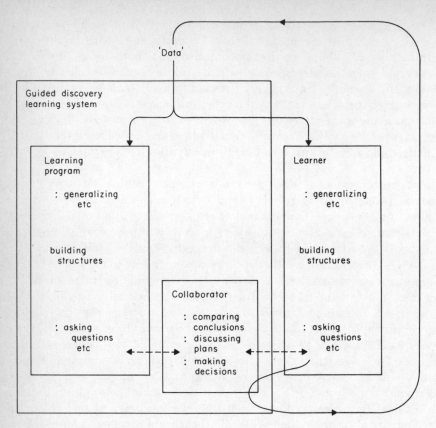

Figure 3   Design of a guided discovery learning system

system would not itself know what is to be learned by the learner; there is no 'target' body of knowledge and no expert system within the GDL system. The 'expertise' of the GDL system lies not in the subject matter but in the learning process itself. Notice that if the 'collaborator' module did nothing at all we would simply have a conventional discovery learning situation, using simulation, information retrieval or LOGO. Our aim is to investigate the problems that would arise in implementing ICAL systems intermediate between overbearing tutorial systems and open-ended learning environments.

It must be emphasized that Fig. 3 is not offered as the design of an 'ideal' ICAL system. Clearly, there is a place for expert systems in the direct exposition of known rules, especially for adults. Figure 3 represents a research strategy to ensure that we focus on the needs of the learner when designing ICAL systems.

CONCLUSIONS

The prevailing methodology for implementing intelligent teaching systems is based upon the idea of an expert system. There are several problems with this approach. To balance the present emphasis on subject expertise and to focus attention on the needs of the learner, we have proposed a 'guided discovery learning' style of ICAL, based upon machine learning research. By developing tutoring systems which 'learn with a student' (because they have no built-in subject expertise), we hope to focus more directly on the learner's activities, beliefs and understanding, and also on the learning process itself. As a learner explores the subject domain, the tutoring system would try to build (using its own model of learning) a detailed model of the learner's state of understanding.

REFERENCES

1. SERC/DoI (1983) *Intelligent Knowledge-Based Systems: a programme for action in the UK*, SERC/DoI, London.
2. Brown, J. S. and Burton, R. R. (1978) Diagnostic models for procedural bugs in basic mathematical skills, Cognitive Science, 2, 155–192.
3. Burton, R. R. and Brown, J. S. (1979) An investigation of computer coaching for informal learning activities, *International Journal of Man-Machine Studies*, 11, 5–24.
4. Goldstein, I. P. (1979) The genetic graph: a representation for the evolution of procedural knowledge, *International Journal of Man-Machine Systems*, 11, 51–77.
5. Sleeman, D. H. and Smith, M. J. (1981) Modelling student's problem solving, *Artificial Intelligence*, 16, 171–187.
6. Young, R. M. (1980). Production systems for modelling human cognition, in *Expert Systems in the Microelectronic Age* (ed D. Michie), Edinburgh, Edinburgh University Press.
7. Brown, J. S., Burton, R. R. and Bell, A. G. (1975) *SOPHIE*: a step toward creating a reactive learning environment, *International Journal of Man-Machine Studies*, 7, 675–696.
8. Clancey, W. J. (1983) *GUIDON, Journal of Computer-Based Instruction*, 10, 8–15.
9. Clancey, W. J. (1984) Methodology for building an intelligent tutoring system, in *Methods and Tactics in Cognitive Science* (ed. Kintsch, W.), Hillsdale, NJ, Lawrence Erlbaum.
10. Fisher, R. and Howe, J. (1982) The potential for expert system based training aids. DAI Report No. 121, University of Edinburgh.
11. Carbonell, J. R. (1970) AI in CAI: an artificial intelligence approach to computer-assisted instruction, *IEEE Transactions on Man-Machine Systems*, 11, 190–202.

12. Michalski, R. S., Carbonell, J. G. and Mitchell, T. M., (eds.) (1983) *Machine Learning: an Artificial Intelligence Approach*, Palo Alto, Tioga.

13. Mitchell, T. M., Utgoff, P. E. and Banerji, R. (1983) Learning by experimentation: acquiring and refining problem-solving heuristics, in *Machine Learning: an Artificial Intelligence Approach* (eds. Michalski. R. S., Carbonell, J.G. and Mitchell, T. M.), Palo Alto, Tioga.

14. Lenat, D. B. (1982) *The Role of Heuristics in Learning by Discovery*, Palo Alto, Tioga.

15. Greiner, R. and Lenat, D. B. (1980) A representation representation language, *Proceedings of First National AAAI Conference*, Stanford.

7 EVALUATING CAL

This section is concerned with evaluation. In choosing the papers we had two aims in mind: firstly to provide 'case studies' which illustrate the different approaches to evaluating the use of computers in education, and secondly that these same studies should give practical guidance on evaluation.

Evaluation methodologies cover a spectrum from quantitative to qualitative methods. The papers in this section are mainly located towards the qualitative end. We believe that a strictly quantitative approach is not appropriate for evaluating the use of computers in the classroom: it is possible, however, to draw from a range of traditions as Atkin advocates, and as the papers by Phillips and Kerry illustrate.

Clearly, choice of methodology depends on the researcher's concerns: an interest in measures of attainment will necessitate quantitative measures whilst focussing on processes tends towards the qualitative end or a more eclectic approach. It is very difficult to gather hard evidence of success in skills such as problem solving, creativity and effective co-operation—although as you saw in Paper 5.4, measures of co-operation can be successfully devised. We do not even know whether creativity can be successfully 'taught' or 'fostered'. The authors of the four papers approach evaluation in quite different ways. For Phillips an important objective is developing good ideas for using a computer in the classroom—and in trialling the programs with teachers, unexpected ways of using program emerge. The ITMA teams' approach is at variance with that of Kerry in that they don't believe it possible for teachers to successfully observe their own classes. Note, however, that in the project Kerry discusses this emerged as a solution to a logistical problem of gathering enough data. Note also the emphasis on checking the validity and reliability of these reports—including 'triangulation': i.e. checking on the results by a different method, in this case, visits to the participating classroom by an observer. Atkins's system of analysing 'open' questionnaire or interview responses also involves a 'double-check'—an independent judge going through the categories. Finally the evaluation criteria offered by Blease should, by virtue of being so comprehensive, help you to address the particular questions you are interested in.

7.1 *ITMA's approach to classroom observation*

- Richard Phillips

Investigations on Teaching with Microcomputers as an Aid (ITMA) is a group which conducts research and develops materials. The group is based at Plymouth and Nottingham, and is partly funded by the Microelectronics Education Programme (MEP). Before explaining ITMA's approach to classroom testing, it is worth briefly describing our approach to CAL.

Traditionally, computers in education have been operated by a single student at the keyboard. More recently, it has become common for pupils to work in small groups. Both these styles of use normally exclude the direct involvement of the teacher. Our main interest is in an approach which involves a teacher, a microcomputer, and a group of pupils working together. We have observed many hundreds of lessons conducted in this style and believe it is unusually effective for promoting major extensions of pupils' understanding and problem-solving ability.

The computer can provide rich environments for problem-solving and investigation, it is a powerful visual aid, and it can remove many of the less important cognitive loads from the teacher and pupils. However, its depth of understanding is limited; it is poor at many activities which teachers can do better, such as managing a discussion, encouraging strategic thinking, regulating the pace and offering appropriate levels of guidance.

We believe that teachers should teach with computers; neither the computer, nor the teacher, is as effective working alone.

CLASSROOM OBSERVATION

The appropriate way to test computer software must depend on the way it is to be used. Some educational programs are intended to be self-contained learning packages. These could be tested almost as well in the home as in the school, because their purpose is to work well without a teacher. On the other hand, most ITMA programs depend heavily on the presence of the teacher and so, for us, classroom observation is an essential part of the development of our material. It amounts to much more than 'testing'. With classroom use, material will often develop in exciting and unexpected ways.

What do we do? Well, if possible, we avoid observing just a single program. It seems more natural to give teachers a collection of programs (not necessarily just ITMA ones) and let them choose what they use. Clearly, this is not always possible, but it does help overcome some of the unnatural aspects of a one-off lesson with a computer.

In selecting teachers, our major concern is that we should sample as wide a range of teaching styles as possible. Successful program teaching units should work well in everybody's classroom. We also hope that some of our teachers will be innovators. They will show us things that can be done with a program which we had not thought of. Clearly, we try to pick teachers who are sufficiently committed to use the computer regularly over the period of the trials, but we tend to avoid computer enthusiasts, and always try to include some teachers who have not used a computer before.

We have never found it very useful to ask teachers to report on their own lessons. Even the most skilful and imaginative teachers seem unable to report effectively on their own performance. We always use observers. We make a point of observing whole lessons, even if the computer is in use for only a few minutes. We do not usually make any use of audio or video recording—these techniques do not make it any easier to get the essential details of a lesson. They simply allow one to put off the problem until a later date. We think it is better to get the important information on paper while the lesson is in progress.

The observers are mostly members of the ITMA team. Everyone has a few hours training to learn the SCAN (systematic classroom analysis notation) recording system. Observation techniques are, however, mostly learnt by working alongside more experienced observers, through discussing lessons and through reading other people's reports.

Our observers are instructed to collect three types of information:

1. Answers to a set of specific questions, some of which are purely factual while others involve some elements of judgement (see Fig. 1)
2. A detailed, event-by-event description of substantial segments of the lesson, recorded using SCAN notation[1]
3. A free commentary on the key features of the lesson.

This lesson information is often supplemented by interviews with the teacher, and with samples of pupils' work.

SCAN is a shorthand notation which allows observers to record the structure of the lesson as it is happening. It focuses particularly on the quality of

Confidential

Date | Teacher | School | Observer

Class (Year, number, ability etc)

Program(s)

Please attach securely: SCAN sheets your report teacher-produced materials etc

Keep this page at the top.

Activities

	1	2	3	4	5	6	Whole Lesson
Type of Activity							
Minutes of lesson							
Rate general pupil interest. (1 = Total Boredom, 8 = Strong interest)							
Rate general familiarity of material and level of demand (α, $\alpha\beta$, β, $\beta\gamma$, γ)							
Rate level of guidance. (1 = Structured, 3 = Open)							
Estimate for the pupils the percentage of task-related activity.							

Your global rating of the value of CAL in this lesson:

$$-3 \quad -2 \quad -1 \quad 0 \quad +1 \quad +2 \quad +3$$

CAL a substantial hindrance

CAL a great help

Short Check List for Report

Report the whole lesson—not just the program use. Does this follow work in a previous lesson? Will it continue in a later lesson?
Was the computer used as a whole-class teaching aid, or in some other style?
Did CAL take a natural place in the topic being followed? Who operated the keyboard?
Did CAL promote discussion? Did it promote written work? Was the teacher experienced with the computer? What resources were used (besides the computer)?
Comments on program and documentation.
Comment on the roles played by the teacher, pupils and computer.

Figure 1. A general purpose form used by ITMA for classroom observation

the dialogue: for example, it categorizes teachers' questions according to both the demand made of pupils and the level of guidance offered by the teacher. Observers find that SCAN is an effective memory aid, enabling the finer details of a lesson to be recalled easily when writing a report.

As soon as possible after each lesson, the observers write a brief narrative account of the lesson, and comment on its main features. They also complete some rating scales, which attempt to give a crude and subjective measure of such factors as the level of demand of the lesson, the level of guidance, and the amount of pupil interest.

The result is a detailed description of the lesson, which any member of the team can draw on for research or development purposes. When writing a report, it is not our business to criticize the pupils or the teacher. When lessons do not seem to go as well as they might, we look for changes in the hardware, software and documentation which might help to put things right.

THE BENEFITS OF OBSERVATION

After watching half a dozen lessons, where different teachers have employed the same program, a large number of useful facts emerge, of a very diverse kind.

This is what might be described as ergonomic information—facts which cast light on the efficiency of the man–machine interface. These relate mostly to the control of the program through the keyboard, and the intelligibility of the screen display. For instance, on several occasions, we noticed difficulty when an important change in the screen display took place rapidly and in isolation. This could happen when, for example, a transformational geometry program illustrates a reflection. The problem is that it seems very difficult to get everyone in a class to watch the screen at the moment the change occurs. It is not that the class is inattentive, but rather that, when the screen remains static for long periods, pupils will only sample it intermittently. The problem seems to disappear with the incorporation of an animated change, or sequence of changes, to the screen display.

This is just one example, and there are many other ergonomic problems of a similar kind.[2] The designers of hardware and documentation, as well as writers of educational software, need to watch these factors carefully, as they can easily nullify any educational value in a program.

An important question to ask about any program teaching unit is 'Will teachers use it?' By asking teachers to select programs to use from a collection, we get a rough idea of the relative attractiveness of different programs. There are obvious dangers in reading too much into this choice. For example, teachers are unlikely to select a program which is complicated to use, unless someone has demonstrated it to them before.

Perhaps a more valid indication comes from asking teachers whether they would use a program again. In some of our trials, one week after using a program, we asked teachers to answer this single question:

Would you use this program again after this project is over? They could choose one of the following answers:

- I would never use this program again.
- I am unlikely to use this program again.
- I would use this program again, but only if a suitable computer were always freely available in the classroom.
- I would use this program again, even if the computer had to be carried up two flights of stairs before the lesson.
- I would use this program again, even if the computer had to be booked a week in advance and carried up two flights of stairs before the lesson.
- I would use this program again, even if a computer had to be specially borrowed from another school.

In order to encourage teachers to be honest, we asked them to seal their answers to this question in envelopes, which were not opened until the trials were over.

The ITMA approach avoids asking teachers to complete lengthy questionnaires. Because teachers are already busy, questionnaires tend to elicit a minimum of information.

Trials can help one assess the probability of a particular program being used, and they can also indicate the likelihood of different styles of use. For example, there has recently been a lot of interest in what MEP calls 'content-free programs'. These are programs where teachers may create their own disk or cassette files containing particular questions, examples of data for use in a lesson. Because many teachers produce their own workcards and other materials, it seems likely they would want to use a computer file in a similar way. However, in practice, we have found this hardly ever happens. It may be because teachers do not have easy access to a computer. Although teachers do not seem to make full use of content-free programs in lesson preparation, it is more common for files to be created during a lesson, usually by groups of pupils.

Perhaps the most important purpose of observation is to develop good ideas for using a program in a classroom. For example, during some secondary mathematics trials, a number of teachers chose to use some mathematics games (for example, 'Subgame' and 'Ergo'). Some teachers used these at the end of the lesson when other work had been completed. But teachers at two Nottingham schools experimented with a different way of using them. They began the lesson by getting the whole class to play the game on the computer. The teacher took a fairly passive role and typed in any moves which were suggested. After playing a couple of games, the teacher asked for suggestions on how to win, but did not comment on anything which was said. The class played one more game and then the computer was switched off. For the remainder of the lesson, pupils continued to play the game in twos or threes. They took turns in being the player or the 'computer'. This activity seemed very useful in a number of ways. It developed a broad understanding of the mathematics underlying the game; it encouraged discussion and strategic thinking; and it adapted very well to the different levels of ability within the class.

Since these trials, we have seen many lessons using this approach. It works well with a number of programs. But the important point is that none of these programs were designed for this type of use—it was only through observation that the full value of this method was discovered.

Most ITMA programs have developed through classroom observation in this kind of way. We expect programs to develop through successive drafts of the code, but, more importantly, we expect them to develop as ideas, and classroom observation is the most effective way of achieving this. A good example is the development of 'Clues', described earlier by Graham Field.

The business of observing program teaching units in use in the classroom is, of course, very time-consuming. We believe it is well worthwhile, both in order to develop program teaching units and to understand the full implication of microcomputers in teaching. There is no space here to discuss the broader research approach to classroom observation. Two ITMA reports, however, may be of interest: one concerns classroom roles[3] and the other tries to predict future trends.[4]

REFERENCES

1. Beeby, T., Burkhardt, H. and Fraser, R. (1979) 'Systematic classroom analysis notation (SCAN) for mathematics lessons', Shell Centre for Mathematical Education, University of Nottingham.
2. Phillips, R., Burkhardt, H., Coupland, J., Fraser, R., Pimm, D. and Ridgway, J. (1984) 'Computer aided teaching', *Ergonomics* **27**, 1984.
3. Fraser, R., Burkhardt, H., Coupland, J., Phillips, R., Pimm, D. and Ridgway, J. (1984) 'Learning activities and classroom roles', unpublished ITMA paper from Shell Centre for Mathematical Education, University of Nottingham.
4. Phillips, R., Burkhardt, H., Coupland, J., Fraser, R, and Ridgway, J. (1984) 'The future of the microcomputer as a classroom teaching aid: an empirical approach to crystal gazing', *Computers and Education* **8**, 1984.

7.2 Self-report case-studies: an experiment in own classroom data collection by teachers

● Trevor Kerry

BACKGROUND

In September 1981 the Schools' Council established a two-year project called 'Developing Pupils Thinking Through Topic Work' to be directed by Professor J. F. Eggleston and Howard Bradley. The brief was to explore the current practice of teachers in topic work lessons (also variously called project work, thematic work, environmental or integrated studies), and then to experiment with in-service training materials and methods. Early on, a policy decision was taken to spend most of the first year on the research, with training materials emerging directly from this research activity for trialling in year two. This article examines in detail one aspect of the research methodology and its application—an aspect which may have wider applications in the field of data collection for curriculum development.

THE SCOPE OF THE PROJECT

Topic work is an important weapon in the primary teacher's armoury. Teachers tell us that anything from 10% to 75% of the week is spent on it. My role as project co-ordinator of the School's Council Project was to find ways in the research phase by which to probe more deeply into teachers' practice, and then to try to use the discoveries in the in-service phase to articulate principles or guidelines that other teachers might find valuable. In practice the co-ordinator, directors and a research student, along with volunteer researchers, worked together using a variety of methods to probe approaches and methods. Some of this work has been reported elsewhere: a summary of the project's work can be found in Kerry;[1] and studies of classroom process are recorded in Miles[2] and Eggleston.[3]

Much of the concern of the Project was about the cognitive demand of learning experiences presented to pupils in this kind of cross-disciplinary lesson. Part of the purpose of the research activity, therefore, had to centre upon how teachers articulated those learning processes and on what they themselves believed they were aiming for and achieving. It was desirable for the research team to talk to teachers face-to-face whenever possible, and to study their classrooms at first hand. But to increase the sample size, and more importantly to maximize the range of teacher approaches to topic work covered by our work, we had to find ways to enable teachers to give us insights into their thinking processes. In the event this was done through the use of open-ended questionnaires, through unstructured interviews, and by the use of the self-report procedures described later in this article. These self-report procedures evolved from more traditional research approaches, as will be seen, and represent an interesting and novel approach to involving teachers in research/development curriculum projects.

THE RESEARCH PHASE

From the beginning the research activity of the project, exploring teachers' practice in topic work lessons in primary schools, was seen as taking place in two main stages.

The first stage was to survey a range of practice by means of a semi-structured questionnaire mailed to heads and teachers in a stratified random sample of schools in rural, suburban and urban areas of the East Midlands. This questionnaire was detailed in that it asked for demographic data and for definitions of topic work: it asked, too, about aims, curriculum and teaching methods, planning and preparation procedures, class management, about assessments and record-keeping and about follow-up activities. It also solicited the professional advice the respondent would give to students or inexperienced practitioners. Most questions allowed a freehand response; though some (e.g. those concerned with demographic information or specific procedures) involved a more economical box-ticking response to save the respondent's time.

This questionnaire was seen as a crucial examination of the individual teacher's practice. In due course responses to the questionnaires were received and analysed: and the findings are reported elsewhere.[4] In the event the questionnaire provided the basis for the compilation of a document which would guide observers in the second major phase of the research—case-studies in primary classrooms.

In order to provide in-service materials for teachers the hope was to watch teachers at work during topic work lessons, to tape record their reflections upon the lessons and lesson-planning, to talk to pupils on tape and to collect examples of pupils' work so that the in-service clientèle could discuss its value, especially in terms of the development of pupils' thinking. To achieve this within the framework of a short-life project was a tall order. A team of seven case-study workers (one full-time project officer and six part-time volunteers) was established and they studied some twenty teachers across eight schools. The quantity and range of data generated was considerable: but the question remained as to whether the still quite small case-study sample could be augmented. Within this second research phase, therefore, a decision was made to augment the researchers' cases by experimenting with a system of self-report case-studies in which teachers would be asked to scrutinize and report on their own classroom practice, i.e. to case-study themselves. But would it work? This paper investigates the methodology of these self report studies and comments on their value as seen by other teachers.

SETTING UP THE SELF-REPORT CASE-STUDIES

Few teachers, except those most recently emerged from B.Ed. Honours courses, have been taught to think in research terms. Therefore, the setting up of a self-report system of case-studies had to be meticulously planned. The first step was to try to put together a self-report package, a guideline document, which would give the respondents a framework within which to record their activities sensitively and in detail. It had to be probing, with a structure shared by all respondents, but flexible enough to allow for individual initiatives in recording unique classroom events. It had, too, to solicit information about the key areas highlighted by the original questionnaire as in need of exploration and included in those case-studies conducted by trained observers. Inevitably, the package would look sizeable; but an eye would be kept on length so that it did not discourage too many potential users. The final research package consisted of four parts, which are described in the following paragraphs.

1. The first section of the self-report case-study asked teachers to complete a questionnaire, in fact the identical questionnaire which had been used in the first research phase. There were several good reasons for this. The questionnaire was known to explore thoroughly and economically a teacher's basic attitudes to, and procedures within, topic lessons. There was already a pool of existing information resulting from the use of the

questionnaire and so the data from the self-reports could be compared with this as a way of seeing the self-report respondent's position within a wider scheme of topic work teaching, and to determine what was 'typical' and what was 'distinctive' about the teacher in question. The feeling was also that this was a stock-taking exercise for the teacher, a kind of self-analysis which was open-ended enough not to distort his or her thinking, but stimulating enough to get the respondent into an appropriate frame of mind for self-reporting.

2. If section one served as a background to the teacher's topic work in general, then part 2 of the self-report package concentrated on the specific topic to be taught and reported upon by the respondent. Christened the Topic Outline Proforma it asked for the topic title, an outline of the content (including flow diagrams, examples of worksheets), and the resources available. Then it went on to explore the progress the teacher intended the pupils to make during the topic socially and in terms of knowledge gained, skills practised and attitudes to learning or subject matter. Questions were included about provisions for the most and least able, the planned duration of the topic, its links with other curriculum areas and the processes for monitoring and assessing pupils' progress. Two final questions looked at the teacher's expected outcomes of the project and the roles he or she expected to play.

The first two parts of the self-report package could be completed before any classroom teaching took place. The questionnaire could be timed well in advance of the lessons covered by the self-report activity, and the Topic Outline Proforma could be absorbed with a minimum effort into the teacher's standard preparation procedures. In these ways, the workload was spread and interference minimized. Parts 3 and 4, however, needed attention during the period of the teaching of the topic itself.

3. Part 3 was designed as a diary sheet to record the events of a lesson. Respondents were not asked to complete a diary sheet for every topic lesson taught, but for one such lesson per week for the topic's duration. The diary sheet was seen as central to the whole affair, since it would replace the case-study worker's lesson notes of the main case-study sample. It asked for responses to these questions or instructions:

(a) What were your intentions, aims or objectives for this lesson?
(b) Describe briefly your lesson organisation for the session (use of space, or of whole class or individualized learning. etc.).
(c) What particular *teaching strategies* were used, e.g. problem-solving, class discussion?
(d) What task or tasks were the pupils set?
(e) By the end of the lesson what new information, skills and concepts had the pupils acquired?
(f) Looking back, with what aspects of the lesson were you most and least satisfied?

(g) Please include worksheets, etc., as examples of work done.

(h) Add any comments of your own.

For teachers to respond to this was a sizeable time-demand, but crucial to the whole operation.

4. The fourth part of the self-analysis document was a weekly summary sheet which asked the teachers to look back over the week and to record anything which had affected their own planning of the pupils' learning. Specific questions probed the learning difficulties of individual pupils, resource production and management, and things to be borne in mind when planning the next week's work.

The complete package as it came to the teachers in the self-report group, then, contained a questionnaire, a topic outline proforma, six diary sheets to record six individual lessons, and six weekly summary sheets. The case study was to extend over a six-week period or up to half a term if the topic lasted that long. In addition, the document was equipped with clear but detailed instructions for use. Though sizeable, half of it could be completed and put aside before the classroom teaching began. In the event, eleven teachers out of twenty-one (52%) invited to take part did so. The next question was whether their self-reporting would be adequate for our purposes.

SOME CRITERIA FOR JUDGING SUCCESS

Adelman *et al.*[5] remarked that 'case study is an umbrella term for a family of research methods having in common the decision to focus an enquiry round an instance'. Nisbet & Watt[6] add 'the method attempts to give a fair and accurate account of a specific case in such a way as to allow the reader to penetrate the superficial record, and also to check the author's interpretations by examining an appropriate selection of objective evidence from which the case study has been built'.

Our self-report case-studies differed from most in a significant way. While most case-studies are compiled by an observer-researcher and written up by him for an audience, ours were to be compiled by the teacher-subject and given to the researchers as fodder for in-service materials. By definition, the role of the subject as researcher would call into question the objectivity of these cases. While they did not need to satisfy the ultimate canons of objective research—they were to augment other more conventional case-studies and to do so in a curriculum developmental, rather than in a purely research, role—nevertheless, some degree of objectivity was required to inform professional practice.

To judge the worth of these case-studies, then, this objectivity needed to be scrutinized. In effect, the project researchers need to answer a number of questions about these self-report studies:

(a) Were they detailed enough both to be an accurate portrayal of the topic work being examined and to be valuable as potential development material for use in curriculum initiatives for the in-service training other teachers?

(b) Were they sensitive enough to be a realistic and credible account of what happened in the topic work lessons described?

(c) Was there evidence of self-analysis by the teachers in their self-reporting?

(d) Were the accounts honest?

(e) Would actual use of extracts from these self-report cases be proven in the in-service role at the evaluation stage?

If the answers to the foregoing questions were satisfactory, then it would appear that this could well be a useful methodology for similar research-and-development projects which needed to increase sample sizes at the research stage against a background of limited man-power.

SATISFYING THE CRITERIA FOR SUCCESS IN SELF-REPORTING

Perhaps the best way to assess the effectiveness of the self-report case-studies is to illustrate or comment upon how they satisfied each of the criteria verbalized in the foregoing questions.

As regards detailed and accurate portrayal of classroom life, the respondents went to considerable lengths to supply even minute details. In one case-study the teacher augmented his written returns with a tape of a concert of American music which resulted from the topic on the United States. Not content with this, he felt that he should also include a tape of the rehearsal for the concert since so many teaching points were made in it. A second teacher, who had pursued the theme 'Castles', had turned the classroom (inside and outside) into a castle: the door had a portcullis attached, lights were turned into chandeliers, windows had mock bars across them. All this he documented on colour-slide and added a suitable commentary. Here were ready-made results from topic work lessons, described and commented upon by their chroniclers, and ready for use by other teachers as stimulus materials.

The written accounts were often sensitive too, and sensitive enough to make them credible. A short quotation from the diary sheet illustrates the judgement. The teacher is writing about a topic on a favourite theme. How we used to live 1936–1953:

> The aim of this (first) lesson was to introduce the children to the topic. I aimed to stimulate their interest for the forthcoming television series around which our topic will develop. I intended to give the class a broad introduction to the period to be studied and suggested ways in which they might be able to make

personal contributions. This was a class lesson based on a discussion introduced by me. The second part of the lesson involved the children compiling individual questionnaires to be taken home later and discussed with grandparents or older relatives. The class discussion centred mainly around a question and answer technique, with the pupils contributing any previous knowledge.

After an initial explanation of how to compile a questionnaire, each child composed a list of questions that they would like to ask a grandparent about life in 1936. These were then marked before the children took home a neatly written, corrected copy of the questionnaire.

By the end of the lesson I wanted the pupils to have set the topic period into a time-scale they could relate to. The class discussion required skills: and while most of the pupils had these some pupils transferred recently from the remedial unit did not, and had to begin to learn these. The exercise of posing questions made the pupils think, and careful thought was needed to make sure they were phrased in such a way that the children could compare life in the 1980s with 1936.

I was satisfied that the children showed great enthusiasm for the topic and are looking forward to meeting the Hodgkins family on the T.V. series. They were also keen to discuss the school work with their relatives.

Copies of the pupils' questionnaires are attached (i.e. to the original self-report account). On reflection, in future I would review ways to correlate this information and compare the pupils' results more effectively.

Such an account seems to satisfy all the criteria reviewed so far: detail, accuracy, realism and credibility. It begins, towards the end, to satisfy that of self-analysis, too. Other accounts exemplify this last criterion. A topic on Owls was progressing satisfactorily in a small rural primary school on an isolated fen. The teacher completed a series of weekly diary sheets as things progressed, and here is an extract from one of them:

It is obvious that some children are working at a much slower pace than others, but rather than having half-finished pieces of work I have been giving these slow ones more time. Some children, mostly in order to catch up a bit, are not thinking for themselves but are copying ideas from the more able. This insistence on finishing work might be a distinct disadvantage, making the project drag out; but at least the slow pupils are producing and finishing work—eventually: and this is giving them satisfaction. My problem now is finding work matched to individual abilities and this I must bear in mind in next week's planning . . .

This extract is certainly self-analytical; and it seems honest. Even more honest, perhaps, was the way teachers were prepared to record things which were demonstrably less than perfect:

Due to the start of the World Cup and rehearsals for the school play—both of which are incorporated into the children's curriculum work—the topic has now been curtailed . . . some parts that were planned will not now be dealt with.

The pragmatism was characteristic of the accounts and it is perhaps an additional measure of their authenticity that they include the highlights and the shadows, the successes and the warts, of classroom reality.

CROSS-CHECKING THE DATA

Having established, however, that teachers were prepared to keep sustained records of their own classroom activities, that they could remain faithful to a research Proforma in so doing, and that the resulting reports satisfied the criteria of success indicated in the previous section, it was still felt to be important to cross-check the data for validity. If the self-report case-studies were to be proved valid then they could be used in two ways: to augment the research reports of the project and to help in compiling in-service training materials based on real classroom events. To this end the project personnel maintained a programme of informal visits to the classrooms of participating teachers and recorded impressions and incidents they witnessed to compare with the teachers' own accounts. Two examples of this cross-checking process may suffice to illustrate its nature.

At Wheeldon School the class teacher of year 3 was tackling a topic of 'Castles', the project observer visited the school four times during this topic. On each occasion a description of the events taking place in the classroom was compiled, either in note form or on tape. These observations were then compared with the teacher's completed proforma. In addition, colour-slides of the pupils' work were produced: hard evidence that the resulting display work described by the teacher and seen by the observer actually existed and that the classroom genuinely had been transformed into another era! Placed side-by-side the teacher's account and the observer's impressions allowed a comparison of perspective under the various headings of the self-report proforma listed in an earlier section of this paper.

The observer made three visits to Hamlets JMI, the location of the 'Owls' topic described above. He specifically noted the pupils' emerging written work in the class, their dissection and display of the contents of owl pellets, and the fact that the pupils showed a considerable range of achievement which meant that—after the passage of some weeks—they were becoming widely separated in quantity and demand of the tasks set. He also picked up the problems of diminishing available time to complete the topic noted by the teaching head himself in the extract quoted in the previous section; though the observer felt that an additional significant factor in this was the presence of the telephone in the ever-open office adjoining the classroom—a phenomenon perhaps too familiar to the head himself to seem worthy of record.

The observer was also able to *add* data to the self-report studies by including descriptions of school facilities, the local environment, and his impressions of school ethos gained, for example, over a school lunch or during break in the staffroom.

Evidence from these observer visits suggested that what the teachers *did* record was substantially accurate in all cases. In just one instance the observer felt that there was an important omission, notably that the pupils were consistently uninterested in the work in progress; a phenomenon not mentioned by the teacher's self-report. It was possible in this instance to triangulate the data by placing a second, unprimed, observer into this class: and wholly independently she made a similar comment about disaffection.

Overall, then, these self-report studies seemed both to satisfy the criteria of success which the project team required as a pre-condition for using them as research material, and also to be substantially corroborated by independent observation. It was concluded, therefore, that, once teachers had become used to conforming to the guidelines supplied, these self-report case-studies were no more liable to a charge of bias than any other form of ethnographic reporting. In our case the monitoring of each case by an independent observer considerably strengthened the value of the data.

SELF-REPORT DATA IN IN-SERVICE TRAINING MATERIALS

Having established the validity of the data, therefore, it was desirable to put it to use to meet the project's requirements for the production of in-service training materials. Here, the procedure was to compile a resource bank of materials around those areas of topic work identified as being problematical by the research phases described earlier. These areas were; preparation for topic teaching: classroom processes, including class management and such teaching skills as questioning and task-setting: managing the curriculum at school and classroom level; and evaluating and assessing pupils' learning in topic lessons.

Under each of these major themes the project team identified issues, usually in the form of questions. Issues on the theme of classroom processes would include, for example, 'What are the teacher's underlying intentions for pupil learning in topic lessons?' and 'What tasks do teachers set to pupils during topic lessons?' Each issue was illustrated by extracting from a case-study, a self-report case-study or from the questionnaire responses, some aspect of teaching in progress that pinpointed the issue. This might be in the form of a teacher's written account, or in the form of a tape or a slide sequence or a list. To this account was added a series of questions to get the user to think more deeply about the strengths, weaknesses, or omissions of the extract, and to structure alternatives for his or her own situation.

Thus was compiled an in-service training bank of items individually culled from the research data (including the self-report cases), re-written into a format that could be used in a study-group of teachers and heads, and collected under the four major themes indicated above. Use of the bank was carefully monitored during a trial period. This aspect of the project's work is strictly outside the scope of the present article and is reported elsewhere[7, 8]. Suffice it to say that teacher-users of the bank commented specifically on the immediacy and helpfulness of the individual items in it which had been culled from self-report case-studies, though of course they were not aware of their origin in this form of data collection.

It would appear, therefore, that research materials' collected in this way for adaptation in in-service training materials are more than adequate for the purpose, and satisfy most criteria of acceptability normally applied to conventional case-studies.

THE PARTICIPANTS' VIEWPOINT

It was not possible logistically to talk in depth to every teacher who completed a self-report case-study package. But it was possible to chat informally with some and to interview others more formally. In these ways the project team was able to gain some impression of whether the teachers found the exercise valuable.

Two points were universal: it was time-consuming, but the effort expended had been worthwhile because it had forced the participant to think more carefully about his or her own practice. In effect, then, involvement even at the research level had in-service implications.

A number of other points were made, among them that the rather structured form of the self-report, necessary to ensure some conformity between the kinds of data collected by the self-reporters and to ensure relevance to the central concerns of the research, was rather cumbersome for descriptions of some infant classes and vertically grouped classes. The self-reporters usually just abandoned the proformas and wrote freehand accounts.

But the in-service spin-offs of having some teachers in a school taking part in an exercise like this were frequently reported. There was an increased likelihood of inter-staff discussion about the subjects to be covered in topic work, how to teach the material and of longer-term curriculum planning. In a three-teacher school where two teachers were involved, it was remarked of the effect on the non-participant teacher.

> The idea of Paula putting her coat on and going with pupils to the woods in the rain was unheard of before this: but now *everyone* is much more excited . . .

CONCLUSION

The argument of this study has been that self-report case-study can be valuable to the participant and also a valid method of data collection for the kind of research which underpins in-service development and training materials. To some extent the success of this methodology depended upon the compilation of a sound guideline document with its related instructions. It depended, too, upon the professionalism and commitment of the teachers who participated, but not upon any special training. Applied research often requires quick but reliable methods of data collection; and in this context self-reporting may have an increasingly important place.

REFERENCES

1. Kerry, T. (1984a) Developing children's thinking through topic work, *Education 3–13*, Vol. 12(1).
2. Miles, A. (1984) A closer look: a case study of topic work in the classroom, *Education 3–13* Vol. 12(1).
3. Eggleston, J. F. (1984) What did the children learn? *Education 3–13* Vol. 12(1).
4. Bennett, N. (1984) *Recent Advances in Classroom Research* (British Journal of Educational Psychology, Monograph).
5. Adelman, C., Jenkins, D. and Kemmis, S. (1977) 'Rethinking case-study' notes from the second Cambridge Conference, *Cambridge Journal of Education*, 6, pp. 139–150.
6. Nisbet, J. and Watt, J. (1978) *Rediguide 26: Case Study* (University of Nottingham, School of Education).
7. Kerry, T. (1984b) Effective training for topic work teaching, *Education 3–13* Vol. 12(1).
8. Kerry, T. (1984c) Trialling INSET materials for topic work teaching, *Cambridge Journal of Education*, 14, pp. 25–30.

7.3 Practitioner as researcher: some techniques for analysing semi-structured data in small-scale research

- M. Atkins

INTRODUCTION

Increasingly, practitioners in the field are turning to small-scale research projects in an attempt to improve their understanding of the professional processes in which they are engaged. Their concern may be to evaluate the effectiveness of new materials, techniques and strategies, or to collect data on the experiences, problems, expectations, beliefs and values of those with whom they deal. Although the concept of practitioner as researcher is not new[1] the increasingly sophisticated use of in-service training has highlighted the possibilities of small-scale research as part of the facilitation of heightened professionalism in many areas.

When practitioners turn to the methodology of social science research it may well appear that the greatest developments are taking place at either end of the methodological range. At the 'quantitative' pole lie the advanced techniques of multidimensional measurement; at the 'qualitative' pole lie the ethogenic techniques of researchers such as Harré[2] and Marton.[3] As Table 1 (opposite) it is tempting to view these methodological poles as vehicles for different types of research with different foci and different modes of operation.

Such a schematic polarization can be helpful provided it does not become stereotyped with mid-points on the range lost to view. The danger for the practitioner lies in the impression given that alignment with one or other 'camp' has to precede development of a research strategy. The over-riding criterion which should guide the selection of methodology—fitness for the research task in hand—may then be overturned. Indeed, both extreme positions have weaknesses as well as strengths. Rigid adherence to the quantitative position may lead the practitioner to take for granted certain factors in a situation which should have been rendered problematic. Similarly, over-reliance on the ethogenic approach may result in neglect of those external factors which are giving a situation the very characteristics to which the subjects are responding.

Table 1 Focus on methods

Quantitative focus on	Qualitative focus on
Study and explanation of manifest behaviour	Discovery and understanding of personal meaning
Search for 'laws' governing human behaviour; deterministic	Illumination of intersubjective construction of reality
Claim for objective truth	Claim for relative truths
Prediction on basis of statistical generalizability	General held to be inherent in particular. Reliance on informed judgment of reader to assess generalization to other known contexts
Repeated patterns, trends and central tendencies in phenomena	Relationships and distinctions between cases. The unique an acceptable subject of research
Outcomes, results and products	Processes
Natural science paradigms	Arts pardigms
Measurement and testing instruments to collect data	Researcher as own instrument in collection of evidence
Detachment of researcher	Involvement/participation of researcher

In any case a rigid distinction between the quantitative and qualitative approaches is conceptually unsound. As Eisner[4] has pointed out, all scientists are concerned with the 'qualities' of the situation they are studying. Further, scientists of all persuasions may employ analogy (in the derivation of hypotheses), intuition and hunch. Conversely, the term 'scientific' should apply to any research design which has been appropriately conceived for the task in hand and appropriately applied in practice. A good piece of ethogenic research should not be 'unscientific' in the pejorative sense of 'haphazard', 'irrational' or 'illogical'. Finally, both approaches are necessarily bounded by the cultural domain of which they are a part and neither is value free. Theories derived from either can be used to predict and control but equally can be superseded or discarded as better models are formulated on the basis of new evidence and data.

In those situations, therefore, where the practitioner wishes to obtain both quantitative and qualitative data and evidence an eclectic approach to research methodology should be encouraged. Indeed, applying the concept of triangulation, the use of techniques from contrasting repertoires may strengthen rather than weaken confidence in the results.

There is a further, more practical reason for the practitioner researcher to eschew the polar extremes in the methodological range. Both poles make demands on specialist skill and resources which the practitioner is unlikely to possess in full. The use of multivariate analysis techniques may require a large data base and access to mainframe computer facilities. Such techniques also demand knowledge of advanced statistical concepts and an understanding of the assumptions on which the techniques are based. Without such knowledge the practitioner is unable to judge the nature and limit of interpretation which the results can bear. Conversely, transcription and analysis of personal accounts of social episodes can make considerable demands on time and require specialist knowledge of psycho- and sociolinguistics and phenomenology. Once again a mid-point on the range which will enable the practitioner to acquire and use methodological skills successfully is required. In particular, research techniques are needed which build on and refine existing methods currently employed by the practitioner in collecting information and obtaining feedback on his or her professional practice. The techniques which commend themselves most obviously in this context are semi-structured instruments which enable the practitioner to combine closed and open items yielding, respectively, quantitative and qualitative data.

Chief among the semi-structured research techniques which the practitioner is likely to adopt in a small-scale research project are the self-report questionnaire and the interview. For both instruments are familiar in concept and practice to professionals in the field and can be tackled at different levels of analysis from lesser to greater sophistication. As indicated above, they can be designed to accommodate both quantitative and qualitative items and yield both nominal and ordinal data. The strengths and weaknesses of these instruments have been frequently rehearsed in handbooks on research design[5]: the pitfalls, and strategies for increasing reliability and validity, are also well understood.

There remain, however, particular problems in tackling the content analysis of responses to open questions or items.[6] The information yielded tends to be 'rich' and 'interesting' but if it is treated phenomenologically as an 'account' and subjected to the full rigours of linguistic analysis the number of respondents with whom the practitioner can deal in a small-scale study is very limited. Indeed, the sample size may become too small to enable other data-handling techniques to be applied to items yielding ordinal data. If, on the other hand, a numeric approach to the content analysis of open items is adopted (for example coding the response as it is given into prespecified binary categories such as 'yes', 'no') much of the value of the material is lost and a measure of unchecked interpretation and inference on the part of the interviewer has been introduced at the point of recording.

The problem, therefore, is to find a method of content analysis for open items which retains the advantage of 'rich' data while still rendering the responses into a form which can be handled easily and reliably for analysis. The method of content analysis set out below has been devised and used by the author[7] both for handling semi-structured interview responses and for handling open items on self-report questionnaires.[8] The examples given in this article are drawn from the analysis of interviews with 68 sixth formers conducted at the beginning and end of their one-year-courses. These interviews were the main instruments in a case study of City and Guilds Foundation Courses offered in a sixth form college.[9] It should be noted that these interviews were deemed to yield data and evidence which had an objective status beyond the episode of the interview itself. The interview questions, though prespecified and piloted in advance, invited students to give their views, beliefs and feelings about the college and the course in an unstructured response which was recorded verbatim, if possible, on the interview schedule itself. The accuracy of this written record was checked in a sample of interviews against an audio-tape of the interviews. (While professional researchers may have the facilities to audiorecord and transcribe every interview in full, for the practitioner as researcher a compromise such as the one just described may be more realistic and still achieve a reasonable level of reliability.)

PROCEDURE FOR CONTENT ANALYSIS OF OPEN ITEMS

When a record of responses has been obtained the following procedure can be adopted for analysing the open items both in questionnaires and in interview schedules.

Each open question on the schedule is taken in turn. Each response which has been recorded is read. As the responses suggest a category it is written down and the response coded under it. Each subsequent response is read with the existing categories in mind and a new category added if no previous category seems correct. In this way a complete set of categories for a question is built up and all responses are coded according to them. Typically, a question generates two different levels of response: an overall, or 'gross' answer such as 'agree', 'disagree' or 'satisfied', 'dissatisfied' and a number of sub-categories containing the reasons for the overall answer. An example of this procedure is given below with a random sample of ten students' responses to the interview question 'What advantages, if any, do you see in this course for yourself?'

STUDENT NUMBER

(1) None—(except that) after one year on City and Guilds I can go on to a mechanics' course—I don't know where.

(2) More qualifications for apprenticeships. I can't take 'O' levels—my grades are too low. This course is a kind of 'O' level—but for a knitwear mechanic. If I get distinctions, I've a better chance of getting a job.

(3) I now know something about knitwear—I can help Dad. I can go on to 'O' level next year—the course is a step to 'O' level.

(4) I can get out and meet different kinds of people on placements—I'm treated as an adult. I've never done community service before and I enjoy it.

(5) I'm doing biology—I need this. I wasn't good at it at my last school. I got a CSE 5 but I should pass it this year.

(6) I can prepare for 'O' levels.

(7) If I get a hospital placement then I can understand more about hospital life. It's the right course for me.

(8) The placements. And I get on better with my teachers.

(9) None. I really need an 'O' level course, but I'm resigned to doing City and Guilds.

(10) None. It's a waste of a year. I could be studying what I really want— nursing. No-one listens to me. I don't know how to get the application forms for other colleges.

Reading through these responses, the researcher might decide that there were two overall or 'gross' categories:

(1) No advantages
(2) At least one advantage.

Using these two gross categories the researcher would place students 1, 9 and 10 under category (1) and students 2, 3, 4, 5, 6, 7 and 8 under category (2). (There might be some dispute about the correct category for student 1. His initial response was modified. However, it transpired later in the interview that he himself had no particular desire to take a further mechanics' course so he was left as category (1).) Two subcategories are suggested by students who saw no advantage in the course: that it was not an 'O' level course, and that it was not a truly vocational course. Student 9 would be coded under the first, and student 10 under the second. Rather more subcategories are needed to do justice to the answers of the students who saw at least one advantage in the course for themselves:

- The student will get a qualification he needs for the job he wants to do (student 2)
- The student will learn practical aspects of the job he wants to do (students 3, 7, 8)
- The course will be a good preparation for 'O' level (students 3, 6)
- The course will help the student to mix with adults (student 4)
- The student will understand his work better (student 5)

The author expressed the categories which emerged from the responses, as can be seen above, in a manner which reflected the purposes of the research. But when using this procedure undue subjectivity can be reduced by applying an explicit set of rules to both the derivation of categories and to the coding process.[10] Thus, in the content analysis of the open questions on the interview schedules, the categories were drawn up to be:

(1) Exhaustive—all answers were put into categories, but sometimes an answer was split between several questions.
(2) Exclusive—apart from the subcategories being contained in the gross categories, no two subcategories were the same. At some points in analysis, however, subcategories were combined in a higher-order generalization.
(3) Independent—assigning a response to one category did not affect the classification of other data.
(4) At the same level of analysis—every effort was made to code the manifest content of what was said rather than an interpretation of its latent meaning. The flexibility of the interview itself, however, meant that some questions were answered partially in response to other questions, i.e. the 'context unit' of analysis could be more than one question.

In the example given above the unit of analysis adopted was the single assertion. This is a more difficult unit to handle in analysis than, say, a single word but more appropriate for this type of data. In the majority of answers, the single assertion will be one sentence. On occasion, however, a sentence has to be broken down into its thematic units and sometimes more than one sentence may form the assertion. Further, in the author's case study procedure, if an interviewee made more than one assertion which fell into the same category only one endorsement was coded. This applied particularly to questions on students' extra-curricular interests. If this coding rule is adopted, however, the assumption on which it rests needs to be noted: the impression from the whole is greater than the sum of its parts.

When all the responses to a particular question have been placed in categories, the endorsements for the gross and sub-categories are counted up and tabulated. There is a danger here of creating the impression that because something is mentioned often in the sample as a whole it is important or at least a worthy focus of attention. This may, of course, be questioned: the absence of a category, or low endorsement for a category, may be just as revealing as a large number of endorsements. Moreover, such an enumeration system makes no recognition of intensity of feeling; each response and each category is given equal weight. To overcome this problem the researcher may wish to record particular emphases as well as the actual wording of the response at the time of interview and reproduce both as a verbatim quotation in exemplification of a point made on analysis or interpretation.

RELIABILITY AND VALIDITY

How reliable and valid, then, is this kind of content analysis of open items? Since the practitioner as researcher commonly works alone there will be few problems with inter-interviewer inconsistency in administering the questions, while the sample of tape-recorded interviews should provide a check on self-consistency. No coding into predetermined categories is required at the point of data collection, thus reducing the need for two independent interviewers to be present to check each other's judgment.

Turning to the categories, a test—retest technique can be applied by the researcher to some questions during the analysis and at least the first ten responses on each question should always be re-checked in the light of later categories. Although these techniques may indicate to the practitioner that the analysis is reliable, further assurance can be sought by use of independent judges that the categories have been fairly derived from the responses and that the coding operation has been conducted according to the explicit rules (and has not been 'skewed' by personal, unconscious, subjective considerations).

The first independent judge can be given a sample of the most open-ended questions from the interview or questionnaire schedules. The rules for forming categories should be explained, including the desirability of deriving gross as well as sub-categories from the responses. A random sample of respondents' answers should then be presented to the judge who should be asked to write down the categories which seem to be suggested by the responses. Clearly, identical *wording* of the categories is not to be expected, but directly equivalent gross categories should be obtained where these apply. For example, on a one-in-three sample of the interview question 'looking back on the course so far, has it been what you wanted or not?', the judge suggested three gross categories: 'favourable', 'unfavourable' and 'mixed'. The author had used 'satisfaction', 'dissatisfaction' and 'qualified satisfaction/dissatisfaction'. Turning to the subcategories, there were again differences in wording where the meaning was similar. In a very few instances, however, the judge did suggest a category which had not been used by the author. (The reverse situation also occurred, but this is to be expected with a one-in-three sample). As a further example, the judge's categories are now shown below alongside those of the researcher for a further student question.

Can you tell me why you came to college?

Judge	Author
Failed to get a job	To avoid unemployment having failed to get a job
College preferable to the dole	
Family wanted student to come to college	To maintain family tradition of continuing full-time education
Student wanted more qualifications to get the job(s) he wanted	To get qualifications needed for a specific job
Student wanted to get a higher qualification especially 'O' level	To get more qualifications generally
	To get qualifications needed to proceed to 'O' level or equivalent
The course was right for the student's career	To learn about a specific job or the skills needed for it.
Student wanted more education	To get more education generally
Student wanted time to grow up before starting work	To gain in maturity
Student wanted a second chance after things had gone wrong at last school	To have a second chance after wasting opportunities at school
	To have a second chance after a period of illness at school
Student unable to get her first choice of college so had come to college	(no equivalent: this part of answer taken with biographic details)
Friends suggested student should try college	(no equivalent)
(not found in sample)	To get a good job generally
(not found in sample)	To gain increased status in eyes of others

The results obtained through use of an independent judge in the case study questions indicated that the identification of the gross categories was very reliable; the sub-categories had a lower level of reliability but were certainly not fictitious.

A second independent judge can be given the researcher's list of gross and sub-categories for several questions (and the coding rules if appropriate) and asked to code a number of responses into the categories. The researcher then checks to see if the judge's allocation corresponds to his/her own. In the author's case study three questions were chosen at random from each of the interview schedules. A proportion of responses, totalling 154, also drawn at random, were allocated by the judge to the categories provided. Agreement between the independent judge and author occurred on 123 of these responses (80 per cent). Taking the gross categories alone, the intercoder agreement was 98 per cent. This again seems to indicate that considerable confidence can be placed in the gross category figures and confirms the author's belief that they can be reliably used as the basis for statistical data-handling techniques, particularly tests of association. It should also be reasonable to use the sub-categories as a basis for interpretation, indicating trends or patterns of interest in the data, even though too much reliability should not be claimed for the actual figures.

In this part of the analysis use can be made, if desired, of software programmes designed for a microcomputer. In the case study, for example, a Commodore PET was used to run chi-squared tests on gender, racial type, and type of Foundation Course being taken. T tests of difference in proportion between student answers to similar questions at the beginning and end of year were also conducted on students' career choices. Finally, cluster analysis was conducted on selected items.[11]

The method for dealing with responses to open-ended items outlined above has been shown to be reasonably reliable (and to have a reasonable degree of internal validity), yielding a range from 'hard' data at the gross category level to 'soft' evidence at the more detailed sub-category level. The procedures given, however, do not exhaust the battery of techniques for increasing confidence in the results obtained. Within the instrument itself comparison of results to open and closed items on the same topic or issue can prove to be a useful device. Consistency encourages confidence. Inconsistency signals the need for further analysis. Thus it transpired in the case study that though the majority of students agreed on a closed question that they had learned information relevant to adult life roles, in answer to an open item they revealed that they did not regard the information as particularly necessary or useful in their own case.

Application of the principle of triangulation can also help the practitioner researcher in some small projects. He or she may be able, for example, to undertake some observation of the subjects of his/her research to provide a check on the interpretation of the analysis of interviews or questionnaires. Documentary analysis can also be helpful as a complementary source of data and evidence. Equally important, where the practitioner as researcher has a small sample, it may improve the generalizability of the findings if that sample can be related on key variables to national surveys and statistics. Questionnaire and interview items can be deliberately inserted into the research instrument for this purpose. Thus, in the author's case study, it was possible to relate the student sample on some biographical and attitudinal characteristics (e.g. CSE performance, social class, gender distribution, types of motivation, career aspirations) to large-scale surveys of 17 + courses[12] and to national data held by the City and Guilds Institute on their Foundation Courses. It is also possible to provide the reader with information about the institutional setting of the small-scale research project which, again, enables comparisons with other settings or the national picture to be made. In the case study, for example, it was possible to locate the sixth form college in question on a national range of characteristics of sixth form colleges including size, type of course offered, and proportion of non-A-level students.

CONCLUSION

An eclectic approach to small-scale research can be justified methodologically and may well offer the practitioner-researcher an appropriate strategy for his or her research project. Carefully used and contexted, semi-structured instruments can yield qualitative and quantitative data, the interpretation of which can be usefully generalized. They also present no insuperable problems in the resources or specialist skill needed. Responses to open items do, however, require a carefully formulated approach to categorization and coding if the researcher wishes to use them as a basis for descriptive statistical analysis as well as illuminative insight. Such a strategy is possible and yields acceptable degrees of reliability and validity especially when combined with other procedures for maximizing confidence in the results obtained.

REFERENCES

1. Stenhouse, L. (1980) *An Introduction to Curriculum Research and Development* (Heinemann, London, 1975) and Stenhouse, L. *The Teacher as Focus of Research and Development* (Monograph, Centre for Applied Research in Education, University of East Anglia).
2. Harré, R. (1978) 'Accounts, actions and meaning—the practice of participatory psychology' in Brenner, M., Marsh, P. and Brenner, M. (Eds.): *The Social Context of Method* (London, Croom Helm, 1978).
3. Marton, F. (1981) 'Phenomenology: describing conceptions of the world around us', *Instructional Science* (10), pp. 177–200.
4. Eisner, E. W. (1981) 'On the differences between scientific and artistic approaches on qualitative research', *Educational Researcher* (April), pp. 5–9.
5. Kerlinger, F. N. (1973) *Foundations of Behavioural Research* (Holt, Rinehart, Winston, London, second edition) Cohen, L. Manion, L. *Research Methods in Education* (Croom Helm, London, 1980), pp. 241–262.
6. See L. Cohen, L. Manion, *op. cit. supra.*
7. Atkins, M. J. (1982) 'Foundation Courses in a Sixth Form College: A Case Study', unpublished Ph. D., School of Education, Nottingham University.
8. Atkins, M. J. and Brown, G. A. (1983) *Identifying Student Learning Needs* (Further Education Unit, Department of Education and Science: Craft, M. and Atkins, M. J. (1983) *Training Teachers of Ethnic Minority Community Languages* (School of Education, University of Nottingham, 1983).
9. Atkins, M. J. (1982): *op. cit.*

10. Holsti, O. R. (1969) *Content Analysis for the Social Sciences and Humanities*, London, Addison-Wesley.
11. Youngman, M. B. (1979) *Analysing Social and Educational Research Data*, Maidenhead, McGraw Hill.
12. Dean, J., Steeds, A, (1981) *17 Plus: The New Sixth Form in Schools and F. E.*, Windsor, NFER-Nelson.

Acknowledgement

I am grateful to Dr George Brown for his helpful comments and suggestions on a draft of this article.

7.4   *Choosing educational software*

•   Derek Blease

To decide what teachers really need to know in order to make informed decisions about educational software is not as easy as it may seem. There are many things which make demands on teachers' time and which threaten to keep them out of their classrooms. Gaining sufficient knowledge of computers and their software is just one of many things that they must do to keep up with developments in educational ideas and methods. Of course, in-service courses play an important part here, trying to acquire the necessary skills is not something which is easily done 'on the job'. However, there is still a shortage of courses for inexperienced teachers which satisfactorily develop these necessary skills.[1] If the opportunity to merely browse through a selection of available software is insufficient, then it is important for us to decide exactly what it is that the well prepared teacher needs to know. [. . .]

It is not difficult to find examples of software which could almost have been designed to put the newcomer off altogether. Add this to the normal pressures of an average day in school and one can see how easily inexperienced users can be forced into making decisions about programs which they and their pupils may live to regret. Spielman[2] [. . .] describes what many teachers may recognise as a fairly common experience; [. . .]

> He loads the program and gets it running. What he almost certainly does not do is sit down and read the documentation first. Indeed, it is quite likely that he has already mislaid it, but he has got a computer in front of him and, not unreasonably, he might expect sufficient guidance to be on tap from the computer itself.
>
>   What all too often happens, however, is something like this. The program starts off with an indulgent display of exhibitionism: ornate titles, animated logos, warnings against infringement of copyright, accompanied possibly by a rendering of 'I Wonder Who's Kissing Her Now?'—a pleasant diversion the first time one encounters it, perhaps, but a feature which quickly palls if it has to be endured every time the program is run.

[. . .] Now this may sound all very amusing, and indeed some of it is just a little larger than life, but it does raise a number of important issues which should be of interest to program writers and users alike.

Documentation has always posed problems and [. . .] some software authors are more understanding of these problems than others. Indeed, some documentation is so tortuous and complicated that its very appearance is enough to put off all but the most determined. [. . .]

'Obstacle courses' can appear in a variety of forms, although, with the benefit of hindsight many program designers are giving this more serious attention than in the past. Programs which offer a series of menus setting out the various options available can be very useful, provided that the options are clearly stated. [. . .] As an alternative to the 'menu driven' program, some favour the 'command driven' style. This requires the user to learn, or have handy on a piece of paper, a whole list of commands, so that when prompted by the program, they can state their preference. This is all very well, but it does prove to be somewhat confusing to the unfamiliar user, and presents a somewhat less friendly user interface than the well planned menu. If they are not familiar with how a particular set of programs are structured this presents real problems for busy teachers trying to select suitable programs for their own use. [. . .]

Spielman[3] suggests that educational programs should include what he calls a 'browse mode' especially for teachers. This would make it easier and quicker to see how the program runs, and to linger on the most interesting parts while quickly skipping over parts of less interest. Of course, some programs do already offer something similar. The teacher's notes for 'Dragon World' include a section containing the solutions to the many tasks which have to be performed. This enables the teacher to move rapidly through the program and to experiment with different solutions at any point. [. . .]

WHAT TEACHERS NEED TO KNOW

In very general terms, there are four groups of really important things that teachers need to know about before they can become efficient software selectors:

1. What you might call 'basic housekeeping'. This includes all of the day to day things a computer user must be able to do to set up the hardware, load and run programs, make back-up copies of tapes or discs, protect files from accidental erasure and so on. These are such rudimentary skills, but they are vitally important. [. . .]
2. What the range of possibilities really is for educational programs. This comes in two parts. Firstly, teachers need to have experienced the full

spectrum of educational programs, from tutorials to content-free tools, with sufficient time to experiment until they can come to appreciate for themselves the educational contribution that good examples of each might make. Secondly, some experience of a programming language like LOGO to help them appreciate the potential of the hardware itself, in other words what the computer is capable of doing, and also to appreciate how versatile a learning aid a program like LOGO really is.

3. To have a clear idea in their own minds about their curriculum objectives and the role they want the computer program to play. This can work in two ways. Firstly when a teacher is looking for a program to do a specific job, and secondly when a teacher, with general curriculum objectives in mind, is viewing a range of programs to see where some of them might perform a useful role in the already existing scheme.

4. What makes a program a good program. Of course this issue is closely tied to the question of objectives, but there is another important element which must be considered. There are a number of things which must be looked out for which will highlight many of the technical, as well as the educational strengths and weaknesses of a program. [. . .]

CHECKLISTS AND RATING SCALES

[. . .]

In the January 1984 issue of *Primary Teaching and Micros* there are a suggested 'Eight Steps to Evaluation';

1. Package title, source, machine, memory size, special equipment required.
2. Subject area, topic, target age, target ability, class, group or individual use.
3. Brief description.
4. Definition of educational aims and objectives.
5. Appropriate use of sound, colour, graphics.
6. Documentation, screen instructions, user adaptable?, ease of use.
7. Achievement of educational objectives, robustness, educational value.
8. Technique used, what sort of program is it?

Here we have a list of important things to look out for, although little help is given in coming to terms with why some of the things listed are so important. However, the eight steps are intended for use by individual teachers to help them look more closely at programs in a more systematic way. [. . .] The important thing is to remember that these checklists have their limitations, but that, at the same time, they can provide an all important framework within which the software reviewer can work. What might one realistically expect from using a reasonable checklist? [. . .]

There are two weaknesses of checklists which seem to contribute most to the confusion of potential users;

1. The selection criteria are generally inadequately defined or explained.
2. There are almost always some selection criteria which are inappropriate to the program being studied. This is because most checklists are designed to suit all purposes, and ignore the need to consider the more specialized strengths and weaknesses of different kinds of programs. There are specific things that we need to know about drill and practice programs which do not apply to simulations, information retrieval packages need to be assessed in a different way to adventure games, and so on. [. . .]

In attempting to come to terms with these weaknesses we need to look at, and explain in detail, those assessment criteria which might apply to all kinds of educational programs irrespective of their function, and then to consider separately those which pertain more specifically to tutorials, games, simulation games, experimental simulations, content-free tools and programming languages respectively.

GENERAL SELECTION CRITERIA

At this point it would be very tempting to try to produce yet another 'original' checklist to add to the already numerous examples available in the literature. However, what seems more sensible is to take the most commonly occurring criteria from a few of the better ones, and to look at them in detail. [. . .] The main headings which I shall use for these general criteria are arranged roughly in the order that a teacher might be expected to want to consider them. However, this does not mean that they need necessarily be taken in that order;

1. Documentation. (i) Technical. (ii) Program information.
2. Presentation and layout.
3. Friendliness and flexibility.
4. Achievement of stated aims.
5. Robustness.

If, at this stage, you feel that there are things which have been left out, remember that they are quite likely to appear later as specific criteria for one or more of the six program types mentioned above.

Documentation

(i) Technical

Does the program have any accompanying documentation?

This may seem to be rather an obvious question to ask, and in fact it does seem to crop up quite regularly. Of course, it is important to know the answer to this question, but in most cases no indication is given as to whether it is necessarily a good thing or not. If you read the documentation first it can save you a great deal of time, but as I have mentioned before, there is always a great temptation to try the program first and then to refer to the instructions when you get stuck. Good documentation will start by setting out clearly, and in simple terms, what sort of computer the program is written for and what special features it may require, e.g. high resolution graphics, colour, a particular size of memory expressed in units called 'K', i.e. 16K, 32K, 64K and so on. Next it should give you a set of simple instructions on how to get the program running before going into a detailed discussion of its finer points. Sometimes these points are covered by separate questions like;

Are there any simple loading and running instructions?

This is important, to save you time, but if there do not appear to be any you can still get by. Most software publishers adopt a standard loading and running procedure for all their programs. So, if you used one, you can probably get into any of the others by using the same method. If in doubt, you should always try the simplest method first, which is recommended by the computer manufacturer in your user's handbook.

Does the program require anything other than the most elementary knowledge of the computer to get it up and running?

It should not be necessary to be a computer expert in order to use it as a teaching and learning resource in the classroom. If you are invited to type in all sorts of strange things before the program will work, it probably means that the program has not been thoroughly planned and thought out. Take care, it could mean that other parts of the program design, which are less visible, leave something to be desired. A really good program, in this context, is one which will load and run automatically following one simple command, or even better, at the press of a key.

Are hardware requirements made explicit in the simplest of terms?

Once again the question of 'expertise' arises here. The information you require should be readily available in the User's Handbook. If not, then you may need to seek the advice of a colleague, or the person who supplied the computer. Once you have the information, it would be as well to write it on a sticky label and attach it to the computer or the monitor for future reference. At some stage or other you may need to know about some of the following:

1. Memory size, expressed in multiples of 'K', e.g. 16K, 32K etc. The higher the number, the bigger the memory. Longer and more sophisticaed programs generally require more memory.
2. Version of BASIC. e.g. Basic 2, or RML BASICSG, and so on.
3. Operating system version number. The operating system of a computer

gets things organised so that the computer can follow the instructions contained in your program. e.g. OS.1.2, or CPM 1.4, etc.

4. Does it have a disc filing system (DFS)? All microcomputers that you will come across in school will be able to load and save programs using tape cassette, but not all of them are equipped to use a disc drive.

5. Does the computer have a network filing system (NFS)? Some computers can be connected together in a 'network' so that they can all be controlled centrally, using one disc drive and printer etc. You need to know if your computer is a part of such a network. Sometimes a computer which is equipped to be a part of such a network, but is not connected to one, can experience certain problems with some programs. If this occurs you may need to seek expert advice.

6. What kind of graphics facility does your computer have? Is it High Resolution (HRG), Medium Resolution (MRG), or Low Resolution (LRG)? The higher the resolution the finer the detail that can be drawn on the screen, but at a price. The better the graphics, the more memory space it occupies.

7. Does it have a facility for sound? Also, it will not be long before you will need to know whether it has a facility for speech, and if so, which system does it employ?

8. Is your computer display in colour or black and white?

I have deliberately not referred to particular makes of computer here because there are so many varieties. However, I hope that you have now got some idea of what to look out for. It is probably a good idea to collect together all of this information before you start trying to assess programs. Attach one copy to your computer, and keep another copy with you for when you visit your teachers' centre or software supplier. If you do this it won't be long before you don't need to refer to it because you will have remembered it.

Are instructions given for making a back-up copy of the tape or disc? If not, do the publishers offer a replacement service for corrupted discs and tapes?

Some publishers urge you to make a back-up copy before you use the program, allowing you to keep the original safely locked away. This is a good idea because you can always prepare a fresh back-up copy if the first one becomes damaged, saving time and inconvenience. However, some publishers, being so anxious about software piracy and copyright, protect their programs in such a way that they are very difficult to copy. If they do this, then they should make it very clear in the documentation how you should go about obtaining a replacement. However, remember that you have already paid for the program once, and so the cost of a replacement should be little more than the cost of a blank disc or cassette.

Does the documentation include a list of other machines for which a version of the program is available?

This can save you a great deal of time, especially if you can only view a version intended for a different machine from your own. If your computer is included in the list, you will be pretty safe in ordering the right version.

(ii) Program information

Are the aims and objectives of the program made clear?

It is very important that you should be able to find this out easily before you make any serious attempts to judge the suitability of the program. Unless you know what the designer had in mind for the program, it will be very difficult to assess whether it may or may not fulfil those objectives if used with the class you have in mind. However, sometimes the objectives of a program are deliberately left vague. This is done to enable the user to adapt more readily to the needs of the curriculum. This is perfectly acceptable, provided that is made clear in the documentation, and you realise that assessing the suitability of the program will take you somewhat longer as you come to consider how you might use it to its best advantage. Beware, however, this does not apply to all programs, especially those which have been written by amateurs who may not have considered the question of objectives at all.

Does it specify the age and ability range for which it was designed? What degree of flexibility does it provide?

Sometimes it is quite difficult to decide which age groups would benefit from a program until you have spent some time trying it out. It is a great help if the documentation includes some discussion of this together with the results of any school trials which might help you to make a decision. Some programs have a very specific target age and ability group, these are the ones you must be most careful about. Some tutorial and drill programs may depend very much upon the users having covered certain skills to a certain level. Laboratory simulations generally require the user to have at least grasped the basic principles of the process or experiment before exploring it further. You also need to know something about the difficulty of the concepts involved, something which might appear in the detailed discussion of the program content. However, it is not only content which is important. You need to know whether the style and complexity of the language used on the screen is at a level with which your class will be happy and can cope.

More flexible programs will cater for a wider age and ability range, and you may feel that they are somewhat better value for money, having a wider range of use in the school. This can be best illustrated with drill and practice programs like 'Rally' (published in 1984 by Longman) and a programming language like LOGO.

What kind of program is it?

By this time you may already have come to some conclusions about this, since it may be quite implicit in the statement of aims and objectives. However, this is not always as clear as it might be, and if the author has taken the trouble to discuss the program type in the documentation there is a reasonable chance that some thought has been given to the underlying perspective on learning. However, take care as this may not always be the case. Some discussion of the program type may give you valuable clues as to how the author sees the program being used in the classroom, whether it is intended for use with a whole class, a small group or individually. Of course, you will have the final say here in the light of your own experience as a teacher, but if the author has included results of trials carried out in schools it will give you much more to go on.

Does the program allow for any alterations to be made? If so, are the instructions unambiguous and easy for the non-expert to follow?

I include this one while having certain reservations about it. [. . .] There are some programs which allow the user to modify programs to suit their own needs simply through a list of options, these I think are probably the best, and there are others which invite you to 'tinker with the code'. This is not uncommon with some laboratory simulations where Data can be modified to suit local conditions. If the instructions are clear about how to list the program and which lines to change, it can be reasonably straightforward if you are not easily put off by what you see on the screen. [. . .] Probably the best advice for the newcomer to these things is 'if in doubt, then leave well alone'.

Does the documentation contain instructions for a 'browse mode' or details of a 'sample run'?

Very often it is helpful to see what would happen at various points in the program without having to work all the way through it. Some programs allow this by either giving special instructions for the teacher to 'browse', or alternatively, the documentation contains a printout of a sample-run to illustrate how the program works. This is by far the commonest way, often being broken down into sections accompanied by some detailed explanation, and some suggestions of how that part of the program might be used. [. . .]

If a 'browse' option or a sample run are missing from the documentation, it might be inconvenient, but it should not affect your decision about the suitability of the program itself.

Presentation and layout

Here, we are particularly interested to see that text, graphics and sound have been used to their best advantage. Try to adopt the same critical eye that you use when reviewing and selecting text or library books for your class or school. Your own professional judgment is just as important here as when you plan a blackboard or transparency layout or when you prepare a worksheet or class handout.

Text

Are instructions clear and unambiguous?

Writing instructions which are unambiguous and easy to follow is sometimes more difficult than it sounds. You can never be sure that the reader is going to see the problem from the same angle as you do, or that the style and complexity of language with which you are comfortable will necessarily be understood by others. This is a common problem faced by teachers, and it is always important to ensure that the children can cope with the language, both written and spoken, which they encounter during the course of their studies. This is a particular problem with computer programs because, to avoid constant repetition, instructions may be abbreviated or replaced by a symbol. This is further complicated because it is quite rare to be able to browse through the program or to return briefly to the beginning to have another look at the instructions without having to start all over again. Where instructions do appear on the screen they should be in a prominent enough place not to be missed, but at the same time they ought not to detract from the activity in hand. Any text which appears in the top or bottom left hand corners of the screen probably means that the program designer has not given it much thought, since this is where the computer will automatically print it in the absense of any other instructions.

Where instructions are not printed in full, it should be obvious what the child is expected to do. The classic examples of where this is a problem is in many arcade-type games where the instructions are briefly displayed at the beginning, but are inaccessible during the program run. In the case of 'command driven' programs, for example, all commands must be readily to hand in a list which the child can have by the computer. Also it should be possible to list them on the screen without disturbing the program run. This is usually done by including a command like 'HELP' or 'COMMANDS', which produces the list on the screen, followed by an invitation to choose a command from the list. Where instructions are abbreviated, their full meaning should be obvious, not just to you, but to the children in the ability range that you have in mind. When symbols are used, their meaning should appear all together on one convenient page in the program documentation so that they are available for easy reference. It is important to you, when you try the program for the first time, that this information is contained in the initial instructions for getting the program going. As children use the program, they should find that they come to learn what the symbols mean and so do not have to refer to the instructions. For this reason it is important for you to ensure that the use of symbols is consistent, that they always mean the same thing, and that they always appear in the same place. A very good example of this can be found in the programs of the Loughborough Primary Micro Project (LPMP, pubished by Ladybird-Longman), where a coloured rectangle in the corner of the screen means 'press the space bar', and a different coloured text is used to denote that input is required from the keyboard. The full explanation of the instructions is prominently displayed in the documentation and is expressed in simple language.

Is each frame attractively presented avoiding irrelevant detail?

Screen layout is of paramount importance. You should be able to expect that each screen display has been carefully planned to have the maximum effect. This is just as important for the positioning of text as it is for diagrams and pictures. One of the worst faults, which was sadly all too common in the early days, is for text simply to scroll up the screen as the program progresses. There is only one kind of program where that is acceptable, and that is with a word processor, where the user should be able to scroll up and down the screen at will.

Have coloured and double height characters been used to their best advantage?

Very often coloured text can be used to enhance or to accentuate a point, but the careless choice of colours can cause problems. Sometimes this just means that the result is unattractive, the colours clash or tend to merge making it difficult to read the words. More seriously, however, you should make sure that the choice of colours will not create problems for sufferers from colour blindness, especially the red-green form, which is a sex-linked character, being transmitted from women to their sons, and therefore much more common in boys. So, beware of combinations of shades of red and green in particular, since the problem is probably more common than you think. Children are very good at finding ways of hiding disabilities of this kind. I have a friend who drove a fire engine for years before they discovered that he suffered from red-green colour blindness. He used to respond to traffic lights by noting which lamp was alight, not by its colour. Unfortunately a computer display provides insufficient information to allow for colour blind children to compensate in this way.

Not all computers can conveniently produce double height characters, but most can be programmed to make large characters using their graphics facility. There are many occasions when this is advantageous, especially in programs designed for young children or for those with sight or perceptual problems.

Graphics

Is the use of graphics appropriate to the aims and objectives of the program?

You can approach this one in a number of ways.

Particularly you will want to consider whether your aims and objectives differ in any way from those stated by the program designer. If they do, it could be that the graphics are too childish or too adult for your group:

1. Is the style of graphics suitable for the age and ability group you have in mind?
2. Do the graphics serve to clarify or enhance the points being made?
3. If there are no graphics, would the program have been improved by their inclusion?

[. . .]

If pictures and diagrams are included, could they be represented more effectively by some other means? e.g. a printed sheet, a map or a photograph.

Sometimes, of course, the quality of the graphics is less important than the point being made. This may be especially true when the graphics are included to create atmosphere or simply to provide some variety to the visual effect, 'Granny's Garden' and 'Dragon World', both published by 4MATION, are good examples of this. However, on other occasions the quality of the picture is all important, and in some cases it might be that the microcomputer is just not up to it. Most maps and some diagrams fall into this category, but, when the object of the program is to exploit the computer's ability to process information rapidly and to represent it as a graph or a bar chart, you have to accept the computer's limitations. Apart from the question of whether the computer itself is up to the job, it is important to remember your objectives and what the program is trying to do. [. . .] If you think that the program could be enhanced by the inclusion of some pictures, diagrams or worksheets there is no reason why you should not think of the program merely as a starting point, and put them together in a study pack of your own.

Sound

If sound effects are included, do they constitute an essential and integral part of the program?

Sound effects can be very useful in helping to create realism and atmosphere. A flight simulator like 'Aviator' (published in 1983 by Acornsoft) would not be the same without the sound of the engine to give some clue as to the appropriate throttle setting. Some programs, however, include music or toots and bleeps which are totally outside the user's control, and seem to be there for no apparent reason. Probably worst of all is the program which makes a bad attempt at playing the 'Hallelujah Chorus' every time it is used. Try to think what the effect would be of using a program with sound effects in your classroom while other activities are in progress. Do you have a separate area where the computer can be used without disturbing anyone else?

> *Does the program provide a simple means whereby the volume can be controlled or the sound can be turned off completely?*

The best programs will provide these options as a matter of course, in fact some will even allow you to make adjustments throughout the program run. [. . .]

Friendliness and flexibility

'User friendliness' is a term which arises very commonly in computing circles these days. Rather than being concerned with friendliness in an anthropomorphic sense, it relates to the ease and convenience with which any program can be used, whatever its purpose. A useful, and sometimes amusing, perspective is applied to 'user friendliness' by Elithorn,[4] who draws upon his extensive experience in the use of computers for assessment testing in experimental psychology to describe what he calls 'truly ergonomic' programs. He outlines a number of 'rules', which, he considers, essential starting with one which already has been 'well learnt in educational circles'. This is that programs must be 'tailored' in such a way that they suit the needs of the user. In fact the very process of software selection, in which we are engaged, is simply a way of deciding whether a particular program is suffi-ciently suitable for the needs of the pupils we have in mind. Elithorn goes further, as I have done, to suggest that this tailoring process 'should be applied to the instructions as well as to the task itself'. 'Help' options are important here too. Elithorn agrees that you should always ask yourself whether the program would be easier to use 'if it had a help option available during run time'. Blank screens and obscure messages should be avoided. He writes:

> The basic principle is clear: any break in transmission should be as short as possible, or long enough to be a planned rest period or a coffee break. In starting up, for example, it is quite practicable to load a small program which will present either the instructions, or for the second time user, a summary of the key issues while the main body of the program is loading. (p. 12–13)

[. . .] A good example of an unacceptable blank screen is in 'Quest' (published in 1983 by AUCBE), an excellent data-base program, but when undergoing a search of a large data file, the screen can remain completely blank for several minutes during which time the user might be led to think that the program had stopped working altogether. A 'truly ergonomic' program has consistency as a key component. This means that, 'Command key press responses which cause a major state change, as for example quitting the program, should not be used elsewhere in the program for routine commands'. (p. 13). This whole problem of creating and handling errors is a major bugbear in educational computing. Many programs written by amateur programmers do not take this seriously enough. It must be accepted, as a matter of course, that users will make mistakes. Elithorn's final point is that these mistakes should not prove fatal. We will take this point up further when we look at the problems of program robustness later on in this chapter.

Here are some questions you might want to ask youself about the program;

Does the program provide helpful messages to correct errors?

Sometimes the only indication that you get is a cryptic message from the machine's operating system which is far from helpful. You can look up the meaning in the user manual, but even then you can't always be sure of what to do about it when you have. Good programs will tell you where you have gone wrong in plain English, and then allow you to have another go without spoiling what you already achieved.

Is sufficient help provided so that pupils can understand the program without your constant intervention?

One great asset of a computer in the classroom is that it can free the teacher to concentrate on someone else in the knowledge that those using the computer are gainfully occupied. However, if it is constantly necessary to sort out queries because the program is unclear, the object is defeated. It is not just a question of poor instructions or unclear messages, it is also important to consider the level and complexity of language used, and whether it is suitable for those whom you want to use it.

Is the program sufficiently versatile so that the user can control what it does?

This varies, of course, as one moves from tutorials to content-free tools, but some element of choice in terms of pace and level of difficulty is desirable in most programs.

Is the program sufficiently flexible to be applicable in a variety of teaching/learning situations?

This raises the question of value for money. Obviously some programs are designed to do a very specific job, and if you want that job done by your computer, you must accept the cost. However, as a general rule, programs which offer several levels of difficulty, or a variety of applications to different sets of data or problems can possibly be used on more occasions and by more teachers in the school than those which have more specific and narrow applications.

Achievement of stated aims

Without actually using the program, and keeping your own pupils in mind, to what extent do you think the program would achieve its/your aims and objectives?

Of course at this stage there is no way of knowing for certain whether the program will ever achieve its stated aims in the classroom because you will not have had a chance to try it. For this reason this is probably the most difficult section to deal with satisfactorily. Firstly, you will need to examine the program documentation carefully to ascertain what the author says are the program's aims. You will then need to consider your own aims and objectives, and decide whether these coincide with those of the author. If they do then you need to use your own professional judgement, keeping in mind the group of children who will use the program, to decide whether it has a chance of achieving those aims and objectives. You will also need to draw upon your past experience of using computer programs in the classroom, particularly with the group of children in question. If you haven't tried any programs with this group, or this is your own first time, the decision will be rather more difficult to make. If your own aims and objectives differ from those of the program author, you will need to decide whether you could possibly use it to suit your requirements without too much difficulty. In which case you need to decide whether the program has a chance of achieving your aims and not those of the author. Once again, there will always be a degree of uncertainty, but at least you should be able to get as far as deciding whether the program is worth a trial, and as you gain experience of using programs in the classroom, the task will become easier.

If you can get hold of any case-studies written by teachers who have already used the program in the classroom, this will be a great help. There are now a number of these, called 'MEP Classroom Reports', published jointly by MEP and the Council for Educational Technology (1984 onwards).

Robustness

The essence of robustness in any computer program is the degree to which it can cope with three groups of problems:

1. Input errors
2. Unusual or unexpected inputs
3. Accidental use of other keys on the keyboard.

What we are looking for then, in a good program, is the ability to deal with any of these problems without interrupting the smooth running of the program. If you are really going to test this thoroughly, you need to try every occasion when pressing a key might cause an interruption, throughout the program run. Just because the program can handle it in one place doesn't necessarily mean that it is equipped to do so everywhere.

Is it easy for the user to correct typing errors?

This has already arisen when we looked at user friendliness, but it is worth looking at again.   One of the major problems here is caused when the RETURN key (it may be the ENTER key on your computer), is pressed following the entry of text or data. It is usually possible to correct errors before pressing RETURN, provided that you notice them in time, but if you don't, you may have to start the program all over again. A good program will allow you to make changes to the input, through a menu option, or a command, wherever that input could have serious and far reaching effects on the result. Some programs require inputs which do not need the RETURN key to be pressed at all. These are entries of one character only, and are often used in response to a series of options in a menu, or as a simple yes/no answer to a question. Once the key is pressed there is no turning back unless the response is then 'Are you sure Y/N?' You might expect a well planned program to be consistent in its use of input methods.

Are possible errors trapped? When numerical input is required, what happens if you type in a word? What happens if you type in a number when a word is required?

In either case, if the program comes to an abrupt halt it means that error trapping has not been properly considered by the programmer. If you decide to continue with a program like this you are likely to find that children will be constantly asking for your help, and much time could be wasted.

When textual input is required, what is the longest sentence you can input? Does the program crash if you enter a longer one?

The most characters that many computers will allow in an input is 255, including spaces, after which the program will crash. Some will be less, but the program should handle this so that it is impossible to enter too many. This is often done by printing a simple message like 'That sentence is too long, try another', or something like that. Of course these comments do not apply to word processors and text editors as they are specially written to handle large blocks of text.

*Can you get all the way through the program without entering anything,
just pressing the RETURN key each time a word, number or sentence is
required?*

A good program will always contain routines which check inputs to make
sure that they are within the expected range or are of the expected kind. If the
input does not fit the question, the user should be told why it was unsuitable,
and invited to try again.

*When numerical input is required, what happens if you type in very large
or very small numbers?*

Can the program cope with an input of zero or a negative number?

If the program has to perform some calculations, numbers outside its
expected range can cause unusual results or cause the program to crash altogether. Very large or very small numbers can create results which are beyond
the scope of the model, division by zero will cause the program to crash
unless the input is properly checked by a special routine before any calculations are performed.

*Are all non-essential keys automatically turned off by the program itself?
Try pressing some wrong keys, e.g. ESCAPE, BREAK, SHIFT/BREAK,
the CONTROL key in conjunction with any others.*

While the program is running the only keys which should have any effect are
those essential to the activity. If any other key is pressed by mistake, nothing
should happen. With most computers it is a simple matter to cater for this
when the program is being written. The key which probably causes the most
problems is the BREAK key, especially if it is situated in a prominent position, or is near to other keys which might be regularly used as the program is
running. Some programs overcome this problem by using it to return the
user to the main menu, at any time, without causing a break.

SPECIFIC SELECTION CRITERIA

Having looked at those selection criteria which might apply generally to
nearly all programs, we need to consider those which may be especially
important to particular kinds of programs.

(i) Tutorial and drill and practice programs

Although there are some significant differences between these two kinds of
program, they have several things in common which are concerned with

content, accuracy, input style, feedback, pupil records, and other non computer-based work.

Is the content fully described?

Is the content of the program appropriate to the designer's stated aims and objectives?

Is the content and presentation appropriate to your class and the use you have in mind?

Is the micro appropriate for teaching this topic?

These first four are all closely related. In fact they could probably be combined into one, but I have separated them for the sake of clarity. Obviously it makes the selection task easier if you can read about the program content before you try it. But also, in school, it is useful to be able to refer to the documentation now and again to remind yourself of the content. The question of appropriate content has arisen elsewhere, but this time you need to decide whether, in your opinion, the content matches the designer's and your own aims and objectives sufficiently to be worth using. However, you might feel that there are better ways of covering the same ground, and will consequently reject the program.

Is the content/information accurate?

Is the content/information accurate enough for the use you have in mind?

The question of accuracy is a very important one, and can arise in two ways. Firstly, if the program is simply imparting information like most tutorials do, you have to be sure that that information is correct. Secondly, if the program requires some numerical input from the user in order to perform a calculation, you need to be sure that the range of acceptable inputs is controlled by the program so that the outcome is an acceptable fit to observations made in the real world. Of course, sometimes certain approximations or simplifications are acceptable in order that an idea is easier to grasp. This is not uncommon in science and economics for example. You only need to be sure that the information is accurate enough for your purposes, given that you have a particular group of pupils in mind.

Does the input format suit your purposes? Are there options from which you can choose?

Remember the example of drill and practice programs involving multiplication. Would you prefer the children to be able to enter their answers as they work them out, or do you want them to perform paper and pencil tasks? A good program will give you the option, or at least justify the choice of input format in the documentation.

Does the program provide immediate and appropriate feedback to the user?

Behaviourist theories of learning stress the importance of regular and positive feedback to the learner. This means that all desirable behaviour or correct responses need to be rewarded. However, undesirable behaviour or incorrect responses are best ignored in the sense that an absence of positive feedback is feedback enough. Some programs, in trying to supply negative feedback to discourage incorrect responses, actually defeat their own objective since the so-called negative feedback is often more entertaining than the positive variety. The result is that the undesirable responses are encouraged.

Does the program keep a score or a record of the learner's progress?

This is useful from a diagnostic point of view, although a scoring or points system is probably more useful as a motivating factor. Learners can try to improve their own personal scores, or they can compete against one another. It is useful sometimes, however, to be able to turn off the scoring facility, especially if you think that it could cause too much anxiety in a particular child. A more detailed record of the learner's progress is very useful for the teacher as a diagnostic aid, and can be the subject of discussion between the teacher and the learner at a later stage. Once again, however, it ought to be available as an option since it can sometimes be seen as 'spying' and ought not to be used without the pupil's knowledge.

Does the program suggest pencil and paper tasks, or other work that might be carried out away from the computer?

Work cards, references for private study, art and craft, drama and so on are all activities which can be used to follow up a tutorial or a drill and practice program. Some of the best program packs contain a whole range of ideas like this which will help you to integrate the program fully into the normal range of classroom activities.

For Tutorial programs in particular

Is the content broken down into appropriately small and logical stages?

Does the program allow the user to revise previous pages or follow remedial loops?

Will the program take free-format answers in an acceptable number of forms?

These three points are more specific to the smooth running and convenience of use of tutorial programs. Each frame needs to be simple enough for the user to be almost guaranteed success, and the frames must be presented in a logical sequence. Whenever a difficulty arises it should be possible to revise or to be automatically sent round a remedial loop until the point has been clarified and understood. When input is required from the learner, it is important that the program is sufficiently versatile to accept answers in a variety of forms, even to the extent of catering for the more common spelling mistakes if accurate spelling is not the major purpose of the activity.

For drill and practice programs in particular

Does the program provide a variety of levels of difficulty?

Are the examples or exercises randomly generated?

Obviously the more levels of difficulty available in a program, the more use you will have for it. Also, any one pupil will be spared the boredom of working through the same examples over and over again. This is further aided if the examples themselves are randomly generated so that they never follow a set sequence. If all of the examples are contained in the program as Data, they very soon become exhausted and the pupils come to learn which one is coming next. You should expect to find details of how the examples are generated, somewhere in the program documentation.

(ii) Arcade-type games

Are the instructions clear and always available?

Remember that it is a good thing to be able to refer to the instructions while the program is running.

Does the program provide a sufficient range of levels of difficulty and speed?

Is the content of the program available for inspection and/or change?

Is the content accurate?

Especially in the case of matching, sequencing and reading exercises, it is useful to be able to preview the content in the form of a word or sound list. Some programs will allow you to make changes or additions to this list, which of course makes them move versatile. If they do not, then you must decide whether the list is sufficiently comprehensive for your purposes.

Does the program provide appropriate feedback to the player?

Does the program keep a score or a record of the player's progress?

The same comments apply here as they did when we looked at tutorial and drill and practice programs.

Is the visual display likely to be attractive, exciting and absorbing?

Remember that arcade-type games are often used to add interest and excitement to an otherwise dull activity. Children become so absorbed in playing the game that they forget that, in order to progress, they are actually having to learn and practice new skills.

(iii) Simulation games

Is it appropriate to use the computer for this topic?

Is the content of the program appropriate to your aims and to the group you have in mind?

Are commands and instructions available throughout the program run?

These three have all arisen before, leading on to the next question which is particularly relevant to adventure type simulations,

Does the program (or the documentation) give sufficient and appropriate clues if the user gets stuck?

Is the nature of the model made explicit?

You will find this particularly helpful when you are trying to select an appropriate simulation game for your class. It should help you finally to make decisions about how appropriate the program is.

Is there provision to change data if appropriate?

This does not necessarily apply to all simulations, but in cases like 'Micro Map' (published in 1985 by Ladybird-Longman) it is a great asset.

Can a game be 'saved' and resumed later?

Sometimes complicated simulation games take longer to complete that you have time available. It is very frustrating if every time, you must start again from the beginning. If the current game can be saved on tape or disc, next time the players can just start where they left off.

Does the program give any suggestions as to how it might relate to events in the real world?

Suggestions for follow-up work which include a wide range of other activities may be very helpful in getting the pupils to relate their work with the computer to their everyday experiences.

(iv) Laboratory simulations

Is the nature of the mathematical model made specific?

Is the range and degree of accuracy of the model discussed in the documentation?

In laboratory simulations the mathematical model is of particular importance since very often the purpose of such a simulation is for the user to come to understand more fully the theoretical basis of the model itself. For this reason, you must be sure that it does not over-simplify the problem or make it so complicated as to defeat its own, or your, objectives.

Is there provision for changing the data?

The best programs will allow you to do this by selecting the appropriate option, but alas, some might expect you to follow instructions and 'tinker with the code'.

Could this topic be covered more effectively with real practical work?

Remember that laboratory simulations can only effectively replace first-hand experience if that experience would prove to be too expensive, too dangerous or too time-consuming.

(v) Content-free tools

The essence of all good content-free tools, that is data-bases, teletext emulators, word processors and programming languages is that they are relatively 'transparent'. That is, they are convenient to use without getting in the way. Of all these, it is probably the data-bases which create the most initial confusion so I will make some particular comments about these,

Data-bases

When creating files,

Are the instructions clear and easy to follow?

What is the maximum number of records and fields?

What is the maximum field size?

Is there an option to edit and delete records?

Can the number of records be increased after the file has been created?

If you want to create fairly large data files you will need to select a data-base which stores its files on disc rather than in its own memory. This means that you can handle a large number of records relatively quickly. Make sure that the maximum number of fields is not too small, some of the best data-bases for school use allow up to at least twenty. If you have some idea of the kind of data you might collect you will have an idea of how large each field will need to be. Remember that if you have many large fields in a data file, you will have less room available for individual records. Finally, it is always useful to be able to add more records at a later date, so make sure that the program allows this as well as an option to edit, add and delete records.

When interrogating files,

Are the instructions for formulating a query clear and unambiguous?

Is there a 'help' option to explain the commands and to describe the fields?

Does the search option allow you to formulate both simple and complex queries?

What is the longest query acceptable?

When you first come to use a data-base you will need all the help you can get. It is therefore important that the instructions and 'help' routines are as explicit as possible. It is always useful to be able to perform a search for several attributes at the same time, so make sure that the program you choose allows for this unless you are going to be working with very young children, where perhaps one or maybe two will be enough. If you refer to the section on data-bases in the source article you will find a list of the kinds of search facilities to look out for.

USING OTHER PEOPLE'S ASSESSMENTS

It is hoped that the discussion of the selection criteria in the previous sections will, in conjunction with your own experience of using a computer in the classroom, help you review and select suitable software. I have tried to cover as many of the points that arise in most checklists, but of course there is always the chance that you might find others which you would prefer to add or even use instead. Clearly, the comments and guidelines which I have offered represent my own feelings about software selection in the light of my own experience and research, and there are bound to be those who would wish to take me to task on some of them. However, if you adopt them as general, though not hard and fast, guidelines, you will not go far wrong.

There will be times, however, when you have the opportunity to see program assessments or reviews written by other teachers who may have had the opportunity to use the program in the classroom. Here are a number of fundamental questions which you could ask yourself about them to help you assess their validity, and therefore their usefulness when deciding whether the program would suit your needs.

1. How reliable is the information? To what extent does it represent the behaviour of the audience of the age and ability range for which it was intended? Does it give any indication of the problems encountered by poor performers?
2. How accurate is the information? As far as you can tell, has the full range of effects (positive and negative), been accurately identified and reported?

To what extent have the effects claimed actually been measured? How well does the evaluator know the program?
3. How discriminating is the information? To what extent does it reflect differences in responses among the target audience? Does it indicate the conditions which resulted in different responses?
4. How useful is the information? Has it told you anything you wouldn't already have known? Does it suggest practical changes that could be made, or problems to be avoided when using the program?
5. To what extent does it take the context into account? How did the program relate to other media or fit into the curriculum? How was the program used by the teacher and/or the learners?

(Adapted from Bates[5])

REFERENCES

1. Jones, A. and Preece, J. (1984) 'Training Teachers to Assess Computer Software', *Computer Education*, November, pp. 17–20.
2. Spielman, B. (1982) 'Simple Software', *Educational Computing*, Vol. 3, no. 4, pp. 18–19.
3. Spielman, B. (1981) 'Programs and Busy Teachers', *Computers in Schools*, Vol. 4, no. 2.
4. Elithorn, A. (1982) 'User Friendliness', *Computers in Schools*, Vol. 4, pt. 4, July, pp. 11–14.
5. Bates, T. (1981) 'Towards a Better Framework for Evaluating the Effectiveness of Educational Media', *British Journal of Educational Technology*, Vol. 12, no. 3, pp. 215–233.

8 EDUCATIONAL COMPUTING WHERE NEXT?

The four papers in this final section look beyond the CAL work currently being done in schools to discuss some of the ways in which the field might develop over the next few years. Seely Brown's paper addresses two key issues for the learner-centred teacher. One is the importance of attending to the process rather than to the products of creative activity. The second is the computer's potential for recording and communicating this process to both teacher and child. This in turn allows far greater opportunities for children to take control of their own learning, either within schools or beyond. Some examples of the ways in which this might be done are outlined.

Holland's paper illustrates how the value of an already established innovation (the use of Logo) can be increased by taking it into a new curriculum area. Clearly there are plenty of opportunities for this sort of curriculum 'in-filling' without having to wait for new developments in educational software. The classroom teacher is in many ways very well placed to take the lead in innovations of this kind.

Feurzeig's paper deals with some current research intended to help students to develop concepts and problem solving strategies in algebra. Again Logo programming is one of the methods used, but it appears here alongside the provision of microworlds and an expert instructional system. This illustrates the way in which (within a large research project) a variety of computer-based approaches can be used pragmatically to tackle different aspects of the teaching problem.

Kaye evaluates the prospects in the near future for on-line services for schools. Drawing upon overseas experience, he argues that the technology in Britain is still not sufficiently reliable and accessible to schools for the educational benefits to be fully seized. However given the tremendous potential of these systems for providing teachers and children with access to much greater supplies of information this must be a major area of interest in the future.

8.1 Process versus product: a perspective on tools for communal and informal electronic learning

• John Seely Brown

The revolutionary impact of computational devices on learning is just beginning. The new generation of microcomputers has finally turned the tide—
computer systems can be shaped to the mind of the user rather than to the
hardware of the machine. In the past, computers limited the user to modes of
communication that made the machine's job easier. But now, as computer
cycles become plentiful and as memories become gigantic, our focus can shift
to the student and how to make easier his job of communicating ideas,
conjectures, intentions, etc. We therefore must free ourselves from prior
notions of how to use computers in instruction—notions based primarily on
timesharing programs, or equivalent programs shoehorned into yesterday's
micros. If we are to realize the potential of this new technology for creating
qualitatively different kinds of learning environments, we must be willing to
explore new paradigms for the use of computers in learning. Furthermore,
precisely because the environments that we explore are so new, we must
carefully examine each one with an open mind, not only to identify what is
good and what is bad, but most importantly to discover why whatever
appears to be winning is winning.

What follow are some thoughts, in progress, described here to foster discussion of how massive, inexpensive computation can alter radically both the
form of learning and content of what is learned. The change in form will see
a move away from formal textbook learning to informal learning-by-doing

(or learning-while-doing), a move that is particularly well suited to help students who fail in the classroom but seem adept at experiential learning. The change in content will have two dimensions. One is an increased emphasis on *domain-independent* skills (e.g. problem-solving and information-browsing) in conjunction with *metacognitive* skills (skills that have to do with learning how to learn, e.g., learning from one's errors). The second centers on devising ways to impart procedural abstractions that form the core of computer literacy—a topic about which we will have little to say in this article.

What follows is a set of examples of learning environments. Some already exist, some are under construction, and some are figments of our imaginations. More important than the specific examples is the underlying web of ideas concerning cognitive, pedagogical, and, perhaps most importantly, sociological issues—issues aimed at constructing learning environments that transcend the home and the school and permeate the community at large.

EMPOWERING ENVIRONMENTS

Currently, there are many imaginative proposals for computer systems that are aimed at promoting a student's creativity. These systems are usually thought of as empowering environments. They are intended to amplify a kid's creative capabilities by providing him with powerful electronic tools (e.g. a painting system or a music-editing system) with which to manipulate and control a given expressive medium. From this perspective, a kid is bursting with creative energy but lacks the formal resources, techniques, and tools to pursue his creative urges. The computer provides a rich environment of such resources and tools.

Consider a music-editing system with which a student composes separate voices using a keyboard to enter the notes. He can replay any segment as often as he wishes. He can make changes via an editor that first transforms the notes into musical notation and then paints the score onto the screen for 'symbolic editing.' Each voice can be perfected in isolation and then combined, enabling the student to explore the subtle interactions between the voices. This music-editing system is not fantasy. Indeed, it is off-the-shelf technology. But so what? Does this environment really encourage young musicians to develop an artistic discipline any more than traditional musical environments do? In some ways yes and in others no.

Certainly computers add to the creative process quantitatively; that is, they give an artist a new medium to explore. And they may, initially at least, increase motivation because they are flashy and novel. But will they fundamentally enhance the creative process? Will they have the 'staying power' that will encourage a kid to develop the self-discipline for self-expression? That is, will the medium progressively unfold its richness so that the user will be encouraged in his struggle to shape his work of art to better express his feelings and ideas? Or will the tools that comprise these electronic empowering environments be so powerful, or the medium so sparse, that the techniques for mastering the medium will be nearly transparent? This may be too conservative a view, but we see potential paradoxes in the very notion of empowering environments for creativity. We must ask ourselves: will an artistic environment comprised of tools so powerful and easy to use, accompanied by techniques so transparent and quickly mastered, really stimulate creativity? Or is the true struggle for self-expression not just one of mastering a tool, but rather of discovering what one wants to 'say' *through* the work of mastering the tool? In this regard, I am reminded of some lines from Robert Browning's poem 'Andrea del Sarto (Called 'The Faultless Painter').'

> Well, less is more, Lucrezia: I am judged,
> There burns a truer light of God in them,
>   (i.e. they that have to struggle)
> In their vexed beating stuffed and
>   stopped-up brain,
> Heart, or whate'er else, than goes on to
>   prompt
> This low-pulsed forthright craftsman's
>   hand of mine.
> Their works drop groundward, but
>   themselves, I know,
> Reach many a time a heaven that's shut
>   to me, . . .

In brief, designing empowering environments that will entice a kid into developing his full creative potential, rather than simply mesmerize him with his ability easily to produce something flashy, will take some care. Let us start down that path by asking what are the points of leverage that the computer, or computation, can provide, and what are the ways it can go astray?

There seem to be two critical issues that define where empowering environments can draw their power and, interestingly, these two issues turn out to be heavily interwoven. The first involves a distinction between *product* and *process*—a distinction that will permeate nearly every computer activity discussed in this paper. The second involves viewing the computer more as a communication device than as a computational engine—an admittedly fuzzy distinction but one that will, nevertheless, turn out to have force.

Process versus product

By focusing in the design of empowering environments on the product of a creative effort, we are missing the real source of power for computer-based tools: the computer can record and represent the process underlying the created product. By making explicitly available to the user the series of steps and missteps that leads to the creation of a particular object or result, we create a basis on which to build extraordinarily powerful editing, merging, undoing, and transforming tools. Tools designed to manipulate this 'histori-cal' information, or *audit trail*, can be used to carry out intellectual and creative tasks of great complexity.

But there is another intriguing reason why reifying the process turns out to provide a tremendous leverage point. It provides a way greatly to enhance the communication to others of what one has done by enabling the user to communicate aspects of how it was done. Before delving into this, let's step back and examine the reason why communication tools are crucial for enabling empowering environments to achieve their maximum potential.

Motivation and creativity

I think there is little doubt that tools alone, no matter how powerful or sexy, will not in themselves suffice. The right kinds of powerful tools will capture a kid's imagination and let her exercise her creative powers. But why will she be willing to struggle with mastering the subtleties of the medium? To do so, she must be highly motivated. Indeed, sustained motivation is crucial before new levels of creativity can be attained. But, for most of us, motivation stems from communal support mechanisms as much as from purely internal drives, and it is here, *in the sociological realm*, that we encounter both the paradox and the power of empowering environments.

First the paradox: Let's accept for the moment that a great deal of the satisfaction we get from creating something stems from having others around us enjoy, understand, and appreciate what we have done. Indeed approval, if not appreciation, from one's peers can carry most of us a surprising distance and spur us on to new heights. But here lies the rub: As empowering environments enable each of us to become more and more creative and original, the art form, or theory, or just-plain-neat discovery that we make may become more and more specialized; consequently the subculture that can appreciate it will become smaller and smaller. If this is true, the chance diminishes that the subculture surrounding each budding creator will provide a sustaining communal support structures. The more creative we become and the more we develop our own unique artistic dimension, the less likely it is that our neighbours or proximal peers can provide us with meaningful support and motivation. We can see the effects of this in music by examining the subculture for electronic music and comparing its communal support structures (or lack thereof) with those of the more traditional and culturally understood forms of music (jazz, rock, classical, etc.).

The potential of empowering environments to sustain advanced individual growth probably won't be realized unless specialized subcultures develop. Subcultures need to arise on their own; they will be richer if they are not constrained by the interests, beliefs, and values of one's geographically surrounding folk. In other words, as our communal support mechanisms tend to contract for lack of immediate 'neighbours' who can appreciate our rather unique adventure, we need to be able to reach out to a larger geographic area in search of those who might be interested in our particular 'art form.' Ideally, we would like to be able to form our own subcultures based on shared interests and insights and not constrained by the geographical limitations of classroom, home, or local community! Such subcultures can arise from using a different property of the new technology. Computers and computer networks provide a beautiful opportunity for subcultures to form and grow independent of geography but dependent on shared beliefs, interests, etc.

Tomorrow's networks will have 'bulletin boards' open to computer browsing that will help identify common interests. New subcultures will form, and new ideas or creations will spread to broader audiences. But for this to happen, the object or act of creation itself must be easily transmittable on the network. This brings us back to the local empowering environment where the process of a creative act is retained and made representable. By maintaining an explicit audit trail of the steps that led to the created 'object,' not only can more powerful tools be constructed but, perhaps more importantly, the ability for one to understand what another has done is greatly enhanced. The viewer or recipient can 'replay' the process underlying the creation and thereby grasp more fully the significance of the 'product'. Both the 'bandwidth of communication' and the potential depth of understanding are expanded when one can transmit not just the finished piece of work, but also information about the process that led to its final form. (Oh, how often I have wished to see the aborted tries and reformulations that underlie the highly polished proof of some neat mathematical result.)

In summary, the computer as a communication facilitator and network, if designed properly, could enable the wide dissemination of not only the 'art' of subcultures, but also the methods, techniques, and underlying structures of the creative processes of those subcultures. By being able to study, copy, play, and replay a creative process, members of a subculture, although geographically isolated, can learn from each other. By drawing on a larger population, the student as artist, creator, or budding theoretician has a better chance of finding like souls who will appreciate, motivate, and, of course, compete with her in her endeavours.

ROBOTIC OLYMPICS AS A LEARNING ENVIRONMENT

One of the challenges facing educational theorists is to find effective ways to combine the motivational aspects of arcade-style games with more educationally useful material. There have been numerous attempts to achieve this goal by embedding drill-and-practice activities within the framework of games, especially competitive arcade-style games. Our purpose here is not to explore this particular dimension. (There has been at least one classic study, by Thomas Malone, of what makes computer-based games fun, which sets the stage for that kind of investigation.) Rather, we would like to suggest a radically different approach to constructing educationally significant, captivating games—in particular, games aimed at encouraging kids to articulate (precisely) *strategic and tactical problem-solving knowledge*, as well as strategies for resource-limited reasoning and diagnosis. The hope is that we might be able to find ways to help students discover knowledge about knowledge, thereby setting the stage for acquiring truly domain-independent skills, such as how to reflect on the knowledge they already have and to identify the causes underlying the mistakes they make. Of course, the catch is constructing a gaming environment that has sufficient pull that kids will be willing, even eager, to struggle with the task of making precise the knowledge that, heretofore, was intuitive, vague, and often unconsciously held.

Robotic olympics

Toward this end, we have been exploring a notion for building games that we have come to call 'robotic olympics.' Briefly stated, our idea involves transforming current arcade-style games into ones in which each human player is actually the 'coach' responsible for programming a set of automated, robot-like players that meet in 'combat' on the arcade screen/computer. Each of the programmed players is a miniature robot, an 'intelligent' agent whose behaviour is governed by its knowledge base. The knowledge base consists of a set of rules specifying how best to respond to changing circumstances of the game (i.e. the position of the other team members, the position of the opponents, and the global state of the environment, such as how much time is left in the game, the current score, whose turn it is, and so on). As the game unfolds in real time—that is, with one set of programmed players playing against another set—the human player acts as a real-time coach, sending top-level commands that the automated players can interpret and use to redirect their strategies and tactics.

To make this kind of activity practical, we postulate the need for two kinds of programming/gaming environments. The first resides in a home computer where each player, in the quiet of his home, constructs and checks out devilish knowledge bases (programs) for his robot players that, after sufficient honing, he decides are smart enough to submit to open challenge. At that point, he carries his trusty home computer module down to the arcade, down loads and initializes his programmed, intelligent robot squad, and with them takes on all challengers. A variant of this scenario involves computer networks in which a computer 'game server' links up and referees the play of automated teams, with each team operating from a home computer.

This version has some attractive features but misses the educational and motivational aspects of groups of people meeting together to discuss and try out their current creations.

For either of these scenarios to work, numerous issues must be addressed. First, programming a set of robots to play intelligently will require specialized languages that facilitate the expression of both strategic and tactical knowledge; otherwise the programming becomes unmanageable. Are such languages available today? Yes, there are some interesting new languages on the horizon that could be ideal for this task—but more about that later. Second, how can students get 'in touch' with the kinds of strategic and tactical knowledge that must be made explicit and precise? Or is this task just too monumental for most kids to do? Proabably not, given some recent advances in the cognitive sciences toward providing frameworks for representing meta-knowledge. Third, given that constructing such automated players is nontrivial, how can we make the overall environment so enticing as to encourage kids to spend the substantial cognitive effort to 'play' in this arena? The answer, we will argue, could turn crucially on the existence of the right sort of sociological conditions, conditions that public television might play a role in creating.

Before we delve into these issues in any depth, let us describe a scenario that we consider typical of the robotic olympics, followed by a brief description of a system that has some of the desired properties. Picture a flashy arcade football game, two teams competing. But, as we said earlier, the human players do not manipulate the play directly as in current arcade-style games; instead, they have worked out 'intelligent' programs for the members of their teams to follow. At home they function as coaches, constructing new plays, diagnosing the strengths and weaknesses of past competitors, and so forth. They articulate their ideas into knowledge bases that define the strategies and tactics for each member of their teams.

Of course, the set of rules, or knowledge base, for the offence is radically different from the one for the same team playing the defense. [. . .] Crucial to success is a thorough recognition of the tradeoffs concerning where the resource-limited robots must direct their outward and inward attentions. [. . .] Costs, in this case in terms of real-time computer resources that are consumed, must be explicitly recognized and acted on.

When the player finally thinks he has a winning set of plays and a well-orchestrated set of automated players, he ventures down to his local 'intelligent' arcade and loads his knowledge bases into each of the robot players in a massive arcade host (an AI-type LISP machine, for example, with spectacular graphics). The game commences and the player acts as real-time coach, watching the developments of the game and perhaps giving the top-level instructions. But this must be done in real time and through a limited channel of communication. This last twist is necessary to make the human player an active but limited participant in the actual play, thus maintaining his interest as the game unfolds and allowing him to tap some of his own real-time resources. Alternatively, he might play the role of quarterback, performing the real-time strategic decision-making for his automated teammates. Both of these possibilities provide him the opportunity, if not the need, to construct his own language and protocols for communicating with his team during the game. Since the primitive language that the players start with is apt to be too verbose for real-time use, he must provide ways for them to interpret the shortened, goal-oriented language that he must invent to coach effectively.

Why football as a target? Several reasons: First, we have tried to sketch out an activity that requires kids to focus on and make absolutely explicit both strategic and tactical knowledge. This is desirable because it increases the possibility that the game-playing activity will induce them to think about their own problem-solving activity. Kids are more likely to be willing and able to articulate this kind of knowledge, or meta-knowledge, if they can tap some of their own real-world experience—that is, ground in their experiential knowledge that which they are trying to make explicit and technical. The relatively pervasive athletic literacy could provide the grounding, for many people, of a new kind of cognitive and metacognitive literacy, as well as a deeper appreciation of what it takes to make such knowledge explicit and precise.

Athletic literacy

The endeavour of kids, teenagers, and adults to make articulate their intuitive notions about football could affect the way they watch football on television. Instead of the passive experience it is now, it might become an active experience of trying to analyze how the game is played, what plays are effective and why, etc. Thus we might be able to create a staircase situation in which one's pre-articulate knowledge or intuitions ground the articulated, technical constructs embodied and used in the knowledge-base language for programming plays. In turn, the experience of formulating and witnessing the entailments of one's articulated strategies makes one a more sensitive observer, thereby enhancing the (athletic) literacy base for grounding further, potentially more abstruse, terms that can be used for building better automated/robotic players. In such a setting, 'Monday-morning quarterbacking' takes on a new sense of reality and educational significance.

Computer literacy

One benefit of the robotic olympic notion of games is that the players learn computer programming. However, the type of computer programming that they learn is likely to lead to a concept of a program that is quite different from the notion of a program as a set of lock-step procedures. The notion of debugging a program would also undergo a change. The ability of a program to handle all sorts of unusual situations would take on a very real and important meaning. A football team that anticipated only the most obvious opponent's plays would surely be a loser.

Motivation

Just as important to learning is the sociological setup of the game. How can a student's interest be captured and maintained during this educational recreation? We believe that one avenue is to create the proper sociology surrounding the olympics. A yearly tournament—perhaps orchestrated and publicized by public television—might be held at the local, regional and national levels. It may be possible to have the best teams combine their programs in some way before the next level of competition, so as to encourage cooperation among the players as they try to merge the good aspects of their separate teams.

Following each competition, the tournament committee could publish the winning team's program so that other players could discover how the best teams did it and the winner could get recognition and feedback about the specifics of his program. Publicizing not only the outcome but also the process would encourage players to learn how to read other players' 'code' and in time would result in a large data base of encoded knowledge about tactics and strategies. (Unfortunately it also might encourage the writing of obscure, hard-to-figure-out rules, but one hopes that players would build on the comprehensible rules while the obscure ones would fade into further obscurity.)

In some instances, such as war games, the publication of winning designs has some negative effects. One such effect is that an optimal way to play the game may be discovered. Doug Lenat, with the help of his computer program Eurisko, designed a fleet for a national war game that won so easily it necessitated rewriting the rules for the next year. The real game of football overcomes the topping-out phenomenon because a large part of the game is determined by what the other team does. The rules in robotic football can be structured to provide a similar importance to team interaction. For example, if last year's winning team ran a wishbone offence, and all of the players of the game had a year to study it, it isn't likely to be a winner again this year. Here the resource-limited nature of the game is important, because adding something to a successful program to cover a special case that it missed means that something else must be removed. This means that a 'perfect' team cannot be constructed simply by adding new material; the program must be restructured to combine old knowledge with new, within the resource limits.

Another possible negative effect of publicizing the winning programs is that the winning stratum of programs might become so good that a new player coming into the game for the first time could not compete effectively without first 'studying' a large data base or copying an existing program. If this happens, the game can be made approachable for beginning players by staging tournaments that place limits on the complexity of a team's program by reducing the amount of computation given at each turn and by changing the rules of the game. Using these parameters, it should be possible to build a series of tournaments that mimic the Pop Warner, high school, college, and pro levels in football. The device of adjusting the game rules could also be used to 'tune' games to encourage development of specific strategies along the lines of the 'increasingly complex microworlds' paradigm.[1]

As we mentioned earlier, one of the road blocks to making our vision of robotic olympics a reality is the programming language in which the robots are constructed. The recent development of the Loops language brings us closer to our goal. Loops is an extension of the Interlisp-D programming environment that includes object-oriented and rule-oriented language facilities.[2] It was orginally designed for use in a clever sociological experiment proposed by Conway and Stefik to engineer knowledge in the VLSI community. The idea was to form a community knowledge base of rules for aiding VLSI design that were usable, readable, and modifiable by users in the community. Thus the rules would be an explicit representation of the community knowledge that would, over time, grow. As a method of teaching Loops, Bobrow, Stefik and Mittal invented a beautiful game called Truckin which is the first operative example of a robotic olympics game. Truckin is based on the activity of transporting goods by truck. During the game a truck moves from one place to another, buying and selling goods, trying to make money. At each turn, decisions must be made about what to buy, what to sell, and where to go next. These decisions are complicated by having to worry about running out of gas, being robbed, having goods get damaged or spoiled, stopping at weigh stations, and having to be at a certain location at the end of the game. After a specified number of moves, the truck at the ending location with the most money wins. The trucks are not directly controlled by human players. Instead their moves are determined by a set of Loops rules provided by the human players prior to the game. Thus, the students learning Loops do so by constructing programs for their 'robots.' Even though the Truckin activity is still in its infancy, many of the positive benefits that we envision for robotic olympics are observable.

COMMUNICATING IDEAS AND ARGUMENTS

The new generation of microcomputers provide the first realistic (cost-effective) opportunity to construct a communication medium that breaks away from a fundamentally linear structuring of ideas. We can now start to experiment, on a large scale, with ways to transcend the straitjacket of linear documents through an electronic medium that captures the more weblike structure of complex ideas. Two-dimensional structures are what we seem naturally to construct on blackboards when we are grappling with a set of interrelated ideas. Likewise, when we are trying to write an essay or report we often spread out 3" × 5" note cards on our tabletops and experiment with tentative arrangements, constantly reshuffling until a coherent framework emerges. Why not create an 'electronic blackboard' that can provide a medium to directly reflect the structure of a set of ideas or arguments? But simply representing a network of ideas through nodes with connections hardly seems that new or that substantial an advance over the proverbial blackboard. We need to go a step further and provide (epistemological) primitives for structuring the network, that is, for identifying different types of nodes and different types of interconnections. Let's explore this further.

Recently, *The New Republic* devoted most of an issue to an article called 'The Great Nuclear Debate.' The intention of this article was to return the debate to its 'intellectual and moral fundamentals.' The article was written by a first-class author, passed through a first-class system of editors, and presented to the public as a vehicle to clarify a muddled yet urgent issue and to provide a compelling new argument. Unfortunately, several of us found the article virtually impenetrable on the first several readings because of the *inherent complexity of the arguments.* Here was an issue of utmost importance, presented in the 'best' form available, and we couldn't really understand it, couldn't keep all its threads straight in our minds! It was only after painstakingly analyzing the argument in its linear form and discovering its underlying *nonlinear* structure that we were able to grasp much of its meaning. But what if, instead of being hammered into a linear document, the article had been presented in a form that more directly reflected the complex web of its logical structure? Instead of spending our time and effort trying to identify the structure of the argument we could have evaluated it. But, as we mentioned before, casting the essay into a web of interconnecting points isn't the whole answer. At a minimum we need to have a systematic way to structure arguments, that is, to make explicit the elements of an argument (subarguments, assumptions, presuppositions, caveats, etc.) and the relationships between those elements (orderings, dependencies, etc.). For much of this work, we can look to the fields of rhetoric, logic and cognitive psychology.

The anatomy of an argument

What are the essential components of argumentation? What is the microstructure of logical syllogisms? Stephen Toulmin analyzes the 'anatomy' of the argument 'organism' and proposes this basic pattern:[3]

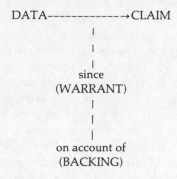

A Claim is made based on certain Data. The leap from Data to Claim is justified by a Warrant that has a defensible Backing. For example:

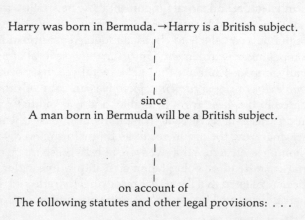

We won't discuss this in detail here. The point is that, using the argument patterns described above, we can create a recursive framework for casting complex essays.

Tools for facilitating comprehension

Unfortunately, just making the structure of the argument explicit and embedding it in a manifold that reflects that structure does not necessarily mean that the result is easier to understand than the original document. By making everything more explicit and by representing all the possible inter-connections between subarguments (for example, arguments for a position, arguments against that position, arguments attempting to defeat arguments for that position, and so on), we might create such a monstrous structure that it exceeds our capacity to understand. What this suggests is that we need also to consider tools that allow the reader to do more than just 'fly over the web.' We need comprehension, as well as creation, tools. Such tools would act as impedance matchers between the properties of the medium and the properties of the mind (and culture). Thus, the reader can examine the different elements of an argument, perhaps initially looking at just the arguments and not the counter-arguments, or checking the presuppositions, or looking at the caveats, etc. Because the structure is explicit and clear, the reader can direct the tools to find and show just what she wants. She can repress not only certain degrees of detail, but also certain *kinds* of detail. Even more powerful tools can be created if the argument is based on a microstructure, such as the Toulmin pattern described above. The reader could extract the essence of the argument by browsing the Claim parts of the document. She could examine the evidence by browsing the Data. She could check the reasoning by browsing the Warrants. If she found something unacceptable, she could dive deeper. The argument structure is recursive—underlying each Datum and Warrant is another argument structure. The reader would be able to track down her points of contention.

The structuring of community information systems

But the scope of this medium can be expanded even farther. Suppose complex political issues were represented using the above kinds of mechanisms in a community information system coupled to home computers. Would public issues so structured and embedded in such an electronic medium be more easily understood by more people? Indeed, what if major issues were presented to people so that they could grasp their subtleties rather than resort to platitudes? Would that draw people into more active and rational involvement with political issues? If the anatomy of an issue is not clear, it is difficult to respond to it rationally and emotional responses or apathy are apt to dominate.

An anecdote: After reading 'The Great Nuclear Debate' we employed a research itern, Cece Blase, to analyze the article and attempt to cast it in a framework based on Toulmin's pattern. She eventually covered an entire wall with paper nodes and connectors. But the fascinating development was that as soon as the anatomy of the arguments became clearer, she began to respond to the assumptions that were being made, questioning and challenging them. We could barely get her to finish 'diagnosing' the rest of the article. Before starting the analysis, the arguments had inspired very little reaction in her. Perhaps Cece's experience generalizes. What appears to be apathy might only be the result of unclear, ill-defined arguments. If we can create tools to make an argument clear, perhaps we can involve more people in responding to it and developing it.

Active reading

The potential of a new communication medium to increase individual involvement in public issues suggests the possibility of creating a community information 'space,' browsed through the tools, or 'eyes,' residing on one's personal computer. Important to the success of such a communication device is the notion of adding context, or writing, mechanisms, to enable readers not only to view a public document but also to add their own ideas, criticisms, and observations. Each reader could have his or her own context layer containing personal comments. Likewise, each context layer could be browsed by other readers of the document. Suppose this 'public essay' was really a public electronic entity accessible by every cable television in a community. Structuring essays concerning issues of great importance in an argument-based electronic form would give each member of the community a better chance to understand the complexities and subtleties underlying a particular community issue. Furthermore, by making this a two-way system, we could create a *growing* public document that encourages readers to become active in developing a more refined analysis of an issue. Such a system might help return activity-based learning, or active hypothesis formation, to the heretofore passive absorption of public issues presented on television or in newspapers. And, perhaps, these issues are sufficiently complex that they really do require a new medium for expression and understanding—a medium that not only reduces the cognitive load in understanding arguments, but also creates a kind of *sociological pull* encouraging participation in refining those arguments.

AUTHORINGLAND—FROM CHAOS TO ORDER

Currently, text-editing systems are loaded up with devices to craft the surface structure, or appearance, of a document: to change fonts, to move text around in a document, to change the spacing, to print special characters, etc. But do these mechanisms actually help one write clearly? Admittedly, they improve the cosmetic quality of the final document and they make the mechanics of preparing it faster and easier, but they also focus the user's attention on the end product, rather than the process of writing. They provide a perpetually 'clean' version of the document, with tools for *local tinkering* and *superficial crafting*. However, at the beginning of the writing process, doesn't the writer want tools for high-level, global tinkering—tools for dealing with rough, unrefined ideas? Isn't writing at this point more a stream of consciousness, only moving toward ordered thinking in the later stages? Conjecture: A blank piece of paper (and a blank screen with a blinking waiting caret) may result in writer's block because both encourage the author to view writing as a top-down logical process. Blockage comes from the belief that one must start with an outline, which, by its very nature, presupposes a good logical analysis of the topic.

In the same way, current 'structured editors' that require an author first to specify an outline and then to refine and expand that structure are apt to hurt rather than stimulate the writing process. What we need instead are tools to help us discover the structure, to accept unconditionally our ideas, notes, brainstorms, tentative structurings—the raw material out of which we will construct a paper, document, or essay. For example, we can design an 'active scratch pad' on which an author can jot down fleeting ideas that might be lost if he had to spend the cognitive resources to determine where they belong and how they relate to other ideas. At this stage the electronic environment is like a fishnet, catching and supporting ideas without demanding that they be in some prespecified form. The next stage requires tools to help the author browse, edit, expand, refine, and articulate his ideas—to discover the inherent structure and subtleties of the argument. Only at the last stage do we need tools to craft the surface of the document, to prepare it for presentation. We now have the computing resources to create a writing environment—an Authoringland—that enhances the process of writing, that helps an author move from pre-articulate intuitions to articulate arguments, from chaos to order in his thinking and writing.

The annotation system (Annoland)

Let's look at a specific system we have been experimenting with, [designed by John Sybalsky and myself.] Annoland was designed to help us move from chaos to order in writing. Annotations can be thought of as pencilled-in notes on a paper document: They are amplifications, remarks about content, notes to oneself, etc. Unlike a system of handwritten annotations, however, Annoland gives structure to the world. An annotation is about a certain piece of text, and travels with it come what may. There are different kinds of annotations (e.g. comments on style, comments on content, points to check, etc.) and these various annotation types are distinguished by Annoland to prevent confusion. There is a reference to each annotation in the body of the document similar to a footnote number. This 'pointer' leads to the content of the annotation. Since an annotation is itself a piece of text, it can also be annotated; those annotations can in turn be annotated, and so on. In this way, one can track a 'dialogue' of comments, or can build a structure of points about stylistic issues that can be checked later. This many-layered structure is hard both to navigate and to locate oneself in, if all you can see is the local structure. Hence, Annoland provides a window that displays the overall structure in the form of a graph, identifying the annotations and how they are related. Each node of the graph represents a single annotation, and can be 'touched' to see the annotation itself; the arc between two nodes is labelled to show their relationship. In working with a document, one often needs to find a particular annotation and what it was about, but not where it was. Annoland provides a summary of the annotations for each document. This summary can be used as a table of contents, listing enough of each annotation to indicate its content. When an annotated document is saved, the annotations follow along; when it is loaded for editing, the annotations are retrieved as well, and the graph and summary windows are re-created.

Tools for multiple-authorship

There seems to be a total lack of tools to help coauthors write a paper, yet computational resources for such tools now exist on micros. For example, we can build a system that keeps track of all the versions of a paper, along with what changes were made when and by whom. We can create an environment that structures documents so that they can be browsed along different dimensions. One author can browse the changes another made. He can look at and efficiently compare and contrast different versions. Facilities can be devised for leaving flags to call attention to certain passages, for reminders, for messages to other authors, etc. We need such tools, not only because more papers are being co-authored, but also because, from an educational perspective, we want to construct tools that facilitate cooperation among students in problem-solving and writing. Perhaps the real power of informal learning lies in group co-operation such as helping each other debug and clarify an understanding of a given situation. Explaining one's idea to a teammate, classmate, or colleague is certainly hygienic. Arguing out, on paper, the pros and cons of an idea is inevitably educational.

Integrated environments for stimulating writing

But what if the goal of writing isn't to create order from a fertile but chaotic stream of consciousness? What if the goal is to teach writing skills, rather than producing a certain document? What if we want to teach kids to write, but they don't seem to have any ideas, chaotic or otherwise? How do we stimulate them? The computer provides the perfect opportunity to integrate writing into other endeavours. For example, we can create a physics learning environment consisting of a computer-simulated lab, along with tools for taking notes, for designing experiments, for recording data, for analyzing data, for writing up the report, for drawing graphs, and so on. All the tools can be integrated into one environment, making clearer the significance of each aspect of a scientific process, and the relationships between them. For example, instead of being a detached and dreary task, note-taking could be part of the lab, integrated into each phase of the experiment. The environment could be geared toward idea generation, to learning about physics and math and how to express ideas in different ways, including through writing.

LEARNING FROM DOING HOMEWORK IN ALGEBRA

The last example for this article illustrates the instructional value to be gained from reifying the *process* as opposed to the *product* of some set of actions. In this case 'process' refers to the solution process or steps that a student performs in attempting to simplify a given algebraic equation. Before describing the system, let's first discuss why it was constructed.

Educators and cognitive scientists have observed that students are asked to spend numerous hours doing the homework problems listed at the end of each chapter in math and science books. It is accepted doctrine that one must engage in solving the problems before one will have mastered the knowledge in the chapter. Intuitively we all agree, yet there has been surprisingly little analysis of what precisely is being learned. (There are, of course, exceptions, such as the provocative work being conducted by Larkin and VanLehn.)[4, 5] Perhaps even more surprising is that while every pedagogist stresses the need for doing such homework, there is nearly a total absence of explicit strategies or heuristics for learning from the doing of homework. Whatever is learned is learned tacitly and often by accident. It seems that computer systems could be a major aid in helping a student learn more directly from the homework he or she has done. In addition, the right kind of system could help students *learn how to learn* from what they have done, that is, to learn from the false paths taken while trying to solve the problem. What we would like, in short, is a computer system to help students improve both domain-specific skills and, more importantly, certain metacognitive skills.

Recently [Kelly Roach, Kurt VanLehn and I] built an experimental teaching system for high school algebra that helps kids learn from the actual doing of the homework. The central idea for the system is actually quite simple, although the details of making it truly habitable, given the two-dimensional nature of mathematical expressions, has turned it into a relatively complex system. The student is presented with an algebraic equation to solve. She is provided with a menu of algebraic transformations (such as cancel, commute, or distribute), any one of which she can select and instantiate on the equation as a whole or on one of its subexpressions. Once the transformation is instantiated, she can execute it, thereby producing another expression that she hopes is on the path to the solution.

The details of what the particular transformations are and how they get instantiated are unimportant for this discussion. What is important is that an audit trail of each of the selected transformations, or solution steps, is kept as a data structure that can be displayed, edited, annotated, and even replayed, thereby providing a kind of animation of the solution path. This audit trail or record is also graphically represented as a problem-solving tree (or space). The resulting structure reifies the solution path with all the backtracking points and retries that the student generates in the course of trying to solve the equation. What is interesting is how this structure or solution space can become an object of study in its own right—that is, a meta-object. For example, the student can now browse her own solution space, looking at branch points where she first applied a transformation that led her down a garden path, before returning and trying another transformation that started her down a path that worked. Having distinguished the faulty branch points from the one that led to success (which can only be accomplished after the solution is constructed), she may then be able to identify the features of the equation that point to the optimal transformations to apply to its solution. Extracting and analyzing these features is a first step to discovering strategic knowledge about equation solving. Stepping back and playing with the solution space as an object of study in its own right is a first step to discovering metacognitive strategies about how to learn from what one has done.

It is evident that providing a means to study and replay one's problem-solving attempts does not, in itself, ensure that students will be willing to examine the structure in detail. However, there are numerous games and activities that can help focus a student's attention on the structure of her own problem-solving space. For example, suppose the task is to find the shortest solution path relative to a given set of possible transformations. Such a task becomes eminently feasible and even fun to do in this medium because it is so easy to browse and edit the current solution space. Indeed, a task might be to examine someone else's proposed solution and to try to improve on it. Furthermore, since the solution space is not only easy to edit but also easy to annotate, a student might be given the task of going back and justifying why she chose to do what she did at each step along the way—a reasonable task especially after the fact. [. . .]

Of course, this kind of system has to be augmented with a set of activities that focus a kid's attention on the structure of the search space. An example of such an activity would be to have one student examine the solution space of another student in an attempt to find a shorter solution, perhaps by extending one of the partial solutions that had been abandoned. Another task might be to have a student complete a partial solution in a specially constructed solution space, perhaps annotating on an associated electronic notepad what was good and bad about the strategic decisions made in the original solution space. Needless to say, there are many possibilities of how to make the solution space come alive as an object in its own right.

CONCLUSION

We have presented a set of ideas of how the new generation of powerful microcomputers can radically alter both the form and content of learning. The threads that tie these ideas together are the concepts of *process versus product* and *the computer as a communication device.*

We have argued that computer learning environments provide a beautiful opportunity to reify the process one goes through in solving a problem. But having computers record and make replayable the process that a user went through in crafting his solution (or piece of art) does not, in itself, suffice to provide a new kind of learning environment. Tools must be added to the computing/learning environment that help structure the process as an object in ways that bring the important parts of (one's thought) processes to the surface. Tools are also required to help the user browse this object, filtering out irrelevant portions, highlighting and annotating other portions, and so on. The right collection of tools should help the overall system to act as a mirror for the user's thought processes, enabling him to reflect on his own thinking and improve his metacognitive skills.

We must also recognize the critical role of the computer as a device capable of communicating the products of creative efforts along with the process that underlies their creation. The computer as a communication facilitator not only permits the wide dissemination of knowledge and the development of supporting subcultures, but also provides the opportunity to engineer the sociological element of learning environments—a topic that deserves some serious research. [. . .]

ACKOWLEDGEMENTS

I am greatly indebted to Richard Burton, with whom I have had countless discussions on all aspects of this article and who has made numerous suggestions on all the earlier drafts. Steven Locke and Susan Newman have aided greatly in helping me clarify these ideas and express them in semi-English. Danny Bobrow and Mark Stefik have provided many useful comments on the robotic olympics section. Lynn Conway has always acted as a source of inspiration, especially given her knack for generating ideas concerning the sociology of innovations.

REFERENCES

1. Burton, R., Brown, J. S. and Fischer, G. Analysis of Skiing as a Success Model of Instruction: Manipulating the Learning Environment to Enhance Skill Acquisition, in *Everyday Cognition: Its Development in Social Context*, B. Rogoff (ed.), Cambridge, Massachusetts, Harvard University Press, in press.
2. Stefik, M., Bobrow, D., Mittal, S. and Conway, L. (1983) Knowledge Programming in LOOPS: Report on an Experimental Course, *AI Magazine*.
3. Toulmin, S., (1964) *The Uses of Argument*, London, Cambridge University Press.
4. Larkin, J. H. (1982) Enriching Formal Knowledge: A Model for Learning to Solve Textbook Physics Problems, in *Cognitive Skills and Their Acquisition*, Anderson, J. R. (ed.), Hillsdale, New Jersey, Lawrence Erlbaum Associates, pp. 311–344.
5. VanLehn, K. (1983) Human Procedural Skill Acquisition: A Theory, A Model and Psychological Validation, to appear in Proceedings of the National Conference on Artificial Intelligence, American Association for Artificial Intelligence, Menlo Park, California.

8.2 Algebra slaves and agents in a Logo-based mathematics curriculum

• Wallace Feurzeig

For many students the ideas and methods of algebra appear obscure and mysterious, their sense and purpose unclear, and their applicability to anything genuinely real or interesting very remote. Students often fail to acquire an understanding of the key concepts, despite their inherent simplicity. Even when they gain the notion of variables, expressions and equations, students often lack the strategic knowledge required to motivate and direct the global planning and detailed execution of an attack on a problem. These conceptual and strategic difficulties are compounded by the needs for precise performance of the arithmetic and symbolic operations required in manipulating expressions. Extended operations like subtracting an expression from both sides of an equation or expanding a product of three terms, are very difficult for beginning students. Their buggy performance in carrying out the detailed manipulative work greatly confounds and frustrates their acquisition and assimilation of the most important and central ideas.

In an effort to confront these difficulties and show how they can be overcome, we are developing a Logo-based introductory algebra course for sixth graders. Our approach has three major components: work on Logo programming projects in algebraically rich contexts whose content is meaningful and compelling to students, the use of algebra microworlds with concrete iconic representations of formal objects and operations, and the introduction of the algebra workbench, an expert instructional system to aid students in performing extended algebraic operations.

The algebra workbench will employ a set of powerful symbolic manipulation tools for performing the standard manipulations of high school algebra. It will have two main modes of use: demonstration mode, which uses an expert tutor program to solve algebra problems incrementally, explaining its strategy and its step by step operations in straightforward terms along the way; and practice mode, in which the student tries to solve a problem with the assistance of the tutor, which performs the operations requested by the student at each step and which can be called at any point to advise the student of the correctness of a step, to perform or explain any step, to evaluate the student's solution, or to perform a problem that she poses.

These powerful aids make it possible to effectively separate out the difficulties in performing the formal and manipulative aspects of algebra work from those encountered in learning the central conceptual and strategic content. Distinctly different kinds of instructional tools and activities—Logo programming, expert tutors, or algebra microworlds—can thus be brought to bear where each is most appropriate and effective.

1. INTRODUCTION

We plan to introduce and develop the key and central concepts of algebra— variable, formal expression, function, equation, inverse—in terms of Logo ideas and programming activities. Many projects will be centered on areas of interest to students, e.g. developing programs to generate gossip, Knock-Knock jokes, or secret codes. These will lead in a natural way to projects that address the standard content of introductory algebra. For example, work on writing programs to generate conversational dialogs will provide a starting point for projects on generating algebra story problem quizzes.

The Logo knowledge and skills required to develop the programs will be taught along the way, as an integral part of the project work. Students will only be expected to write programs with relatively simple structures—they will be given the more difficult Logo procedures needed for building complex programs. Also, we will introduce an iconic representation of Logo programs as function machines that can be inspected, connected together in various ways, and run. This multi-level graphic representation shows the procedure structure of complex programs with great clarity. It should greatly aid students' understanding of Logo's control structure and semantics and help them in the process of program design and construction.

There are several reasons for giving Logo a central role in the course. Our experience is that building mathematical structures is a uniquely valuable way of understanding them. Programming is the tool of choice for building algebraic objects and processes because of its interactivity and generality and Logo is the programming language of choice because of its essential mathematical character (e.g. its recursive functional structures which account for its power and elegance) together with its easy accessibility to beginning students of mathematics. A related consideration is that the experience of creating problems, equations or functions gives great insight into how to analyze, manipulate and solve them. In the traditional school math course, students are always asked to solve or transform complex constructs, never to construct or create them. The use of Logo makes it possible to show very concretely the value of *doing* as a clue to *undoing* in many algebraic contexts. The theme of building objects and processes as a precursor and aid to undoing and solving them occurs repeatedly throughout the course. Some of the Logo teaching modules used in the course are described in Sections 2 and 4.

Logo programming activities have paramount importance in the teaching of algebra concepts and problem solving strategies but we are working with other kinds of instructional tools as well. The student's programming projects are complemented by the use of a graphic microworld, the *marble bags microworld*, specially designed to introduce the algebraic manipulation of expressions and equations through a very concrete iconic representation.

The objects in this microworld are pictures of marbles and bags (bags contain some unknown number of marbles); the operations include addition or subtraction of specified numbers of bags or marbles, and multiplication or division of the current collection by a specified integer. Students are introduced to marble bag stories and diagrams. They are shown how to create and solve simple marble bag stories (story problems). They are introduced to standard algebraic notation as a rapid way of writing marble bag stories. As a student works on a problem, the system can show the correspondence between the iconic, English, and standard algebraic representations of the operations and results. The marble bag microworld will be further described and illustrated in Section 3.

The marble bag microworld and the Logo modules on equations and functions provide strong introductions to algebra expression manipulation and problem solving strategies. Students will have a firm understanding of the meaning of algebraic expressions but relatively little experience in dealing with problems involving extended expressions and requiring extensive symbolic manipulation. Problems such as simplifying algebraic expressions whose terms have many factors, transforming complex expressions into canonical form, factoring polynomials, determining whether two expressions are equivalent and solving systems of two simultaneous linear equations greatly strain the newly acquired fragile manipulative skills of beginning students. The task of consolidating and extending their strategic skills is greatly complicated by the need to carry out the associated manipulations at the same time.

The use of another kind of instructional tool based on an expert symbol manipulation program enables the strategic and manipulative components to be effectively separated. We plan to develop such an expert instructional system, the *algebra workbench*. In practice mode, when the student works on a problem, the system will serve as his agent or slave by carrying out the algebraic operations he requests, enabling him to focus on the strategic planning and the operational decisions. The system will also include an expert algebra tutor. The tutor will be available to advise the student and critique the student's work. In demonstration mode, the tutor will work through a problem, explaining its strategy and actions along the way. The student will be able to intervene and propose alternative steps. Our tentative design plan for the algebra workbench is described and its use is illustrated, in Section 5.

The course will thus employ three distinctly different kinds of instructional facilities—Logo programming, an algebra microworld, and an expert tutoring system. A comprehensive mathematics program with serious learning goals requires all three. In Section 6 we discuss the educational strengths and limitations of programming, microworlds and 'intelligent' tutors, and suggest some ways their capabilities might be extended.

2. FROM ENGLISH TO ALGEBRA

We begin the course by having students work on programming tasks that seem to them to be part of the subject of English rather than mathematics. There are two main reasons for this. Students have a great deal of knowledge of the formal structure of English, but relatively little real knowledge and experience of mathematical structures. We can build on their knowledge of English structure as a starting point for developing the idea of algebraic structure. Along the way, it is easy to find linguistic tasks that have more than a little interest for students. The first unit in this module is the development of Logo programs to generate gossip.

The initial version of gossip presented to the students is a Logo program that randomly selects a name from a list of names, randomly selects an action from a list of actions, and then puts the name and action together as a sentence and outputs it. The program is:

```
to gossip
output (sentence who doeswhat)
end
```
where **who** and **doeswhat** are the following Logo procedures:
```
to who
output pick [sam jane sally bill chris]
end

to doeswhat
output pick [cheats [loves to sing] giggles
[talks your ears off] [likes smelly feet]]
end
```

To run **gossip**, say five times, one types:

    repeat 5 [print gossip]

and Logo responds with

    jane talks your ears off
    sally giggles
    bill loves to sing
    chris likes smelly feet
    sally loves to sing

or some of the other constructed sentences embedded in the procedures.

The Logo procedure **pick** which does the random selection from its associated list, is given to the students as a primitive. The other procedures, gossip, **who** and **doeswhat**, are intended as models for the students. When their operation is understood, students modify and extend these in projects to create their own gossip. First they rewrite **who** and **doeswhat** using their own name and action lists. Then they extend gossip so that it includes two actors and takes the form **who doeswhat towhom.** Further extensions generate more complex sentence structures involving noun phrases and verb phrases and, later, perhaps, noun phrases with embedded verb phrases. To vary the form of their productions, students can write a supergossip procedure which uses pick to randomly select a different one of the several varied gossip procedures they have written, each time it generates a new sentence.

Icon machine Logo is introduced from the start. The icon machine picture of the two-person gossip procedure, for example, is shown in Fig. 1.

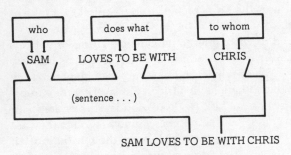

Figure 1   The gossip machine

The picture shows the internal structure of the gossip machine, whose parts include the **who, doeswhat, towhom,** and **sentence** machines. The **who, doeswhat** and **towhom** machines have an output (called a spout in icon machine notation) but no inputs. These kinds of machines are called *sources*. Machines with one or more inputs (referred to as hoppers in icon machine notation) but with no output, are called *sinks*. Machines with neither inputs or output are called *solos*. Machines like **sentence** (a Logo primitive in this case) which have one or more inputs and an output as well, are called *processes*. Sources can input to sinks or processes and processes can input to other processes as well as to sinks. Thus, complex Logo procedures can be diagrammed as icon machines in a way that shows their structure very clearly. The correspondence between Logo machine diagrams and Logo program text is one-to-one. The icon machine notation is due to Paul Goldenberg, one of my colleagues on the Logo algebra project.

Students are next shown how to write interactive procedures in Logo. This enables them to create programs that communicate with a user in activities such as exchanging Knock-Knock jokes. Their programs generate dialogues such as:

Person:	**Knock, Knock**
Computer:	**Who's there?**
Person:	**Miss**
Computer:	**Miss who?**
Person:	**Mississippi**
Computer:	**Ha Ha Ha Ha**
	Now it's my turn
	Knock Knock
Person:	**Who's there?**
Computer:	**Boo**
Person:	**Boo Who?**
Computer:	**There, there, don't cry, baby**

The student enables the computer to become a participant by writing a procedure that stores a list of the Knock-Knock jokes acquired by the computer from previous games with students. When it is the computer's turn to tell a Knock Knock joke, it uses the Logo **pick** procedure to select a joke at random from this database.

Students are then prepared to write interactive quiz programs of various kinds. They generate quizzes in areas of individual interest such as movies, food, cars, sports, and music. The students enjoy having their classmates try their programs, especially when others have difficulty answering their questions. However, around this time the kids begin to wonder if they are in an English course or an algebra course, and sometimes sound as though they are being deprived of the math they were promised, even though they often dislike math! Some even suggest the idea of writing mathematics quiz programs. They see that they can write programs that generate sentences in math instead of English, e.g. sentences such as $72 - 29 = ?$ They are shown how to randomly generate all the standard forms of arithmetic problems for use in quizzes.

Their programs combine English and arithmetic phrases to generate arithmetic story problems such as:

I GET 3 PIES
I GIVE AWAY 4 FISH
I WIN 7 ELEPHANTS

I TAKE 5 CAKES
I SELL 8 MARSHMALLOWS
HOW MANY THINGS DO I HAVE NOW?

In this program, **pick** is used to randomly select the names of the objects, the numbers, and the addition and subtraction words from associated lists.

At this point the students are given the project of writing algebra quiz programs that present problems such as:

5*BOX + 4 = 49
What is the value of BOX?

This brings up a critical difficulty, however. They do not know how to solve such algebra problems—how, then, will they be able to tell whether the answers given by the users are correct? We show them a 'trick' that will enable their *program* to know the correct answers, even though the students do not know how to *solve* the problems. Their program will choose three numbers at random, say 3, 7 and 4. It will then compute 3*7 + 4 to get 25, conceal the 7, and output the problem 3*BOX + 4 = 25 whose answer the program knows to be 7. thus, the program can pose a problem to users and evaluate the correctness of their answers even though the student who has written the program could not do so himself.

In their initial programs students usually program responses such as 'THAT IS WRONG' to incorrect answers, some adding epithets such as 'DUMMY', 'KNUCKLEBRAIN' or 'STUPIDHEAD'. If they have a real-time clock available they sometimes append helpful remarks such as 'BESIDES, IT TOOK YOU 23 SECONDS AND THAT IS REAL SLOW KID.'

In the ensuing development they are urged to program more informative and helpful responses, for example, to show the user that his answer is indeed wrong. On the next round, the typical responses are of the form

6 CAN'T BE THE RIGHT ANSWER BECAUSE 3*6 + 4 = 22 AND 22 IS NOT 25 IS IT?

They are urged to be even more helpful. A little later their programs may produce responses such as

6 IS TOO SMALL. THE ANSWER MUST BE BIGGER BECAUSE 25 IS BIGGER THAN 22

To give students further insight leading to the realization that there *exists* a formal procedure for solving linear equations, we go back to work on sub-problems of simpler forms, such as BOX + 3 = 10 then 4*BOX = 20. When they return to progressively harder problems students work with 'big' numbers as coefficients and incorporate signed numbers. Some succeed in working out the general algorithm, though we do not count on that happening.

A preliminary version of this unit was tested in early Logo teaching experiments with seventh grade students in the middle mathematics track of a junior high school in Lexington, Massachusetts.[1] This work established the effectiveness of preceding the formal work on algebra equation solving by work on formal English language tasks already meaningful to students. It also showed that students could acquire the required level of competence in Logo programming. Transcripts of two student program runs from the last phase of that work are reproduced in Figs. 2 and 3.

The program MULTEACH (Fig. 2) shows one of the wonderful things that often happened with this algebra quiz activity—the intense engagement of the students and the injection of their personalities into their work through the mixing of English text with the algebra. This student was regarded as highly mathophobic. As the transcript shows, however, he was capable of doing significant math in the context of Logo.

ALGE (Fig. 3) is one of the more advanced programs. This student found the standard algorithm on his own and was happy to show off its use in responding to wrong answers on problems chosen to impress his classmates. We especially enjoyed his comment 'AN EASY WAY TO GET THE ANSWER IS' when the computations involved two- and three-place signed numbers. (The program does have a bug, however, as seen in the first problem. It does not recognize that 4 and +04 are numerically equal.)

```
—MULTEACH
4 * /BOX/ = 20
WHAT IS /BOX/?
*5
VERY GOOD.  YOUR A SMART LITTLE DEVIL.  BUT YOU TOOK 3 SECONDS
WOULD YOU LIKE TO  NO  MORE
*YES
ITS BEEN LIKE THIS, YOU SEE ALONG TIME AGO MY MOTHER SAID I WAS
NOT AGING LIKE ALL THE OTHERS, SO WE GOT A CUPUTER DOCTOR TO HELP
ME, AND HE DID.  SO.  NOW YOU NO WHY I AM SO OLD
8 * /BOX/ = 32
WHAT IS /BOX/?
*4
VERY GOOD.  YOUR A SMART LITTLE DEVIL.  BUT YOU TOOK 2 SECONDS
WOULD YOU LIKE TO NO MORE
*NO
BOY ITS NOT OFTEN YOU HERE A STORY LIKE MINE, BUT SINCE YOU DO NOT
I NOW RETURN YOU TO YOUR SO CALLED HUMAN FUN HA HA HA
8 * /BOX/ = 48
WHAT IS /BOX/?
*8
/BOX/ IS 6
IF YOU THINK YOUR SO SMART WHY DID YOU GET IT WRONG.  OR WHERE YOU
THINKING OF TRICKING THEY OLDEST COMPUTER IN THE WORLD.  PLEASE DO
NOT I AM 588 YEARS OLD AND DO NOT WISH TO DIE NOW.
WOULD YOU LIKE TO NO MORE
*NO
BOY ITS NOT OFTEN YOU HERE A STORY LIKE MINE
```

Figure 2   The MULTEACH program

```
-ALGE
-38 = /BOX/ + +28 = -124

WHAT IS BOX?
*4
IT TOOK YOU 21 SECONDS TO ANSWER ME YOU KNUCKLEBRAIN THAT IS SLOW!
WRONG
THE REAL ANSWER IS +04
AN EASY WAY TO GET THE ANSWER IS TO SUBTRACT +28 FROM -124 AND THEN TR
TO DIVIDE -38 INTO -152


-78 x /BOX/ + +97 = -3023

WHAT IS /BOX/?
*+35
IT TOOK YOU 33 SECONDS TO ANSWER ME YOU KNUCKLEBRAIN THAT IS SLOW!
WRONG
THE REAL ANSWER IS +48
AN EASY WAY TO GET THE ANSWER IS TO SUBTRACT +97 FROM -3023 AND THEN
TRY TO DIVIDE -78 INTO -3120


-31 x /BOX/ + +50 = -2802

WHAT IS BOX?
*+92
IT TOOK YOU 19 SECONDS TO ANSWER ME YOU KNUCKLEBRAIN THAT IS SLOW!


GOOD
-54 x /BOX/ + +09 = -477

WHAT IS BOX?
*2
YOU MUST BE A BRAIN TO ANSWER ME IN 5 SECONDS
WRONG
THE REAL ANSWER IS +09
AN EASY WAY TO GET THE ANSWER IS TO SUBTRACT +09 FROM -477 AND THEN
TRY TO DIVIDE -54 INTO -486
```

Figure 3   The ALGE program

3. THE MARBLE BAG MICROWORLD

This module approaches the manipulation of algebraic expressions and the
solution of linear equations in another way. Students work on problems in
an algebra microworld that uses a concrete iconic representation for the
objects to be constructed and manipulated—marbles and bags. Marble
stories and diagrams are introduced through the device of a guessing game.
The teacher proceeds with a student along the following lines.

> Do you know the day of the month you were born on? O.K. don't tell me
> what it is, just remember it.

> Now double it. Ready?
> Add 3 to that.
> Then subtract 2 from that.

Then double the result. Now, tell me what you have. You said 50, right? Then I say you were born on the 12th. Am I correct? (How did I do it?)

Students are shown how to do such number puzzles by using a new notation called bags and marbles. A bag represents the number to be guessed (the student's original number). Marbles represent 'ones'—for example, the number 6 is represented by six marbles. After, becoming familiar with this notation on paper, students are introduced to the marble bag microworld. This program is being developed in Logo on the Macintosh computer.

Figure 4 shows the student interface, as currently planned. The top half of the display shows the operations and operands that can be selected with the mouse. The arithmetic operations can be specified either in symbolic notation (top middle window) or in English (including the additional operations **pick a number, double and halve**). The operands can be the numbers from 1–10 or **your original number**. Other possible operands are a bag or (from one to three) marbles (these icons are shown in the top left window). The operations can, of course, be repeated.

The use of the marble bag microworld is illustrated for the birthdate guessing problem presented above. The two bottom left windows show the problem history. The first operation, **pick a number**, gave rise to the display of a bag. The operation **multiply by 2** resulted in the display of two bags. The final operation, another **multiply by 2**, produced the last collection of four bags and two marbles.

The work can also be displayed in standard algebraic notation, as in the third bottom window. Finally, the working out of the problem can be shown, as in the rightmost bottom window. To figure out the number of marbles in the bag, one works backwards either from the icon representation or the algebraic notation. Using the icons, if four bags and two marbles equal 50 marbles then two bags and one marble must equal 25 marbles, and so on.

Students go on to create marble bag stories of increasing complexity. They will use the microworld to represent stories in either representation and to solve them in both. Figure 5 shows work on a fairly advanced story.

The marble bag approach is based on the work of Wirtz *et al.*[2] The algebra bag microworld is being designed by my colleagues Paul Goldenberg and Ricky Carter. The design is not finished—questions such as the icon representation of negative numbers (perhaps as antimarbles?) have yet to be decided.

4. FUNCTIONS, SECRET CODES, BLACK BOXES AND STORY PROBLEMS

This section briefly describes some of the other Logo modules we are developing to deepen and extend the approaches made through the work in simple computational linguistics and algebra bag problems. The notion of a func-

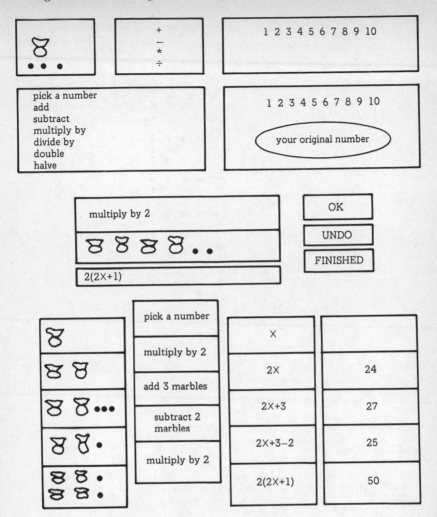

Figure 4 Marble Bag Interface

tion and the power of functional composition were already introduced in the context of Logo function machines (icon Logo). The module on functions is designed to show the connection between functional inversion and equation solving. Students gain extensive experience in constructing functions and reducing them to their constituents (*doing* and *undoing*).

The module has two main units—codes and functions guessing (black boxes). The activities in both units include the construction of complex functions from simpler ones by chaining (composition) with the goal of creating difficult decoding and function guessing and inversion problems, and posing them to other students ('try to break my secret code', 'guess my

Story line	Algebraic shorthand summarizing the story line so far	Marble picture	Algebraic description of marble picture	example
Think of a number	x		x	5
Add 4	x + 4		x + 4	9
Triple that	3(x + 4)	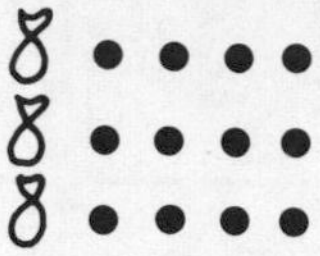	3x + 12	27
Add your original number	3(x + 4) + x	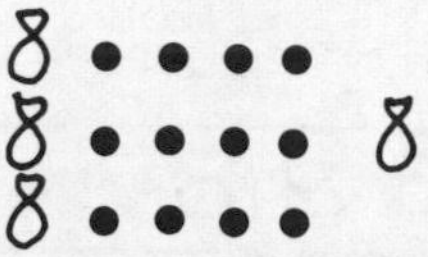	4x + 12	32
Subtract 8	3(x + 4) + x − 8	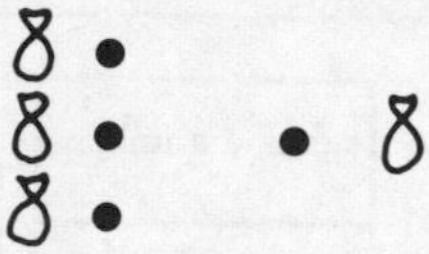	4x + 4	24
Now divide by 4	$\dfrac{3(x + 4)\ 3\ x - 8}{x}$		x + 1	6

Corresponding word problem.

Ayoka has some marbles.
Benjamin has four more marbles than Ayoka.
Carlos has three times as many marbles as Benjamin.
Darlene has as many marbles as Ayoka's and Carlos's combined.
Emmett has eight marbles less than Darlene.
Emmett has four times as many marbles as Felicia.
And Felicia? She has exactly six marbles.
How many marbles does Ayoka have?

Figure 5 Marble Bag Algebra

rule'). In this respect, the activities are similar to the previous interactive quiz work ('try to answer my questions', 'solve my algebra quiz problems').

Secret codes

The first codes developed are letter substitution ciphers for encoding text. We start with ciphers that displace each letter by a fixed number, modulo 26.

Thus, a displacement of -1 turns IBM into HAL and PA into OZ. Students gain experience with hand encoding and decoding of displacement ciphers. They represent displacement ciphers as function machines and as graphs. They observe that deciphering and enciphering are inverse functions. They then write Logo displacement cipher procedures, using two given pseudo-primitives **numberof: letter** and **letterof: number**, which work as follows. **numberof** takes a letter as input and outputs its associated alphabet position (A outputs 1, B outputs 2, . . ., Z outputs 26). **letterof** takes a number as input, interprets it mod 26, and outputs its letter equivalent. Using these, students construct displacement cipher encoding procedures. For example, the procedure for a displacement of -1 might be called **mycode** and written as follows:

> **to mycode: letter**
> **output letterof minus 1 numberof: letter**
> **end**

where **minus 1** is the procedure

> **to minus 1: number**
> **output: number** -1
> **end**

The use of icon machines should assist students in developing procedures such as **mycode** that have long function chains.

Next, students write procedures to encode words, sentences and entire messages (these are represented as lists) using an auxilliary pseudo-procedure **scramble,** which accomplishes the encoding for a given encipherment procedure and message. For example,

scramble "mycode [try to understand] outputs **sqx sn tmcdqrszmc**

Students then write the decoding procedures associated with their encoding procedures. The decoding procedure for **mycode** is:

> **to mydecode: letter**
> **output letterof plus 1 numberof: letter**
> **end**

scramble "mydecode [sqx sn tmcdqrszmc] outputs **try to understand**

In the last part of the unit on secret codes, displacement ciphers (which have the form $x + b$) will be generalized to linear-form ciphers (which have the form $a*x + b$). To avoid ambiguity, we will only work with encoding functions that are single-valued. In the last phase, students will be given a text encoded by a linear-form cipher together with the original message. Their task will be to try to determine the specific encoding function used. They will find this to be enormously difficult until we show them how it can be done graphically by the following procedure. The two axes are labelled by the alphabet and corresponding letters from the two texts are plotted against each other. This will produce a display of the algebraic form Y = a*X + b. An analysis of the graph will reveal the encoding function.

This unit was designed by Larry Davidson. Paul Goldenberg and Ricky Carter contributed further extensions and refinements.

Functions as black boxes

A function has three components: its input list (which may be empty), its definition (which describes the computational process), and its output. In the usual situation, the inputs and definition are known, and its output is determined by performing the computation, i.e. running the program.

The function evaluation problem is: given a function (e.g. a Logo procedure which has an output) and given its input list, find the output. Two related problems are defined when either the input list or the function definition is unknown. The inversion problem is: given a function and given its output, find its inputs. The black box problem is: given a function's inputs and its output, find the function.

There is no effective solution procedure for the black box problem. However, when one restricts the form of the unknown function, e.g. to linear algebraic forms as with the linear-form ciphers, projects to develop function guessing strategies ('guess my rule' games) and function guessing machines (in icon Logo and as Logo procedures) become feasible. For example, students will be shown how to write a procedure to compare the behaviour of the unknown function (which although 'buried', so that it is made non-inspectable, is nevertheless runnable) with that of a guessed function, to see whether they produce the same outputs across a wide range of inputs. Students often find these activities highly interesting. They can be used to give real mathematical insight into the behaviour of algebraic functions.

The inversion (or missing input) problem gives rise to a number of projects. The code deciphering work described above is a special case. Students learn that this problem does not always have a unique solution, that in some cases no inputs satisfy the required conditions and in other cases there are multiple solutions. It becomes apparent that the key question is whether or not the function has an unique inverse. If so, students are shown that the missing input is computed by running the inverse function with the original output (or output list) as its input. There is a particularly compelling demonstration of this, one that operates on functions composed of lengthy chains, but in a domain that is concrete and real to students. It involves the Logo turtle in a genuine problem solving task, the path reversal problem.

This task introduces the powerful algorithm for inverting functional chains in the problem context of bringing home a wandering Logo turtle. The task is introduced to students (possibly working in pairs) by a Logo program showing a simple schematic floor plan with two or more rooms and a turtle

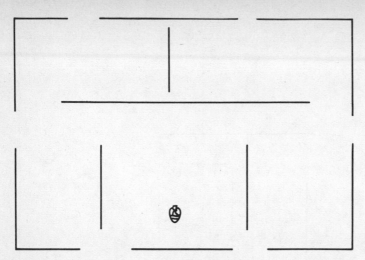

Figure 6 The Turtle in its Home Room

(see Fig. 6). The turtle starts off on a trip, moving from one room to another by a series of turtle commands. Sometime later when it is no longer visible from its starting point (home) the task is to bring it back home by invoking an appropriate series of commands. To make the situation more realistic and compelling, the 'lights' are turned off in all rooms except the starting one (see Fig. 7) in which we are waiting for the return of our missing traveller. Thus, we can no longer see the path taken by the turtle after it left home room. All we can see is that it went forward, turned on its lamp, turned right 90 degrees, went forward, hooted its horn, turned left 45 degrees and went forward and out of the room.

We do, however, have a complete list of the turtle 'moves'—the commands that took it from home to its current invisible place. How might this help us? If the students are stymied, they are asked how they might bring the turtle to where it was 'the time before last'. This hint is usually sufficient to inspire the 'aha'. They see that the solution is to undo the actions that the turtle took in proceeding on the way to its destination, and that this is accomplished by performing the *opposite* actions in the reverse of the original order. Otherwise (and, of course, after they are successful) the entire floor plan can be illuminated with the additional constraint imposed that the return path is to be identical to (i.e. to retrace) the starting path. In working out the path reversal procedure, students have to resolve certain issues, e.g. what might be an appropriate 'opposite' command for **horn**? (Logo has no unhorn command though **LampOn** has an opposite **LampOff**). Why should sound be treated differently than light. (Students might decide that **horn** is a perfectly reasonable opposite for itself).

After they construct the command sequence for returning the turtle along the specific path used to introduce the problem, students are given the more

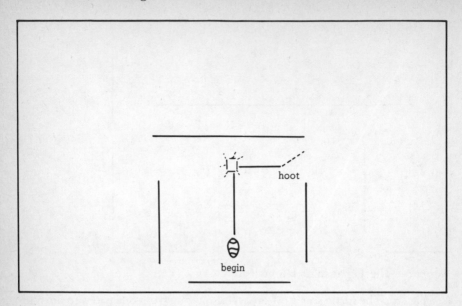

Figure 7   The Turtle Leaves Home

general task of writing a Logo program to reverse *any* path defined by a sequence of turtle commands. (Note: the general problem of developing a program to reverse turtle paths generated by arbitary Logo programs—including procedures—is very difficult indeed. It is not essential to our focus here, on developing the fundamental functional inversion algorithm).

Students might be given the top level program:

to ReversePath
Travel
Return
end

They will be given the skeletons for the **Travel** procedure and for the **Opposite** subprocedure used in **Return**. Once they have an articulate understanding of the algorithm, we will make the programming task interesting but accessible to them.

At this point we make an observation drawn directly from the path reversal algorithm, concerning the problem of solving linear equations in algebra. The process of solving an equation (one might call this undoing the equation) should be the inverse of the process used in generating (i.e., doing) the equation originally. Consider, for example, how we generate an equation such as $3*X + 8 = 35$.

We **start** with X.
Then we **multiply** that by 3.
Then we **add** 8 to that.
And we **end** with 35.

To undo this, we should do the opposite operations in the reverse order. Thus

We **unend** i.e. **start** with 35.
Then we **unadd** i.e. **subtract** 8 from that, to get 27.
Then we **unmultiply** i.e. **divide** that by 3, to get 9.
And we **unstart** i.e. **end** with X. So X = 9.

So the same algorithm is effective here. Students can now write procedures for solving simple linear equations without resort to the 'trick' used in the work on generating algebra quiz problems.

Algebra story problems

The solution of word or story problems is one of the most difficult subjects in school algebra. Solving age, distance, work and mixture problems and the other standard story fixtures in this domain appears to many students to be an unapproachable art form, not a learnable skill. English is soft and fuzzy; math is hard and precise. The idea of transforming an English story into mathematical equations seems implausible. In classroom teaching, the students are given the impression that there is a general solution procedure for story problems and that, if they applied it, they would be able to solve all such problems. Somehow, though, like the standard prescription for doing science by 'the scientific method', the way to do story problems is never clearly articulated in a way that students can comprehend.

We start with the observation that, as with purely formal mathematical structures and processes, it is valuable to construct the objects one is interested in analyzing. This is a recurring theme throughout the course. Our attack thus begins by reversing the traditional approach. Instead of asking students to turn stories into equations, we start by having them create their own stories from equations. Consider for example the simple age problem: 'Sam is 3 years older than Tom. The sum of their ages is 29. How old are they?' Many beginning students never learn to translate this problem into formal language. Our experience is that students find it a great deal easier to generate the same story problem from the equations

$$S = 3 + T$$
$$S + T = 29$$

when they write Logo programs for automatically generating such stories.

Students will develop a variety of algebra story problem generators in Logo. These will be driven by equations of several different forms, including:

$$BOX + NUMBER1 = NUMBER2$$
$$NUM1*BOX + NUM2 = NUM3$$
$$1/NUM1 + NUM2 = 1/BOX$$

as well as linear systems with two independent variables and the students' own forms. These generators will be developed along the following lines. For the first form above, the procedure will be

> to MakeSimpleEquation
> output (sentence BOX PlusOrMinus Number Equals Number)
> end

where the constituents of **sentence** are selected randomly using **pick**. Similar procedures will generate equations of the other forms.

Students develop extended algebra quiz programs using their varied equation generators. Then they are given starting models of story problems associated with each of the equation forms. For example, standard work problems like 'Dick can plow a field in 3 hours. Harry can plow it in 2 hours. How long does it take when they work together?' can be described by the last of the equation forms shown above. The reasons for the correctness of the correspondences between the story forms and equation forms are discussed and motivated in each case, taking into account the appropriate domain-specific world knowledge.

Next, students will generate story problems of these kinds, using a given procedure, **MakeStory**, as a tool. **MakeStory** takes two lists as inputs, the first is an equation, the second a template. For example,

**MakeStory [Tom + 7 = 19] [Item 3 [years from now] Item 1 [will be]
[Item 5 [years old.] [How old is] Item 1 [?] [empty]]**

generates the story

7 years from now Tom will be 19 years old. How old is Tom?

The use of **MakeStory** is illustrated to generate diverse story problems from all forms of equations. Students then use **MakeStory** to build a variety of story problems corresponding to each of the wordified story forms. Using **MakeStory** as a subprocedure, they write the following procedures as building blocks for the story problems in each domain:

MakeAgeStory, MakeRateStory, MakeWorkStory, MakeMixtureStory

These do not need to be the same—within each category students may use different forms of their own design. Using these procedures, they develop story problem quizzes and superquizzes.

Another unit in the story problem module teaches use of the icon machine construction lab to build simple function machines as components of story problems. These machines can then be connected together to create complete runnable models which, if all goes well, will in the course of development, generate the solutions. For example, consider the following mixture problem:

The sixth grade class wants to give a party. They want to know how many

quarts of lemonade to make. They have paper cups which hold six ounces each. They have invited 48 people.

Using the icon machine lab, students develop a number of machines. One might be designed to convert ounces to quarts, an **OuncesToQuarts** machine. Others might convert servings to ounces, number of people to quarts, and so on. By constructing and connecting the machines, we feel that students will often get a clearer understanding of this kind of problem structure.[3]

The story problem module is currently being developed. In another unit, we anticipate the use of the marble bag microworld as a nice vehicle for representing and manipulating many kinds of story problems, along the lines described in Section 2.

5. THE ALGEBRA WORKBENCH

The work described in the previous sections, based on Logo programming tasks and (marble bag and icon Logo) microworld activities, provides a very substantial conceptual and strategic foundation for algebra. In a sense, all that remains is to provide supports for the weak manipulative skills of the burgeoning sixth grade algebraists. For, without adequate fluency in performing algebraic manipulations (which we would like to regard as the essentially mechanical component) students will only be able to handle the simpler problems and their growth in problem solving will be significantly limited by their incapacity to do the necessary arithmetic.

We want to keep the focus of this course on the conceptual and strategic aspects, if necessary at the expense of the manipulative. Of course we know that the distinction is not completely tenable operationally, that one needs knowledge and skill in manipulation as a part of understanding algebra concepts such as expression. Nevertheless, it is possible to a great extent, to emphasize either aspect. I'm sure that it would be possible, for example, to train some persons to be superb formal manipulation engines with only the slightest knowledge of the conceptual content of what they were doing. (I don't know why anyone would want to do this, but I sometimes think that some school math teachers effectively strive for that goal). We prefer the other road, that of training superb mathematical thinkers who may have to rely on machines to do their computation (given that they know how to use their machines responsibly). So, instead of dividing the course to allow for significant time in both dimensions, we like the idea of developing an algebra calculator for students, freeing up more time for real problem work.

We are designing an instructional system for formal symbolic manipulation at the level required for introductory algebra, a system that will serve the student as agent or slave, and also as a tutor in the powerful, though often narrow, fashion of an expert. It will be implemented on a Macintosh computer. It will be less powerful than advanced symbol manipulation systems such as Reduce and Macsyma, which require larger computational hardware, but it will only need to provide mathematical manipulative facilities appropriate to high school algebra. It will also incorporate instructional facilities and a simple student interface employing windows, menus, and a mouse device.

We know of two such relatively sophisticated systems currently under development. An intelligent tutoring system called Algebraland is being implemented by Caroline Foss at Xerox PARC.[4] Another algebra tutor program being built at the Rand Corporation, is based on integrating a tutor with Reduce and GED, a graphical editor for algebraic expressions.[5] Algebraland and the RAND algebra tutor are being implemented on personal Lisp machine systems. Our algebra workbench will have more restricted computational and display capabilities as dictated by the less powerful Macintosh hardware.

Our tentative student interface is similar to the one planned by McArthur, though it has fewer windows and a much simpler operations menu. Our graphical display is shown in Fig. 8. As of now, we anticipate using only two special pull-down menus, the ones labelled **YourWork** and **AskTutor**. The student workspace display window shows a problem described by McArthur. The top node of the problem tree shows the problem. The tree forks whenever the student returns to the associated node to take an alternate path, possibly following assistance from the expert. Below the bottom rightmost node, which shows the most recent result, is a blank rectangle that shows where the student's next step will be displayed.

Three other windows are not shown—the tutor response window, which is a small text window showing the tutor's most recent response, the tutor response history window (usually obscured by the student workspace display window) showing the set of tutor responses during the session, and the student operations window. The operations include addition, subtraction, multiplication and division of or by an indicated expression, to both sides of an equation; combining, cancelling, or distributing indicated terms in an expression; a 'do it' command to invoke execution; an 'undo' command to revoke the last command or operation; a command to go on to the next problem step; a command to go back to a previous indicated step; and a quit command.

The problem types include simplify expression, transform expression, compare expressions for equivalence, solve equation, and solve system.

The algebra workbench has two instructional modes. In **student mode**, the student can take complete initiative in solving a problem. He can choose a problem or be assigned one. He works through the problem step by step, calling on the **algebra expert** to perform the operations. He can work it through entirely on his own or invoke the **tutor** whenever he wants help. He can ask the tutor if any specified step is correct. He can ask the tutor to do a step for him and to explain its work. He can, of course, ask the tutor if his

File Edit Your Work Ask Tutor

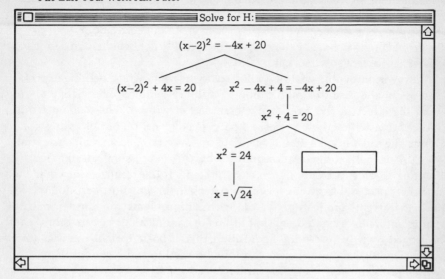

Figure 8 Algebra Workbench. Student Display Window

answer is correct. He can ask for another problem. And, finally, he can call on the tutor to do a problem—this invokes the **tutor mode**, also called demonstration mode.

In tutor mode, the tutor works through a problem, step by step, explaining its actions, both strategically in terms of its current subgoals and locally in describing the current step. The student can ask the tutor to do a problem, either one chosen from a list of problems, or one that he constructs corresponding to a specified problem form. As the tutor carries out a demonstration, it explains the actions that it takes at each step in the context of strategic goals such as: expand composite expressions containing a variable into terms; group together like terms; order the terms by increasing powers of the variable; collect like terms into a single expression; isolate the variable. These are essentially the strategies suggested by Bundy and Welham.[6]

The tutor invokes standard solution algorithms, the same ones that the student is taught. It does not employ the rich variety of simplifying patterns and short cuts that competent human problem solvers bring to bear. But it is capable of accepting non-standard simplifications of these kinds. The student can intervene at any step to ask whether a specified alternate step would be acceptable. If the student's suggested step is both valid (i.e. algebraically equivalent) and productive (i.e. not demonstrably more complicated than the tutor's), the tutor accepts it and proceeds with its demonstration from that new step. Otherwise it rejects it as invalid or unproductive and explains why.

The algebra expert performs the manipulations requested by the student in student mode as well as those invoked by the tutor in demonstration mode. By enabling students to concentrate on *what* operations are to be performed in carrying out a plan and relieving them from concern about *how* to do them, we intend primarily that the algebra workbench will help in acquiring strategic problem solving skill.

However, knowing what operation to do means having a definite expectation about the result of performing it, and this requires knowledge about what the effect of the requested manipulation will be. The student is not allowed to ask directly for a desired outcome like 'get rid of this expression'. Rather, he must invoke an intermediate operation to accomplish each goal, like 'divide both sides of the equation by this expression' (designated by pointing to an expression in the current step). If the result is not what the student expected, he can ask the tutor to explain the way the operation works and its current application. Work with subproblems that are primarily manipulative (like expanding, simplifying or canonicalizing expressions) can be staged to help foster the acquisition of the basic formal manipulative skills. The algebra workbench can thus be used to teach the mechanics of formal problem work as well as strategic concepts.

The preceding work with the Logo programming modules introduced algebraic structures and showed the connection between functions and equations ('Functions, Codes, Black Boxes and Equations'). Work with the marble bags microworld motivated algebraic notation and directly prepared the way for the introduction of the algebra workbench. The workbench will be used as an integral part of the subsequent course modules to support and supplement extended work on equation solving and algebra story problems.

6. EXPERT TUTORS, MICROWORLDS, AND LOGO PROGRAMMING

The algebra workbench is an example of a kind of instructional facility that might reasonably be called an *expert tutoring system.* It incorporates a domain expert: a program capable of solving algebra problems expressed in standard formal algebraic notation. It also incorporates a tutor, a program that uses the algebra expert and is capable of:

— solving problems in a step by step fashion using the same methods that beginning students are expected to learn.
— explaining its actions and strategies in an understandable fashion as it proceeds.
— monitoring, advising, assisting, and critiquing the work of students as they attempt to solve algebra problems on the system.

The marble bag microworld is a *mathematical microworld.* Only recently have workers begun to give definite meaning to the concept of computer microworld. The key notion is that of a clearly delimited task domain or problem space whose elements are objects and operations on objects that create new objects and operations. Microworlds are designed to give experiences with 'powerful ideas' through exploring 'phenomena that are inherently interesting to observe and interact with'.[7] A precise definition of computer microworlds based on Piaget's notion of structure, in terms of states and state transformations, has been proposed.[8] A mathematical microworld is a computer microworld whose elements are mathematical objects and operations. It is a restricted form of mathematical programming language in that 'the result of programming is not a 'program', it is a new mathematical object'.[9]

Computer microworlds and CAI systems, including 'intelligent' tutoring systems, are designed from distinctly different educational viewpoints. The microworld focus is on exploration and investigation rather than knowledge acquisition, on constructing rather than receiving knowledge, on learning rather than teaching. This does not imply a simplistic view of the self-sufficiency of learning or teaching on either side, it is more a matter of emphasis on what is perceived to be crucial.

One can easily parody either viewpoint taken as a complete paradigm. The teaching (tutoring) extremist regards the student, the object and intended beneficiary of instruction, as an empty vessel into which knowledge is to be poured. The learning extremist has a more romantic view, that given a rich environment for exploration, the student will discover and recreate knowledge. One sees teaching as the way to learning. The other views the only really worthwhile learning as learning without teaching. These one-sided views are narrowly partial and faulty. The process of learning substantial and complex areas of knowledge such as the mathematics of algebra, benefits richly from the interplay of different and varied instructional experiences. Expert tutors and computer microworlds, intelligently realized, can each make unique and valuable contributions to mathematics education, but neither can carry the entire instructional task by itself.

Instructional computer scientists are, however, attempting to make current systems more powerful and comprehensive. Work toward the development of *intelligent tutoring systems* is well known. Such systems are intended to greatly extend the instructional capabilities of expert tutors like the algebra workbench by improving user interaction, working within the user's conceptualization of the domain, incorporating capabilities for diagnosis of bugs and underlying difficulties, and basing tutoring strategies on improved theories of learning.[10]

Work on the development of *intelligent microworlds*, as envisaged by Thompson is less familiar. The notion is to incorporate within the microworld, knowledge both of the domain and of the student user. Domain knowledge would include descriptions of the properties of the microworld objects and operations and theorems about the subject matter. Knowledge of the student would include descriptions of misconceptions, conceptual gaps and learning difficulties. The system, as envisaged by Thompson, could provide students with (multi-level) explanations of the actions it takes in response to student commands. It would allow the student to predict the outcome of a command and have the expert comment on the prediction. It would also include commands to facilitate and guide exploration, hypothesis formulation and generalization.

These developments (of intelligent tutors and intelligent microworlds) might converge so that the two kinds of instructional systems become a great deal closer in what they can do as their capabilities grow. Nevertheless they will retain significant vestiges of their different origins—one from a teaching, and the other from a learning paradigm. The intelligent microworld will still be focused on exploration, though the emphasis will be on guided exploration so as to help ensure that learning really occurs, and the intelligent tutor will still be focused on teaching, though with much greater freedom for the learner so as to help ensure that learning really occurs. It should be noted that the systems envisaged thus far will not be intelligent in one essential respect: they themselves do not learn.

Little has been said lately of *Logo programming*, the center piece and primary instructional actor in our course. Unlike the visions of how learning will be enhanced by computer-based instructors, whether tutors or microworlds, we have a very different view of the role of Logo. We see students' work with Logo as providing a *conceptual framework* for the teaching and learning of mathematics. Logo provides a principled foundation for mathematics—the concepts underlying programming (as articulated in Logo) are essentially isomorphic to the concepts underlying mathematics. Logo is the great tool—students can use it to build a rich variety of mathematical worlds. We envisage an approach to mathematics in which the entire curriculum is developed in terms of programming concepts and activities, with occasional assists from microworlds and tutors and, even, a human teacher. The introductory algebra course is an example.

REFERENCES

1. Feurzeig, W. (1969), 'Programming languages as a conceptual framework for teaching mathematics'. Bolt Beranek & Newman Report No. 1889.
2. Wirtz, R. W., Botel, M., Sawyer, W. W. and Beberman, M. (1967), *Math Workshop*, London, Encyclopedia Britannica Press.
3. Goldenberg, E. P. (1985) 'Learning to think algebraically: a Logo contribution to solving word problems,' Unpublished paper.
4. Brown, J. S. (1984) 'Process versus product—a perspective on tools for communal and informal electronic learning,' in *Education and the Electronic Age*, proceedings of a conference sponsored by the Educational Broadcasting Company.
5. McArthur, D. (1985) Developing Computer Tools to Support Performing and

Learning Complex Cognitive Skills, to appear in D. Berger *et al.* (Ed.), *Applications of Cognitive Psychology*, Hillsdale, NJ, Lawrence Erlbaum Associates.

6. Bundy, A. and Welham, B. (1981) 'Using meta-level inference for selective application of multiple rewrite rules', *Artificial Intelligence*, 16(2), 189–211.

7. Lawler, B. (1984) 'Designing computer-based microworlds,' in M. Yazdani (Ed.), *New Horizons in Educational Computing*. Chichester, U.K., Ellis Horwood Limited.

8. Groen, G. J. (1985) 'The epistemics of computer based microworlds,' *Proceedings of 2nd International Conference on Artificial Intelligence and Education*, University of Exeter, U.K.

9. Thompson, P. W. (1985) 'Mathematical microworlds and ICAI,' in *Proceedings, Conference on Moving Intelligent CAI Into the Real World*, Burroughs Canada Technical Report PPD Mt1—85—3.

10. Sleeman, D. H. and Brown, J. S. (1982) *Intelligent Tutoring Systems*, New York, Academic Press.

8.3 Computers and music education

- S. Holland

INTRODUCTION

This chapter forms part of a project on the application of Artificial Intelligence theories and techniques to support the learning of composition skills. It deals with two present day applications of computers to the teaching of music; Music Logo and a graphics music game. It also considers speculations about how Artificial Intelligence might be used to foster music composition in the future.

MUSIC LOGO

Strong claims are made for Logo by its proponents. Speaking in the context of the way in which the notions underlying differential calculus crop up naturally in Logo when trying to 'teach' a turtle to move in a circle or spiral, Papert says that 'I have seen elementary school children who understand clearly why differential equations are the natural form of laws of motion.[1] To attribute the development of such understanding to Logo would be a very strong claim, (and one that Papert only makes implicitly) since this is an understanding that escapes some graduate mathematicians, physicists and engineers. The validity of the claims made for Logo are hotly contested. Papert says that the sort of growth he is interested in fostering can take decades to bear fruit, and would not necessarily show up on 'pre-and post' tests.

In one sense, any attempt to do for part of music what turtle geometry does for part of mathematics could be considered as a Music Logo, but Music Logo is usually identified with the work of Jeanne Bamberger and her colleagues, working in association with Seymour Papert, Terry Winograd, Hal Abelson and others at MIT.

According to Bamberger, one aim of Music Logo is to describe music in a way that allows redefining of its elements by the user, and leads to extendable concepts. The representation should have very wide scope, yet be uniform and simple. It should allow any student to create his own tools to explore and create music that makes musical sense to him, whatever that sense may be. Music Logo should not only develop the skills that underly intelligent listening, performance, analysis and composition, but should also encourage non-musical learning and understanding. If Turtle Logo was ambitious, then Music Logo is even more ambitious. Logo could at least draw on a concept developed over twenty centuries that most mathematicians would agree underlies much of mathematics (the function) with a well-developed notation (functional notation) and an existing computational embodiment (Lisp). Where do we find as well-developed equivalents for music? The unlikelihood, some would say absurdity, of any such formalism existing for music does not make Music Logo impossible, but it does suggest that its stated aims will be hard to satisfy—especially the requirements for uniformity and wide scope.

We now describe two experiments by Jeanne Bamberger that make a start of creating a Music Logo.[2, 3]

The first experiment is called Tune Blocks. This starts with a four voice synthesizer connected to a computer. A simple tune (say a nursery rhyme) has already been broken into motives or perhaps phrases, depending on the precise variant of the game being played. The phrases are labelled, say, B1 to B5, and if you type in B1, then the synthesizer plays the corresponding phrase. In one game, you are simply given a set of phrases, and invited to arrange them, using sequence and repetition, in an order that 'makes sense' to you. The game sounds trivial, but strong claims are made for it. First of all, anyone can try it—there are virtually no prerequisites. Secondly, it involves active manipulation of and listening to musically meaningful elements (i.e. phrases or motives as opposed to isolated notes or arbitrary fragments). Thirdly, it promotes 'context-dependant' as opposed to isolated listening (e.g. block 1 followed by block 2 may give both blocks a new slant). Listening to what people say as they play the game, Bamberger reports that whereas a phrase is initially perceived in only one way e.g. 'went down' or 'went faster', as the game procedes, it comes to be perceived in a variety of ways, for example 'same downward movement as block 1, but doesn't sound like an ending'. Players produce a wide variety of resulting pieces, and comparing other people's pieces, especially if they come from different musical cultures, is one of the pleasures of the game. Bamberger sees the use of neutral tags like B1, B2 as opposed to more visual representations as a positive advantage to tune blocks, as it means that visual sense cannot be used as a substitute for listening. There is variation of the game in which the player is given a complete piece, programmed in advance, which he can hear at will, and the challenge this time is to recreate the original tune from its constituent phrases. Bamberger points out that in this version, the student is likely to discover the melody's overall structure (e.g. A B A) as an effortless by-product of play. Players begin to ask themselves leading questions like 'Why does B1, B3, B2' seem incomplete, although it sounds as though it has ended?'.

The second group of experiments concerns rhythm. It starts from the fact that most people can clap along with the rhythm of a melody or its underlying regular beat (some can tap both at once using hands and feet). The Time Machine attempts to represent the interaction of these two streams of motion in a way at once intuitive and concretely representable. The gadgetry is very simple. The player strikes a drum, which leaves a trace on a VDU screen. Figures 1, 2 and 3 should make clear the relation between what is struck on the drum and what appears on the screen. Pieces can be recorded and played back later with synchronised sound and display. One crucial feature is that the time machine can play a regular beat against which you can input your piece; both the rhythm and the beat will appear on the screen (see Fig. 4) as you play. Once recorded, the beat trace can be concealed while you listen to both streams of sound at once. Bamberger claims that one activity in particular—trying to picture how they mesh, and then revealing the beat trace to check your guess—can transform how people perceive pieces. Players often originally perceive 'Mary had a little lamb' (American version), both aurally and visually as consisting of three 'chunks'—as in Fig. 3. Bamburger shows that the single suggestion of *linking visually all the marks that occur during the lifetime of each beat* (Fig. 4A) can lead to the recreation of conventional rhythm notation, and can lead to the perception (though some people already perceive this anyway) that the first chunk contains a sub-chunk identical to the second and third chunks.

Given sufficiently extendable representations, musically sensible transformations could be carried out in a Music Logo at various levels of musical structure, and it could be argued that this is an important part of what composers do. Bamberger quotes from Schoenberg:[4]

Even the writing of simple phrases involves the invention and use of motives, though perhaps unconsciously . . . The motive generally appears in a characteristic and impressive manner at the beginning of a piece . . . Inasmuch as almost every figure within a piece reveals some relationship to it, the basic motive is often considered the 'germ' of the idea . . . However, everything depends upon its use . . . everything depends upon its treatment and development. Accordingly variation requires changing some of the less important ones (features). Preservation of rhythmic features effectively produces coherence. For the rest, determining which features are important depends on the compositional objective.

Bamberger mentions briefly experiments with slightly more extendable representations; in particular a language for representing and changing separately the pitch and durational aspects of a melody. But for more complex

Time Machine Traces

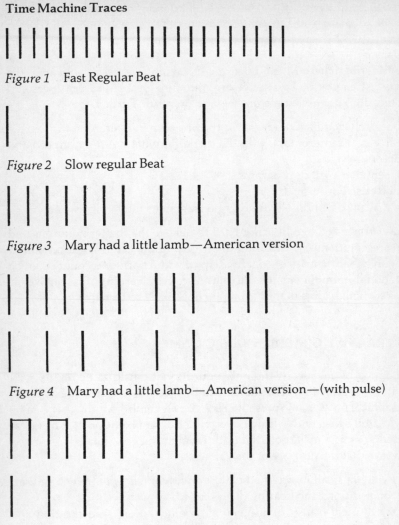

Figure 1   Fast Regular Beat

Figure 2   Slow regular Beat

Figure 3   Mary had a little lamb—American version

Figure 4   Mary had a little lamb—American version—(with pulse)

Figure 4a   Mary had a little lamb—American version—(with pulse & linked track)

Source: Redrawn from Bamberger, 1974

musical structures, Music Logo needs more extendable representations than those suggested so far, if it is to easily permit musical manipulation. However, the implied claims made for the effects on users' perceptions of using even relatively crude tools like Tool Blocks and the Time Machine are strong.

Bamburger reports how, for a set of students who had played the two games for several weeks, the experience of listening to Haydn's symphony no. 99 was transformed by a perception of the piece's evolution from a 5-note motive. The new perception, for some, dramatically extended their musical taste.

In considering where Music Logo might take us we need to identify the underlying strengths of Logo as a programming system: Green (personal communication) itemises some of the good points of Turtle Logo:

1. a moderately compact notation for the objects and operators
2. a clear visual representation (in the turtle) of what the program did and the order of events
3. incremental growth of programs
4. parameterised program fragments
5. an easy way to compose two program fragments into a bigger one.

In the case of Music Logo, it is not hard to believe that better notations and visual representations can be found than conventional staff notation, and it is imaginable that theories of tonality, rhythm and harmony could be given computational embodiment and recast as discovery learning areas but Music Logo has such high aims that fulfilling them is likely to be hard.

AN INTERACTIVE GRAPHICS MUSIC GAME

Music Logo is by no means the only educational music game or the only music discovery learning environment. In this section, we describe an interactive graphical music game presented by Martin Lamb.[5] Although the game has many similarities with Music Logo (which Lamb mentions), it has relatively modest aims and is rooted in traditional music notation.

Lamb says that the purpose of the game is:

1. to provide musically untrained children with a means of inventing their own compositions and hearing them immediately and
2. to teach musical transformations (e.g. augmentation, transposition and inversion) by letting children manipulate their visual analogues and immediately hear their effect.

The game is best described using pictures. The student begins with a set of blank staves (Fig. 5). The player points to the word 'Draw' on the display, using a pointing device, and then, holding down a button on the pointing device, can sketch a freehand curve on the staves (Fig. 6). The program immediately plays a line of music with the same shape (pitch for height) as the drawn curve, but smoothing overhanging areas. (Fig. 7). The curve then breaks up into discrete triangle shapes, each representing a note (Fig. 8) (Our diagram does not show—as Lamb's program does—that a note can lie on a line or a space, or midway between the conventional positions, to indicate black notes. Also the length of each triangle should be proportional to the length of the note.) Pointing to 'transform', a group of notes can be selected by circling them (Fig. 9), and an inner circle can be drawn to exclude notes. A copy of the selected notes can then be moved about the screen (Fig. 10). Using one of two physical sliders, the selected fragment can be continuously stretched or squashed relative to a horizontal axis (time relations are preserved). The image can be squashed beyond a completely flat position continuously through to its mirror image. When the image reaches exact inversion, it indicates this by glowing more brightly. Similarly, using the other slider, a fragment can be squashed vertically into a chord, beyond simultaneity if desired to its exact retrograde and further (interval relations are preserved). The reaching of the exact retrograde point is indicated when the mirror-image fragment glows more brightly. At any point, the transformation can be played at the pitch at which it is floating, or moved down to a different pitch level. It is possible to move or delete notes, as well as copy them, and there is an undo command.

More than one voice can be entered onto the screen by sketching more than one curve, and music can also be entered using a keyboard. The display

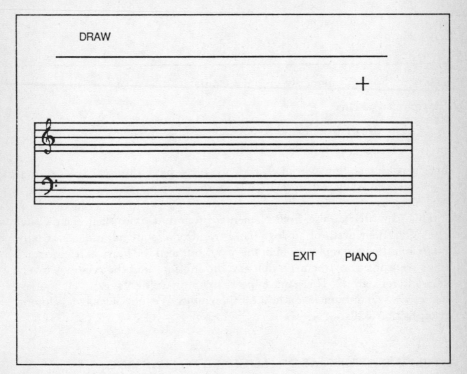

Figure 5   Lamb's Interactive graphics Game

Initial set up

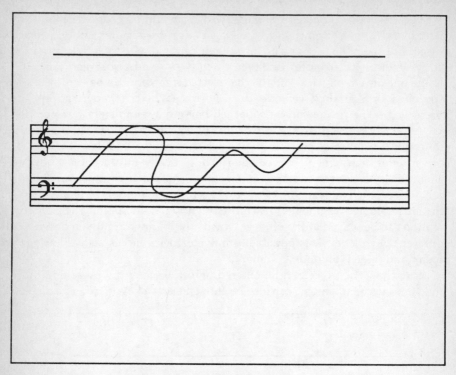

Figure 6   Lamb's Interactive graphics Game

Player draws a curve

Source: (Redrawn from Lamb, 1982)

uses a colour coding system. Different voices have different colours, but material derived by transformation from the same material is displayed in a single colour.

This game harmonises four elements; pitch and time, their clear visual analogue, their gestural analogue and traditional staff notation. Not only pitch and time are represented in this way, but also the musical transformations transposition, augmentation and diminution, and the relations inversion and retrograde. This game appears to amply fulfill its relatively modest objectives. What is unclear is how far these objectives go towards developing composition skills.

APPLYING ARTIFICIAL INTELLIGENCE TO LEARNING COMPOSITION SKILLS?

Very few people compose music. Until the last decade or so, the rarity of the

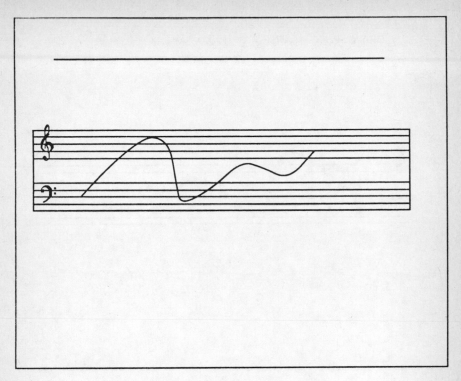

Figure 7   Lamb's Interactive graphics Game

Computer smooths curve

Source: (Redrawn from Lamb, 1982)

prerequisites—ability to play instruments, access to musicians to perform works, the ability to read and write music—put all but the most rudimentary music composition skills out of the reach of most people. The advent of cheap electronic and computer musical instruments, tape recorders and music editing software has removed many of these barriers. Ideas can be recorded on tape without knowledge of notation; access to a wide palette of sonorities is much more widely available using comparatively inexpensive FM synthesis and sound sampling techniques. Intricate, many-voiced ideas can be tried out and performed not only by those lacking conventional instrumental skills but even by the severely disabled using sequencers, music editors and computer musical instruments. This technology is likely to get cheaper and more widely available. There is not only a technology-driven revolution, but a revolution in ideas about teaching music (at least in Great Britain). Where the majority were previously expected only to sing and 'appreciate' music, composition of simple original music is now considered to be an objective for all school children from age five to sixteen.[6] It appears

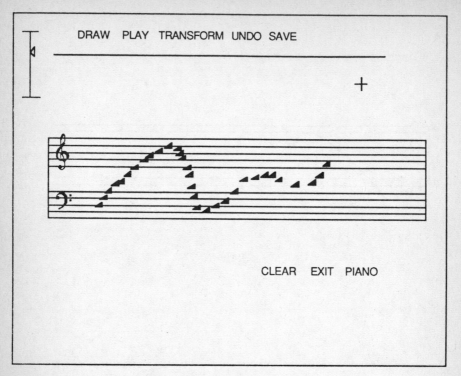

Figure 8   Lamb's Interactive graphics Game

Computer changes curve into discrete notes

Source: (Redrawn from Lamb, 1982)

that a golden age of access for all to the materials for composition is dawning. But there is more to music composition than simple access to materials. Consider the analogy of creative writing. Literacy and writing implements are now commonplace, but creative writing, or even good writing remains relatively rare. There is a big gap between making sounds and composing music. Knowledgable guides are rare. Some good sources of guidance are the mutual help of peers, masterworks (and favourite works) and understanding and perceptive teachers. But in the words of Paynter,[7]

> Unfortunately, relatively few music school teachers have had any serious compositional training. Most music courses in conservatoires and Colleges of Higher Education tend to emphasise instrumental performance, and the majority of University Music courses are still heavily biased towards musicology . . . Opportunities to invent and develop musical ideas are rarely given, except within very narrow stylistic limits.

Some people learn to compose well with little help from teachers, but one

Figure 9   Lamb's Interactive graphics Game

User has selected transform. Circled notes are to be transformed
Notes in inner circle are to be excluded

Source: (Redrawn from Lamb, 1982)

suspects that despite the technological and educational changes, personal
experience of music composition is likely to remain for many people at a
limited level. Let it be stressed that there is no suggestion here that Artificial
Intelligence should or could make good the shortage of human guides. The
speculations that follow envisage *much* more modest roles for Artificial
Intelligence as enabler, tool and occasional catalyst. So far the term 'Artificial Intelligence (AI)' has not been defined. AI can be seen as two inter-
weaving strands: one is the "study of ideas that enable computers to be
intelligent",[8] the other is an attempt to understand the principles that make
any intelligence, human or machine, possible. But music engages the
emotions more obviously than the intellect. Hofstadter writes:

Question: Will a computer ever write beautiful music?
Speculation: Yes but not soon. Music is a language of the emotions, and until
programs have emotions as complex as ours, there is no way a program will
write anything beautiful. There can be 'forgeries'—shallow imitations of the

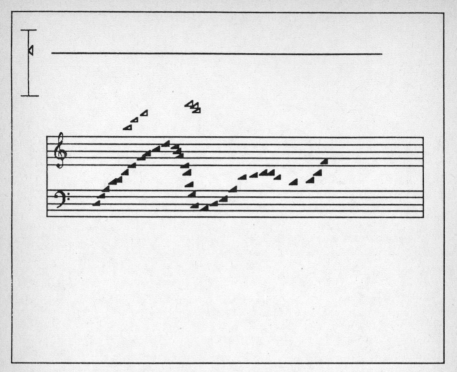

Figure 10   Lamb's Interactive graphics Game

Notes to be transformed are displayed as hollow triangles

Source: (Redrawn from Lamb, 1982)

> syntax of earlier music—but . . . there is much more to musical expression than
> . . . syntactical rules. To think . . . (that a music box might) . . . bring forth
> from its sterile circuitry pieces which Chopin or Bach might have written had
> they lived longer is a grotesque and shameful misrepresentation of the depth of
> the human spirit.[9]

Would the truth of this speculation (with which this author is sympathetic) mean that AI is an unsuitable tool for our purposes? No—no more than it makes unsuitable pen and paper and piano strings. However it is a useful reminder of how far Artificial Intelligence may have to go to get any real understanding of music. Marvin Minsky speculates that understanding how the human mind works may prove easier than—and a necessary prerequisite to—understanding how music works. But, as Minsky points out, science proceeds from surface descriptions to deeper explanations. In the sections that follow, we will try to see how Artificial Intelligence at its present stage of development offers some tools that might for some purposes be more useful than pen, paper and piano strings. First we look at the possibilities of intelligent tutors for traditional music education.

The first requirement for an intelligent tutoring system (ITS) for any task is that it has to have some ability to perform or at very least discuss articulately the task in hand. *This demands explicit knowledge of the task.* To summarize their two other usual features in a nutshell, intelligent tutoring systems are firstly also expected build up knowledge of what a particular student knows so that opportunities can be seized to get points across in the most appropriate way or to diagnose misconceptions, and secondly they are expected to have explicit knowledge of ways of teaching. The very first requirement, for explicit knowledge of the task, raises the question, 'For what areas of music composition do we have explicit knowledge?'. This appears to narrow the possibilities *for this style of AI contribution* down to few areas, some of which are listed below such as:

1. Music Theory
2. Aural training
3. Harmonisation
4. Some highly formalized and rather artificial styles of composition.

It seems entirely reasonable to suggest that intelligent tutoring systems might be built for factual aspects of music theory. These would probably not differ all that much from intelligent tutoring systems for, say, geography.[10] A more specifically musical application might be an intelligent tutor for aural training, although it is not immediately apparent how the skills of, say, recognising a major seventh could be broken down into subskills. Although a remote possibility, it would be worth finding out whether work by cognitive psychologists or others on the perception of music might suggest subskills or mechanisms involved in musical listening that could be exploited in an intelligent aural training tutor. Equally, taxonomies of students' errors in ear training, if they exist, might be exploited for diagnosis by an intelligent tutor, but let us leave the rudimentary skills and see what opportunities may be available at higher levels of skill involved in music composition.

One of the very few areas of composition for which explicit rules of thumb can be found in textbooks is harmonization. In principle, there seems no reason why an intelligent tutor for harmonization should not be built, but a number of cautions should be borne in mind. The essential problem is that the tutor will know nothing about music other than whatever formalisms or rules of thumb we can explicitly give it. If, for example, the tutor spots the student using consecutive fifths, what should the tutor do? Parallel fifths should generally be avoided, but they have been used to good musical effect, at any rate by great composers. A good tutor should not criticise unless he (she or it) can suggest a better way of doing things[11]. Unfortunately, we have no way of making a machine distinguish good music from bad.

If we are determined to keep within the intelligent tutoring system paradigm, which tends to imply that the tutor, if not ncessarily in control, may at any rate tend to offer the result of its deliberations from time to time, then either we need to pick our area or case studies very carefully, or we need to make sure the tutor's limitations are understood and accepted. However, if we turn to other paradigms of support for learning, we will see that AI-accessible areas of music composition are potentially much wider.

One area where Artificial Intelligence may be able to make an indirect contribution to the learning of composition skills is by allowing music editors to be more intelligent and responsive. Buxton *et al.*[12] give the example of a conductor requesting 'play a little more staccato in the lower brass'. The request is easily put into words, but to put in the corresponding markings using most present day score editors and hear the result could take many distinct operations. The problem is that most music editors are note-based. They may allow operators (e.g. transpose, delete) to be applied to combinations of, for example, all notes within a given block of time, all notes in a particular voice, or all notes lying in a certain pitch range, but they do not allow operators to be applied, except laboriously, to musical objects such as phrases, ostinati and themes. How can an editing program 'know' what musical structures underly a score? Buxton *et al.* describe one partial solution using a hierarchical tree structure. Other approaches may be worth exploring, but the only one we will mention here is the object-oriented approach. In an object-oriented music editor, completely arbitrary collections of musical events could be designated to be a single object, and operated on as such. Objects could be dismantled, regrouped, and re-operated on at will.

Turning to longer term prospects, Marvin Minsky[13] is reported as asserting that 'a good way to train composers would be to give them the rules of a highly constrained system (such as a Beethoven piano sonata) and let them alter the constraints that produce it.' This remains a speculation, of course, because no one yet knows how to specify a Beethoven sonata as a constraint system. In the area of jazz improvisation, however, Levitt[14] has written a program that 'negotiates mutual harmonic, melodic and thematic constraints to produce a solo from a chord progression and melody' using AI techniques. Christopher Fry's 'Flavours Band'[15] allows the representation of a musical style independently, to some extent, of any particular piece of music. This allows experiments such as playing the melody and chords of 'Norwegian Wood' in the 'style' of John Coltrane. Given the lack of tools presently capable of implementing Minsky's suggestion vis-a-vis Beethoven sonatas, what tools we do have might be employed honourably as games, as sketched below.

Seeing that we know so little about music composition, and that knowledge is so fragmented, games are one way of allowing us to build and pass on memorable experiences out of those few insights that we do possess. The problem is not to find material for games; the psychology of music, branches of music theory and almost any piece of AI that captures some musical knowledge all offer possibilities. The problem is to find or make explicit a principled framework to order the possibilities.

The scholarly literature on games as education has not yet been examined as part of this survey. However, one example of the power of games can be cited, if an example is needed. Illich[16] writes of

> . . . educational games which can provide a unique way to penetrate formal systems. Set theory, linguistics, propositional logic, geometry, physics and even chemistry reveal themselves with little effort to certain persons who play these games. A friend of mine went to a Mexican market with a game called 'Wff 'n Proof' which consists of some dice on which twelve logical symbols are imprinted. He showed children which two or three combinations constituted a well formed sentence, and inductively, within the first hour some onlookers also grasped the principle. Within a few hours of playfully conducting formal logical proofs, some children are capable of introducing to others the fundamental proofs of propositional logic. The others just walk away . . . In fact for some children, such games are a special form of liberating education, since they heighten their awareness of the fact that formal systems are built on changeable axioms and that conceptual operations have a gamelike nature.

Games that encourage or assist music composition are not new[17]. Random methods have been used by working composers, perhaps most famously Mozart and Cage. If we imagine a continuum extending from random methods at one extreme, through to (human) creative musical intelligence at the other, AI methods can be viewed at present as encapsulating generative intelligence slightly intelligence-wards of the completely random.

Just as improvisers will sometimes ask for a motif from the audience, then develop the fragment into a complete piece, a game could begin with the player singing, playing or selecting a fragment. However, given the 'intelligent human, dumb machine' situation, instead of the machine going away and coming back with a complete piece, the process would involve much more give and take. The machine might begin with more knowledge about elements, form, grammar, and constraints, but the player would have a virtual monopoly on aesthetic judgements. The player could direct the game when confident, or ask for suggestions when stuck. Other possible starting points include setting a piece of text, film, script or picture to music, or trying to capture the elements of a style as previously discussed.

The games being considered here have a precedent in creative writing aids. Sharples[18] had children use games employing context-free grammars and associative networks as modest tools for creative writing. 'By specifying first an appropriate vocabulary, then syntactic structure and the agreement of meaning the child can use the computer to generate interesting and increasingly refined sentences, poems and stories'. Sharples work was based on a cognitive theory of the writing process.[19]

Minsky notes how areas previously considered personal and inaccessible were systematically explored for the first time earlier this century: Freud and dreams; Piaget and children's play. Since it has not yet happened, it is hard to predict when and to what extent comparable breakthroughs might be made in our understanding of music, and whether Artificial Intelligence will play a part. However, Artificial Intelligence already provides the most explicit tools and ideas currently available for modelling and describing mental processes, although the scope and depth of these tools is as yet undeveloped.

Given due caution, it appears possible that modest contributions are likely to be forthcoming from Artificial Intelligence to support the learning of music composition.

REFERENCES

1. Papert, S. 1980 Mindstorms. The Harvester Press, Brighton.
2. Bamberger, Jeanne, (1972) Developing a Musical Ear: A New Experiment. LOGO Memo 6, A.I. Laboratory. Massachusetts Institute of Technology.
3. Bamberger, Jeanne, (1974) Progress Report: Logo Music Project. A.I. Laboratory, Massachusetts Institute of Technology.
4. Schoenberg, A. 1967, Fundamentals of Music Composition. Faber & Faber, London.
5. Lamb, Martin, 1982. An interactive Graphical Modeling Game for teaching Musical Concepts. In Journal of Computer-Based Instruction Autum 1982.
6. HM Inspectorate, 1985. Music from 5–16 (Curriculum Matters 4). HMSO, London.
7. Paynter, J. 1982. Music in the secondary School curriculum. Cambridge University Press, London.
8. Winston, P., 1984. Artificial Intelligence. Addison-Wesley, London.
9. Hofstadter, Douglas R., 1979. Godel, Escher, Bach: an eternal golden braid. Penguin Books, London.
10. Barr, A. and Feigenbaum, E., Eds., 1982. The Handbook of Artificial Intelligence, Vol. II. Pitman, London.
11. Burton R. R. and Brown J. S., 1982. An Investigation of Computer coaching for informal learning activities. In Intelligent Tutoring Systems, Sleeman D. and Brown J. S., Eds. Academic Press 1982.
12. Buxton, W. et al., 1981. Scope in Interactive Score Editors. Computer Music Journal, Vol. 5 No. 3 p. 50–56.
13. Minsky, Marvin., 1981. Music, Mind and Meaning. In Computer Music Journal Vol. 5 No. 3 p. 28–44.
14. Levitt, David, 1984. Constraint Languages. In Computer Music Journal Vol. 8, No. 1.
15. Fry, Chris, 1984. Flavours Band: A language for specifying musical style. Computer Music Journal, Vol. 8 No. 4.
16. Illich, Ivan. 1976. Deschooling society. Pelican, London.
17. Eno, Brian, 1978. Oblique Strategies. Opal, London.
18. Sharples, Mike, 1983. The use of Computers to Aid the Teaching of Creative Writing. In AEDS Journal, Vol. 16, No. 2, pp. 79–91. (Reprinted in this collection).
19. Bereiter, C., Scardamalia, M. (1982) 'From conversation to composition: the role of instruction in a developmental process'. In 'Advances in Instructional Psychology' Volume 2, R. Glaser (Ed.). Lawrence Erlbaum Associates, Hillsdale, N.J.

8.4 *On-line services for schools: an appraisal*

- Tony Kaye

INTRODUCTION

Not so many years ago, it was claimed by some educational experts (few of whom had much experience of classroom teaching!) that educational television would 'revolutionize' teaching and learning in schools. It would provide a window on the world, broaden both pupils' and teacher' horizons, and even lead to fundamental changes in the teacher's role, shifting the emphasis from that of dispenser of information to that of *animateur*, discussion leader, and problem-solver. It would be a shame if similarly sweeping claims were to be made for the newer information technologies, yet there is a strong element of hyperbole in much of what is currently said about the potential for education of computer-mediated communications. *Networking* and *interactivity* are concepts which are being actively promoted, often in the absence of any serious analysis of real needs and potential outcomes.

After a brief description of the relevant technology, this paper will examine the ways in which computer communications have been applied in practice in school education, drawing on examples from projects in a range of different countries. Finally, a number of questions will be raised about the future potential of these technologies, and the ways in which they can best be appropriated by teachers and pupils for their own needs.

COMPUTER-MEDIATED COMMUNICATION

Computer-mediated communication methods can permit users to contact other users and databases easily, regardless of space or time constraints. They do this through networks which connect users' terminals or micro-computers to a host computer (a mainframe, a mini-computer, or even a micro-computer) on which information is stored. Networks can range from the very local, such as within one building, to the international, joining together participants in several different countries. At the present time, and certainly for the wider networks, users are restricted on the whole to input of textual material and data files, although techniques for coding, storing, and manipulating graphical information should soon be more widely available. Systems which use videotex standards (e.g. Prestel in the UK, *Télétel* in France, or Telidon in Canada) can present information from the host machines using graphic features and colour.

In the last few years, there have been a number of educational applications, in schools and elsewhere, of three specific technologies in the general area of computer communications: computerized data-bases, electronic mail, and computer conferencing.

Computerized data-bases and information banks

Information can be stored on files in a data-base program installed on the same host computer which is used for an electronic mail or computer conferencing system, or alternatively, users can access a variety of existing relevant public or private data-bases held on other computers. It is rapidly becoming more economic and efficient to search for specialist information on such electronic data-bases than it is to use libraries and other information sources. Setting up a data-base for a specific group of users is a fairly straightforward matter; even for small groups of widely dispersed members it may well be more economic to make information available in this way rather than through more conventional means such as photocopying and mailing. Furthermore, information held in electronic data-bases can be quickly and easily edited and up-dated. Users can locate required information through a range of search methods and, if needed, download the material onto their own microcomputer for subsequent printing. Traditionally, videotex data-bases were designed with a branching tree structure, which entails tedious and time-consuming election of successive menus before arriving at the desired information. Increasingly, however, key word and natural language search techniques are being developed, which make these systems much quicker to use.

ELECTRONIC MAIL

The basic unit of an electronic mail system is a 'message'—a discrete item of text produced by a sender and addressed to one or more named readers. Messages can vary in length from a few words to very many pages of text, although, in practice, many electronic mail systems impose an upper limit on the size of an individual message. In most systems, the text of each message is accompanied by a 'header' containing information about the message (sender, addressee/s, time and date sent, title or key words, message size expressed in number of characters or number of lines, and status—e.g. new, unread, read, answered etc). Messages are routed by the system to the addressee's mailbox (which is, of course, a computer file) on the host computer, and wait there to be read the next time the addressee logs in to the system. At this point, the latter can then read the message, reply to it, leave it in the mailbox for later attention, delete it, forward it to someone else, and/or file it.

Most electronic mail systems allow users to search for messages according to a number of parameters—including information held both in the message 'header' and in the text of the message. Thus a user can ask to view all messages in his or her mailbox from a particular person, or sent since a specific date, or containing a particular word or sequence of words in either the message title or text. Some systems include a 'recorded delivery' feature, where the sender of a message is automatically notified when the recipient has accessed it.

Group communication—as opposed to messaging between individuals— can be achieved in two ways in electronic mail systems. A circulation list can be set up for sending a message to a named list of individuals, but this becomes cumbersome if it involves more than a few people, and replies copied to everyone else on the list by each person get mixed up with all one's other mail. The alternative is for the system operator to set up a bulletin board on a particular topic (effectively, a mailbox for that topic) to which all concerned send their messages, which are then available to all members registered on the particular bulletin board.

Computer conferencing

Computer conferencing systems, although based on electronic mail, offer, in addition to person-to-person messaging, more sophisticated group communication facilities than topic-based bulletin boards. Individual users can join 'conferences' on specific subjects of interest; a given user may be a member of several such conferences—each conference containing the cumulative total of messages sent to it by the various conference members. As in electronic mail, conferencing on such a system is asynchronous—it does not require that all members be present and active at the same moment in time. Unlike face-to-face conferencing, or telephone or video-conferencing, participants are not put 'on the spot' to respond immediately to questions and to other participants' interventions. These can be read and reflected on at ease, and one's own contribution sent in when it is ready and at a time which is convenient. The conference transcript becomes a valuable record which can be consulted at leisure, and even edited and used as a basis for a subsequent report, as all contributions to a conference are automatically stored on the system.

The more sophisticated systems offer a range of facilities to enhance various forms of group communication; these may include conference management tools, polling options, co-operative authoring, and the ability to 'customize' the system with special commands for particular groups.

There are a number of conferencing systems which are currently available commercially—the best known include PARTICIPATE, PortaCOM, eFORUM, CONFER, COSY, and NOTEPAD; some were originally developed for Government and military applications, others for business use, others for enhancing communication amongst communities of university researchers and scientists.

Special features of computer-mediated communication

In a way it is regrettable that terms like 'mail', 'conferencing', and 'information banks' are used to describe these technologies, because they provide metaphors which are inappropriate. Electronic mail is qualitatively different from written mail—messages can be sent and received instantaneously, searched and filed by a range of parameters, edited into word-processed documents, and manipulated in all sorts of ways that would be impossible, or extremely time-consuming, with handwritten or typed mail. Conferencing software, in addition to providing chances for group communication where previously none might have existed, also permits forms of group communication that are quite different from face-to-face meetings, or audio or video conferences. Many of the cues that regulate communication in the latter situations (body language, eye movements, intonation, accent etc.) are missing. Comments can be made when it suits the participants, allowing time for reflection, and have to be evaluated on their objective content and meaning alone. Conference systems can provide for serendipity—queries or messages sent in to a conference might provoke responses from people one did not know existed: informal networks and interest groups can spring up overnight in a way that would be impossible using other communication channels. A computerised information bank, in contrast to the relatively inert connotation of the term, permits active searching and manipulation of its contents under the user's control, and allows the user to perform operations which would be impossible with a paper-based information source (for example, it is possible to access and compile information from the French electronic telephone directory in ways that are impossible with printed directories, even if one had the complete set of printed volumes available). Combinations of message and data-base systems provide the potential for performing on-line transactions (e.g. bookings, reservations, payments) which might be too expensive, troublesome, or time-consuming to carry out by any other means.

It is a prerequisite that features such as these, unique to computer communication systems, need to be identified and exploited in the educational environment if these technologies are to find a useful role. But this is not the only condition that needs to be fulfilled, as will be shown later in this article.

SOME EXAMPLES OF APPLICATIONS FOR SCHOOL EDUCATION

The few examples discussed below do not pretend to be an exhaustive analysis of all uses of on-line technologies for school level education. They have been chosen from amongst those known to the author at the end of 1986, to illustrate particular points about the nature of computer-mediated communication, and its strengths and weaknesses for schooling.

Databases galore: the British example

At the time of writing, it is difficult to tell how successful the various initiatives launched in the UK in 1985 and 1986 are likely to be. Prestel Education and the Times Network for Schools (TTNS) were both set up in 1985, and the National Educational Resources Information Services Data-base (NERIS), funded by the Department of Trade and Industry (DTI) is due to go on-line in 1987. The DTI had distributed 12,000 modems to schools by mid-1986: by the end of this equipment project, costing over £1 million, every middle and secondary school in the UK will have at least one modem.

The principal emphasis in all this activity is on databases, as it has always been with Prestel: the assumption is made that people will only—or mainly—want to use on-line facilities for accessing and searching for information. The Prestel Education database holds thousands of pages of information, from more than 150 educational organisations, ranging from the British Library to the Health Education Council. It provides a gateway to the ECCTIS service hosted at the Open University, with up-to-date information on all post-secondary education courses in the UK, and also allows users to download tele-software (e.g. from Micronet) for subsequent use on school micros. Prestel Education, although appreciated for its videotex colour and graphics screens, and the chance of downloading free software, is heavily criticised by some teachers, who find little of use for their teaching in the databases available.[1]

The NERIS database, which will be available free of charge to schools, is designed to provide detailed information about learning materials and other resources, and how to obtain them, and will concentrate initially on maths, science, geography, and social and personal development education. It is hoped that teachers and pupils will find this emphasis on learning resources and materials valuable—some materials will be directly available on-line for subsequent downloading and printing, for example, and could then be used straight away in the classroom.

TTNS has been rather more adventurous than Prestel Education in the range of services it offers, with electronic mail facilities, a trial of a computer conferencing system (PARTICIPATE), and the chance for Local Education Authorities and schools to set up their own databases, with pupils able to submit entries directly. Commercial sponsers of TTNS (e.g. the TSB, the Stock Exchange, and the Banking Information Service), as well as the Army and the Navy, have provided databases on the system. By mid-1986, TTNS had 2,000 subscribers, 10% of which were primary schools, the remainder secondary schools, teacher centres, and other educational institutions. TTNS users are able to access services such as ECCTIS, AFEIS (the Advanced and Further Education Information Service) and PCAS (the Polytechnics Central Admissions System), and will provide a gateway to NERIS, as well as access to educational bulletin boards. TTNS uses Telecom Gold mail facilities, which means that users could have access to the international Dialcom network (bought by BT in 1986) used by over 16 countries in the world, including the USA, West Germany, Italy, Mexico, Japan, Israel, and Australia. This enables relatively low-cost 'twinning' experiments, such as the one between 10 primary schools in Devon and primary schools in Tasmania, enabling the children and teachers in the schools to exchange messages on a daily basis if they wish. However, such initiatives are relatively rare, even marginal—the principal emphasis for on-line services in the UK remains that of retrieval of information from databases.

A personal communication tool: the French example

The French public videotex system, *Télétel*, had a user base of about 2 million installed Minitel* terminals at the end of 1986, the great majority of these being in private homes (total Prestel subscribers in the UK at the same time numbered less than 70,000, most of them professional users). Minitels are also widely used in offices, shops, government departments, and educational institutions, including schools. The terminals are provided free of charge to domestic telephone subscribers, by the PTT, as a replacement

---

* The basic Minitel, available free of charge to telephone subscribers, is a dumb terminal with a 9" black and white screen, a built-in 1200/75 baud modem, and an AZERTY alphanumeric keyboard. It is connected between the telephone socket and the telephone itself, has a very small 'footprint', and is of extremely robust design. It is rapidly becoming an everyday item of household equipment. Other more sophisticated terminals can be hired or purchased.

for the printed telephone directory. The PTT's database of 23 million telephone subscribers is made freely available for on-line searches of phone numbers, street directories, and yellow pages information. At the end of 1986, there were around 2,000 services, in addition to the electronic telephone directory; new services can be set up relatively simply by anyone with the necessary finance and equipment, with the minimum of control or intervention by the PTT. Many of these services are instantly available without the need for subscriptions or passwords; charges are debited automatically to the user's telephone bill.

Although the planners of *Télétel* (as with Prestel) started out on the assumption that people would mainly want to use the system for searching out information in data-bases, carrying out transactions (ordering goods, home banking etc), and other worthy purposes, they have very soon been proved wrong. Although such services exist and are widely used, the really popular services are those providing chat, messaging, and dating facilities, as well as computer games.[2] The Minitel has thus been appropriated by a large sector of the public as a personal communication tool, like the telephone, and also as a source of entertainment. This point is stressed here, because it is quite different from the ethos of videotex services in Britain, and is relevant to the educational uses of on-line technologies in France.

Télétel services can be accessed by micro-computers with Minitel emulation software, of course, but there has not been the same level of domestic purchase of micro-computers in France as, for example, in Britain. In schools, the situation is different—in addition to standard Minitel terminals, some 10,000 schools have now been equipped with Exel 100 microcomputers with Minitel emulation, which will allow for easy down-loading and stocking of CAL software and other material.

In the September 1986 directory of public *Télétel* services, there were 51 entries listed under education and teaching. Service providers include private language schools, universities, regional Ministry of Education Documentation Centres, publishers, and associations (e.g. PTA's). Many of these services are concerned with school education, and contain CAL teaching materials, educational games, message services, and databases with information and documents useful to teachers and pupils. The diversity of the services available makes generalizations difficult: for the purpose of illustration, we can look at one well-established service from the formal education sector (*La Télémédiathèque du Centre Régional de Documentation Pédagogique de Bordeaux*), and, in contrast, a recent initiative (*SOS Devoirs*) from a private videotex service provider.

The *Centre Régional de Documentation Pédagogique (CRDP)* in Bordeaux established the *Télémédiathèque* in 1982, serving all the primary schools in the region.[3] A variety of databases are available, the most important being a bibliographic database of teaching and learning resources. The actual materials are held in Bordeaux, but teachers and pupils can search by key word or author for material they need, check immediately on-line whether it is available, and if so, reserve it. The material is then mailed to the school the same or the next day. This resources service had always been available in theory to any teacher, but in practice the time it took to locate and reserve documents by conventional means (visits, phone calls, letters) meant that it was little used. Since the launching of the on-line search and reservation facility, demand for materials by teachers has shot up, and the holdings of the Documentation Centre have had to be considerably increased. Alongside this transactional service, there are a number of others available on *Télémédiathèque*

- a regularly up-dated newsletter with national and regional items of interest to schools, and a service containing administrative announcements for teachers and directors of schools;
- educational games and programmed revision and CAL sequences for use by children on-line;
- an electronic mail service, available to all staff and pupils in the system; this is very heavily used, both by children between different schools, and by staff for administrative purposes.[4]

Although the primary locus of use of *Télémédiathèque* services is the school, it must not be forgotten that the widespread domestic penetration of Minitel terminals means that pupils and parents can also access the services from home. There have even been instances of individual teachers or schools setting up their own on-line services (with electronic mail facilities, and text materials such as homework assignments and revision exercises) on, for example Apple II micro-computers, accessible at local phone call rates, and available for children to use from home or school.[5] This provides a totally new potential for bringing the school into the home—which will work to the advantage of the children from more prosperous and middle-class families, who tend to be the ones who take up the offer of free terminals, and can afford the extra telephone charges for some public and all commercial services.

Our second example of educational services (*SOS Devoirs*) is one specifically targeted on schoolchildren at home. Set up by a prospering private videotex server (CRAC) which also runs chatline, dating, games, and other services, *SOS Devoirs* gives children the chance to obtain help with their homework—either in real time (in the early evening each day) or via a store and forward electronic mail facility. In the latter case, the user logs in again the next day to get the advice asked for, using an 'order number' allocated when the request was made. Sitting at the other end of the service are students and teachers earning extra money by answering questions directly on-line, and by preparing and inputting to the electronic mail service their answers to queries put in their mailboxes. These staff are given clear directives by the director of CRAC not to give complete answers to homework questions, but rather to guide the pupil to construct their own answers as they would if they were teaching in a classroom. The real time early evening service is public in the sense that all users see the questions put in by other users on-line at the same time, as well as the answers given, so there is some potential here for cooperative learning and group interaction. Other services available on *SOS Devoirs* include CAL sequences, educational games, and revision materials in each of the main school subjects, at each level.

Overcoming distance—an Australian example

Distance education for schoolchildren living in isolated areas has a long history in Australia, and it is hardly surprising that thought is now being given to using on-line technologies, in addition to correspondence tuition, radio, and telephone, to help improve its quality. Vivian[6] reports a trial of a videotex electronic mail service by the Sydney Correspondence School, for ten year old children from nine isolated families. Six teachers were involved, in the fields of mathematics and language teaching; a database of 700 videotex frames of course material was developed for the trial. Staff and pupils used IBM PC's with colour monitors, Voca Dex 1100 facsimile machines, 1200/75 baud modems, and the telephone system. The trial identified a number of technical and user problems which are not uncommon with on-line services used by the general public in countries outside France (e.g. poor quality phone lines, faulty equipment, corrupted disks, delays in calling up videotex screens; difficulties in assembling, connecting, and learning to use the equipment etc). Despite these difficulties, the response from parents, children, and teachers was on the whole enthusiastic, and it is worth describing briefly here how the system was operated.

Lessons were downloaded from the database onto disk, a rather lengthy procedure, involving saving each screen individually (taking at least 11 seconds per screen). The lesson material could then be consulted at will from disk—as printers were not provided, no paper copies were available, so lessons could not be rapidly scanned or reviewed; calling up the videotex screens from disk was also a lengthy procedure.

Pupils' handwritten homework assignments, including drawings and sketches were faxed (i.e. sent down the phone lines by facsimile transmission) to the School; the teachers' responses and comments were likewise faxed back. This involved the teacher concerned in making a phone call five minutes beforehand, to ask for the fax machine at the receiving end to be turned on ready to receive the transmission. The 'live' phone call, by the way, also provided an opportunity for much appreciated voice contact and discussion between parents, pupils, and teachers. The drastically improved turnaround time on assignments that faxing permitted (down from a few weeks to a few hours or a day) was a great bonus: it allowed the teacher to re-teach, extend, or take another approach to the child's work, much as would be done in a classroom situation. Conventional correspondence tuition, because of the long delays imposed by surface mail, does not permit this.

Some children learned to use file transfer and word processing techniques and were able to communicate with other children in the trial via PC-TALK, as well as by fax. They used this in the language course, for example, to send their homework stories to each other, and comment on them. This again was very much appreciated—one can imagine how motivating it is for completely isolated children, trying to study at home alone, to share their experiences with others in the same situation (and how such high levels of motivation can overcome the frustrations of using complicated and occasionally unreliable equipment, with a relatively poor user interface!).

The teachers involved, despite some initial technophobia, gained new skills in using communications technologies, and on the whole were keen to see these ideas explored further. Particular issues which were raised as important included the integration of electronic communication with audio-cassettes, voice telephone communication, written correspondence, and print materials, and the impact of this new technology on the organization of courses and the scheduling of teachers' workloads.

A worldwide intercultural network

The relatively low cost of international data transmissions, compared to voice telephone calls, and the convenience of asynchronous communication (which overcomes the problem of communication across different time zones) has of course been a stimulus to the use of electronic mail for contacts between schools in different countries. We have already mentioned the primary schools in Devon using TTNs to link with schools in Tasmania. And there are a number of schools in the UK, for example, which maintain electronic mail links with schools in France as part of their language studies. Perhaps one of the most ambitious projects in this area is the one reported by Cohen and Miyake,[7] of an intercultural network involving college and secondary level students in sites in California, Alaska, Mexico, Israel, and Japan. The network involved off-line preparation of messages and other text materials, which were transmitted at off-peak hours directly to the students in the other sites. The educational emphasis was on cross-cultural comparisons—students, for example, called and summarized news items from their own press, and sent them to the other sites for comparison; students queried each other about their societies and living conditions, and were thus able to compare the responses obtained from 'real representatives of other cultures' with the information obtained from their text books. Those taking language courses were involved in message translation; the students in Japan effectively obtained a functional learning environment for studying English as a foreign language, which considerably increased their motivation—using English as a tool to communicate with American students was seen as far more interesting than studying the language *per se*.

The authors of this study point out that the mere presence of a computer network does not automatically create a learning environment; students need to be provided with a series of structured activities which use the network to achieve common goals, as well as the chance for informal communication. It is important that teachers involved should be given the chance to learn about the potential of this technology at their own pace, progressing from a fairly small-scale and loosely structured involvement to more complex interactions and projects as they become familiar with the medium.

DISCUSSION

We started off this chapter with a reference to the high expectations held by some for educational television in schools. Nowadays, the great majority of schools in the UK have access to TV receivers, to a daily diet of broadcast programmes, and to video-recorders. Television (or video) has taken its everyday place as one amongst a variety of resources which teachers and pupils can use if they wish. And yet one suspects that, despite its relative availability, the resource is not exploited as much or as well as it might be because of the sheer bother involved in arranging for use and maintenance of the equipment and videotapes in the ordinary school situation. Furthermore, TV is a one-way communication medium, well adapted for use in the group (class) situation.

Compare this with the technologies discussed in this chapter. It makes little sense to raise expectations about the potential of computer-mediated communications in school education unless a certain minimum number of prerequisite conditions are satisfied. On-line technologies are essentially adapted to individual (*not* group) use, so, to fully exploit their potential, schools would require more terminals/communicating micro-computers and phone lines than TV receivers. One modem in each school, located in the Library or the Computer Room or the Headmaster's office may help in keeping the school's phone bill down, but it firmly labels on-line work as a marginal activity in the school curriculum. However, this issue, which in the UK is essentially one of cost—both of equipment purchase and telephone use and other on-line charges—is only one of a series of increasingly intractable barriers to using these technologies in the classroom.

Even if, in British schools, the necessary funds were made available to overcome this initial barrier to access, there would then be the problem of learning to use the technology, in its current state. Computer communications must be made totally transparent to the user if any but the most dedicated hackers are to maintain interest. At the present time, the 'hassle factor' is too high: even when the right communications software, cables, modem, and telephone socket have been brought together, and all the correct communications parameters set up on the machine, actually learning to use many current electronic mail or conferencing systems, or to find the information one wants in a database, can be an extremely frustrating experience. As Gaines and Shaw[8] point out, 'the art of conversation with computers. . . . has not yet developed': electronic mail and data-base systems generally run on mainframe computers, and the programmers of these machines are often quite unaware of the difficulties ordinary people have in understanding the dialogue structures they have designed for human/computer communication. Only when, and if, computer communications become more commonplace, and *much* easier to use, will ordinary teachers and pupils start being able to exploit them on any scale for rewarding educational activities. The Australian trial reported earlier was probably only rated as a success because the motivation levels of the parents and children involved were so high—a strong Hawthorne effect evidently helped overcome the frustration and bother caused by the actual use of the equipment.

In France, these first two barriers—availability of equipment, and the interface problem—have to a large extent been overcome because of the Government commitment to *Télétel*, and because the massive user base has opened up a lucrative new market for on-line services for the general public. This has, in turn created an environment for the development of relatively transparent interfaces, with good user/computer dialogue structures. The French system is thus, potentially, a very important test-bed for the development of new ideas about uses of computer communications, and it might be worthwhile briefly analysing what is happening there before going on to look at the specific issue of the value of these technologies for educational purposes.

Most on-line services can be put into one of three categories: information services (for searching out information), transactional services (which allow users to effect reservations, bookings, orders, payments etc), and personal communication services (e.g. messaging, conferencing). In Britain, and in Canada, the emphasis—certainly in terms of use by the general public and by schools—has been on the first of these, namely the electronic publishing of databases (i.e. the use of videotex as a centralised medium, like TV). But this technology . . . 'could be used to develop a decentralised communication medium, like the telephone, that would allow people to create information and to communicate directly with each other'.[9] It is interesting that in France the initial perceptions of user needs by the planners of the public videotex service—namely that the bulk of traffic would be for access to information services—were to some extent mistaken. What in fact has happened is that the services which allow people to communicate with each other (e.g. electronic mail and 'chat' services), and to perform transactions (e.g. home shopping, home banking, reservations etc) are used much more heavily than was originally anticipated. In the *Télémédiathèque* project, as we have seen, the most heavily used services are the transactional ones (for finding and ordering resource materials) and the electronic mail facility; the various information databases on the system are less popular. In a way this corresponds to many of the impressions one gains in this country of teachers' and pupils' poor opinions of the value of database information on Prestel Education and TTNS (unless, of course, it is really *valuable* and *time-sensitive* information, like the places remaining open for polytechnic entries on PCAS the day after "A" Level results are published!). Maybe we have placed too much emphasis in Britain on using on-line facilities for informational purposes, and should be giving more thought to the other two categories of service. In any case, with the increasing availability and decreasing costs of compact disc technology (which could allow schools and LEA's to hold their own software copies of databases) it would seem to make sense to reserve on-line access for those categories of information which really require frequent and regular up-dating.

If more emphasis is to be put on transactional and personal communication services, then it is important first of all to identify the needs for such services. The first step should be an analysis of pre-existing human communication networks in the overall school situation, both within and outside the classroom, to see whether, and how, computer communications could improve or transform them. This is what has happened, successfully, with *Télémédiathèque*'s documentation service for primary schools, and what the Australian trial of electronic mail for Correspondence School pupils was concerned with. Another successful example is the use of the COSY conferencing system in Ontario to allow local School Board computer studies coordinators to continuously share and develop ideas on the use of microcomputers in the schools throughout the Province—something that without COSY as a group communication medium, could only have taken place at occasional and expensive face-to-face meetings.[10]

Perhaps only as a second step should one then be starting to look for entirely new things to do with this technology—like the setting up of international educational networks, or the capability for pupils to get help with their schoolwork, or access messages and revision material, from home. There is no doubt that the educational potential of computer communications is considerable: use of terminals to access remote databases and compose text material could evidently foster independent learning strategies amongst pupils; the combination of good conferencing and word-processing software can be a wonderful tool for inter-personal and group communication. particularly in the development of writing skills and joint production of text material. As such, these technologies can help foster cooperative learning and creative abilities. However, it is not clear that the applications in this area in the conventional school situation will be all that important in the near future after all, schoolchildren normally work together in the classroom situation anyway, and their real needs for textual communication with other learners and resources at a distance are not significant.

It is more likely that the really useful applications of these technologies in education will be for distance education and training—particularly in the field of the distance education of adults, where it is possible that students might be able to have access to suitable equipment of their own at home.[12] Here the needs for inter-personal communication—both amongst students, and between students and tutors and the institution—are much greater than in the classroom situation. And in the training sector, it is likely to be the companies and other organizations with the necessary funds, and with a distributed population of trainees, who will be the first to use these methods. For electronic communication to have the same sort of educational potential for pupils in the classroom would require fairly significant changes in the school curriculum—changes which would place more than curiosity value on contact with children and resource people working in other schools and institutions, maybe in other countries. At the moment experiments of this sort are very much due to the initiative and enthusiasm of a few individual teachers, rather than being an essential part of the syllabus.

In the school system as a whole, if one looks outside the actual classroom, the main application area for computer communications in the immediate future is probably that of professional development and in-service training of teachers. Conferencing and electronic mail facilities could play a valuable role in accessing teaching resources, in providing a framework for peer support, in establishing special interest groups for teachers of the same discipline in different schools, for planning and organizing activities between schools, and as the on-line element of professional development programmes offered at a distance.[13]

CONCLUSIONS

There is no doubt that, until recently, many schools have ignored the educational potential of using micro-computers to access remote databases and to communicate with other learners and resource people through electronic mail and computer conferencing systems. Recent efforts in Britain to remedy this situation (the DTI initiative on supply of modems and the construction of the NERIS database) have no doubt been prompted to some extent by disillusionment with much of the educational software available for stand-alone applications, and the thought that on-line use might extend the value of the equipment already installed in schools.

Despite the technical and other problems involved (e.g. poor human/computer dialogue design, noisy phone lines etc), many teachers appreciate the ability to use on-line facilities to download new software and other resource material for subsequent use in the classroom, and some LEA's (e.g. Derby, Hants) have made extensive use of the messaging and database facilities offered through TTNS. However, it is argued here that the full potential for the use of on-line communication and transactional, facilities cannot be realised in the school situation unless resources are made available for the necessary equipment and on-line costs, *and* unless the school curriculum places a premium on human communication networks which can be supported by on-line technologies. This depends to a large extent on national policy on the development of new technologies for use by the general public. Where an effective policy which permits and encourages decentralised initiatives has been implemented, as in France with the *Télétel* system, then significant applications are likely to develop in the school situation. In the absence of such a policy, and the massive initial investment needed to get it off the ground, the key educational applications of computer communications are more likely to occur in the field of the training and education of adults at a distance. In the school context, it is thus more likely that this technology will find a role as a component of in-service training programmes for teachers, rather than as an educational tool for use by pupils in the classroom.

REFERENCES

1. Leah, T. (1986) 'Modems in schools', *Telelink*, August 1986, pp. 11–16.
2. Marchand, M. *et al.* (1987) *Les paradis informationnels: du Minitel aux services de communication du futur*, Paris, Masson/CNET-ENST.
3. La Borderie (1982) *Le système Télémédiathèque*, Montpellier, IDATE, Actes des IVe Journées Internationales.
4. Mercier, N. *et al.* (1984) *Les besoins de communications à distance dans le monde de l'enseignment*, Montpellier, IDATE.
5. Minitel Magazine (1986) *Et sur les bancs de l'école?*, no. 16, Aug/Sept 1986, pp. 51–52.
6. Vivian, V. (1986) 'Electronic mail in a children's distance course: trial and evaluation', *Distance Education*, Vol. 7, no. 2, pp. 237–260.
7. Cohen, M. and Miyake, N. (1986) 'A worldwide intercultural network: exploring electronic messaging for instruction', *Instructional Science*, Vol. 15, no. 3, 257–273.
8. Gaines, B. and Shaw, M. (1984) *The art of computer conversation: a new medium for communication*, Englewood Cliffs, Prentice Hall.
9. Peterson, L. (1984) 'Creating a convivial communications society', *Telecommunications Policy*, September 1984, pp. 170–172 (Reprinted in this collection).
10. Ord, J. and Tobin, J. (1985) 'Electronic Communications: Computer conferencing, computer networks, interactive cable', *Working Papers of the Office of Development Research*, no. 85–4, Toronto, TVOntario.
11. Bacsich, P., Kaye, A. and Lefrere, P. (1986) 'An international survey of

information technologies for education and training', *Oxford Surveys in Information Technology*, 3, pp. 271–318.

12. Kaye, A. (1986) 'La télématique comme outil de communication en formation à distance', *Le Bulletin de l'IDATE*, no. 23, pp. 43–52.

13. Harasim, L. and Johnson, M. (1986) *Research on the educational applications of computer networks for teachers and trainers in Ontario*, Toronto, Ontario Ministry of Education.

Index

$26.00